THE
Official Guide
—— TO THE ——
NEW *TOEFL*® iBT

THE
Official Guide
—— TO THE ——
NEW *TOEFL*® iBT

McGraw-Hill

New York | Chicago | San Francisco | Lisbon | London | Madrid | Mexico City
Milan | New Delhi | San Juan | Seoul | Singapore | Sydney | Toronto

Contents

THE
Official Guide
──── TO THE ────
NEW *TOEFL*® iBT

Introducing the TOEFL iBT

> **READ THIS CHAPTER TO FIND OUT**
>
> ➤ **what's new about the TOEFL iBT**
>
> ➤ **what kinds of questions are on the new test**
>
> ➤ **how you can use this book to help you get a better score**

This *Official Guide* has been created to help English language learners understand the TOEFL® Internet-based test (iBT) and prepare for it. By preparing for the new test, you will also be building the skills you need to communicate with confidence and succeed in an academic setting.

All About the TOEFL Test

Start your preparation for the TOEFL iBT by reading the following important information about the test, testing requirements, and your TOEFL scores.

WHAT IS TOEFL?

The Test of English as a Foreign Language (TOEFL) is used to measure English language proficiency. If you are applying to a college or university where English is the language of instruction, your TOEFL scores will help admissions staff determine if your skills in English are adequate for enrollment into the program of study you have selected. The TOEFL test is administered in more than 180 countries, making it the most accessible test in the world. Internet-based testing makes it possible to expand greatly the number of test centers and increase access. The TOEFL test is also the most accepted test in the world. More than 5,000 colleges, universities, and licensing agencies in 90 countries accept TOEFL scores. So, for example, students can use the test to study in the United Kingdom and other European countries, Australia, New Zealand, Hong Kong, Singapore, Japan, and Korea, in addition to the United States and Canada.

WHO CREATES THE TOEFL TEST?

The TOEFL is created by ETS ("Educational Testing Service"). ETS also created this book as the official guide to the test.

WHAT IS THE TOEFL iBT?

The TOEFL iBT is a new version of the TOEFL test. It is an Internet-based test (iBT) delivered in secure testing centers around the world. The new TOEFL iBT test is scheduled to be phased in from September 2005 through June 2006. The phase-in date for the United States is September 2005; for Canada, France, Germany, and Italy, it is October 2005. The test will be introduced in the rest of the world on a rolling basis. To find out when it will be available in your country, visit www.ets.org/toefl.

The TOEFL iBT replaces the TOEFL computer-based test (CBT) and the paper-and-pencil (PBT) version of the test. Information comparing scores from TOEFL iBT to TOEFL CBT and TOEFL PBT is available on pages 350 to 359.

WHO IS REQUIRED TO TAKE THE TOEFL TEST?

If your first or native language is NOT English, it is likely that the college or university that you wish to attend will require you to take this test. However, you should check with each institution to which you are applying for admission.

HOW IS THE TOEFL TEST USED IN THE ADMISSIONS PROCESS?

Your test scores will be considered together with other information you supply to the institution to determine if you have the appropriate academic and language background to be admitted to a regular or modified program of study. Often your field of study and whether you are applying as a graduate or undergraduate student will determine what TOEFL scores you need.

IS THERE A MINIMUM ACCEPTABLE SCORE?

Each institution that uses TOEFL scores sets its own minimum level of acceptable performance. These minimums vary from one institution to another, depending on factors such as the applicant's field of study, the level of study (undergraduate or graduate), whether the applicant will be a teaching assistant, and whether the institution offers English as a Second Language support for its students.

How to Use This Book

This book gives you instruction, practice, and advice on strategies for performing well on the TOEFL iBT.

➤ Chapter 1 provides an overview of the test, information about test scores, an introduction to the on-screen appearance of the different parts of the TOEFL iBT, along with general test-taking suggestions.

➤ Chapters 2, 3, 4, and 5 provide in-depth discussions of the kinds of questions that appear in each part of the TOEFL iBT. Each chapter also includes practice questions and explanations of correct answers so that you will understand the actual communicative skills that are being tested in each section. Finally, Chapters 2 to 5 provide you with sample test sections that will give you an estimate of how you would perform on the actual TOEFL test.

➤ Chapter 6 is a brief writing handbook that helps you identify errors in your writing and presents strategies for academic writing, both for tests like the TOEFL iBT and for other kinds of writing that occurs in college and graduate school.

You can use this book to familiarize yourself with the appearance, length, and format of the TOEFL iBT. You can also experience a free, online practice version of the TOEFL iBT at the TOEFL online practice community, called **TOEFL® Practice Online,** at toeflpractice.ets.org. Members have access to the following:

➤ Sample Speaking questions and responses
➤ Sample Writing questions
➤ Reading and Listening questions
➤ Discussion boards where learners and teachers can exchange ideas
➤ Daily study tips

TOEFL Practice Online can help you become familiar with the tools available in the TOEFL iBT and what it is like to answer the questions under timed conditions. This *Official Guide* will help you understand language skills you will need to succeed on the test and in the classroom.

Use the practice tests in this book and the free online practice at toeflpractice.ets.org to determine which of your skills are the weakest. Then follow the advice in each skill chapter to improve those skills. You should use other materials to supplement the practice test questions in this book.

Because the TOEFL iBT is designed to assess the actual skills you will need to be successful in your studies, the very best way to develop the skills being measured on the TOEFL iBT test is to study in an English program that focuses on

➤ communication using all four skills, especially speaking
➤ integrated skills (e.g., listening/reading/speaking, listening/reading/writing)

However, even students who are not enrolled in an English program should practice the underlying skills that are assessed on the TOEFL iBT. In other words, the best way to improve performance is to improve your skills. Each chapter of this book gives you explicit advice on how to connect your learning activities to the kinds of questions you will be asked on the test. Perhaps you want to improve your reading score on the TOEFL iBT. The best way to improve reading skills is to read frequently and to read many different types of texts in various subject areas (sciences, social sciences, arts, business, etc.). The Internet is one of the best resources for this, but any books, magazines, or journals are very helpful as well. It is best to progress to reading texts that are more academic in style, the kind that would be found in university courses.

In addition, you might try these activities:

➤ Scan the passages to find and highlight key facts (dates, numbers, terms) and information.
➤ Increase vocabulary knowledge, perhaps by using flashcards.

➤ Rather than carefully reading each word and each sentence, practice skimming a passage quickly to get a general impression of the main idea.

➤ Choose some unfamiliar words in the passage and guess the meaning from the context (surrounding sentences).

➤ Select all the pronouns (*he, him, they, them*, etc.) and identify which nouns each one refers to in the passage.

➤ Practice making inferences and drawing conclusions based on what is implied in the passage as a whole.

All About the TOEFL iBT

The new TOEFL iBT differs in important ways from previous versions of the test. Read the following to learn about those differences and about the important features of the new test.

WHY IS THE TOEFL TEST CHANGING?

➤ *To measure the ability to communicate successfully in an academic setting.* The new test will better measure what colleges and universities need to know: a prospective student's ability to use English in an academic setting. The new Speaking section evaluates a person's ability to use spoken English, and the new integrated Writing and Speaking tasks measure the ability to combine and communicate about information from more than one source.

➤ *To reflect how language is really used.* The new integrated tasks that combine more than one skill are designed to reflect how people really use language. By preparing for the new TOEFL test, you will be building the skills you need to use language in an academic setting and communicate with confidence.

➤ *To keep up with the best practices in language learning and teaching.* In the past, language learning focused on learning *about* the language (especially grammar), and students would receive high scores on tests without having the ability to communicate. Now teachers and learners understand the importance of learning to *use English to communicate,* and activities that focus on communication and integrating (combining) skills are very popular in many English language programs.

WHAT ARE THE MAIN FEATURES OF THE TOEFL iBT?

➤ *It tests all four language skills that are important for effective communication: speaking, listening, reading, and writing.* The TOEFL iBT emphasizes the student's ability to use English effectively in academic settings.

➤ *It will be delivered via the Internet in secure test centers around the world.* The "iBT" in the title of the test stands for "Internet-based testing." Once the new test is introduced in an area, the computer-based and paper-based tests will no longer be offered there.

➤ *Some tasks require test takers to combine more than one skill.* To succeed academically in English-speaking colleges and universities, students need to be able to combine their language skills in the classroom. Integrated questions, or "tasks," in the new test help learners build the confidence needed to communicate in the academic environments they plan to enter. The new integrated tasks ask test takers to

- read, listen, and then speak in response to a question
- listen and then speak in response to a question
- read, listen, and then write in response to a question

➤ *The new TOEFL test includes a Speaking section.* This section includes six tasks, and test takers wear headphones and speak into a microphone when they respond. The responses are digitally recorded and transmitted to ETS's Online Scoring Network, where human scorers, trained and certified by ETS, rate them. The scorers are carefully monitored for accuracy, so test takers and score recipients can be assured of the reliability of the Speaking scores.

➤ *The Writing section has been expanded.* The new test requires test takers to type a response to material they have heard and read, and to compose an essay in support of an opinion. Trained and certified human scorers also rate the responses to the Writing tasks via ETS's Online Scoring Network.

➤ *The new test is about 4 hours long.* All test sections will be completed in one day, so there is no need to travel to the test center twice.

➤ *Note taking is allowed.* Test takers can take notes on any section of the test, and they can use those notes when answering the questions. Test takers' notes are shredded before they leave the test center for security purposes.

➤ *The new scores help to explain test takers' English language ability.* ETS provides comprehensive scoring information that includes scores for four skills and a total score. Competency descriptors for each skill and level can be found on pages 365–373 and are available at www.ets.org/toefl. These descriptors help to explain what the new scores mean. In addition, test takers will receive helpful performance feedback on their score reports.

➤ *The new scores are reported online.* Test takers can view scores online fifteen business days after the test, as well as receive a copy of their score report by mail. Colleges and universities will be able to view online scores starting in 2006, but they will also continue to receive scores via their current method of delivery.

FORMAT OF THE TOEFL iBT

The new TOEFL iBT consists of four sections: Reading, Listening, Speaking, and Writing. All sections are taken on the same day, and the entire test is about four hours long. The test is not computer-adaptive. Each test taker receives the same range of questions. Instructions for answering questions are given within each section. There is no computer tutorial.

The following chart shows the range of questions and the timing for each section. The time limit for each section varies according to the number of questions.

The New Test Format

Test Section	Number of Questions	Timing
Reading	3–5 passages, 12–14 questions each	60–100 minutes
Listening	4–6 lectures, 6 questions each 2–3 conversations, 5 questions each	60–90 minutes
BREAK		5 minutes
Speaking	6 tasks: 2 independent and 4 integrated	20 minutes
Writing	1 integrated task	20 minutes
	1 independent task	30 minutes

QUESTION TYPES

The TOEFL iBT features many of the question types used on the computer-based test. However, the new questions that ask you to integrate (combine) two or more skills are probably the most distinguishing feature of the new test. Questions that assess integrated skills require you to

➤ read, listen, and then speak in response to a question
➤ listen and then speak in response to a question
➤ read, listen, and then write in response to a question

These new questions measure your ability to use English to communicate effectively and succeed in an English-speaking academic environment.

TOOL BAR

The tool bar in each section allows you to navigate through the test with ease. Following are examples of testing tools from the Listening and Reading sections of the new test. The section is always listed in the upper left-hand corner of the tool bar.

This is what the tool bar looks like on the Listening section.

➤ You will always know what question you are on and how much time is remaining in the section. It is possible to hide the clock at any time by clicking on **Hide Time**.
➤ **Volume** allows you to adjust the volume of the Listening.
➤ **Help** allows you to get relevant help. When you use the **Help** feature, the clock does not stop.
➤ **Next** allows you to proceed to the next question.
➤ Once you click on **Next**, you can confirm your answers by clicking on **OK**. In the Listening section, you cannot see a question again once you click on **OK**.

The tool bar for the Reading section has some different features.

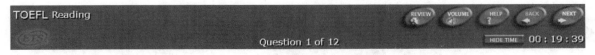

➤ You can view the entire passage when answering questions. For some questions, you need to click on **View Text** to see the entire passage.

➤ You can view all your answers by clicking on **Review**. This allows you to return to any other question and change your answers. You can also see which questions you have skipped and still need to answer.

➤ In the Reading section you can also click **Back** at any time to return the previous question.

OVERVIEW OF THE TOEFL® iBT READING SECTION

Length of Each Passage	Number of Passages and Questions	Timing
Approximately 700 words	3–5 passages, 12–14 questions per passage	60–100 minutes

Reading Passages

You must read through or scroll to the end of each passage before receiving questions on that passage. Once the questions appear, the passage is located on the right side of the computer screen, and the questions are on the left. (See the illustration that follows.)

You do *not* need any special background knowledge to answer the questions in the Reading section correctly; all the information needed to answer the questions is contained in the passages. A definition may be provided for difficult words or phrases in the passage. If you click on the word, a definition will appear in the lower left part of the screen. This is how the reading passage and a question look on the computer screen:

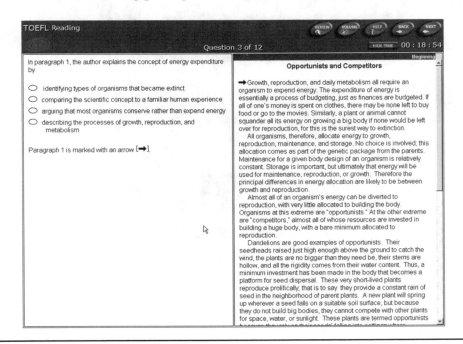

The 60 to100 minutes allotted for this section include the time spent reading the passages and answering the questions.

OVERVIEW OF THE TOEFL® iBT LISTENING SECTION

Listening Material	Number of Questions	Timing
4–6 lectures, 3–5 minutes long each, about 500–800 words	6 questions per lecture	60–90 minutes
2–3 conversations, about 3 minutes long, about 12–25 exchanges	5 questions per conversation	

The Listening section measures your ability to understand spoken English from North America and other English-speaking parts of the world. In academic environments students need to listen to lectures and conversations. Listening materials in the new test include academic lectures and long conversations in which the speech sounds very natural. You can take notes on any listening material throughout the entire test.

Academic Lectures

The lectures in the TOEFL iBT reflect the kind of listening and speaking that goes on in the classroom. In some of the lectures, the professor does all or almost all the talking, with an occasional question or comment by a student. In other lectures, the professor may engage the students in discussion by asking questions and getting the students to speak. The pictures that accompany the lecture help you know whether one or several people will be speaking.

A lecture where the professor is the only speaker

A lecture where the professor and students will speak

Conversations in an Academic Setting

The conversations on the TOEFL iBT may take place during an office hour with a professor or teaching assistant, or they may be with the person in charge of student housing, a librarian, a bookstore employee, a departmental secretary, or the like.

Pictures on the computer screen help you imagine the setting and the roles of the speakers.

Conversation example

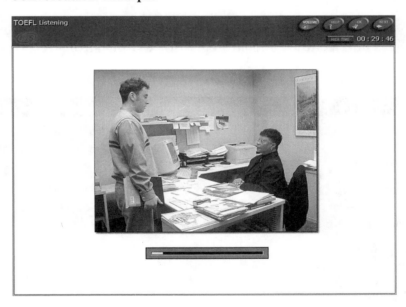

Other Important Features of the TOEFL iBT Listening Section

➤ Note taking is allowed. After testing, notes are collected and shredded before you leave the test center.

➤ Conversations and lectures are longer than on previous versions of the TOEFL test, and the language sounds more natural.

➤ One lecture may be spoken with a British or Australian accent.

➤ One new multiple-choice question type measures understanding of a speaker's attitude, degree of certainty, or purpose. These questions require you to listen for voice tones and other cues and determine how speakers feel about the topic being discussed.

Chapter 3 gives you detailed information about the lectures, conversations, and question types in the Listening section.

OVERVIEW OF THE TOEFL® iBT WRITING SECTION

Task	Number of Tasks	Timing
Read/Listen/Write	1	20 minutes
Independent—answer based on personal knowledge and experience	1	30 minutes

There are two different writing tasks in the TOEFL iBT Writing section:

➤ An integrated task in which you read a short passage for 3 minutes (about 230 to 300 words), you listen to a short lecture that directly addresses the points made in the reading (2 minutes), and you write a summary of what the speaker said about the reading passage.

➤ An independent writing task in which you are asked to give an opinion about a general topic or a topic of interest to students. You are asked to support your opinion with specific reasons and examples. This task is very similar to the essay on the TOEFL CBT and the paper-and-pencil Test of Written English (TWE).

Chapter 5 gives you detailed information about both writing tasks, the topics of the reading passages and lectures, and strategies for writing strong responses.

OVERVIEW OF THE TOEFL® iBT SPEAKING SECTION

Tasks	Number of Tasks	Timing of Each Response
Independent—answer short questions on general topics about your opinions	2	Preparation time: 15 seconds Speaking time: 45 seconds
Read/Listen/Speak—answer questions about information you have read and listened to	2	Preparation time: 30 seconds Speaking time: 60 seconds
Listen/Speak—answer questions about a discussion and a short lecture you have listened to	2	Preparation time: 30 seconds Speaking time: 60 seconds

The Speaking section is approximately 20 minutes long, including questions and answers. It includes six tasks.

➤ The first two tasks are **independent speaking tasks** that focus on topics familiar to the test taker.

➤ The remaining four tasks are **integrated tasks**, and you must combine more than one skill when responding. You first listen to and read some brief material. You can take notes and use those notes when responding to the speaking tasks. Then a question is asked that requires you to relate the information from the reading and the listening material.

For all speaking tasks you use a headset with a microphone. You speak into the microphone to record your responses. Responses are digitally recorded and sent to ETS's Online Scoring Network.

Chapter 4 gives you detailed explanations and examples of each of the speaking questions.

ABOUT YOUR SCORES

Score Scales

Since the TOEFL iBT is significantly different from the previous version of the test, the score scale is also different. Scores from the TOEFL iBT provide information about performance in the four skill areas:

Listening	0–30
Reading	0–30
Speaking	0–30
Writing	0–30
Total Score	**0–120**

The total score is the sum of the four skill scores.

Rating of Speaking and Writing Responses

Speaking The responses to all Speaking tasks are digitally recorded and sent to ETS's Online Scoring Network. The responses from each test taker are scored by at least three different human raters. Some of the tasks are scored by two raters in order to check for the reliability of the ratings. The response for each task is rated on a scale of 0 to 4 according to the standards (rubrics) on pages 242 to 246. The sum of all six ratings is converted to a score scale of 0 to 30.

Raters evaluate the test taker's ability in topic development, delivery, and language use. For topic development, raters consider whether the test taker has addressed the task and conveyed relevant information. They also consider whether the test taker has effectively synthesized and summarized the information in the integrated tasks. Raters evaluate whether the delivery of the response is clear and smooth, and whether the delivery is consistent throughout the response for overall intelligibility. Last, raters evaluate the range and accuracy of the test taker's vocabulary and grammar.

Writing The responses to all Writing tasks are sent to ETS's Online Scoring Network. Each task is rated by two human raters on a score scale of 0 to 5 according to the standards (rubrics) on pages 253–254 and 261–262. If the two ratings differ by more than one point, a third rater evaluates the response and resolves the score. The sum of the scores on the two writing tasks is converted to a scaled score of 0 to 30.

The response to the integrated writing task is scored on the quality of writing (organization, appropriate and precise use of grammar and vocabulary) and the completeness and accuracy of the content. The independent writing essay is scored on the overall quality of the writing: development, organization, and appropriate and precise use of grammar and vocabulary.

Score Reports

Score reports for the TOEFL iBT provide better information than ever before about an individual's readiness to participate and succeed in academic studies in an English-speaking environment. Score reports include

➤ four skill scores
➤ total score

Scores are reported online fifteen business days after the test. Test takers and score-receiving institutions and agencies can view the scores online free of charge. Paper copies of score reports are mailed shortly after scores are posted online. Test taker score reports also include performance feedback, which indicates whether the test taker's performance was high, medium, or low, and describes what test takers in these score ranges know and can do. In the future, the performance feedback will also include suggestions for improvement.

English Language Competency Descriptors

The TOEFL iBT English Language Competency Descriptors (pages 365 to 373) provide useful information about what a student can do in English at various score levels, and help everyone understand what the test scores mean. These descriptors are also available on the TOEFL Web site at www.ets.org/toefl.

Test Preparation Tips from ETS

Once you have built your skills and practiced for the test, you will be ready for the TOEFL iBT test. Here are some good test-taking strategies recommended by ETS:

➤ **Carefully follow the directions** in each section to avoid wasting time.
➤ **Click Help** to review the directions **only when absolutely necessary** because the test clock will not stop when the Help function is being used.
➤ **Do not panic.** Concentrate on the current question only, and do not think about how you answered other questions. This is a habit that can be learned through practice.
➤ **Avoid spending too much time on any one question**. If you have given the question some thought and you still don't know the answer, eliminate as many answer choices as possible and then select the best choice. You can review your responses in the Reading section by clicking **View**. However, it is best to do this only after all the questions have been answered so you can stay focused and save time.
➤ **Pace yourself** so you have enough time to answer every question. Be aware of the time limit for each section/task, and budget enough time for each question/task so you do not have to rush at the end. You can hide the time clock if you wish,

but it is a good idea to check the clock periodically to monitor progress. The clock will automatically alert you when five minutes remain in the Listening and Reading sections, as well as the independent and integrated tasks in the Writing section.

Registering for the TOEFL iBT

STEP 1: GET A COPY OF THE TOEFL iBT INFORMATION BULLETIN

The *TOEFL iBT Bulletin* is a free publication that contains all the information test takers need to register to take the TOEFL iBT. It explains test-scheduling procedures and provides information about fees and identification requirements. The *Bulletin* can be downloaded or ordered on the TOEFL Web site (www.ets.org/toefl).

Paper copies of *Bulletins* can be found locally at many educational advising centers, universities, and libraries. If you do order a *Bulletin* online, it will be shipped from ETS in Princeton, New Jersey, United States. Allow up to eight weeks for delivery outside of the United States.

STEP 2: CHECK THE TOEFL WEB SITE FOR THE LIST OF TEST CENTERS

You should check the TOEFL Web site at www.ets.org/toefl for the latest list of test centers and testing schedule for the TOEFL iBT. Copies of the test center list and testing schedule will be available at many advising centers, universities, and libraries.

STEP 3: REGISTER ONLINE, BY PHONE, OR BY MAIL

Registration information is on the TOEFL Web site at www.ets.org/toefl and in the TOEFL *Information and Registration Bulletin* for Internet-based testing. The easiest way to register is online in the Learners and Test Takers section of the TOEFL Web site. When you register, you will be required to establish a user name and password. You will be alble to return to the site to:

➤ update personal/contact information (e.g., change your password or modify your address)
➤ view your registration
➤ reschedule or cancel your registration
➤ place orders for services, such as additional score reports
➤ check previously placed orders
➤ view your scores

You can also register by phone or by mail. To register by mail, complete the registration form in the *Bulletin*. The *Bulletin* and the registration form can be downloaded from the TOEFL Web site.

You must register online or by phone at least seven days before your test date. If you are registering by mail, your registration form must be received by ETS or your Regional Registration Center for weeks before your requested first-choice test date.

Questions Frequently Asked by Students

THE NEW TOEFL® TEST

Why is the TOEFL test changing?

The new test better measures what colleges and universities need to know: a prospective student's ability to use English in an academic setting. The new Speaking section evaluates a person's ability to use spoken English, and the new integrated Writing and Speaking tasks measure the ability to combine those important communication skills.

What is different about the TOEFL iBT?

The TOEFL iBT has a new Speaking section, which includes independent and integrated tasks. There is no longer a Structure section. Grammar is tested on questions and tasks in each section. Note taking is allowed throughout the test. The lectures and conversations in the TOEFL iBT Listening section are longer, but test takers can take notes. The speech in the listening material sounds more natural, and one lecture may use a British or Australian accent. Also, there are new questions that measure understanding of a speaker's attitude, degree of certainty, and purpose. The TOEFL iBT Reading section has new questions that ask test takers to categorize information and fill in a chart or complete a summary. In the TOEFL iBT Writing section, typing is required. There is an integrated task in addition to the current independent task, and the rubrics used for rating are different from those used for the current test.

LAUNCH SCHEDULE

When will the new test be available?

To ensure test score integrity and a quality administration for all test takers, ETS will introduce the new TOEFL test to countries worldwide in phases rather than all at once. The test is scheduled to be introduced in the United States on September 24, 2005. It will be offered in Canada, Germany, Italy, and France starting on October 22, 2005. The rest of the world will follow in 2006. TOEFL computer-based testing (CBT) and paper-based testing (PBT) will continue to be available until the launch of iBT in other parts of the world.

When do TOEFL CBT and PBT stop?

ETS will stop administering the computer-based and paper-based versions of the test in locations around the world whenever the new Internet-based test is introduced in that particular location.

How can test takers find out when the new test will be available in their countries?

A timeline is available on the TOEFL Web site. ETS will also inform score users and test takers of the schedule at student fairs, through educational advisors and other means.

TEST DELIVERY

How is the new test administered?

The new test is administered on fixed dates in a network of secure Internet-based test centers. Internet-based testing makes it possible to greatly expand the number of test centers in what is already the world's largest testing network. Most areas where the TOEFL iBT test is offered will have 30 to 40 administrations a year, but the number will vary based on the number of test takers and the test center capacity.

Test center information is posted at www.ets.org/toefl and is updated regularly. *Information and Registration Bulletins* are available at many educational advising centers, colleges, universities, and libraries.

Why use Internet-based testing (iBT)?

Internet-based testing makes it possible for ETS to capture and score test taker speech in the most efficient, standardized, and objective manner. Internet-based testing will also make it possible to greatly increase the number of test centers, which is good for test takers.

Is it possible to take just a specific section of the test?

You must take the entire test to receive a score.

TEST BENEFITS

Is the new test really different?

The TOEFL iBT is an entirely new approach to learning and assessing the kind of English used in higher education. For the first time ever, the TOEFL test will assess test taker ability to integrate English skills and will reflect how people actually communicate in English in college and university settings.

Is the new test more difficult than the previous test?

The TOEFL iBT Reading and Listening sections are not dramatically different from those on the previous TOEFL tests. The integrated tasks on the TOEFL iBT Speaking and Writing sections may be considered more challenging because they are new to test takers. However, to succeed academically in English-speaking colleges and universities, students need to be able to speak and write in response to what they have read and listened to. The integrated tasks in the new test will help learners build the confidence needed to communicate in the academic environments they plan to enter.

What other benefits does the new test provide?

The inclusion of Speaking, the use of integrated skills, and the emphasis on communicative competence will have a great impact on how English is taught in the future. Students and other test takers will develop a higher level of English ability as a result and will have confidence that they will be able to communicate and succeed.

Who else benefits from the new test?

Admissions officials and faculty at English-speaking colleges and universities as well as administrators of certification and licensing agencies are provided with better information on their applicants' English communication abilities.

TEST SCORES

How is the TOEFL iBT Speaking section scored?

Each of the six tasks is rated from 0 to 4, and the sum of these scores is converted to a scaled score of 0 to 30. Human scorers rate the responses. They evaluate the test taker's ability in topic development, delivery, and language use.

Scoring guides (rubrics) for the TOEFL iBT Speaking section are available on pages 242 to 246.

How is the TOEFL iBT Writing section scored?

The two tasks are rated from 0 to 5, and the sum of these scores is converted to a scaled score of 0 to 30. Human scorers rate the responses. They evaluate the integrated writing task on the overall quality of the writing (development, organization, appropriate and precise use of grammar and vocabulary) and the completeness and accuracy of the content. Scorers evaluate the independent writing essay on the overall quality of the writing: development, organization, appropriate and precise use of grammar and vocabulary.

Scoring guides (rubrics) for the TOEFL iBT Writing sections are available on pages 253 to 254.

Is there a new TOEFL score scale?

Yes, the new score scale is as follows:

Listening	0–30
Reading	0–30
Speaking	0–30
Writing	0–30
Total Score	**0–120**

The total score is the sum of the four skill scores.

What happens to scores from previous tests?

ETS will report previous scores for two years after the original test date.

Will institutions still accept previous scores?

Requirements vary from institution to institution. Please check with your prospective institution or agencies to determine their specific requirements.

Is there a chart comparing TOEFL CBT scores with scores for the new TOEFL iBT?

Yes. These score comparison tables can be found starting on page 352.

TEST TAKER RESOURCES

Is a sample test available?

Yes, a complete TOEFL iBT sample test can be viewed free of charge at www.ets.org/toefl. There is also an online tour with sample test questions from each of the four sections.

How can learners practice for the TOEFL iBT?

Practice tests are available at TOEFL Practice Online at toeflpractice.ets.org. Join the online community for free and get access to Speaking samples, discussion boards, and daily study tips. After they complete the practice test, members receive instant scores and performance feedback. Additional practice is available for Listening, Reading, and Writing for those who need to improve these skills.

Those wishing to receive a Speaking score can take the Speaking practice for an additional fee. Visit www.ets.org/test for more information.

TOEFL iBT Reading

The TOEFL iBT Reading section includes 3 to 5 reading passages, each approximately 700 words long. There are 12 to 14 questions per passage. You have from 60 to 100 minutes to answer all questions in the section.

TOEFL iBT Reading Passages

TOEFL iBT reading passages are excerpts from college-level textbooks that would be used in introductions to a discipline or topic. The excerpts are changed as little as possible because the goal of the TOEFL iBT is to assess how well students can read the kind of writing that is used in an academic environment.

The passages will cover a variety of different subjects. Don't worry if you are unfamiliar with the topic of a passage. All the information needed to answer the questions will be in the passage. All TOEFL passages are classified into three basic categories based on author purpose: (1) Exposition, (2) Argumentation, and (3) Historical.

Often passages will present information about the topic from more than one perspective or point of view. This is something you should note as you read because usually you will be asked at least one question that allows you to show that you have understood the general organization of the passage. Common types of organization you should be able to recognize are

➤ classification
➤ comparison/contrast
➤ cause/effect
➤ problem/solution

TOEFL iBT passages are approximately 700 words long, but the passages used may vary somewhat in length. Some passages may be slightly longer than 700 words, and some may be slightly shorter.

TOEFL iBT Reading Questions

TOEFL iBT Reading questions cover Basic Information skills, Inferencing skills, and Reading to Learn skills, There are 10 question types. The following chart summarizes the categories and types of TOEFL iBT Reading questions.

TOEFL READING QUESTION TYPES

Basic Information and Inferencing questions
(11 to 13 questions per set)

1. Factual Information questions (3 to 6 questions per set)
2. Negative Factual Information questions (0 to 2 questions per set)
3. Inference questions (0 to 2 questions per set)
4. Rhetorical Purpose questions (0 to 2 questions per set)
5. Vocabulary questions (3 to 5 questions per set)
6. Reference questions (0 to 2 questions per set)
7. Sentence Simplification questions (0 to 1 questions per set)
8. Insert Text question (0 to 1 questions per set)

Reading to Learn questions (1 per set)

9. Prose Summary
10. Fill in a Table

The following sections will explain each of these question types one by one. You'll find out how to recognize each type, and you'll see examples of each type with explanations. You'll also find tips that can help you answer each TOEFL Reading Question type.

BASIC INFORMATION AND INFERENCING QUESTIONS

Type 1: Factual Information Questions

These questions ask you to identify factual information that is explicitly stated in the passage. Factual Information questions can focus on facts, details, definitions, or other information presented by the author. They ask you to identify specific information that is typically mentioned only in part of the passage. They generally do not ask about general themes that the passage as a whole discusses. Often the relevant information is in one or two sentences.

How to Recognize Factual Information Questions

Factual information questions are often phrased in one of these ways:

➤ According to the paragraph, which of the following is true of X?
➤ The author's description of X mentions which of the following?
➤ According to the paragraph, X occurred because . . .
➤ According to the paragraph, X did Y because . . .
➤ According to the paragraph, why did X do Y?
➤ The author's description of X mentions which of the following?

THE OFFICIAL GUIDE TO THE NEW TOEFL iBT

Tips for Factual Information Questions

➤ You may need to refer back to the passage in order to know what exactly is said about the subject of the question. Since the question may be about a detail, you may not recall the detail from your first reading of the passage.

➤ Eliminate choices that present information that is contradicted in the passage.

➤ Do not select an answer just because it is mentioned in the passage. Your choice should answer the specific question that was asked.

Example

PASSAGE EXCERPT: ". . . Sculptures must, for example, be stable, which requires an understanding of the properties of mass, weight distribution, and stress. Paintings must have rigid stretchers so that the canvas will be taut, and the paint must not deteriorate, crack, or discolor. These are problems that must be overcome by the artist because they tend to intrude upon his or her conception of the work. For example, in the early Italian Renaissance, bronze statues of horses with a raised foreleg usually had a cannonball under that hoof. This was done because the cannonball was needed to support the weight of the leg. In other words, the demands of the laws of physics, not the sculptor's aesthetic intentions, placed the ball there. That this device was a necessary structural compromise is clear from the fact that the cannonball quickly disappeared when sculptors learned how to strengthen the internal structure of a statue with iron braces (iron being much stronger than bronze) . . ."

According to paragraph 2, sculptors in the Italian Renaissance stopped using cannonballs in bronze statues of horses because

○ they began using a material that made the statues weigh less
○ they found a way to strengthen the statues internally
○ the aesthetic tastes of the public had changed over time
○ the cannonballs added too much weight to the statues

Explanation

The question tells you to look for the answer in paragraph 2. You do not need to skim the entire passage to find the relevant information.

Choice 1 says that sculptors stopped putting cannonballs under the raised legs of horses in statues because they learned how make the statue weigh less and not require support for the leg. The passage does not mention making the statues weigh less; it says that sculptors learned a better way to support the weight. Choice 3 says that the change occurred only because people's taste changed, meaning that the cannonballs were never structurally necessary. That directly contradicts the passage. Choice 4 says that the cannonballs weakened the structure of the statues. This choice also contradicts the passage. Choice 2 correctly identifies the reason the passage gives for the change: sculptors developed a way to strengthen the statue from the inside, making the cannonballs physically unnecessary.

Type 2: Negative Factual Information Questions

These questions ask you to verify what information is true and what information is NOT true or not included in the passage based on information that is explicitly stated in the passage. To answer this kind of question, first locate the relevant information in the passage. Then verify that three of the four answer choices are true and that the remaining choice is false. Remember, for this type of question, the correct answer is the one that is NOT true.

How to Recognize Negative Factual Information Questions

You can recognize negative fact items because either the word "NOT" or "EXCEPT" appears in the question in capital letters.

➤ According to the passage, which of the following is NOT true of X?
➤ The author's description of X mentions all of the following EXCEPT

Tips for Negative Factual Information Questions

➤ Usually a Negative Factual Information question requires you to check more of the passage than a Factual Information question. The three choices that are mentioned in the passage may be spread across a paragraph or several paragraphs.
➤ In Negative Factual Information questions, the correct answer either directly contradicts one or more statements in the passage or is not mentioned in the passage at all.
➤ After you finish a Negative Factual Information Question, check your answer to make sure you have accurately understood the task.

Example

PASSAGE EXCERPT: "The United States in the 1800's was full of practical, hardworking people who did not consider the arts—from theater to painting—useful occupations. In addition, the public's attitude that European art was better than American art both discouraged and infuriated American artists. In the early 1900's there was a strong feeling among artists that the United States was long overdue in developing art that did not reproduce European traditions. Everybody agreed that the heart and soul of the new country should be reflected in its art. But opinions differed about what this art would be like and how it would develop."

According to paragraph 1, all of the following were true of American art in the late 1800's and early 1900's EXCEPT:

⬭ Most Americans thought art was unimportant.
⬭ American art generally copied European styles and traditions.
⬭ Most Americans considered American art inferior to European art.
⬭ American art was very popular with European audiences.

Explanation

Sometimes in Negative Factual Information questions, it is necessary to check the entire passage in order to make sure that your choice is not mentioned. However, in this example, the question is limited to one paragraph, so your answer should be based just on the information in that paragraph. Choice 1 is a restatement of the first sentence in the paragraph: since most Americans did not think that the arts were useful occupations, they considered them unimportant. Choice 2 makes the same point as the third sentence: ". . . the United States was long overdue in developing art that did not reproduce European traditions" means that up to this point in history, American art did reproduce European traditions. Choice 3 is a restatement of the second sentence in the paragraph: American artists were frustrated because of "the public's attitude that European art was better than American art. . . ." Choice 4 is not mentioned anywhere in the paragraph. Because you are asked to identify the choice that is NOT mentioned in the passage or that contradicts the passage, the correct answer is choice 4.

Type 3: Inference Questions

These questions measure your ability to comprehend an argument or an idea that is strongly implied but not explicitly stated in the text. For example, if an effect is cited in the passage, an Inference question might ask about its cause. If a comparison is made, an Inference question might ask for the basis of the comparison. You should think about not only the explicit meaning of the author's words, but the logical implications of those words.

How to Recognize Inference Questions

Inference questions will usually include the word *infer, suggest*, or *imply*.
➤ Which of the following can be inferred about X?
➤ The author of the passage implies that X . . .
➤ Which of the following can be inferred from paragraph 1 about X?

Tips for Inference Questions

➤ Make sure your answer does not contradict the main idea of the passage.
➤ Don't choose an answer just because it seems important or true. The correct answer must be inferable from the passage.
➤ You should be able to defend your choice by pointing to explicitly stated information in the passage that leads to the inference you have selected.

Example

PASSAGE EXCERPT: ". . . The nineteenth century brought with it a burst of new discoveries and inventions that revolutionized the candle industry and made lighting available to all. In the early-to-mid-nineteenth century, a process was developed to refine tallow (fat from animals) with alkali and sulfuric acid. The result was a product called stearin. Stearin is harder and burns longer than unrefined tallow. This breakthrough meant that it was possible to make tallow candles that would not produce the usual smoke and rancid odor. Stearins were also derived from palm oils, so vegetable waxes as well as animal fats could be used to make candles . . . "

Which of the following can be inferred from paragraph 1 about candles before the nineteenth century?

○ They did not smoke when they were burned.
○ They produced a pleasant odor as they burned.
○ They were not available to all.
○ They contained sulfuric acid.

Explanation

In the first sentence from the excerpt the author says that "new discoveries and inventions" made "lighting available to all." The only kind of lighting discussed in the passage is candles. If the new discoveries were important because they made candles available to all, we can infer that before the discoveries, candles were not available to everyone. Therefore, choice 3 is an inference about candles we can make from the passage.

Choices 1 and 2 can be eliminated because they explicitly contradict the passage ("the usual smoke" and "rancid odor").

Choice 4 can be eliminated because sulfuric acid was first used to make stearin in the nineteenth century, not before the nineteenth century.

Type 4: Rhetorical Purpose Questions

Rhetoric is the art of speaking or writing effectively. In Factual Information questions you are asked **what** information an author has presented. In Rhetorical Purpose questions you are asked **why** the author has presented a particular piece of information in a particular place or manner. Rhetorical Purpose questions ask you to show that you understand the rhetorical function of a statement or paragraph as it relates to the rest of the passage.

Sometimes you will be asked to identify how one paragraph relates to another. For instance, the second paragraph may give examples to support a statement in the first paragraph. The answer choices may be expressed in general terms, (for example, "a theory is explained and then illustrated") or in terms that are specific to the passage. ("The author explains the categories of adaptation to deserts by mammals and then gives an example.")

A Rhetorical Purpose question may also ask why the author mentions a particular piece of information (*Example*: Why does the author mention "the ability to grasp a pencil"? *Correct answer*: It is an example of a motor skill developed by children at 10 to 11 months of age) or why the author quotes a certain person.

How to Recognize Rhetorical Purpose Questions

These are examples of the way Rhetorical Purpose questions are typically worded:

➤ The author discusses X in paragraph 2 in order to . . .
➤ Why does the author mention X?
➤ The author uses X as an example of . . .

Tips for Rhetorical Purpose Questions

➤ Know the definitions of these words or phrases, which are often used to describe different kinds of rhetorical purposes: "definition," "example," "to illustrate," "to explain," "to contrast," "to refute," "to note," "to criticize," "function of."
➤ Rhetorical Purpose questions usually do not ask about the overall organization of the reading passage. Instead, they typically focus on the logical links between sentences and paragraphs.

Example

PASSAGE EXCERPT: ". . . Sensitivity to physical laws is thus an important consideration for the maker of applied-art objects. It is often taken for granted that this is also true for the maker of fine-art objects. This assumption misses a significant difference between the two disciplines. Fine-art objects are not constrained by the laws of physics in the same way that applied-art objects are. Because their primary purpose is not functional, they are only limited in terms of the materials used to make them. Sculptures must, for example, be stable, which requires an understanding of the properties of mass, weight distribution, and stress. Paintings must have rigid stretchers so that the canvas will be taut, and the paint must not deteriorate, crack, or discolor. These are problems that must be overcome by the artist because they tend to intrude upon his or her conception of the work. For example, in the early Italian Renaissance, bronze statues of horses with a raised foreleg usually had a cannonball under that hoof. This was done because the cannonball was needed to support the weight of the leg . . . ”

Why does the author discuss the bronze statues of horses created by artists in the early Italian Renaissance?

- ◯ To provide an example of a problem related to the laws of physics that a fine artist must overcome
- ◯ To argue that fine artists are unconcerned with the laws of physics
- ◯ To contrast the relative sophistication of modern artists in solving problems related to the laws of physics
- ◯ To note an exceptional piece of art constructed without the aid of technology

Explanation

You should note that the sentence that first mentions “bronze statues of horses” begins “For example . . .” The author is giving an example of something he has introduced earlier in the paragraph. The paragraph overall contrasts how the constraints of physical laws affect the fine arts differently from applied arts or crafts. The fine artist is not concerned with making an object that is useful, so he or she is less constrained than the applied artist. However, because even a fine-arts object is made of some material, the artist must take into account the physical properties of the material. In the passage, the author uses the example of the bronze statues of horses to discuss how artists had to include some support for the raised foreleg of the horse because of the physical properties of the bronze. So the correct answer is choice 1.

Type 5: Vocabulary Questions

These questions ask you to identify the meanings of individual words and phrases as they are used in the reading passage (a word might have more than one meaning, but *in the reading passage,* only one of those meanings is relevant.) Vocabulary is chosen as it actually occurs in the passage. There is no “list of words” that must be tested. Usually a word or phrase is chosen to be tested as a vocabulary item because understanding that word or phrase is important to understanding a large or important part of the passage. On the TOEFL iBT, words in the passage that are unusual, technical, or have special meanings in the context of the topic are defined for you. If you click on the word in the passage, a definition will appear in a box. In this book, words of this type are defined at the end of the passage. Naturally, words that are tested as vocabulary questions are not defined for you.

How to Recognize Vocabulary Questions

Vocabulary questions are usually easy to identify. You will see one word or phrase highlighted in the passage. You are then asked a question like this:

➤ The word X in the passage is closest in meaning to

In the case of a phrase, the question might be:
➤ In stating X, the author means that

Tips for Vocabulary Questions

➤ Remember that the question is not just asking the meaning of a word; it is asking for the meaning *as it is used in passage.* Do not just choose an answer just because it can be a correct meaning of the word; understand which meaning the author is using in the passage.

➤ Reread the sentence in the passage, substituting the word or phrase you have chosen. Confirm that the sentence still makes sense in the context of the whole passage.

Examples

PASSAGE EXCERPT: "In the animal world the task of moving about is fulfilled in many ways. For some animals locomotion is accomplished by changes in body shape . . ."

The word locomotion in the passage is closest in meaning to

- ◯ evolution
- ◯ movement
- ◯ survival
- ◯ escape

Explanation

Locomotion means "the ability to move from place to place." In this example, it is a way of restating the phrase "the task of moving" in the preceding sentence. So the correct answer is choice 2.

PASSAGE EXCERPT: "Some poisonous snake bites need to be treated immediately or the victim will suffer paralysis . . ."

In stating that the victim will suffer paralysis the author means that the victim will

- ◯ lose the ability to move
- ◯ become unconscious
- ◯ undergo shock
- ◯ feel great pain

Explanation

In this example, both the words tested from the passage and the possible answers are phrases. *Paralysis* means "the inability to move," so if the poison from a snake bite causes someone to "suffer paralysis," that person will "lose the ability to move." The correct answer is choice 1.

Type 6: Reference Questions

These questions ask you to identify referential relationships between the words in the passage. Often, the relationship is between a pronoun and its antecedent (the word to which the pronoun refers). Sometimes other kinds of grammatical reference are tested (like *which* or *this*).

How to Recognize Reference Questions

Reference questions look similar to vocabulary questions. In the passage, one word or phrase is highlighted. Usually the word is a pronoun. Then you are asked

➤ The word X in the passage refers to

The four answer choices will be words or phrases from the passage. Only one choice is the word to which the highlighted word refers.

Tips for Reference Questions
➤ If the reference question is about a pronoun, make sure your answer is the same number (singular or plural) and case (first person, second person, third person) as the highlighted pronoun.

➤ Substitute your choice for the highlighted word or words in the sentence. Does it violate any grammar rules? Does it make sense?

Examples

PASSAGE EXCERPT: ". . . These laws are universal in their application, regardless of cultural beliefs, geography, or climate. If pots have no bottoms or have large openings in their sides, they could hardly be considered containers in any traditional sense. Since the laws of physics, not some arbitrary decision, have determined the general form of applied-art objects, they follow basic patterns, so much so that functional forms can vary only within certain limits . . ."

The word they in the passage refers to

○ applied-art objects
○ the laws of physics
○ containers
○ the sides of pots

Explanation

This is an example of a simple pronoun-referent item. The highlighted word *they* refers to the phrase "applied-art objects," which immediately precedes it, so choice 1 is the correct answer.

Often the grammatical referent for a pronoun will be separated from the pronoun. It may be located in a preceding clause or even in the preceding sentence.

PASSAGE EXCERPT: ". . . The first weekly newspaper in the colonies was the *Boston Gazette*, established in 1719, the same year that marked the appearance of Philadelphia's first newspaper, the *American Mercury*, where the young Benjamin Franklin worked. By 1760 Boston had 4 newspapers and 5 other printing establishments; Philadelphia, 2 newspapers and 3 other presses; and New York, 3 newspapers. The distribution, if not the sale, of newspapers was assisted by the establishment of a postal service in 1710, which had a network of some 65 offices by 1770, serving all 13 colonies . . ."

The word which in the passage refers to

○ distribution
○ sale
○ newspaper
○ postal service

Explanation

In this example, the highlighted word is a relative pronoun, the grammatical subject of the relative clause "which had a network of some 65 offices . . . ." The relative clause is describing the postal service, so choice 4 is the correct answer.

PASSAGE EXCERPT: "... Roots anchor the plant in one of two ways or sometimes by a combination of the two. The first is by occupying a large volume of shallow soil around the plant's base with a *fibrous root system*, one consisting of many thin, profusely branched roots. Since these kinds of roots grow relatively close to the soil surface, they effectively control soil erosion. Grass roots are especially well suited to this   pur- . Fibrous roots capture water as it begins to percolate into the ground and so must draw their mineral supplies from the surface soil before the nutrients are leached to lower levels ... "

The phrase this purpose in the passage refers to

○ combining two root systems
○ feeding the plant
○ preventing soil erosion
○ leaching nutrients

Explanation
In the example, the highlighted words are a phrase containing a demonstrative article (*this*) and a noun (*purpose*). Because a fibrous root system can keep soil in place, it can be used to stop erosion, and grassroots are a fibrous root system. The sentence could be reworded as "Grass roots are especially well suited to preventing soil erosion," so choice 3 is the correct answer.

Type 7: Sentence Simplification Questions
In this type of question you are asked to choose a sentence that has the same essential meaning as a sentence that occurs in the passage. Not every reading set includes a Sentence Simplification question. There is never more than one in a set.

How to Recognize Sentence Simplification Questions
Sentence Simplification questions always look the same. A single sentence in the passage is highlighted. You are then asked

➤ Which of the following best expresses the essential information in the highlighted sentence? *Incorrect* answer choices change the meaning in important ways or leave out essential information.

Tips for Sentence Simplification Questions
➤ Make sure you understand both ways a choice can be incorrect:
  ◆ It contradicts something in the highlighted sentence.
  ◆ It leaves out something important from the highlighted sentence.

➤ Make sure your answer does not contradict the main argument of the paragraph in which the sentence occurs, or the passage as a whole.

Example
PASSAGE EXCERPT: "... Although we now tend to refer to the various crafts according to the materials used to construct them—clay, glass, wood, fiber, and metal—it was once common to think of crafts in terms of function, which led to their being known as the "applied arts." Approaching crafts from the point of view of function, we can divide them

into simple categories: containers, shelters, and supports. There is no way around the fact that containers, shelters, and supports must be functional. The applied arts are thus bound by the laws of physics, which pertain to both the materials used in their making and the substances and things to be contained, supported, and sheltered. These laws are universal in their application, regardless of cultural beliefs, geography, or climate. If a pot has no bottom or has large openings in its sides, it could hardly be considered a container in any traditional sense. Since the laws of physics, not some arbitrary decision, have determined the general form of applied-art objects, they follow basic patterns, so much so that functional forms can vary only within certain limits. Buildings without roofs, for example, are unusual because they depart from the norm. However, not all functional objects are exactly alike; that is why we recognize a Shang Dynasty vase as being different from an Inca vase. What varies is not the basic form but the incidental details that do not obstruct the object's primary function . . . "

Which of the following best expresses the essential information in the highlighted sentence? *Incorrect* answer choices change the meaning in important ways or leave out essential information.

- ⬭ Functional applied-art objects cannot vary much from the basic patterns determined by the laws of physics.
- ⬭ The function of applied-art objects is determined by basic patterns in the laws of physics.
- ⬭ Since functional applied-art objects vary only within certain limits, arbitrary decisions cannot have determined their general form.
- ⬭ The general form of applied-art objects is limited by some arbitrary decision that is not determined by the laws of physics.

Explanation

It is important to note that the question says that *incorrect* answers change the original meaning of the sentence or leave out essential information. In this example, choice 4 changes the meaning of the sentence to its opposite; it says that the form of functional objects is arbitrary, when the highlighted sentence says that the forms of functional objects are *never* arbitrary. Choice 2 also changes the meaning. It says that the functions of applied-art objects are determined by physical laws. The highlighted sentence says that the *form of the object* is determined by physical laws but the function is determined by people. Choice 3 leaves out an important idea from the highlighted sentence. Like the highlighted sentence, it says that the form of functional objects is not arbitrary, but it does not say that it is physical laws that determine basic form. Only choice 1 makes the same point as the highlighted sentence and includes all the essential meaning.

Type 8: Insert Text Questions

In this type of question, you are given a new sentence and are asked where in the passage it would best fit. You need to understand the logic of the passage, as well as the grammatical connections (like pronoun reference) between sentences. Not every set includes an Insert Text question. There is never more than one in a set.

How to Recognize Insert Text Questions

In the passage you will see four black squares. The squares are located at the beginnings or ends of sentences. Sometimes all four squares appear in one paragraph.

Sometimes they are spread across the end of one paragraph and the beginning of another.

You are then asked this question:

Look at the four squares [■] that indicate where the following sentence could be added to the passage.

[You will see a sentence in bold.]

Where would the sentence best fit?
Your job is to click on one of the squares and insert the sentence in the text.

Tips for Insert Text Questions

➤ Try the sentence in each of the places indicated by the squares. You can place and replace the sentence as many times as you want.

➤ Look at both the structure of the sentence you are inserting and the logic. Pay special attention to logical connecting words; they can provide important information about where the sentence should be placed.

➤ Frequently used connecting words:
On the other hand
For example
On the contrary
Similarly
In contrast
Further, or Furthermore
Therefore
In other words
As a result
Finally

➤ Make sure that the inserted sentence connects logically to both the sentence before it and the sentence after it.

Example

PASSAGE EXCERPT WITH EXAMPLE SQUARES: "Scholars offer three related but different opinions about this puzzle. ■ One opinion is that the paintings were a record of the seasonal migrations made by herds. ■ Because some paintings were made directly over others, obliterating them, it is probable that a painting's value ended with the migration it pictured. ■ Unfortunately, this explanation fails to explain the hidden locations, unless the migrations were celebrated with secret ceremonies. ■"

Look at the four squares [■] that indicate where the following sentence could be added to the passage.

All three of them have strengths and weaknesses, but none adequately answers all of the questions the paintings present.

Where would the sentence best fit?

○ Scholars offer three related but different opinions about this puzzle. **All three of them have strengths and weaknesses, but none adequately answers all of the questions the paintings present.** One opinion is that the paintings were a record of the seasonal migrations made by herds. ■ Because some paintings were made directly over others, obliterating them, it is probable that a painting's value ended with the migration it pictured. ■ Unfortunately, this explanation fails to explain the hidden locations, unless the migrations were celebrated with secret ceremonies. ■

○ Scholars offer three related but different opinions about this puzzle. ■ One opinion is that the paintings were a record of the seasonal migrations made by herds. **All three of them have strengths and weaknesses, but none adequately answers all of the questions the paintings present.** Because some paintings were made directly over others, obliterating them, it is probable that a painting's value ended with the migration it pictured. ■ Unfortunately, this explanation fails to explain the hidden locations, unless the migrations were celebrated with secret ceremonies. ■

○ Scholars offer three related but different opinions about this puzzle. ■ One opinion is that the paintings were a record of the seasonal migrations made by herds. ■ Because some paintings were made directly over others, obliterating them, it is probable that a painting's value ended with the migration it pictured. **All three of them have strengths and weaknesses, but none adequately answers all of the questions the paintings present.** Unfortunately, this explanation fails to explain the hidden locations, unless the migrations were celebrated with secret ceremonies. ■

○ Scholars offer three related but different opinions about this puzzle. ■ One opinion is that the paintings were a record of the seasonal migrations made by herds. ■ Because some paintings were made directly over others, obliterating them, it is probable that a painting's value ended with the migration it pictured. ■ Unfortunately, this explanation fails to explain the hidden locations, unless the migrations were celebrated with secret ceremonies. **All three of them have strengths and weaknesses, but none adequately answers all of the questions the paintings present.**

Explanation

In this example, choice 1 is the correct answer. The new sentence makes sense only if it occurs in the first position, after the first sentence. In that place, "All three of them" refers back to "three related but different opinions." The information in the sentence is a commentary on all three of the "opinions"; the opinions are related, but none is a complete explanation. Logically, this evaluation of all three opinions must come either as an introduction to the three opinions, or as a conclusion about all three. Only the introductory position is available, because the paragraph does not include all three opinions.

READING TO LEARN QUESTIONS

Reading to Learn items are a new question category that is being introduced in the TOEFL iBT test. There are two types of Reading to Learn questions: "Prose Summary" and "Fill in a Table." Reading to Learn questions will require you to do more than the Basic Information questions. As you have seen, the Basic Information questions focus on your ability to understand or locate specific points in a passage at the sentence level. The Reading to Learn questions will also involve

➤ recognizing the organization and purpose of the passage
➤ organizing the information in the passage into a mental framework

> distinguishing major from minor ideas and essential from nonessential information
> understanding rhetorical functions such as cause-effect relationships, compare-contrast relationships, arguments, and the like

In other words, these questions will require you to demonstrate an understanding of the passage as a whole, not just specific information within it.

Reading to Learn questions require you to show that you are able not only to comprehend individual points, but also to place the major ideas and supporting information from the passage into an organizational framework or structure such as a prose summary or a table. By answering correctly, you will demonstrate that you can recognize the major points of a text, how and why the text has been organized, and the nature of the relationships within the text. Having an organized mental representation of a text is critical to learning because it allows you to remember important information from the text and apply it in new situations. If you have such a mental framework, you should be able to reconstruct the major ideas and supporting information from the text. By doing so, you will demonstrate a global understanding of the text as a whole. On the TOEFL iBT, each reading passage will have one Reading to Learn item. It will be either a Prose Summary or a Fill in a Table item, never both.

Type 9: Prose Summary Questions

These items measure your ability to understand and recognize the major ideas and the relative importance of information in a passage. You will be asked to select the major ideas in the passage by distinguishing them from minor ideas or ideas that are not in the passage. The correct answer choice will synthesize major ideas in the passage. Because the correct answer represents a synthesis of ideas, it will not match any particular sentence from the passage. To select the correct answer, you will need to create a mental framework to organize and remember major ideas and other important information. Understanding the relative importance of information in a passage is critical to this ability.

In a Prose Summary question, you will be given six answer choices and asked to pick the three that express the most important ideas in the passage. Unlike the Basic Information questions, each of which is worth just one point, a Prose Summary question can be worth either one or two points depending on how many correct answers you choose. If you choose no correct answers or just one correct answer, you will earn no points. If you choose two correct answers, you will earn one point. If you choose all three correct answers, you will earn two points. The order in which you choose your answers does not matter for scoring purposes.

Example

Because the Prose Summary question asks you to show an understanding of the different parts of the passage it is necessary to read the entire passage. Parts of the following passage have already been used to illustrate other question types.

Applied Arts and Fine Arts

Although we now tend to refer to the various crafts according to the materials used to construct them—clay, glass, wood, fiber, and metal—it was once common to think of crafts in terms of function, which led to their being known as the "applied arts." Approaching crafts from the point of view of function, we can divide them into simple categories: containers, shelters, and supports.

There is no way around the fact that containers, shelters, and supports must be functional. The applied arts are thus bound by the laws of physics, which pertain to both the materials used in their making and the substances and things to be contained, supported, and sheltered. These laws are universal in their application, regardless of cultural beliefs, geography, or climate. If a pot has no bottom or has large openings in its sides, it could hardly be considered a container in any traditional sense. Since the laws of physics, not some arbitrary decision, have determined the general form of applied-art objects, they follow basic patterns, so much so that functional forms can vary only within certain limits. Buildings without roofs, for example, are unusual because they depart from the norm. However, not all functional objects are exactly alike; that is why we recognize a Shang Dynasty vase as being different from an Inca vase. What varies is not the basic form but the incidental details that do not obstruct the object's primary function.

Sensitivity to physical laws is thus an important consideration for the maker of applied-art objects. It is often taken for granted that this is also true for the maker of fine-art objects. This assumption misses a significant difference between the two disciplines. Fine-art objects are not constrained by the laws of physics in the same way that applied-art objects are. Because their primary purpose is not functional, they are only limited in terms of the materials used to make them. Sculptures must, for example, be stable, which requires an understanding of the properties of mass, weight distribution, and stress. Paintings must have rigid stretchers so that the canvas will be taut, and the paint must not deteriorate, crack, or discolor. These are problems that must be overcome by the artist because they tend to intrude upon his or her conception of the work. For example, in the early Italian Renaissance, bronze statues of horses with a raised foreleg usually had a cannonball under that hoof. This was done because the cannonball was needed to support the weight of the leg. In other words, the demands of the laws of physics, not the sculptor's aesthetic intentions, placed the ball there. That this device was a necessary structural compromise is clear from the fact that the cannonball quickly disappeared when sculptors learned how to strengthen the internal structure of a statue with iron braces (iron being much stronger than bronze).

Even though the fine arts in the twentieth century often treat materials in new ways, the basic difference in attitude of artists in relation to their materials in the fine arts and the applied arts remains relatively constant. It would therefore not be too great an exaggeration to say that practitioners of the fine arts work to *overcome* the limitations of their materials, whereas those engaged in the applied arts work *in concert with* their materials.

An introductory sentence for a brief summary of the passage is provided below. Complete the summary by selecting the THREE answer choices that express the most important ideas in the passage. Some sentences do not belong in the summary because they express ideas that are not presented in the passage or are minor ideas in the passage. *This question is worth 2 points.*

This passage discusses fundamental differences between applied-art objects and fine-art objects.

-
-
-

1. The fine arts are only affected by the laws of physics because of the limitations of the materials that are used.
2. Applied-art objects are bound by the laws of physics in two ways: by the materials used to make them, and the function they are to serve.
3. Crafts are known as "applied arts" because it used to be common to think of them in terms of their function.
4. In the fine arts, artists must work to overcome the limitations of their materials, but in the applied arts, artists work in concert with their materials.
5. Making fine-art objects stable requires an understanding of the properties of mass, weight, distribution, and stress.
6. In the twentieth century, artists working in the fine arts often treat materials in new ways whereas applied arts specialists continue to think of crafts in terms of function.

Explanation

Correct Choices:

Choice 2: Applied-art objects are bound by the laws of physics in two ways: by the materials used to make them, and the function they are to serve.

Explanation: This answer is correct because it represents the major theme of the first paragraph. It is a broad statement of a general, overriding fact. The paragraph then provides support for that general statement with several specific examples of how the laws of physics apply to all applied-art objects. The examples are presented in over five or six sentences.

Choice 4: In the fine arts, artists must work to overcome the limitations of their materials, but in the applied arts, artists work in concert with their materials.

Explanation: This answer is correct because it summarizes the basic compare-contrast relationship of the entire passage. Although the last sentence of the passage is nearly identical to this answer choice, the able reader with a well-developed mental framework of the passage will recognize that this is not a minor, discrete point. Like the first correct answer choice, this is a broad, general statement, in this case about both applied and fine arts. The first two paragraphs of the passage are devoted to providing support for this statement with numerous examples throughout the passage.

Choice 6: In the twentieth century, artists working in the fine arts often treat materials in new ways whereas applied arts specialists continue to think of crafts in terms of function.

Explanation: This answer is also correct in that it is a general statement about the ongoing and fundamental distinction between applied arts and fine arts. Like the previous correct answer choice it is nearly identical to a sentence in the passage (the first sentence of the last paragraph). It reaffirms that the distinctions discussed and illustrated in the first two paragraphs are real and that the evidence presented about them is sound.

Incorrect Choices:

Choice 1: The fine arts are only affected by the laws of physics because of the limitations of the materials that are used.

Explanation: This answer is incorrect because it is a minor point mentioned in sentence 4 of paragraph 2. The statement is true, but it is made only to support the broader theme (of the second correct answer choice above) about the differences between the two forms of art. Thus, it is used as an example in support of a major idea and is not itself one of the major themes in the passage.

Choice 3: Crafts are known as "applied arts" because it used to be common to think of them in terms of their function.

Explanation: This choice is not correct because it is a minor point. It is mentioned as part of the passage's first, introductory sentence and then is never developed further. It is a true statement from the text, but is merely stated once without further elaboration.

Choice 5: Making fine-art objects stable requires an understanding of the properties of mass, weight, distribution, and stress.

Explanation: This answer choice is also a minor point and is therefore not correct. Like the other incorrect choices, it is true and mentioned in the passage (in paragraph 2, sentence 5). However, it too is raised only as an example. Much like the first incorrect answer choice, it is presented as an example of how fine artists are constrained by physics and is not itself a major theme in the passage.

Type 10: Fill in a Table Questions

In this kind of item, you will be given a partially completed classification table based on information in the passage. Your job is to complete the table by clicking on correct answer choices and dragging them to their correct locations in the table.

Fill in a Table items measure your ability to conceptualize and organize major ideas and other important information from across the passage and then to place them in appropriate categories. This means that you must first recognize and identify the major points from the passage, and then place those points in their proper context.

Just as for Prose Summary questions, the able reader will create a mental framework to organize and remember major ideas and other important information.

Doing so requires the ability to understand rhetorical functions such as cause-effect relationships, compare-contrast relationships, arguments, and the like.

When building your mental framework, keep in mind that the major ideas in the passage are the ones you would include if you were making a fairly high-level outline of the passage. The correct answer choices are usually ideas that would be included in a slightly more detailed outline. Minor details and examples are generally not included in such an outline because they are used only to support the more important, higher-level themes. The distinction between major ideas/important information and less important information can also be thought of as a distinction between essential and nonessential information.

Passages used with Fill in a Table items have more than one focus of development in that they include more than one point of view or perspective. Typical passages have the following types of organization: compare/contrast, problem/solution, cause/effect, alternative arguments (such as theories, hypotheses), and the like.

Correct answers represent major ideas and important supporting information in the passage. Generally these answers will not match specific phrases in the passage.

They are more likely to be abstract concepts based on passage information or paraphrases of passage information. Correct answers will be easy to confirm by able readers who can remember or easily locate relevant text information.

Incorrect answers may include information about the topic that is not mentioned in the passage or that is not directly relevant to the classification categories in the table. They may also be obviously incorrect generalizations or conclusions based on what is stated in the passage. Be aware that incorrect answers may include words and phrases that match or resemble words or phrases in the passage.

Table Rules

Tables can have 2 or 3 columns/rows containing bullets representing either 5 or 7 correct answer choices. So there are four possible types of tables, as follow:

Type 1: 2-column/row table with 5 correct answer choices
Type 2: 3-column/row table with 5 correct answer choices
Type 3: 2-column/row table with 7 correct answer choices
Type 4: 3-column/row table with 7 correct answer choices

There will always be more options than correct answer choices. Some answer choices will not be used.

An answer choice can be used only once in the table. If an answer choice applies to more than one category, or to no category in a table, a row or column labeled "both" or "neither" will be available in the table for placement of that answer choice.

Scoring

To earn points, you must not only select correct answer choices, but also organize them correctly in the table. You may receive partial credit, depending upon how many correct answers you choose.

For tables with 5 correct answers (both type 1 and type 2), you can earn up to a total of 3 points, depending on how many correct answers you select and correctly place. For 0, 1, or 2 correct answers you will receive no credit. For 3 correct answers you will receive 1 point; for 4 correct answers you will receive 2 points; and for all 5 correct answers you will receive the entire 3 points.

For tables with 7 correct answers (both type 3 and type 4), you can earn up to a total of 4 points, depending on how many correct answers you select and correctly place. For 0, 1, 2, or 3 correct answers you will receive no credit. For 4 correct answers you will receive 1 point; for 5 correct answers you will receive 2 points; for 6 correct answers you will receive 3 points, and for all 7 correct answers you will receive the entire 4 points.

Example

(*Note:* The passage used for this example is the same one that was used above for the Prose Summary example question.)

Directions: Complete the table below to summarize information about the two types of art discussed in the passage. Match the appropriate statements to the types of art with which they are associated. **This question is worth 3 points.**

TYPES OF ART	STATEMENTS
The Applied Arts	**Select 3** ➤ ➤ ➤
The Fine Arts	**Select 2** ➤ ➤

Statements

An object's purpose is primarily aesthetic.
Objects serve a functional purpose.
The incidental details of objects do not vary.
Artists work to overcome the limitations of their materials.
The basic form of objects varies little across cultures.
Artists work in concert with their materials.
An object's place of origin is difficult to determine.

Drag your answer choices to the spaces where they belong. To review the passage, click on **View Text.**

Correctly Completed Table

Directions: Complete the table below to summarize information about the two types of art discussed in the passage. Match the appropriate statements to the types of art with which they are associated. **This question is worth 3 points.**

TYPES OF ART	STATEMENTS
The Applied Arts	**Select 3** ➤ Objects serve a functional purpose. ➤ The basic form of objects varies little across cultures. ➤ Artists work in concert with their materials.
The Fine Arts	**Select 2** ➤ An object's purpose is primarily aesthetic. ➤ Artists work to overcome the limitations of their materials.

Explanation

Correct Choices:

Choice 1: An object's purpose is primarily aesthetic. (Fine Arts)
Explanation: This is an example of a correct answer that requires you to identify an abstract concept based on text information and paraphrases of text information.

In paragraph 2, sentence 5, the passage states that the primary purpose of Fine Art is <u>not</u> function. Then, in paragraph 2, sentence 11, the passage mentions a situation in which a sculptor had to sacrifice an aesthetic purpose due to the laws of physics. Putting these statements together, the reader can infer that fine artists, such as sculptors, are primarily concerned with aesthetics.

Choice 2: Objects serve a functional purpose. (Applied Arts)
Explanation: This is stated more directly than the previous correct answer. Paragraph 1, sentences 1, 2, and 3 make it clear how important function is in the applied arts. At the same time, paragraph 2 states that Fine Arts are <u>not</u> concerned with function, so the only correct place for this statement is in the Applied Arts category.

Choice 4: Artists work to overcome the limitations of their materials. (Fine Arts)
Explanation: This is stated explicitly in the last paragraph of the passage. In that paragraph, it is made clear that this applies only to practitioners of the fine arts.

Choice 5: The basic form of objects varies little across cultures. (Applied Arts)
Explanation: In paragraph 1, sentence 5, the passage states that certain laws of physics are universal. Then in sentence 7, that idea is further developed with the statement that functional forms can vary only within limits. From these two sentences, you can conclude that because of the laws of physics and the need for functionality, the basic forms of applied art objects will vary little across cultures.

Choice 6: Artists work in concert with their materials. (Applied Arts)
Explanation: This is stated explicitly in the last paragraph of the passage. In that paragraph, it is made clear that this applies only to practitioners of the applied arts.

Incorrect Choices:

Choice 3: The incidental details of objects do not vary.
Explanation: This idea is explicitly refuted by the last sentence of paragraph 1 in reference to the applied arts. That sentence (referring only to applied arts) states that the incidental details of such objects *do* vary, so this answer cannot be placed in the applied arts category. This subject is not discussed at all in reference to fine art objects, so it cannot be correctly placed in that category either.

Choice 7: An object's place of origin is difficult to determine.
Explanation: This answer choice is implicitly refuted in reference to applied arts in the next to last sentence of paragraph 1. That sentence notes that both Shang Dynasty and Inca vases are identifiable as such based upon differences in detail. By inference, then, it seems that it is not difficult to determine an applied-art object's place of origin. Like the previous incorrect answer, this idea is not discussed at all in reference to fine art objects, so it cannot be correctly placed in that category either.

Improving Your Performance on TOEFL iBT Reading Questions

Now that you are familiar with the ten question types that are used in TOEFL iBT Reading, you are ready to sharpen your skills by working on whole reading sets. In the following pages, you can practice on six reading sets created by ETS for TOEFL iBT. The question types are not labeled, but you should be able to identify them and understand what you need to do to answer each correctly. After each passage and question set you'll find answers and explanations for each question.

In addition to practicing on these sets, here are some other suggestions for improving the skills that will help you perform well on TOEFL iBT Reading:

The best way to improve reading skills is to read frequently and to read many different types of texts in various subject areas (sciences, social sciences, arts, business, and so on). The Internet is one of the best resources for this, and of course books, magazines, and journals are very helpful as well. Make sure to read regularly texts that are academic in style, the kind that are used in university courses.

Here are some suggestions for ways to build skills for the three reading purposes covered by TOEFL iBT.

1. Reading to find information
➤ Scan passages to find and highlight key facts (dates, numbers, terms) and information.
➤ Practice this frequently to increase reading rate and fluency.

2. Reading for basic comprehension
➤ Increase your vocabulary knowledge, perhaps by using flashcards.
➤ Rather than carefully reading each word and each sentence, practice skimming a passage quickly to get a general impression of the main idea.
➤ Build up your ability to skim quickly and to identify the major points.
➤ After skimming a passage, read it again more carefully and write down the main idea, major points, and important facts.
➤ Choose some unfamiliar words in a passage and guess the meaning from the context (surrounding sentences).
➤ Select all the pronouns (*he, him, they, them*, etc) and identify which nouns they refer to in a passage.
➤ Practice making inferences and drawing conclusions based on what is implied in the passage as a whole.

3. Reading to learn
➤ Identify the passage type (e.g., classification, cause/effect, compare/contrast, problem/solution, description, narration, and so on).
➤ Do the following to organize the information in the passage:
  ◆ Create an outline of the passage to distinguish between major and minor points.
  ◆ If the passage categorizes information, create a chart and place the information in appropriate categories. (Remember: On the TOEFL iBT test, you do not have to create such a chart. Instead, a chart with possible answer choices is provided for you, and you must fill in the chart with the correct choices.) Practicing this skill will help you think about categorizing information and be able to do so with ease.
  ◆ If the passage describes the order of a process or is a narration, create an outline of the steps in the process or narration.
➤ Create a summary of the passage using the charts and outlines.
➤ Paraphrase individual sentences in a passage, and then progress to paraphrasing an entire paragraph. Note: The TOEFL iBT Reading section measures the ability to recognize paraphrases. The ability to paraphrase is also important for the integrated tasks in the Writing and Speaking sections of the test.

READING PRACTICE SETS

Practice Set 1

THE ORIGINS OF CETACEANS

It should be obvious that cetaceans—whales, porpoises, and dolphins—are mammals. They breathe through lungs, not through gills, and give birth to live young. Their streamlined bodies, the absence of hind legs, and the presence of a fluke[1] and blowhole[2] cannot disguise their affinities with land-dwelling mammals. However, unlike the cases of sea otters and pinnipeds (seals, sea lions, and walruses, whose limbs are functional both on land and at sea), it is not easy to envision what the first whales looked like. Extinct but already fully marine cetaceans are known from the fossil record. How was the gap between a walking mammal and a swimming whale bridged? Missing until recently were fossils clearly intermediate, or transitional, between land mammals and cetaceans.

Very exciting discoveries have finally allowed scientists to reconstruct the most likely origins of cetaceans. In 1979, a team looking for fossils in northern Pakistan found what proved to be the oldest fossil whale. The fossil was officially named *Pakicetus* in honor of the country where the discovery was made. *Pakicetus* was found embedded in rocks formed from river deposits that were 52 million years old. The river that formed these deposits was actually not far from an ancient ocean known as the Tethys Sea.

The fossil consists of a complete skull of an archaeocyte, an extinct group of ancestors of modern cetaceans. Although limited to a skull, the *Pakicetus* fossil provides precious details on the origins of cetaceans. The skull is cetacean-like but its jawbones lack the enlarged space that is filled with fat or oil and used for receiving underwater sound in modern whales. *Pakicetus* probably detected sound through the ear opening as in land mammals. The skull also lacks a blowhole, another cetacean adaptation for diving. Other features, however, show experts that *Pakicetus* is a transitional form between a group of extinct flesh-eating mammals, the mesonychids, and cetaceans. It has been suggested that *Pakicetus* fed on fish in shallow water and was not yet adapted for life in the open ocean. It probably bred and gave birth on land.

Another major discovery was made in Egypt in 1989. Several skeletons of another early whale, *Basilosaurus*, were found in sediments left by the Tethys Sea and now exposed in the Sahara desert. This whale lived around 40 million years ago, 12 million years after *Pakicetus*. Many incomplete skeletons were found but they included, for the first time in an archaeocyte, a complete hind leg that features a foot with three tiny toes. Such legs would have been far too small to have supported the 50-foot-long *Basilosaurus* on land. *Basilosaurus* was undoubtedly a fully marine whale with possibly nonfunctional, or vestigial, hind legs.

An even more exciting find was reported in 1994, also from Pakistan. The now extinct whale *Ambulocetus natans* ("the walking whale that swam") lived in the Tethys Sea 49 million years ago. It lived around 3 million years after *Pakicetus* but 9 million before *Basilosaurus*. The fossil luckily includes a good portion of the hind legs. The legs were strong and ended in long feet very much like those of a modern pinniped. The legs were certainly functional both on land and at sea. The whale retained a tail and lacked a fluke, the major means of locomotion in modern cetaceans. The structure of the backbone shows, however, that *Ambulocetus* swam like modern whales by moving the rear portion of its body up and down, even though a fluke was missing. The large hind legs were used for propulsion in water. On land, where it probably bred and gave birth, *Ambulocetus* may have moved around very much like a modern sea lion. It was undoubtedly a whale that linked life on land with life at sea.

---

[1] Fluke: the two parts that constitute the large triangular tail of a whale
[2] Blowhole: a hole in the top of the head used for breathing

PARAGRAPH 1

It should be obvious that cetaceans—whales, porpoises, and dolphins—are mammals. They breathe through lungs, not through gills, and give birth to live young. Their streamlined bodies, the absence of hind legs, and the presence of a fluke[3] and blowhole[4] cannot disguise their affinities with land-dwelling mammals. However, unlike the cases of sea otters and pinnipeds (seals, sea lions, and walruses, whose limbs are functional both on land and at sea), it is not easy to envision what the first whales looked like. Extinct but already fully marine cetaceans are known from the fossil record. How was the gap between a walking mammal and a swimming whale bridged? Missing until recently were fossils clearly intermediate, or transitional, between land mammals and cetaceans.

Directions: Mark your answer by filling in the oval next to your choice.

1. In paragraph 1, what does the author say about the presence of a blowhole in cetaceans?

   ○ It clearly indicates that cetaceans are mammals.
   ○ It cannot conceal the fact that cetaceans are mammals.
   ○ It is the main difference between cetaceans and land-dwelling mammals.
   ○ It cannot yield clues about the origins of cetaceans.

2. Which of the following can be inferred from paragraph 1 about early sea otters?

   ○ It is not difficult to imagine what they looked like.
   ○ There were great numbers of them.
   ○ They lived in the sea only.
   ○ They did not leave many fossil remains.

PARAGRAPH 3

The fossil consists of a complete skull of an archaeocyte, an extinct group of ancestors of modern cetaceans. Although limited to a skull, the *Pakicetus* fossil provides precious details on the origins of cetaceans. The skull is cetacean-like but its jawbones lack the enlarged space that is filled with fat or oil and used for receiving underwater sound in modern whales. *Pakicetus* probably detected sound through the ear opening as in land mammals. The skull also lacks a blowhole, another cetacean adaptation for diving. Other features, however, show experts that *Pakicetus* is a transitional form between a group of extinct flesh-eating mammals, the mesonychids, and cetaceans. It has been suggested that *Pakicetus* fed on fish in shallow water and was not yet adapted for life in the open ocean. It probably bred and gave birth on land.

3. The word precious in the passage is closest in meaning to

   ○ exact
   ○ scarce
   ○ valuable
   ○ initial

4. *Pakicetus* and modern cetaceans have similar

   ○ hearing structures
   ○ adaptations for diving
   ○ skull shapes
   ○ breeding locations

---

[3] Fluke: the two parts that constitute the large triangular tail of a whale
[4] Blowhole: a hole in the top of the head used for breathing

5. The word it in the passage refers to

○ Pakicetus
○ fish
○ life
○ ocean

PARAGRAPH 4

Another major discovery was made in Egypt in 1989. Several skeletons of another early whale, *Basilosaurus*, were found in sediments left by the Tethys Sea and now exposed in the Sahara desert. This whale lived around 40 million years ago, 12 million years after *Pakicetus.* Many incomplete skeletons were found but they included, for the first time in an archaeocyte, a complete hind leg that features a foot with three tiny toes. Such legs would have been far too small to have supported the 50-foot-long *Basilosaurus* on land. *Basilosaurus* was undoubtedly a fully marine whale with possibly nonfunctional, or vestigial, hind legs.

6. The word in exposed the passage is closest in meaning to

○ explained
○ visible
○ identified
○ located

7. The hind leg of *Basilosaurus* was a significant find because it showed that *Basilosaurus*

○ lived later than Ambulocetus natans
○ lived at the same time as Pakicetus
○ was able to swim well
○ could not have walked on land

8. It can be inferred that *Basilosaurus* bred and gave birth in which of the following locations?

○ On land
○ Both on land and at sea
○ In shallow water
○ In a marine environment

PARAGRAPH 5

An even more exciting find was reported in 1994, also from Pakistan. The now extinct whale *Ambulocetus natans* ("the walking whale that swam") lived in the Tethys Sea 49 million years ago. It lived around 3 million years after *Pakicetus* but 9 million before *Basilosaurus.* The fossil luckily includes a good portion of the hind legs. The legs were strong and ended in long feet very much like those of a modern pinniped. The legs were certainly functional both on land and at sea. The whale retained a tail and lacked a fluke, the major means of locomotion in modern cetaceans. The structure of the backbone shows, however, that *Ambulocetus* swam like modern whales by moving the rear portion of its body up and down, even though a fluke was missing. The large hind legs were used for propulsion in water. On land, where it probably bred and gave birth, *Ambulocetus* may have moved around very much like a modern sea lion. It was undoubtedly a whale that linked life on land with life at sea.

9. Why does the author use the word luckily in mentioning that the *Ambulocetus natans* fossil included hind legs?

○ Fossil legs of early whales are a rare find.
○ The legs provided important information about the evolution of cetaceans.
○ The discovery allowed scientists to reconstruct a complete skeleton of the whale.
○ Until that time, only the front legs of early whales had been discovered.

10. Which of the sentences below best expresses the essential information in the highlighted sentence in the passage? *Incorrect* choices change the meaning in important ways or leave out essential information.

○ Even though *Ambulocetus* swam by moving its body up and down, it did not have a backbone.
○ The backbone of *Ambulocetus,* which allowed it to swim, provides evidence of its missing fluke.
○ Although *Ambulocetus* had no fluke, its backbone structure shows that it swam like modern whales.
○ By moving the rear parts of their bodies up and down, modern whales swim in a different way from the way *Ambulocetus* swam.

11. The word propulsion in the passage is closest in meaning to

○ staying afloat
○ changing direction
○ decreasing weight
○ moving forward

PARAGRAPH 1

Extinct but already fully marine cetaceans are known from the fossil record. ■ How was the gap between a walking mammal and a swimming whale bridged? ■ Missing until recently were fossils clearly intermediate, or transitional, between land mammals and cetaceans.
　■ Very exciting discoveries have finally allowed scientists to reconstruct the most likely origins of cetaceans. ■ In 1979, a team looking for fossils in northern Pakistan found what proved to be the oldest fossil whale.

12. Look at the four squares [■] that indicate where the following sentence can be added to the passage.

This is a question that has puzzled scientists for ages.

Where would the sentence best fit?

○ Extinct but already fully marine cetaceans are known from the fossil record. **This is a question that has puzzled scientists for ages.** How was the gap between a walking mammal and a swimming whale bridged? ■ Missing until recently were fossils clearly intermediate, or transitional, between land mammals and cetaceans.
　■ Very exciting discoveries have finally allowed scientists to reconstruct the most likely origins of cetaceans. ■ In 1979, a team looking for fossils in northern Pakistan found what proved to be the oldest fossil whale.

○ Extinct but already fully marine cetaceans are known from the fossil record. ■ How was the gap between a walking mammal and a swimming whale bridged? **This is a question that has puzzled scientists for ages.** Missing until recently were fossils clearly intermediate, or transitional, between land mammals and cetaceans.

■ Very exciting discoveries have finally allowed scientists to reconstruct the most likely origins of cetaceans. ■ In 1979, a team looking for fossils in northern Pakistan found what proved to be the oldest fossil whale.

○ Extinct but already fully marine cetaceans are known from the fossil record. ■ How was the gap between a walking mammal and a swimming whale bridged? ■ Missing until recently were fossils clearly intermediate, or transitional, between land mammals and cetaceans. **This is a question that has puzzled scientists for ages.** Very exciting discoveries have finally allowed scientists to reconstruct the most likely origins of cetaceans. ■ In 1979, a team looking for fossils in northern Pakistan found what proved to be the oldest fossil whale.

○ Extinct but already fully marine cetaceans are known from the fossil record. ■ How was the gap between a walking mammal and a swimming whale bridged? ■ Missing until recently were fossils clearly intermediate, or transitional, between land mammals and cetaceans.

■ Very exciting discoveries have finally allowed scientists to reconstruct the most likely origins of cetaceans. **This is a question that has puzzled scientists for ages.** In 1979, a team looking for fossils in northern Pakistan found what proved to be the oldest fossil whale.

13–14. Directions: An introductory sentence for a brief summary of the passage is provided below. Complete the summary by selecting the THREE answer choices that express the most important ideas in the passage. Some answer choices do not belong in the summary because they express ideas that are not presented in the passage or are minor ideas in the passage. *This question is worth 2 points.*

This passage discusses fossils that help to explain the likely origins of cetaceans—whales, porpoises, and dolphins.

◆

◆

◆

Answer Choices

1. Recent discoveries of fossils have helped to show the link between land mammals and cetaceans.

2. The discovery of *Ambulocetus natans* provided evidence for a whale that lived both on land and at sea.

3. The skeleton of *Basilosaurus* was found in what had been the Tethys Sea, an area rich in fossil evidence.

4. *Pakicetus* is the oldest fossil whale yet to be found.

5. Fossils thought to be transitional forms between walking mammals and swimming whales were found.

6. *Ambulocetus'* hind legs were used for propulsion in the water.

Answers and Explanations

1. ❷ This is a Factual Information question asking for specific information that can be found in paragraph 1. Choice 2 is the best answer. It is essentially a rephrasing of the statement in paragraph 1 that blowholes cannot disguise cetaceans' affinities with other mammals. The other three choices are refuted, either directly or indirectly, by that paragraph.

2. ❶ This is an Inference question asking for information that can be inferred from paragraph 1. Choice 1 is the best answer because paragraph 1 says that sea otters are unlike early mammals whose appearances are <u>not</u> easy to imagine. By inference, then, the early appearance of sea otters must be easy (or not difficult) to imagine.

3. ❸ This is a Vocabulary question. The word being tested is *precious*. It is highlighted in the passage. The correct answer is choice 3, "valuable." Anything that is precious is very important and therefore valuable.

4. ❸ This is a Factual Information question asking for specific information that can be found in the passage. Choice 3 is the best answer. Paragraph 3 describes the differences and similarities between *Pakicetus* and modern cetaceans. Sentence 3 of that paragraph states that their skulls are similar. The other three choices describe differences, not similarities.

5. ❶ This is a Reference question. The word being tested is *It*. That word is highlighted in the passage. This is a simple pronoun referent item. Choice 1, "*Pakicetus*" is the correct answer. The word *It* here refers to a creature that probably bred and gave birth on land. *Pakicetus* is the only one of the choices to which this could apply.

6. ❷ This is a Vocabulary question. The word being tested is *exposed*. It is highlighted in the passage. The correct answer is choice 2, "visible." *Exposed* means "uncovered." A skeleton that is uncovered can be seen. *Visible* means "can be seen."

7. ❹ This is a Factual Information question asking for specific information that can be found in the passage. Choice 4 is the best answer because it is the only detail about the skeleton of *Basilosaurus* mentioned in paragraph 4, meaning that it is significant. Choice 1 is true, but it is not discussed in the detail that choice 4 is, and does not represent the significance of the discovery. Choice 3 is not mentioned, and choice 2 is not true.

8. ❹ This is an Inference question asking for a conclusion that can be drawn from the entire passage. Choice 4 is the best answer based on the last sentence of paragraph 4, which describes *Basilosaurus* as a fully marine whale. That implies that everything it did, including breeding and giving birth, could have been done only in a marine environment.

9. **❷** This is an Inference question asking for a conclusion that can be drawn from the passage. Paragraph 5 explains that this discovery provided important information to scientists that they might not have been able to obtain without it. Therefore, you can infer that the discovery was a "lucky" one. The passage offers no support for the other choices. Therefore, choice 2 is the best answer.

10. **❸** This is a Sentence Simplification question. As with all of these items, a single sentence in the passage is highlighted:

> The structure of the backbone shows, however, that *Ambulocetus* swam like modern whales by moving the rear portion of its body up and down, even though a fluke was missing.

Choice 3 is the best answer because it contains all of the **essential** information in the highlighted sentence. Choice 1 is not true because *Ambulocetus* did have a backbone. Choice 2 is not true because the sentence says that the backbone showed how the *Ambulocetus* swam, not that it was missing a fluke. Choice 4 is untrue because the sentence states that *Ambulocetus* and modern whales swam in the same way.

11. **❹** This is a Vocabulary question. The word being tested is *propulsion*. It is highlighted in the passage. Choice 4, "moving forward" is the best answer because it means the action of propelling. The whale in the sentence used its hind legs to push itself forward in the water.

12. **❷** This is an Insert Text question. You can see the four black squares in paragraphs 1 and 2 that represent the possible answer choices here.

Extinct but already fully marine cetaceans are known from the fossil record. ■ How was the gap between a walking mammal and a swimming whale bridged? ■ Missing until recently were fossils clearly intermediate, or transitional, between land mammals and cetaceans.
■ Very exciting discoveries have finally allowed scientists to reconstruct the most likely origins of cetaceans. ■ In 1979, a team looking for fossils in northern Pakistan found what proved to be the oldest fossil whale.

The sentence provided is "**This is a question that has puzzled scientists for ages.**" The best place to insert it is at square 2.
The sentence that precedes square 2 is in the form of a rhetorical question and the inserted sentence explicitly provides a response to it. None of the other sentences preceding squares is a question, so the inserted sentence cannot logically follow any one of them.

13. **❶ ❷ ❺** This is a Prose Summary question. It is completed correctly below. The correct choices are 1, 2, and 5. Choices 3, 4, and 6 are therefore incorrect.

Directions: An introductory sentence for a brief summary of the passage is provided below. Complete the summary by selecting the THREE answer choices that express the most important ideas in the passage. Some answer choices do not belong in the summary because they express ideas that are not presented in the passage or are minor ideas in the passage. *This question is worth 2 points.*

This passage discusses fossils that help to explain the likely origins of cetaceans—whales, porpoises, and dolphins.

- **Recent discoveries of fossils have helped to show the link between land mammals and cetaceans.**
- **The discovery of *Ambulocetus natans* provided evidence for a whale that lived both on land and at sea.**
- **Fossils thought to be transitional forms between walking mammals and swimming whales were found.**

Answer Choices

1. Recent discoveries of fossils have helped to show the link between land mammals and cetaceans.

2. The discovery of *Ambulocetus natans* provided evidence for a whale that lived both on land and at sea.

3. The skeleton of *Basilosaurus* was found in what had been the Tethys Sea, an area rich in fossil evidence.

4. *Pakicetus* is the oldest fossil whale yet to be found.

5. Fossils thought to be transitional forms between walking mammals and swimming whales were found.

6. *Ambulocetus'* hind legs were used for propulsion in the water.

Correct Choices

Choice 1, "Recent discoveries of fossils have helped to show the link between land mammals and cetaceans," is correct because it represents the major idea of the entire passage. The bulk of the passage consists of a discussion of the major discoveries (*Pakecitus, Basilosaurus,* and *Ambulocetus*) that show this link.

Choice 2, "The discovery of *Ambulocetus natans* provided evidence for a whale that lived both on land and at sea," is correct because it is one of the major discoveries cited in the passage in support of the passage's main point, that mammals and cetaceans are related.

Choice 5, "Fossils thought to be transitional forms between walking mammals and swimming whales were found," is correct because like choice 1, this is a statement of the passage's major theme as stated in paragraph 1: these fossils were "clearly intermediate, or transitional between land mammals and cetaceans." The remainder of the passage discusses these discoveries.

Incorrect Choices

Choice 3, "The skeleton of *Basilosaurus* was found in what had been the Tethys Sea, an area rich in fossil evidence," is true, but it is a minor detail and therefore incorrect.

Choice 4, "*Pakicetus* is the oldest fossil whale yet to be found," is true, but it is a minor detail and therefore incorrect.

Choice 6, "*Ambulocetus'* hind legs were used for propulsion in the water," is true, but it is a minor detail and therefore incorrect.

Practice Set 2

DESERT FORMATION

The deserts, which already occupy approximately a fourth of the Earth's land surface, have in recent decades been increasing at an alarming pace. The expansion of desertlike conditions into areas where they did not previously exist is called **desertification**. It has been estimated that an additional one-fourth of the Earth's land surface is threatened by this process.

Desertification is accomplished primarily through the loss of stabilizing natural vegetation and the subsequent accelerated erosion of the soil by wind and water. In some cases the loose soil is blown completely away, leaving a stony surface. In other cases, the finer particles may be removed, while the sand-sized particles are accumulated to form mobile hills or ridges of sand.

Even in the areas that retain a soil cover, the reduction of vegetation typically results in the loss of the soil's ability to absorb substantial quantities of water. The impact of raindrops on the loose soil tends to transfer fine clay particles into the tiniest soil spaces, sealing them and producing a surface that allows very little water penetration. Water absorption is greatly reduced, consequently runoff is increased, resulting in accelerated erosion rates. The gradual drying of the soil caused by its diminished ability to absorb water results in the further loss of vegetation, so that a cycle of progressive surface deterioration is established.

In some regions, the increase in desert areas is occurring largely as the result of a trend toward drier climatic conditions. Continued gradual global warming has produced an increase in aridity for some areas over the past few thousand years. The process may be accelerated in subsequent decades if global warming resulting from air pollution seriously increases.

There is little doubt, however, that desertification in most areas results primarily from human activities rather than natural processes. The semiarid lands bordering the deserts exist in a delicate ecological balance and are limited in their potential to adjust to increased environmental pressures. Expanding populations are subjecting the land to increasing pressures to provide them with food and fuel. In wet periods, the land may be able to respond to these stresses. During the dry periods that are common phenomena along the desert margins, though, the pressure on the land is often far in excess of its diminished capacity, and desertification results.

Four specific activities have been identified as major contributors to the desertification processes: overcultivation, overgrazing, firewood gathering, and overirrigation. The cultivation of crops has expanded into progressively drier regions as population densities have grown. These regions are especially likely to have periods of severe dryness, so that crop failures are common. Since the raising of most crops necessitates the prior removal of the natural vegetation, crop failures leave extensive tracts of land devoid of a plant cover and susceptible to wind and water erosion.

The raising of livestock is a major economic activity in semiarid lands, where grasses are generally the dominant type of natural vegetation. The consequences of an excessive number of livestock grazing in an area are the reduction of the vegetation cover and the trampling and pulverization of the soil. This is usually followed by the drying of the soil and accelerated erosion.

Firewood is the chief fuel used for cooking and heating in many countries. The increased pressures of expanding populations have led to the removal of woody plants so that many cities and towns are surrounded by large areas completely lacking in trees and shrubs. The increasing use of dried animal waste as a substitute fuel has also hurt the soil because this valuable soil conditioner and source of plant nutrients is no longer being returned to the land.

The final major human cause of desertification is soil salinization resulting from overirrigation. Excess water from irrigation sinks down into the water table. If no drainage system exists, the water table rises, bringing dissolved salts to the surface. The water evaporates and the salts are left behind, creating a white crustal layer that prevents air and water from reaching the underlying soil.

The extreme seriousness of desertification results from the vast areas of land and the tremendous numbers of people affected, as well as from the great difficulty of reversing or even slowing the process. Once the soil has been removed by erosion, only the passage of centuries or millennia will enable new soil to form. In areas where considerable soil still remains, though, a rigorously enforced program of land protection and cover-crop planting may make it possible to reverse the present deterioration of the surface.

PARAGRAPH 1

The deserts, which already occupy approximately a fourth of the Earth's land surface, have in recent decades been increasing at an alarming pace. The expansion of desertlike conditions into areas where they did not previously exist is called **desertification**. It has been estimated that an additional one-fourth of the Earth's land surface is threatened by this process.

Directions: Mark your answer by filling in the oval next to your choice.

1. The word threatened in the passage is closest in meaning to

○ restricted
○ endangered
○ prevented
○ rejected

PARAGRAPH 3

Even in the areas that retain a soil cover, the reduction of vegetation typically results in the loss of the soil's ability to absorb substantial quantities of water. The impact of raindrops on the loose soil tends to transfer fine clay particles into the tiniest soil spaces, sealing them and producing a surface that allows very little water penetration. Water absorption is greatly reduced, consequently runoff is increased, resulting in accelerated erosion rates. The gradual drying of the soil caused by its diminished ability to absorb water results in the further loss of vegetation, so that a cycle of progressive surface deterioration is established.

2. According to paragraph 3, the loss of natural vegetation has which of the following consequences for soil?

○ Increased stony content
○ Reduced water absorption
○ Increased numbers of spaces in the soil
○ Reduced water runoff

There is little doubt, however, that desertification in most areas results primarily from human activities rather than natural processes. The semiarid lands bordering the deserts exist in a delicate ecological balance and are limited in their potential to adjust to increased environmental pressures. Expanding populations are subjecting the land to increasing pressures to provide them with food and fuel. In wet periods, the land may be able to respond to these stresses. During the dry periods that are common phenomena along the desert margins, though, the pressure on the land is often far in excess of its diminished capacity, and desertification results.

3. The word delicate in the passage is closest in meaning to

⭕ fragile
⭕ predictable
⭕ complex
⭕ valuable

4. According to paragraph 5, in dry periods, border areas have difficulty

⭕ adjusting to stresses created by settlement
⭕ retaining their fertility after desertification
⭕ providing water for irrigating crops
⭕ attracting populations in search of food and fuel

Four specific activities have been identified as major contributors to the desertification processes: overcultivation, overgrazing, firewood gathering, and overirrigation. The cultivation of crops has expanded into progressively drier regions as population densities have grown. These regions are especially likely to have periods of severe dryness, so that crop failures are common. Since the raising of most crops necessitates the prior removal of the natural vegetation, crop failures leave extensive tracts of land devoid of a plant cover and susceptible to wind and water erosion.

5. The word progressively in the passage is closest in meaning to

⭕ openly
⭕ impressively
⭕ objectively
⭕ increasingly

7. The phrase devoid of in the passage is closest in meaning to

⭕ consisting of
⭕ hidden by
⭕ except for
⭕ lacking in

6. According to paragraph 6, which of the following is often associated with raising crops?

⭕ Lack of proper irrigation techniques
⭕ Failure to plant crops suited to the particular area
⭕ Removal of the original vegetation
⭕ Excessive use of dried animal waste

PARAGRAPH 9

The final major human cause of desertification is soil salinization resulting from overirrigation. Excess water from irrigation sinks down into the water table. If no drainage system exists, the water table rises, bringing dissolved salts to the surface. The water evaporates and the salts are left behind, creating a white crustal layer that prevents air and water from reaching the underlying soil.

8. According to paragraph 9, the ground's absorption of excess water is a factor in desertification because it can

- ⬭ interfere with the irrigation of land
- ⬭ limit the evaporation of water
- ⬭ require more absorption of air by the soil
- ⬭ bring salts to the surface

9. All of the following are mentioned in the passage as contributing to desertification EXCEPT

- ⬭ soil erosion
- ⬭ global warming
- ⬭ insufficient irrigation
- ⬭ the raising of livestock

PARAGRAPH 10

The extreme seriousness of desertification results from the vast areas of land and the tremendous numbers of people affected, as well as from the great difficulty of reversing or even slowing the process. Once the soil has been removed by erosion, only the passage of centuries or millennia will enable new soil to form. In areas where considerable soil still remains, though, a rigorously enforced program of land protection and cover-crop planting may make it possible to reverse the present deterioration of the surface.

10. Which of the sentences below best expresses the essential information in the highlighted sentence in the passage? *Incorrect* choices change the meaning in important ways or leave out essential information.

- ⬭ Desertification is a significant problem because it is so hard to reverse and affects large areas of land and great numbers of people.
- ⬭ Slowing down the process of desertification is difficult because of population growth that has spread over large areas of land.
- ⬭ The spread of deserts is considered a very serious problem that can be solved only if large numbers of people in various countries are involved in the effort.
- ⬭ Desertification is extremely hard to reverse unless the population is reduced in the vast areas affected.

11. It can be inferred from the passage that the author most likely believes which of the following about the future of desertification?

- ⬭ Governments will act quickly to control further desertification.
- ⬭ The factors influencing desertification occur in cycles and will change in the future.
- ⬭ Desertification will continue to increase.
- ⬭ Desertification will soon occur in all areas of the world.

■ The raising of livestock is a major economic activity in semiarid lands, where grasses are generally the dominant type of natural vegetation. ■ The consequences of an excessive number of livestock grazing in an area are the reduction of the vegetation cover and the trampling and pulverization of the soil. ■ This is usually followed by the drying of the soil and accelerated erosion. ■

12. Look at the four squares [■] that indicate where the following sentence can be added to the passage.

This economic reliance on livestock in certain regions makes large tracts of land susceptible to overgrazing.

Where would the sentence best fit?

○ **This economic reliance on livestock in certain regions makes large tracts of land susceptible to overgrazing.** The raising of livestock is a major economic activity in semiarid lands, where grasses are generally the dominant type of natural vegetation. ■ The consequences of an excessive number of livestock grazing in an area are the reduction of the vegetation cover and the trampling and pulverization of the soil. ■ This is usually followed by the drying of the soil and accelerated erosion. ■

○ ■ The raising of livestock is a major economic activity in semiarid lands, where grasses are generally the dominant type of natural vegetation. **This economic reliance on livestock in certain regions makes large tracts of land susceptible to overgrazing.** The consequences of an excessive number of livestock grazing in an area are the reduction of the vegetation cover and the trampling and pulverization of the soil. ■ This is usually followed by the drying of the soil and accelerated erosion. ■

○ ■ The raising of livestock is a major economic activity in semiarid lands, where grasses are generally the dominant type of natural vegetation. ■ The consequences of an excessive number of livestock grazing in an area are the reduction of the vegetation cover and the trampling and pulverization of the soil. **This economic reliance on livestock in certain regions makes large tracts of land susceptible to overgrazing.** This is usually followed by the drying of the soil and accelerated erosion. ■

○ ■ The raising of livestock is a major economic activity in semiarid lands, where grasses are generally the dominant type of natural vegetation. ■ The consequences of an excessive number of livestock grazing in an area are the reduction of the vegetation cover and the trampling and pulverization of the soil. ■ This is usually followed by the drying of the soil and accelerated erosion. **This economic reliance on livestock in certain regions makes large tracts of land susceptible to overgrazing.**

13–14. Directions: An introductory sentence for a brief summary of the passage is provided below. Complete the summary by selecting the THREE answer choices that express the most important ideas in the passage. Some answer choices do not belong in the summary because they express ideas that are not presented in the passage or are minor ideas in the passage. *This question is worth 2 points.*

Many factors have contributed to the great increase in desertification in recent decades.

◆

◆

◆

Answer Choices

1. Growing human populations and the agricultural demands that come with such growth have upset the ecological balance in some areas and led to the spread of deserts.

2. As periods of severe dryness have become more common, failures of a number of different crops have increased.

3. Excessive numbers of cattle and the need for firewood for fuel have reduced grasses and trees, leaving the land unprotected and vulnerable.

4. Extensive irrigation with poor drainage brings salt to the surface of the soil, a process that reduces water and air absorption.

5. Animal dung enriches the soil by providing nutrients for plant growth.

6. Grasses are generally the dominant type of natural vegetation in semiarid lands.

Answers and Explanations

1. ❷ This is a Vocabulary question. The word being tested is *threatened*. It is highlighted in the passage. To threaten means to speak or act as if you will cause harm to someone or something. The object of the threat is in danger of being hurt, so the correct answer is choice 2, "endangered."

2. ❷ This is a Factual Information question asking for specific information that can be found in paragraph 3. The correct answer is choice 2, reduced water absorption. The paragraph explicitly states that the reduction of vegetation greatly reduces water absorption. Choice 4, reduced water runoff, explicitly contradicts the paragraph, so it is incorrect. The "spaces in the soil" are mentioned in another context: the paragraph does not say that they increase, so choice 3 is incorrect. The paragraph does not mention choice 1.

3. ❶ This is a Vocabulary question. The word being tested is *delicate*. It is highlighted in the passage. The correct answer is choice 1, "fragile," meaning "easily broken." *Delicate* has the same meaning as "fragile."

4. ❶ This is a Factual Information question asking for specific information that can be found in paragraph 5. The correct answer is choice 1: border areas have difficulty "adjusting to stresses created by settlement." The paragraph says that "expanding populations," or settlement, subject border areas to "pressures," or stress, that the land may not "be able to respond to." Choice 2 is incorrect because the paragraph does not discuss "fertility" after desertification. Choice 3 is also incorrect because "irrigation" is not mentioned here. The paragraph mentions "increasing populations" but not the difficulty of "attracting populations," so choice 4 is incorrect.

5. ❹ This is a Vocabulary question. The word being tested is *progressively*. It is highlighted in the passage. The correct answer is choice 4, "increasingly." *Progressively* as it is used here means "more," and "more" of something means that it is increasing.

6. ❸ This is a Factual Information question asking for specific information that can be found in paragraph 6. The correct answer is choice 3, "removal of the original vegetation." Sentence 4 of this paragraph says that "the raising of most crops necessitates the prior removal of the natural vegetation," an explicit statement of answer choice 3. Choice 1, lack of proper irrigation techniques, is incorrect because the paragraph mentions only "overirrigation" as a cause of desertification. No irrigation "techniques" are discussed. Choices 2 and 4, failure to plant suitable crops and use of animal waste, are not discussed.

7. ❹ This is a Vocabulary question. A phrase is being tested here, and all of the answer choices are phrases. The phrase is "devoid of." It is highlighted in the passage. "Devoid of" means "without," so the correct answer is choice 4, "lacking in." If you lack something, that means you are without that thing.

8. ❹ This is a Factual Information question asking for specific information that can be found in paragraph 9. The correct answer is choice 4, "bring salts to the surface." The paragraph says that the final human cause of desertification is salinization resulting from overirrigation. The paragraph goes on to say that the overirrigation causes the water table to rise, bringing salts to the surface. There is no mention of the process "interfering" with or "limiting" irrigation, or of the "amount of air" the soil is required to absorb, so choices 1, 2, and 3 are all incorrect.

9. ❸ This is a Negative Factual Information question asking for specific information that can be found in the passage. Choice 3, "insufficient irrigation," is the correct answer. Choice 1, "soil erosion," is explicitly mentioned in paragraph 2 as one of the primary causes of desertification, so it is not the correct answer. Choice 2, "global warming," is mentioned as a cause of desertification in paragraph 4, so it is incorrect. Choice 4, "raising of livestock," is described in paragraph 7 as another cause of desertification, so it is incorrect. The passage includes **excessive** irrigation as a cause of desertification, but not its opposite, insufficient irrigation, so that is the correct answer.

10. ❶ This is a Sentence Simplification question. As with all of these items, a single sentence in the passage is highlighted:

The extreme seriousness of desertification results from the vast areas of land and the tremendous numbers of people affected, as well as from the great difficulty of reversing or even slowing the process.

The correct answer is choice 1. That choice contains all of the **essential** information in the highlighted sentence and does not change its meaning. The only substantive difference between choice 1 and the tested sentence is the order in which the information is presented. Two clauses in the highlighted sentence, "The great difficulty of reversing the process" and "the numbers of people affected," have simply been reversed; no meaning has been changed, and no information has been removed. Choices 2, 3, and 4 are all incorrect because they change the meaning of the highlighted sentence.

11. ❸ This is an Inference question asking for an inference that can be supported by the passage. The correct answer is choice 3; the passage suggests that the author believes "Desertification will continue to increase." The last paragraph of the passage says that slowing or reversing the erosion process will be very difficult, but that it **may** occur in those areas that are not too affected already if rigorously enforced anti-erosion processes are implemented. Taken together, this suggests that the author is not confident this will happen; therefore, it can be inferred that he thinks erosion will continue. The passage provides no basis for inferring choices 1, 2, or 4.

12. ❷ This is an Insert Text question. You can see the four black squares in paragraph 7 that represent the possible answer choices here:

■ The raising of livestock is a major economic activity in semiarid lands, where grasses are generally the dominant type of natural vegetation. ■ The consequences of an excessive number of livestock grazing in an area are the reduction of the vegetation cover and the trampling and pulverization of the soil. ■ This is usually followed by the drying of the soil and accelerated erosion. ■

The sentence provided, **"This economic reliance on livestock in certain regions makes large tracts of land susceptible to overgrazing,"** is best inserted at Square 2. The inserted sentence refers explicitly to relying on "livestock in certain regions." Those regions are the ones described in the sentence preceding square 2, which states that raising livestock is "a major economic activity in semiarid lands." The inserted sentence then explains that this reliance "makes large tracts of land susceptible to overgrazing. " The sentence that follows square 2 goes on to say that "The consequences of an excessive number of livestock grazing in an area are . . ." Thus, the inserted sentence contains references to both the sentence before square 2 and the sentence after square 2. This is not true of any of the other possible insert points, so square 2 is correct.

13. ❶ ❸ ❹ This is a Prose Summary question. It is completed correctly below. The correct choices are 1, 3, and 4. Choices 2, 5, and 6 are therefore incorrect.

Directions: An introductory sentence for a brief summary of the passage is provided below. Complete the summary by selecting the THREE answer choices that express the most important ideas in the passage. Some answer choices do not belong in the summary because they express ideas that are not presented in the passage or are minor ideas in the passage. *This question is worth 2 points.*

Many factors have contributed to the great increase in desertification in recent decades.

- ◆ Growing human populations and the agricultural demands that come with such growth have upset the ecological balance in some areas and led to the spread of deserts.
- ◆ Excessive numbers of cattle and the need for firewood for fuel have reduced grasses and trees, leaving the land unprotected and vulnerable.
- ◆ Extensive irrigation with poor drainage brings salt to the surface of the soil, a process that reduces water and air absorption.

Answer Choices

1. Growing human populations and the agricultural demands that come with such growth have upset the ecological balance in some areas and led to the spread of deserts.

2. As periods of severe dryness have become more common, failures of a number of different crops have increased.

3. Excessive numbers of cattle and the need for firewood for fuel have reduced grasses and trees, leaving the land unprotected and vulnerable.

4. Extensive irrigation with poor drainage brings salt to the surface of the soil, a process that reduces water and air absorption.

5. Animal dung enriches the soil by providing nutrients for plant growth.

6. Grasses are generally the dominant type of natural vegetation in semiarid lands.

Correct Choices

Choice 1, "Growing human populations and the agricultural demands that come with such growth have upset the ecological balance in some areas and led to the spread of deserts," is correct because it is a recurring theme in the passage, one of the main ideas. Paragraphs 5, 6, 7, and 9 all provide details in support of this statement.

Choice 3, "Excessive numbers of cattle and the need for firewood for fuel have reduced grasses and trees, leaving the land unprotected and vulnerable," is correct because these are two of the human activities that are major causes of desertification. The causes of desertification is the main theme of the passage. Paragraphs 6, 7, and 8 are devoted to describing how these activities contribute to desertification.

Choice 4, "Extensive irrigation with poor drainage brings salt to the surface of the soil, a process that reduces water and air absorption," is correct because it is another of the human activities that is a major cause of desertification, the main theme of the passage. Paragraph 6 mentions this first, then all of paragraph 9 is devoted to describing how this activity contributes to desertification.

Incorrect Choices

Choice 2, "As periods of severe dryness have become more common, failures of a number of different crops have increased," is incorrect because it is a supporting detail, not a main idea of the passage.

Choice 5, "Animal dung enriches the soil by providing nutrients for plant growth," is incorrect because it is contradicted by paragraph 8 of the passage.

Choice 6, "Grasses are generally the dominant type of natural vegetation in semi-arid lands," is incorrect because it is a minor detail, mentioned once in passing in paragraph 7.

Practice Set 3

EARLY CINEMA

The cinema did not emerge as a form of mass consumption until its technology evolved from the initial "peepshow" format to the point where images were projected on a screen in a darkened theater. In the peepshow format, a film was viewed through a small opening in a machine that was created for that purpose. Thomas Edison's peepshow device, the Kinetoscope, was introduced to the public in 1894. It was designed for use in Kinetoscope parlors, or arcades, which contained only a few individual machines and permitted only one customer to view a short, 50-foot film at any one time. The first Kinetoscope parlors contained five machines. For the price of 25 cents (or 5 cents per machine), customers moved from machine to machine to watch five different films (or, in the case of famous prizefights, successive rounds of a single fight).

These Kinetoscope arcades were modeled on phonograph parlors, which had proven successful for Edison several years earlier. In the phonograph parlors, customers listened to recordings through individual ear tubes, moving from one machine to the next to hear different recorded speeches or pieces of music. The Kinetoscope parlors functioned in a similar way. Edison was more interested in the sale of Kinetoscopes (for roughly $1,000 apiece) to these parlors than in the films that would be run in them (which cost approximately $10 to $15 each). He refused to develop projection technology, reasoning that if he made and sold projectors, then exhibitors would purchase only one machine—a projector—from him instead of several.

Exhibitors, however, wanted to maximize their profits, which they could do more readily by projecting a handful of films to hundreds of customers at a time (rather than one at a time) and by charging 25 to 50 cents admission. About a year after the opening of the first Kinetoscope parlor in 1894, showmen such as Louis and Auguste Lumière, Thomas Armat and Charles Francis Jenkins, and Orville and Woodville Latham (with the assistance of Edison's former assistant, William Dickson) perfected projection devices. These early projection devices were used in vaudeville theaters, legitimate theaters, local town halls, makeshift storefront theaters, fairgrounds, and amusement parks to show films to a mass audience.

With the advent of projection in 1895–1896, motion pictures became the ultimate form of mass consumption. Previously, large audiences had viewed spectacles at the theater, where vaudeville, popular dramas, musical and minstrel shows, classical plays, lectures, and slide-and-lantern shows had been presented to several hundred spectators at a time. But the movies differed significantly from these other forms of entertainment, which depended on either live performance or (in the case of the slide-and-lantern shows) the active involvement of a master of ceremonies who assembled the final program.

Although early exhibitors regularly accompanied movies with live acts, the substance of the movies themselves is mass-produced, prerecorded material that can easily be reproduced by theaters with little or no active participation by the exhibitor. Even though early exhibitors shaped their film programs by mixing films and other entertainments together in whichever way they thought would be most attractive to audiences or by accompanying them with lectures, their creative control remained limited. What audiences came to see was the technological marvel of the movies; the lifelike reproduction of the commonplace motion of trains, of waves striking the shore, and of people walking in the street; and the magic made possible by trick photography and the manipulation of the camera.

With the advent of projection, the viewer's relationship with the image was no longer private, as it had been with earlier peepshow devices such as the Kinetoscope and the Mutoscope, which was a similar machine that reproduced motion by means of successive images on individual photographic cards instead of on strips of celluloid. It suddenly became public—an experience that the viewer shared with dozens, scores, and even hundreds of others. At the same time, the image that the spectator looked at expanded from the minuscule peepshow dimensions of 1 or 2 inches (in height) to the life-size proportions of 6 or 9 feet.

PARAGRAPH 1

The cinema did not emerge as a form of mass consumption until its technology evolved from the initial "peepshow" format to the point where images were projected on a screen in a darkened theater. In the peepshow format, a film was viewed through a small opening in a machine that was created for that purpose. Thomas Edison's peepshow device, the Kinetoscope, was introduced to the public in 1894. It was designed for use in Kinetoscope parlors, or arcades, which contained only a few individual machines and permitted only one customer to view a short, 50-foot film at any one time. The first Kinetoscope parlors contained five machines. For the price of 25 cents (or 5 cents per machine), customers moved from machine to machine to watch five different films (or, in the case of famous prizefights, successive rounds of a single fight).

Directions: Mark your answer by filling in the oval next to your choice.

1. According to paragraph 1, all of the following were true of viewing films in Kinetoscope parlors EXCEPT:

⬯ One individual at a time viewed a film.
⬯ Customers could view one film after another.
⬯ Prizefights were the most popular subjects for films.
⬯ Each film was short.

PARAGRAPH 2

These Kinetoscope arcades were modeled on phonograph parlors, which had proven successful for Edison several years earlier. In the phonograph parlors, customers listened to recordings through individual ear tubes, moving from one machine to the next to hear different recorded speeches or pieces of music. The Kinetoscope parlors functioned in a similar way. Edison was more interested in the sale of Kinetoscopes (for roughly $1,000 apiece) to these parlors than in the films that would be run in them (which cost approximately $10 to $15 each). He refused to develop projection technology, reasoning that if he made and sold projectors, then exhibitors would purchase only one machine — a projector — from him instead of several.

2. The author discusses phonograph parlors in paragraph 2 in order to

○ explain Edison's financial success
○ describe the model used to design Kinetoscope parlors
○ contrast their popularity to that of Kinetoscope parlors
○ illustrate how much more technologically advanced Kinetoscope parlors were

3. Which of the sentences below best expresses the essential information in the highlighted sentence from the passage? Incorrect answer choices change the meaning in important ways or leave out essential information.

○ Edison was more interested in developing a variety of machines than in developing a technology based on only one.
○ Edison refused to work on projection technology because he did not think exhibitors would replace their projectors with newer machines.
○ Edison did not want to develop projection technology because it limited the number of machines he could sell.
○ Edison would not develop projection technology unless exhibitors agreed to purchase more than one projector from him.

PARAGRAPH 3

Exhibitors, however, wanted to maximize their profits, which they could do more readily by projecting a handful of films to hundreds of customers at a time (rather than one at a time) and by charging 25 to 50 cents admission. About a year after the opening of the first Kinetoscope parlor in 1894, showmen such as Louis and Auguste Lumière, Thomas Armat and Charles Francis Jenkins, and Orville and Woodville Latham (with the assistance of Edison's former assistant, William Dickson) perfected projection devices. These early projection devices were used in vaudeville theaters, legitimate theaters, local town halls, makeshift storefront theaters, fairgrounds, and amusement parks to show films to a mass audience.

4. The word readily in the passage is closest in meaning to

○ frequently
○ easily
○ intelligently
○ obviously

5. The word assistance in the passage is closest in meaning to

○ criticism
○ leadership
○ help
○ approval

PARAGRAPH 4

With the advent of projection in 1895-1896, motion pictures became the ultimate form of mass consumption. Previously, large audiences had viewed spectacles at the theater, where vaudeville, popular dramas, musical and minstrel shows, classical plays, lectures, and slide-and-lantern shows had been presented to several hundred spectators at a time. But the movies differed significantly from these other forms of entertainment, which depended on either live performance or (in the case of the slide-and-lantern shows) the active involvement of a master of ceremonies who assembled the final program.

6. According to paragraph 4, how did the early movies differ from previous spectacles that were presented to large audiences?

○ They were a more expensive form of entertainment.
○ They were viewed by larger audiences.
○ They were more educational.
○ They did not require live entertainers.

PARAGRAPH 5

Although early exhibitors regularly accompanied movies with live acts, the substance of the movies themselves is mass-produced, prerecorded material that can easily be reproduced by theaters with little or no active participation by the exhibitor. Even though early exhibitors shaped their film programs by mixing films and other entertainments together in whichever way they thought would be most attractive to audiences or by accompanying them with lectures, their creative control remained limited. What audiences came to see was the technological marvel of the movies; the lifelike reproduction of the commonplace motion of trains, of waves striking the shore, and of people walking in the street; and the magic made possible by trick photography and the manipulation of the camera.

7. According to paragraph 5, what role did early exhibitors play in the presentation of movies in theaters?

◯ They decided how to combine various components of the film program.

◯ They advised film-makers on appropriate movie content.

◯ They often took part in the live-action performances.

◯ They produced and prerecorded the material that was shown in the theaters.

PARAGRAPH 6

With the advent of projection, the viewer's relationship with the image was no longer private, as it had been with earlier peepshow devices such as the Kinetoscope and the Mutoscope, which was a similar machine that reproduced motion by means of successive images on individual photographic cards instead of on strips of celluloid. It suddenly became public — an experience that the viewer shared with dozens, scores, and even hundreds of others. At the same time, the image that the spectator looked at expanded from the minuscule peepshow dimensions of 1 or 2 inches (in height) to the life-size proportions of 6 or 9 feet.

8. Which of the following is mentioned in paragraph 6 as one of the ways the Mutoscope differed from the Kinetoscope?

◯ Sound and motion were simultaneously produced in the Mutoscope.

◯ More than one person could view the images at the same time with the Mutoscope.

◯ The Mutoscope was a less sophisticated earlier prototype of the Kinetoscope.

◯ A different type of material was used to produce the images used in the Mutoscope.

9. The word it in the passage refers to

◯ the advent of projection

◯ the viewer's relationship with the image

◯ a similar machine

◯ celluloid

10. According to paragraph 6, the images seen by viewers in the earlier peepshows, compared to the images projected on the screen, were relatively

◯ small in size

◯ inexpensive to create

◯ unfocused

◯ limited in subject matter

11. The word expanded in the passage is closest in meaning to

○ was enlarged
○ was improved
○ was varied
○ was rejected

PARAGRAPH 3

■ Exhibitors, however, wanted to maximize their profits, which they could do more readily by projecting a handful of films to hundreds of customers at a time (rather than one at a time) and by charging 25 to 50 cents admission. ■ About a year after the opening of the first Kinetoscope parlor in 1894, showmen such as Louis and Auguste Lumière, Thomas Armat and Charles Francis Jenkins, and Orville and Woodville Latham (with the assistance of Edison's former assistant, William Dickson) perfected projection devices. ■ These early projection devices were used in vaudeville theaters, legitimate theaters, local town halls, makeshift storefront theaters, fairgrounds, and amusement parks to show films to a mass audience. ■

12. Look at the four squares [■] that indicate where the following sentence can be added to the passage.

When this widespread use of projection technology began to hurt his Kinetoscope business, Edison acquired a projector developed by Armat and introduced it as "Edison's latest marvel, the Vitascope."

Where would the sentence best fit?

○ **When this widespread use of projection technology began to hurt his Kinetoscope business, Edison acquired a projector developed by Armat and introduced it as "Edison's latest marvel, the Vitascope."** Exhibitors, however, wanted to maximize their profits, which they could do more readily by projecting a handful of films to hundreds of customers at a time (rather than one at a time) and by charging 25 to 50 cents admission. ■ About a year after the opening of the first Kinetoscope parlor in 1894, showmen such as Louis and Auguste Lumière, Thomas Armat and Charles Francis Jenkins, and Orville and Woodville Latham (with the assistance of Edison's former assistant, William Dickson) perfected projection devices. ■ These early projection devices were used in vaudeville theaters, legitimate theaters, local town halls, makeshift storefront theaters, fairgrounds, and amusement parks to show films to a mass audience. ■

○ ■ Exhibitors, however, wanted to maximize their profits, which they could do more readily by projecting a handful of films to hundreds of customers at a time (rather than one at a time) and by charging 25 to 50 cents admission. **When this widespread use of projection technology began to hurt his Kinetoscope business, Edison acquired a projector developed by Armat and introduced it as "Edison's latest marvel, the Vitascope."** About a year after the opening of the first Kinetoscope parlor in 1894, showmen such as Louis and Auguste Lumière, Thomas Armat and Charles Francis Jenkins, and Orville and Woodville Latham (with the assistance of Edison's former assistant, William Dickson) perfected projection devices. ■ These early projection devices were used in vaudeville theaters, legitimate theaters, local town halls, makeshift storefront theaters, fairgrounds, and amusement parks to show films to a mass audience. ■

○ ■ Exhibitors, however, wanted to maximize their profits, which they could do more readily by projecting a handful of films to hundreds of customers at a time (rather than one at a time) and by charging 25 to 50 cents admission. ■ About a year after the opening of the first Kinetoscope parlor in 1894, showmen such as Louis and Auguste Lumière, Thomas Armat and Charles Francis Jenkins, and Orville and Woodville Latham (with the assistance of Edison's former assistant, William Dickson) perfected projection devices. **When this wide-spread use of projection technology began to hurt his Kinetoscope business, Edison acquired a projector developed by Armat and introduced it as "Edison's latest marvel, the Vitascope."** These early projection devices were used in vaudeville theaters, legitimate theaters, local town halls, makeshift storefront theaters, fairgrounds, and amusement parks to show films to a mass audience.

○ ■ Exhibitors, however, wanted to maximize their profits, which they could do more readily by projecting a handful of films to hundreds of customers at a time (rather than one at a time) and by charging 25 to 50 cents admission. ■ About a year after the opening of the first Kinetoscope parlor in 1894, showmen such as Louis and Auguste Lumière, Thomas Armat and Charles Francis Jenkins, and Orville and Woodville Latham (with the assistance of Edison's former assistant, William Dickson) perfected projection devices. ■ These early projection devices were used in vaudeville theaters, legitimate theaters, local town halls, makeshift storefront theaters, fairgrounds, and amusement parks to shown films to a mass audience. **When this widespread use of projection technology began to hurt his Kinetoscope business, Edison acquired a projector developed by Armat and introduced it as "Edison's latest marvel, the Vitascope."**

13–14. Directions: An introductory sentence for a brief summary of the passage is provided below. Complete the summary by selecting the THREE answer choices that express the most important ideas in the passage. Some answer choices do not belong in the summary because they express ideas that are not presented in the passage or are minor ideas in the passage. ***This question is worth 2 points.***

The technology for modern cinema evolved at the end of the nineteenth century.

- ◆
- ◆
- ◆

Answer Choices

1. Kinetoscope parlors for viewing films were modeled on phonograph parlors.

2. Thomas Edison's design of the Kinetoscope inspired the development of large screen projection.

3. Early cinema allowed individuals to use special machines to view films privately.

4. Slide-and-lantern shows had been presented to audiences of hundreds of spectators.

5. The development of projection technology made it possible to project images on a large screen.

6. Once film images could be projected, the cinema became a form of mass consumption.

Answers and Explanations

1. ❸ This is a Negative Factual Information question asking for specific information that can be found in paragraph 1. Choice 3 is the correct answer. The paragraph does mention that one viewer at a time could view the films (choice 1), that films could be viewed one after another (choice 2), and that films were short (choice 4). Prizefights are mentioned as one subject of these short films, but not necessarily the most popular one.

2. ❷ This is a Rhetorical Purpose question. It asks why the author mentions "phonograph parlors" in paragraph 2. The correct answer is choice 2. The author is explaining why Edison designed his arcades like phonograph parlors; that design had been successful for him in the past. The paragraph does not mention the phonograph parlors to explain Edison's financial success, so choice 1 is incorrect. The paragraph does not directly discuss the situations described in choices 3 and 4, so those answers too are incorrect.

3. ❸ This is a Sentence Simplification question. As with all of these items, a single sentence in the passage is highlighted:

> He refused to develop projection technology, reasoning that if he made and sold projectors, then exhibitors would purchase only one machine—a projector—from him, instead of several.

The correct answer is choice 3. That choice contains all of the **essential** ideas in the highlighted sentence. It is also the only choice that does not change the meaning of the sentence. Choice 1 says that Edison was more interested in developing a variety of machines, which is not true. Choice 2 says that the reason Edison refused to work on projection technology was that exhibitors would never replace the projectors. That also is not true; the highlighted sentence implies that he refused to do this because he wanted exhibitors to buy several Kinetoscope machines at a time instead of a single projector. Choice 4 says that Edison refused to develop projection technology unless exhibitors agreed to purchase more that one projector from him. The highlighted sentence actually says that Edison had already reasoned or concluded that exhibitors would not buy more than one, so choice 4 is a change in essential meaning.

4. ❷ This is a Vocabulary question. The word being tested is *readily*. It is highlighted in the passage. *Readily* means "easily," so choice 2 is the correct answer. The other choices do not fit in the context of the sentence.

5. ❸ This is a Vocabulary question. The word being tested is *assistance*. It is highlighted in the passage. An assistant is a person who helps a leader, so choice 3, "help," is the correct answer.

6. ❹ This is a Factual Information question asking for specific information that can be found in paragraph 4. The correct answer is choice 4. Early movies were

different from previous spectacles because they did not require live actors. The paragraph states (emphasis added):

"But the movies differed significantly from these other forms of entertainment, which depended on either **live performance** or (in the case of the slide-and-lantern shows) the active involvement of a master of ceremonies who assembled the final program."

So the fact that previous spectacles depended on live performances is explicitly stated as one of the ways (but not the only way) that those earlier entertainments differed from movies. The other answer choices are not mentioned in the paragraph.

7. ❶ This is a Factual Information question asking for specific information that can be found in paragraph 5. The correct answer is choice 1, "They decided how to combine various components of the film program," because that idea is stated explicitly in the paragraph:

"Early exhibitors shaped their film programs by mixing films and other entertainments together."

The other choices, while possibly true, are not explicitly mentioned in the paragraph as being among the exhibitors' roles.

8. ❹ This is a Factual Information question asking for specific information that can be found in paragraph 6. The correct answer is choice 4, "A different type of material was used to produce the images used in the Mutoscope." The paragraph says that these machines were very similar but that they differed in one particular way:

". . . the Mutoscope, which was a similar machine that reproduced motion by means of successive images on individual photographic cards instead of on strips of celluloid."

9. ❷ This is a Reference question. The word being tested is *it*. That word is highlighted in the passage. Choice 2, "the viewer's relationship with the image," is the correct answer. This is a simple-pronoun referent item. The sentence says that "it" suddenly became "public," which implies that whatever "it" is, it was formerly private. The paragraph says that the "viewer's relationship to the image was no longer private," so that relationship is the "it" referred to here.

10. ❶ This is a Factual Information question asking for specific information that can be found in paragraph 6. The correct answer is choice 1. The paragraph says that the images expanded from an inch or two to life-size proportions, so "small in size" must be correct. The paragraph does not mention the other choices.

11. ❶ This is a Vocabulary Question. The word being tested is *expanded*. It is highlighted in the passage. Choice 1, "was enlarged," is the correct answer. If something *expanded,* it grew or got bigger. "Enlarged" also means "grew or got bigger."

12. ❹ This is an Insert Text question. You can see the four black squares in paragraph 3 that represent the possible answer choices here.

■ Exhibitors, however, wanted to maximize their profits, which they could do more readily by projecting a handful of films to hundreds of customers at a time (rather than one at a time) and by charging 25 to 50 cents admission. ■ About a year after the opening of the first Kinetoscope parlor in 1894, showmen such as Louis and Auguste Lumière, Thomas Armat and Charles Francis Jenkins, and Orville and Woodville Latham (with the assistance of Edison's former assistant, William Dickson) perfected projection devices. ■ These early projection devices were used in vaudeville theaters, legitimate theaters, local town halls, makeshift storefront theaters, fairgrounds, and amusement parks to show films to a mass audience. ■

The inserted sentence fits best at square 4 because it represents the final result of the general use of projectors. After projectors became popular, Edison lost money, and although he had previously refused to develop projection technology, now he was forced to do so. To place the sentence anyplace else would interrupt the logical narrative sequence of the events described. None of the sentences in this paragraph can logically follow the inserted sentence, so squares 1, 2, and 3 are all incorrect.

13. ❸ ❺ ❻ This is a Prose Summary question. It is completed correctly below. The correct choices are 3, 5, and 6. Choices 1, 2, and 4 are therefore incorrect.

Directions: An introductory sentence for a brief summary of the passage is provided below. Complete the summary by selecting the THREE answer choices that express the most important ideas in the passage. Some answer choices do not belong in the summary because they express ideas that are not presented in the passage or are minor ideas in the passage. *This question is worth 2 points.*

The technology for modern cinema evolved at the end of the nineteenth century.

- Early cinema allowed individuals to use special machines to view films privately.
- The development of projection technology made it possible to project images on a large screen.
- Once film images could be projected, the cinema became a form of mass consumption.

Answer Choices

1. Kinetoscope parlors for viewing films were modeled on phonograph parlors.

2. Thomas Edison's design of the Kinetoscope inspired the development of large screen projection.

3. Early cinema allowed individuals to use special machines to view films privately.

4. Slide-and-lantern shows had been presented to audiences of hundreds of spectators.

5. The development of projection technology made it possible to project images on a large screen.

6. Once film images could be projected, the cinema became a form of mass consumption.

Correct Choices

Choice 3, "Early cinema allowed individuals to use special machines to view films privately, " is correct because it represents one of the chief differences between Kinetoscope and projection viewing. This idea is discussed at several places in the passage. It is mentioned in paragraphs 1, 3, 4, and 6. Thus it is a basic, recurring theme of the passage and, as such, a "major idea."

Choice 5, "The development of projection technology made it possible to project images on a large screen," is correct because this is a major idea that is developed in paragraphs 3, 4, 5, and 6. This development was essentially the reason that the cinema "emerged as a form of mass consumption."

Choice 6, "Once film images could be projected, the cinema became a form of mass consumption," is correct because it represents the primary theme of the passage. It is explicitly stated in the passage's opening sentence; then the remainder of the passage describes that evolution.

Incorrect Choices

Choice 1, "Kinetoscope parlors for viewing films were modeled on phonograph parlors," is incorrect because, while true, it is a minor detail. The Kinetoscope parlors are described in paragraph 2, but the fact that they were modeled on phonograph parlors is not central to the "evolution" of cinema.

Choice 2, "Thomas Edison's design of the Kinetoscope inspired the development of large screen projection," is incorrect because it is not clear that it is true, based on the passage. While it may be inferred from paragraph 3 that the Kinetoscope inspired the development of large screen projection, it seems more likely that the pursuit of greater profits is what really inspired large screen projection development. Since this answer is not clearly supported in the passage, it cannot be considered a "main idea" and is incorrect.

Choice 4, "Slide-and-lantern shows had been presented to audiences of hundreds of spectators," is incorrect because it is a minor detail, mentioned only once in paragraph 4 as part of a larger list of theatrical spectacles.

Practice Set 4

AGGRESSION

When one animal attacks another, it engages in the most obvious example of aggressive behavior. Psychologists have adopted several approaches to understanding aggressive behavior in people.

The Biological Approach. Numerous biological structures and chemicals appear to be involved in aggression. One is the hypothalamus, a region of the brain. In response to certain stimuli, many animals show instinctive aggressive reactions. The hypothalamus appears to be involved in this inborn reaction pattern: electrical stimulation of part of the hypothalamus triggers stereotypical aggressive behaviors in many animals. In people, however, whose brains are more complex, other brain structures apparently moderate possible instincts.

An offshoot of the biological approach called *sociobiology* suggests that aggression is natural and even desirable for people. Sociobiology views much social behavior, including aggressive behavior, as genetically determined. Consider Darwin's theory of evolution. Darwin held that many more individuals are produced than can find food and survive into adulthood. A struggle for survival follows. Those individuals who possess characteristics that provide them with an advantage in the struggle for existence are more likely to survive and contribute their genes to the next generation. In many species, such characteristics include aggressiveness. Because aggressive individuals are more likely to survive and reproduce, whatever genes are linked to aggressive behavior are more likely to be transmitted to subsequent generations.

The sociobiological view has been attacked on numerous grounds. One is that people's capacity to outwit other species, not their aggressiveness, appears to be the dominant factor in human survival. Another is that there is too much variation among people to believe that they are dominated by, or at the mercy of, aggressive impulses.

The Psychodynamic Approach. Theorists adopting the psychodynamic approach hold that inner conflicts are crucial for understanding human behavior, including aggression. Sigmund Freud, for example, believed that aggressive impulses are inevitable reactions to the frustrations of daily life. Children normally desire to vent aggressive impulses on other people, including their parents, because even the most attentive parents cannot gratify all of their demands immediately. Yet children, also fearing their parents' punishment and the loss of parental love, come to repress most aggressive impulses. The Freudian perspective, in a sense, sees us as "steam engines." By holding in rather than venting "steam," we set the stage for future explosions. Pent-up aggressive impulses demand outlets. They may be expressed toward parents in indirect ways such as destroying furniture, or they may be expressed toward strangers later in life.

According to psychodynamic theory, the best ways to prevent harmful aggression may be to encourage less harmful aggression. In the steam-engine analogy, verbal aggression may vent some of the aggressive steam. So might cheering on one's favorite sports team. Psychoanalysts, therapists adopting a psychodynamic approach, refer to the venting of aggressive impulses as "catharsis." Catharsis is theorized to be a safety valve. But research findings on the usefulness of catharsis are mixed. Some studies suggest that catharsis leads to reductions in tension and a lowered likelihood of future aggression. Other studies, however, suggest that letting some steam escape actually encourages more aggression later on.

The Cognitive Approach. Cognitive psychologists assert that our behavior is influenced by our values, by the ways in which we interpret our situations, and by choice. For example, people who believe that aggression is necessary and justified—as during wartime—are likely to act aggressively, whereas people who believe that a particular war or act of aggression is unjust, or who think that aggression is never justified, are less likely to behave aggressively.

One cognitive theory suggests that aggravating and painful events trigger unpleasant feelings. These feelings, in turn, can lead to aggressive action, but *not* automatically. Cognitive factors intervene. People *decide* whether they will act aggressively or not on the basis of factors such as their experiences with aggression and their interpretation of other people's motives. Supporting evidence comes from research showing that aggressive people often distort other people's motives. For example, they assume that other people mean them harm when they do not.

Catharsis: In psychodynamic theory, the purging of strong emotions or the relieving of tensions.

PARAGRAPH 2

The Biological Approach. Numerous biological structures and chemicals appear to be involved in aggression. One is the hypothalamus, a region of the brain. In response to certain stimuli, many animals show instinctive aggressive reactions. The hypothalamus appears to be involved in this inborn reaction pattern: electrical stimulation of part of the hypothalamus triggers stereotypical aggressive behaviors in many animals. In people, however, whose brains are more complex, other brain structures apparently moderate possible instincts.

Directions: Mark your answer by filling in the oval next to your choice.

1. According to paragraph 2, what evidence indicates that aggression in animals is related to the hypothalamus?

○ Some aggressive animal species have a highly developed hypothalamus.

○ Artificial stimulation of the hypothalamus results in aggression in animals.

○ Animals behaving aggressively show increased activity in the hypothalamus.

○ Animals who lack a hypothalamus display few aggressive tendencies.

PARAGRAPH 3

An offshoot of the biological approach called *sociobiology* suggests that aggression is natural and even desirable for people. Sociobiology views much social behavior, including aggressive behavior, as genetically determined. Consider Darwin's theory of evolution. Darwin held that many more individuals are produced than can find food and survive into adulthood. A struggle for survival follows. Those individuals who possess characteristics that provide them with an advantage in the struggle for existence are more likely to survive and contribute their genes to the next generation. In many species, such characteristics include aggressiveness. Because aggressive individuals are more likely to survive and reproduce, whatever genes are linked to aggressive behavior are more likely to be transmitted to subsequent generations.

2. According to Darwin's theory of evolution, members of a species are forced to struggle for survival because

○ not all individuals are skilled in finding food
○ individuals try to defend their young against attackers
○ many more individuals are born than can survive until the age of reproduction
○ individuals with certain genes are more likely to reach adulthood

PARAGRAPH 5

The Psychodynamic Approach. Theorists adopting the psychodynamic approach hold that inner conflicts are crucial for understanding human behavior, including aggression. Sigmund Freud, for example, believed that aggressive impulses are inevitable reactions to the frustrations of daily life. Children normally desire to vent aggressive impulses on other people, including their parents, because even the most attentive parents cannot gratify all of their demands immediately. Yet children, also fearing their parents' punishment and the loss of parental love, come to repress most aggressive impulses. The Freudian perspective, in a sense, sees us as "steam engines." By holding in rather than venting "steam," we set the stage for future explosions. Pent-up aggressive impulses demand outlets. They may be expressed toward parents in indirect ways such as destroying furniture, or they may be expressed toward strangers later in life.

3. The word inevitable in the passage is closest in meaning to

○ unavoidable
○ regrettable
○ controllable
○ unsuitable

4. The word gratify in the passage is closest in meaning to

○ identify
○ modify
○ satisfy
○ simplify

5. The word they in the passage refers to

○ future explosions
○ pent-up aggressive impulses
○ outlets
○ indirect ways

6. According to paragraph 5, Freud believed that children experience conflict between a desire to vent aggression on their parents and

○ a frustration that their parents do not give them everything they want
○ a fear that their parents will punish them and stop loving them
○ a desire to take care of their parents
○ a desire to vent aggression on other family members

7. Freud describes people as steam engines in order to make the point that people

○ deliberately build up their aggression to make themselves stronger
○ usually release aggression in explosive ways
○ must vent their aggression to prevent it from building up
○ typically lose their aggression if they do not express it

The Cognitive Approach. Cognitive psychologists assert that our behavior is influenced by our values, by the ways in which we interpret our situations, and by choice. For example, people who believe that aggression is necessary and justified–as during wartime—are likely to act aggressively, whereas people who believe that a particular war or act of aggression is unjust, or who think that aggression is never justified, are less likely to behave aggressively.

One cognitive theory suggests that aggravating and painful events trigger unpleasant feelings. These feelings, in turn, can lead to aggressive action, but *not* automatically. Cognitive factors intervene. People *decide* whether they will act aggressively or not on the basis of factors such as their experiences with aggression and their interpretation of other people's motives. Supporting evidence comes from research showing that aggressive people often distort other people's motives. For example, they assume that other people mean them harm when they do not.

8. Which of the sentences below best expresses the essential information in the highlighted sentence in the passage? *Incorrect* answer choices change the meaning in important ways or leave out essential information.

○ People who believe that they are fighting a just war act aggressively while those who believe that they are fighting an unjust war do not.

○ People who believe that aggression is necessary and justified are more likely to act aggressively than those who believe differently.

○ People who normally do not believe that aggression is necessary and justified may act aggressively during wartime.

○ People who believe that aggression is necessary and justified do not necessarily act aggressively during wartime.

9. According to the cognitive approach described in paragraphs 7 and 8, all of the following may influence the decision whether to act aggressively EXCEPT a person's

○ moral values
○ previous experiences with aggression
○ instinct to avoid aggression
○ beliefs about other people's intentions

10. The word distort in the passage is closest in meaning to

○ mistrust
○ misinterpret
○ criticize
○ resent

The Psychodynamic Approach. Theorists adopting the psychodynamic approach hold that inner conflicts are crucial for understanding human behavior, including aggression. Sigmund Freud, for example, believed that aggressive impulses are inevitable reactions to the frustrations of daily life. Children normally desire to vent aggressive impulses on other people, including their parents, because even the most attentive parents cannot gratify all of their demands immediately. ■ Yet children, also fearing their parents' punishment and the loss of parental love, come to repress most aggressive impulses. ■ The Freudian perspective, in a sense, sees us as "steam engines." ■ By holding in rather than venting "steam," we set the stage for future explosions. ■ Pent-up aggressive impulses demand outlets. They may be expressed toward parents in indirect ways such as destroying furniture, or they may be expressed toward strangers later in life.

11. Look at the four squares [■] that indicate where the following sentence can be added to the passage.

According to Freud, however, impulses that have been repressed continue to exist and demand expression.

Where would the sentence best fit?

○ **The Psychodynamic Approach.** Theorists adopting the psychodynamic approach hold that inner conflicts are crucial for understanding human behavior, including aggression. Sigmund Freud, for example, believed that aggressive impulses are inevitable reactions to the frustrations of daily life. Children normally desire to vent aggressive impulses on other people, including their parents, because even the most attentive parents cannot gratify all of their demands immediately. **According to Freud, however, impulses that have been repressed continue to exist and demand expression.** Yet children, also fearing their parents' punishment and the loss of parental love, come to repress most aggressive impulses. ■ The Freudian perspective, in a sense, sees us as "steam engines." ■ By holding in rather than venting "steam," we set the stage for future explosions. ■ Pent-up aggressive impulses demand outlets. They may be expressed toward parents in indirect ways such as destroying furniture, or they may be expressed toward strangers later in life.

○ **The Psychodynamic Approach.** Theorists adopting the psychodynamic approach hold that inner conflicts are crucial for understanding human behavior, including aggression. Sigmund Freud, for example, believed that aggressive impulses are inevitable reactions to the frustrations of daily life. Children normally desire to vent aggressive impulses on other people, including their parents, because even the most attentive parents cannot gratify all of their demands immediately. ■ Yet children, also fearing their parents' punishment and the loss of parental love, come to repress most aggressive impulses. **According to Freud, however, impulses that have been repressed continue to exist and demand expression.** The Freudian perspective, in a sense, sees us as "steam engines." ■ By holding in rather than venting "steam," we set the stage for future explosions. ■ Pent-up aggressive impulses demand outlets. They may be expressed toward parents in indirect ways such as destroying furniture, or they may be expressed toward strangers later in life.

○ **The Psychodynamic Approach.** Theorists adopting the psychodynamic approach hold that inner conflicts are crucial for understanding human behavior, including aggression. Sigmund Freud, for example, believed that aggressive impulses are inevitable reactions to the frustrations of daily life. Children normally desire to vent aggressive impulses on other people, including their parents, because even the most attentive parents cannot gratify all of their demands immediately. ■ Yet children, also fearing their parents' punishment and the loss of parental love, come to repress most aggressive impulses. ■ The Freudian perspective, in a sense, sees us as "steam engines." **According to Freud, however, impulses that have been repressed continue to exist and demand expression.** By holding in rather than venting "steam," we set the stage for future explosions. ■ Pent-up aggressive impulses demand outlets. They may be expressed toward parents in indirect ways such as destroying furniture, or they may be expressed toward strangers later in life.

○ **The Psychodynamic Approach.** Theorists adopting the psychodynamic approach hold that inner conflicts are crucial for understanding human behavior, including aggression. Sigmund Freud, for example, believed that aggressive impulses are inevitable reactions to the frustrations of daily life. Children normally desire to vent aggressive impulses on other people, including their parents, because even the most attentive parents cannot gratify all of their demands immediately. ■ Yet children, also fearing their parents' punishment and the loss of parental love, come to repress most aggressive impulses. ■ The Freudian perspective, in a sense, sees us as "steam engines." ■ By holding in rather than venting "steam," we set the stage for future explosions. **According to Freud, however, impulses that have been repressed continue to exist and demand expression.** Pent-up aggressive impulses demand outlets. They may be expressed toward parents in indirect ways such as destroying furniture, or they may be expressed toward strangers later in life.

12. **Directions:** Complete the table below by matching five of the six answer choices with the approach to aggression that they exemplify. *This question is worth 3 points*.

Approach to Understanding Aggression	Associated Claims
Biological Approach	➤ _____
Psychodynamic Approach	➤ _____ ➤ _____
Cognitive Approach	➤ _____ ➤ _____

Answer Choices

1. Aggressive impulses toward people are sometimes expressed in indirect ways.

2. Aggressiveness is often useful for individuals in the struggle for survival.

3. Aggressive behavior may involve a misunderstanding of other people's intentions.

4. The need to express aggressive impulses declines with age.

5. Acting aggressively is the result of a choice influenced by a person's values and beliefs.

6. Repressing aggressive impulses can result in aggressive behavior.

Answers and Explanations

1. ❸ This is a Factual Information question asking for specific information that can be found in paragraph 2. The correct answer is choice 3. The question asks specifically for "evidence that indicates that aggression in animals is related to the hypothalamus." Answer choices 1 and 2 are contradicted by the paragraph. Choice 2 is incorrect because, while the paragraph states that "electrical stimulation" triggers aggressive behavior in many animals, this is not "evidence" in itself, but merely support for the more general statement in choice 3 that increased hypothalmusic activity, in general, is related to aggression.

2. ❸ This is a Factual Information question asking for specific information that can be found in the passage. The correct answer is choice 3, "many more individuals are born than can survive until the age of reproduction." This answer choice is essentially a paraphrase of paragraph 3, sentence 4: "Darwin held that many more individuals are produced than can find food and survive into adulthood." Choices 1 and 2 are not mentioned at all. Choice 4 may be true, but it is not stated in the passage as a fact; an inference is needed to support it.

3. ❶ This is a Vocabulary question. The word being tested is *inevitable*. It is highlighted in the passage. The correct answer is choice 1, *unavoidable*. If something is inevitable, that means that it will occur no matter what; in other words, it is unavoidable.

4. ❸ This is a Vocabulary question. The word being tested is *gratify*. It is highlighted in the passage. The correct answer is choice 3, "satisfy." If a person's desires are gratified, those desires are fulfilled. Thus the person is satisfied.

5. ❷ This is a Reference question. The word being tested is *they*. It is highlighted in the passage. The correct answer is choice 2, "pent-up aggressive impulses." This is a simple pronoun-referent item. The word *they* here refers to something that "may be expressed toward strangers later in life." This is the "outlet" toward which the "aggressive impulses" mentioned may be directed.

6. ❷ This is a Factual Information question asking for specific information that can be found in paragraph 5. The correct answer is choice 2, "a fear that their parents will punish them and stop loving them." The question asks what causes the conflict between the desire to vent aggression and children's fears. The answer is found in paragraph 5 in the sentence that reads, "Yet children, also fearing their parents' punishment and the loss of parental love, come to repress most aggressive impulses." Answer choice 2 is the only choice that correctly identifies the cause of the conflict created by repressing aggression in children.

7. ❸ This is a Rhetorical Purpose question. It asks you why the author mentions that Freud described people as "steam engines" in the passage. The phrase being tested is highlighted in the passage. The correct answer is choice 3, "must vent their aggression to prevent it from building up." Steam engines will explode if their steam builds up indefinitely. The same is true of people, as choice 3 indicates.

The other choices are not necessarily true of both people and steam engines, so they are incorrect.

8. ❷ This is a Sentence Simplification question. As with all of these items, a single sentence in the passage is highlighted:

> For example, people who believe that aggression is necessary and justified—as during wartime—are likely to act aggressively, whereas people who believe that a particular war or act of aggression is unjust, or who think that aggression is never justified, are less likely to behave aggressively.

The correct answer is choice 2. It contains all of the *essential* information in the highlighted sentence. The highlighted sentence compares people who believe particular acts of aggression are necessary and those who don't, in terms of their relative likelihood to act aggressively under certain conditions. This is precisely what choice 2 says: "People who believe that aggression is necessary and justified are more likely to act aggressively than those who believe differently." It compares the behavior of one type of person to that of another type of person. Nothing essential has been left out, and the meaning has not been changed.

Choice 1 changes the meaning of the sentence; it says categorically that "those (people) who believe that they are fighting an unjust war do not (act aggressively)." The highlighted sentence merely says that such people are "less likely" to act aggressively, not that they never will; this changes the meaning.

Choice 3 says, "People who normally do not believe that aggression is necessary and justified may act aggressively during wartime." This is incorrect because it leaves out critical information: it does not mention people who do believe aggression is necessary. This choice does not make the same comparison as the highlighted sentence.

Choice 4, "People who believe that aggression is necessary and justified do not necessarily act aggressively during wartime," also changes the meaning of the sentence by leaving out essential information. In this choice, no mention is made of people who do not believe aggression is necessary. This choice does not make the same comparison as the highlighted sentence.

9. ❸ This is a Negative Factual Information question asking for specific information that can be found in paragraphs 7 and 8. Choice 3 is the correct answer.

Choice 1, "moral values," is explicitly mentioned as one of the influences on aggressive behavior, so it is incorrect. Choices 2 ("previous experiences") and 4 ("beliefs about other people") are both explicitly mentioned in this context. The sentence in paragraph 8 says, "People *decide* whether they will act aggressively or not on the basis of factors such as their experiences with aggression and their interpretation of other people's motives." Choice 3, the "instinct to avoid aggression," is not mentioned, so it is the correct answer here.

10. ❷ This is a Vocabulary question. The word being tested is *distort*. It is highlighted in the passage. The correct answer is choice 2, "misinterpret." To distort

other people's motives is to twist them, or view them incorrectly and thereby not understand them properly. Something that is not understood properly is misinterpreted.

11. ❷ This is an Insert Text question. You can see the four black squares in paragraph 5 that represent the possible answer choices here.

The Psychodynamic Approach. Theorists adopting the psychodynamic approach hold that inner conflicts are crucial for understanding human behavior, including aggression. Sigmund Freud, for example, believed that aggressive impulses are inevitable reactions to the frustrations of daily life. Children normally desire to vent aggressive impulses on other people, including their parents, because even the most attentive parents cannot gratify all of their demands immediately. ■ Yet children, also fearing their parents' punishment and the loss of parental love, come to repress most aggressive impulses. ■ The Freudian perspective, in a sense, sees us as "steam engines." ■ By holding in rather than venting "steam," we set the stage for future explosions. ■ Pent-up aggressive impulses demand outlets. They may be expressed toward parents in indirect ways such as destroying furniture, or they may be expressed toward strangers later in life.

The sentence provided, "According to Freud, however, impulses that have been repressed continue to exist and demand expression," is best inserted at square 2.

Square 2 is correct because the sentence being inserted is a connective sentence, connecting the idea of childhood repression in the preceding sentence to the "Freudian perspective" in the sentence that follows. The use of the word *however* in this sentence indicates that an idea already introduced (the repression of children's aggressive impulses) is being modified. Here, the inserted sentence tells us that Freud thought that even though these impulses are repressed, they continue to exist. This serves as a connection to the next sentence and the "Freudian perspective." Inserting the sentence at square 1 would place the modification ("however, impulses . . . continue to exist") before the idea that it modifies (repression of impulses). This makes no logical sense. Inserting the sentence at square 3 would move the modifying sentence away from its logical position immediately following the idea that it modifies (repression of impulses). Placing the insert sentence at square 4 moves the sentence farther from its logical antecedent and has no connection to the sentence that follows it.

12. This is a Fill in a Table question. It is completed correctly below. Choice 2 is the correct answer for the "Biological Approach" row. Choices 1 and 6 are the correct answers for the "Psychodynamic Approach" row. Choices 3 and 5 are the correct answers for the "Cognitive Approach" row. Choice 4 should not be used in any row.

Directions: Complete the table below by matching five of the six answer choices with the approach to aggression that they exemplify. ***This question is worth 3 points.***

Approach to Understanding Aggression	Associated Claims
Biological Approach	➤ Aggressiveness is often useful for individuals in the struggle for survival.
Psychodynamic Approach	➤ Aggressive impulses toward people are sometimes expressed in indirect ways. ➤ Repressing aggressive impulses can result in aggressive behavior.
Cognitive Approach	➤ Aggressive behavior may involve a misunderstanding of other people's intentions. ➤ Acting aggressively is the result of a choice influenced by a person's values and beliefs.

Answer Choices

1. Aggressive impulses toward people are sometimes expressed in indirect ways.

2. Aggressiveness is often useful for individuals in the struggle for survival.

3. Aggressive behavior may involve a misunderstanding of other people's intentions.

4. The need to express aggressive impulses declines with age.

5. Acting aggressively is the result of a choice influenced by a person's values and beliefs.

6. Repressing aggressive impulses can result in aggressive behavior.

Correct Choices

Choice 1: "Aggressive impulses toward people are sometimes expressed in indirect ways" belongs in the Psychodynamic Approach row based on paragraph 5. That paragraph, in explaining the Psychodynamic Approach, states that "Pent-up aggressive impulses demand outlets. They may be expressed toward parents in indirect ways such as destroying furniture . . ."

Choice 2: "Aggressiveness is often useful for individuals in the struggle for survival" belongs in the Biological Approach row because, as stated in paragraph 3, "An offshoot of the biological approach called *sociobiology* suggests that aggression is natural and even desirable for people." The remainder of that paragraph explains the ways in which aggressive behavior can be useful in the struggle for survival. Neither of the other approaches discusses this idea, so this answer choice belongs here.

Choice 3: "Aggressive behavior may involve a misunderstanding of other people's intentions" belongs in the Cognitive Approach row based on paragraph 8. The theme of that paragraph is that people decide to be aggressive (or not) largely based upon their interpretations of other people's motives. It goes on to say that these interpretations may be "distorted," or misunderstood. Accordingly, this answer choice belongs in this row.

Choice 5: "Acting aggressively is the result of a choice influenced by a person's values and beliefs" belongs in the Cognitive Approach row based on paragraph 7 which states, "Cognitive psychologists assert that our behavior is influenced by our values, by the ways in which we interpret our situations, and by choice." Thus, this is an important aspect of the cognitive approach.

Choice 6: "Repressing aggressive impulses can result in aggressive behavior" belongs in the Psychodynamic Approach row based on paragraphs 5 and 6. Both of those paragraphs explicitly make this point in the section of the passage on the Psychodynamic Approach.

Incorrect Choice

Choice 4: "The need to express aggressive impulses declines with age" is not mentioned in connection with any of the approaches to aggression discussed in the passage, so it should not be used.

Practice Set 5

ARTISANS AND INDUSTRIALIZATION

Before 1815 manufacturing in the United States had been done in homes or shops by skilled artisans. As master craftworkers, they imparted the knowledge of their trades to apprentices and journeymen. In addition, women often worked in their homes part-time, making finished articles from raw material supplied by merchant capitalists. After 1815 this older form of manufacturing began to give way to factories with machinery tended by unskilled or semiskilled laborers. Cheap transportation networks, the rise of cities, and the availability of capital and credit all stimulated the shift to factory production.

The creation of a labor force that was accustomed to working in factories did not occur easily. Before the rise of the factory, artisans had worked within the home. Apprentices were considered part of the family, and masters were responsible not only for teaching their apprentices a trade but also for providing them some education and for supervising their moral behavior. Journeymen knew that if they perfected their skill, they could become respected master artisans with their own shops. Also, skilled artisans did not work by the clock, at a steady pace, but rather in bursts of intense labor alternating with more leisurely time.

The factory changed that. Goods produced by factories were not as finished or elegant as those done by hand, and pride in craftsmanship gave way to the pressure to increase rates of productivity. The new methods of doing business involved a new and stricter sense of time. Factory life necessitated a more regimented schedule, where work began at the sound of a bell and workers kept machines going at a constant pace. At the same time, workers were required to discard old habits, for industrialism demanded a worker who was alert, dependable, and self-disciplined. Absenteeism and lateness hurt productivity and, since work was specialized, disrupted the regular factory routine. Industrialization not only produced a fundamental change in the way work was organized; it transformed the very nature of work.

The first generation to experience these changes did not adopt the new attitudes easily. The factory clock became the symbol of the new work rules. One mill worker who finally quit complained revealingly about "obedience to the ding-dong of the bell—just as though we are so many living machines." With the loss of personal freedom also came the loss of standing in the community. Unlike artisan workshops in which apprentices worked closely with the masters supervising them, factories sharply separated workers from management. Few workers rose through the ranks to supervisory positions, and even fewer could achieve the artisan's dream of setting up one's own business. Even well-paid workers sensed their decline in status.

In this newly emerging economic order, workers sometimes organized to protect their rights and traditional ways of life. Craftworkers such as carpenters, printers, and tailors formed unions, and in 1834 individual unions came together in the National Trades' Union. The labor movement gathered some momentum in the decade before the Panic of 1837, but in the depression that followed, labor's strength collapsed. During hard times, few workers were willing to strike* or engage in collective action. And skilled craftworkers, who spearheaded the union movement, did not feel a particularly strong bond with semiskilled factory workers and unskilled laborers. More than a decade of agitation did finally bring a workday shortened to 10 hours to most industries by the 1850's, and the courts also recognized workers' right to strike, but these gains had little immediate impact.

Workers were united in resenting the industrial system and their loss of status, but they were divided by ethnic and racial antagonisms, gender, conflicting religious perspectives, occupational differences, political party loyalties, and disagreements over tactics. For them, the factory and industrialism were not agents of opportunity but reminders of their loss of independence and a measure of control over their lives. As United States society became more specialized and differentiated, greater extremes of wealth began to appear. And as the new markets created fortunes for the few, the factory system lowered the wages of workers by dividing labor into smaller, less skilled tasks.

*strike: a stopping of work that is organized by workers

PARAGRAPH 1

Before 1815 manufacturing in the United States had been done in homes or shops by skilled artisans. As master craftworkers, they imparted the knowledge of their trades to apprentices and journeymen. In addition, women often worked in their homes part-time, making finished articles from raw material supplied by merchant capitalists. After 1815 this older form of manufacturing began to give way to factories with machinery tended by unskilled or semiskilled laborers. Cheap transportation networks, the rise of cities, and the availability of capital and credit all stimulated the shift to factory production.

Directions: Mark your answer by filling in the oval next to your choice.

1. Which of the following can be inferred from the passage about articles manufactured before 1815?

   ○ They were primarily produced by women.
   ○ They were generally produced in shops rather than in homes.
   ○ They were produced with more concern for quality than for speed of production.
   ○ They were produced mostly in large cities with extensive transportation networks.

PARAGRAPH 2

The creation of a labor force that was accustomed to working in factories did not occur easily. Before the rise of the factory, artisans had worked within the home. Apprentices were considered part of the family, and masters were responsible not only for teaching their apprentices a trade but also for providing them some education and for supervising their moral behavior. Journeymen knew that if they perfected their skill, they could become respected master artisans with their own shops. Also, skilled artisans did not work by the clock, at a steady pace, but rather in bursts of intense labor alternating with more leisurely time.

2. Which of the sentences below best expresses the essential information in the highlighted sentence in the passage? *Incorrect* answer choices change the meaning in important ways or leave out essential information.

   ○ Masters demanded moral behavior from apprentices but often treated them irresponsibly.

   ○ The responsibilities of the master to the apprentice went beyond the teaching of a trade.
   ○ Masters preferred to maintain the trade within the family by supervising and educating the younger family members.
   ○ Masters who trained members of their own family as apprentices demanded excellence from them.

PARAGRAPH 3

The factory changed that. Goods produced by factories were not as finished or elegant as those done by hand, and pride in craftsmanship gave way to the pressure to increase rates of productivity. The new methods of doing business involved a new and stricter sense of time. Factory life necessitated a more regimented schedule, where work began at the sound of a bell and workers kept machines going at a constant pace. At the same time, workers were required to discard old habits, for industrialism demanded a worker who was alert, dependable, and self-disciplined. Absenteeism and lateness hurt productivity and, since work was specialized, disrupted the regular factory routine. Industrialization not only produced a fundamental change in the way work was organized; it transformed the very nature of work.

3. The word disrupted in the passage is closest in meaning to

○ prolonged
○ established
○ followed
○ upset

PARAGRAPH 4

The first generation to experience these changes did not adopt the new attitudes easily. The factory clock became the symbol of the new work rules. One mill worker who finally quit complained revealingly about "obedience to the ding-dong of the bell—just as though we are so many living machines." With the loss of personal freedom also came the loss of standing in the community. Unlike artisan workshops in which apprentices worked closely with the masters supervising them, factories sharply separated workers from management. Few workers rose through the ranks to supervisory positions, and even fewer could achieve the artisan's dream of setting up one's own business. Even well-paid workers sensed their decline in status.

4. In paragraph 4, the author includes the quotation from a mill worker in order to

○ support the idea that it was difficult for workers to adjust to working in factories
○ to show that workers sometimes quit because of the loud noise made by factory machinery
○ argue that clocks did not have a useful function in factories
○ emphasize that factories were most successful when workers revealed their complaints

5. All of the following are mentioned in paragraph 4 as consequences of the new system for workers EXCEPT a loss of

○ freedom
○ status in the community
○ opportunities for advancement
○ contact among workers who were not managers

PARAGRAPH 5

In this newly emerging economic order, workers sometimes organized to protect their rights and traditional ways of life. Craftworkers such as carpenters, printers, and tailors formed unions, and in 1834 individual unions came together in the National Trades' Union. The labor movement gathered some momentum in the decade before the Panic of 1837, but in the depression that followed, labor's strength collapsed. During hard times, few workers were willing to strike or engage in collective action. And skilled craftworkers, who spearheaded the union movement, did not feel a particularly strong bond with semiskilled factory workers and unskilled laborers. More than a decade of agitation did finally bring a workday shortened to 10 hours to most industries by the 1850's, and the courts also recognized workers' right to strike, but these gains had little immediate impact.

6. The phrase gathered some momentum in the passage is closest in meaning to

○ made progress
○ became active
○ caused changes
○ combined forces

7. The word spearheaded in the passage is closest in meaning to

○ led
○ accepted
○ changed
○ resisted

8. Which of the following statements about the labor movement of the 1800's is supported by paragraph 5?

○ It was most successful during times of economic crisis.
○ Its primary purpose was to benefit unskilled laborers.
○ It was slow to improve conditions for workers.
○ It helped workers of all skill levels form a strong bond with each other.

PARAGRAPH 6

Workers were united in resenting the industrial system and their loss of status, but they were divided by ethnic and racial antagonisms, gender, conflicting religious perspectives, occupational differences, political party loyalties, and disagreements over tactics. For them, the factory and industrialism were not agents of opportunity but reminders of their loss of independence and a measure of control over their lives. As United States society became more specialized and differentiated, greater extremes of wealth began to appear. And as the new markets created fortunes for the few, the factory system lowered the wages of workers by dividing labor into smaller, less skilled tasks.

9. The author identifies political party loyalties, and disagreements over tactics as two of several factors that

○ encouraged workers to demand higher wages
○ created divisions among workers
○ caused work to become more specialized
○ increased workers' resentment of the industrial system

10. The word them, in the passage refers to

○ Workers
○ political party loyalties
○ disagreements over tactics
○ agents of opportunity

Before 1815 manufacturing in the United States had been done in homes or shops by skilled artisans. ■ As master craftworkers, they imparted the knowledge of their trades to apprentices and journeymen. ■ In addition, women often worked in their homes part-time, making finished articles from raw material supplied by merchant capitalists. ■ After 1815 this older form of manufacturing began to give way to factories with machinery tended by unskilled or semiskilled laborers. ■ Cheap transportation networks, the rise of cities, and the availability of capital and credit all stimulated the shift to factory production.

11. Look at the four squares ■ that indicate where the following sentence can be added to the passage.

This new form of manufacturing depended on the movement of goods to distant locations and a centralized source of laborers.

Where would the sentence best fit?

⬭ Before 1815 manufacturing in the United States had been done in homes or shops by skilled artisans. **This new form of manufacturing depended on the movement of goods to distant locations and a centralized source of laborers.** As master craftworkers, they imparted the knowledge of their trades to apprentices and journeymen. ■ In addition, women often worked in their homes part-time, making finished articles from raw material supplied by merchant capitalists. ■ After 1815 this older form of manufacturing began to give way to factories with machinery tended by unskilled or semiskilled laborers. ■ Cheap transportation networks, the rise of cities, and the availability of capital and credit all stimulated the shift to factory production.

⬭ Before 1815 manufacturing in the United States had been done in homes or shops by skilled artisans. ■ As master craftworkers, they imparted the knowledge of their trades to apprentices and journeymen. **This new form of manufacturing depended on the movement of goods to distant locations and a centralized source of laborers.** In addition, women often worked in their homes part-time, making finished articles from raw material supplied by merchant capitalists. ■ After 1815 this older form of manufacturing began to give way to factories with machinery tended by unskilled or semiskilled laborers. ■ Cheap transportation networks, the rise of cities, and the availability of capital and credit all stimulated the shift to factory production.

⬭ Before 1815 manufacturing in the United States had been done in homes or shops by skilled artisans. ■ As master craftworkers, they imparted the knowledge of their trades to apprentices and journeymen. ■ In addition, women often worked in their homes part-time, making finished articles from raw material supplied by merchant capitalists. **This new form of manufacturing depended on the movement of goods to distant locations and a centralized source of laborers.** After 1815 this older form of manufacturing began to give way to factories with machinery tended by unskilled or semiskilled laborers. ■ Cheap transportation networks, the rise of cities, and the availability of capital and credit all stimulated the shift to factory production.

⬭ Before 1815 manufacturing in the United States had been done in homes or shops by skilled artisans. ■ As master craftworkers, they imparted the knowledge of their trades to apprentices and journeymen. ■ In addition, women often worked in their homes part-time, making finished articles from raw material supplied by merchant capitalists. ■ After 1815 this older form of manufacturing began to give way to factories with machinery tended by unskilled or semiskilled laborers. **This new form of manufacturing depended on the movement of goods to distant locations and a centralized source of laborers.** Cheap transportation networks, the rise of cities, and the availability of capital and credit all stimulated the shift to factory production.

12. Directions: Complete the table below by indicating which of the answer choices describe characteristics of the period before 1815 and which describe characteristics of the 1815–1860 period. *This question is worth 3 points.*

Before 1815	1815–1850
➤ ➤	➤ ➤ ➤

Answer Choices

1. A united, highly successful labor movement took shape.

2. Workers took pride in their workmanship.

3. The income gap between the rich and the poor increased greatly.

4. Transportation networks began to decline.

5. Emphasis was placed on following schedules.

6. Workers went through an extensive period of training.

7. Few workers expected to own their own businesses.

Answers and Explanations

1. ❸ This is an Inference question asking for an inference that can be supported by the passage. The correct answer is choice 3, "They were produced with more concern for quality than for speed of production."

   A number of statements throughout the passage support choice 3. Paragraph 1 states that "Before 1815 manufacturing in the United States had been done in homes or shops by skilled artisans . . . After 1815 this older form of manufacturing began to give way to factories with machinery tended by unskilled or semiskilled laborers."

   Paragraph 2 states that "Before the rise of the factory . . . skilled artisans did not work by the clock, at a steady pace, but rather in bursts of intense labor alternating with more leisurely time."

   Paragraph 3 states, "The factory changed that. Goods produced by factories were not as finished or elegant as those done by hand, and pride in craftsmanship gave way to the pressure to increase rates of productivity."

   Taken together, these three statements, about production rates, the rise of factories after 1815, and the decline of craftsmanship after 1815, support the inference that before 1815, the emphasis had been on quality rather than on speed of production. Answer choices 1, 2, and 4 are all contradicted by the passage.

2. ❷ This is a Sentence Simplification question. As with all of these items, a single sentence in the passage is highlighted:

   > Apprentices were considered part of the family, and masters were responsible not only for teaching their apprentices a trade but also for providing them some education and for supervising their moral behavior.

   The correct answer is choice 2. Choice 2 contains all of the *essential* information in the highlighted sentence. The highlighted sentence explains why (part of the family) and how (education, moral behavior) a master's responsibility went beyond teaching a trade. The essential information is the fact that the master's responsibility went beyond teaching a trade. Therefore, choice 2 contains all that is essential without changing the meaning of the highlighted sentence.

   Choice 1 changes the meaning of the highlighted sentence by stating that masters often treated apprentices irresponsibly.

   Choice 3 contradicts the essential meaning of the highlighted sentence. The fact that "Apprentices were considered part of the family . . . " suggests that they were not actual family members.

   Choice 4, like choice 3, changes the meaning of the highlighted sentence by discussing family members as apprentices.

3. ❹ This is a Vocabulary question. The word being tested is *disrupted*. It is highlighted in the passage. The correct answer is choice 4, "upset." The word "upset" here is used in the context of "hurting productivity." When something is hurt or damaged, it is "upset."

4. ❶ This is a Factual Information question asking for specific information that can be found in paragraph 4. The correct answer is choice 1, "support the idea that it was difficult for workers to adjust to working in factories." The paragraph begins by stating that workers did not adopt new attitudes toward work easily and that the clock symbolized the new work rules. The author provides the quotation as evidence of that difficulty. There is no indication in the paragraph that workers quit due to loud noise, so choice 2 is incorrect. Choice 3 (usefulness of clocks) is contradicted by the paragraph. The factory clock was "useful," but workers hated it. Choice 4 (workers complaints as a cause of a factory's success) is not discussed in this paragraph.

5. ❹ This is a Negative Factual Information question asking for specific information that can be found in paragraph 4. Choice 4, "contact among workers who were not managers," is the correct answer. The paragraph explicitly contradicts this by stating that "factories sharply separated workers from management." The paragraph explicitly states that workers lost choice 1 (freedom), choice 2 (status in the community), and choice 3 (opportunities for advancement) in the new system, so those choices are all incorrect.

6. ❶ This is a Vocabulary question. The phrase being tested is "gathered some momentum." It is highlighted in the passage. The correct answer is choice 1, "made progress." To "gather momentum" means to advance with increasing speed.

7. ❶ This is a Vocabulary question. The word being tested is *spearheaded*. It is highlighted in the passage. The correct answer is choice 1, "led." The head of a spear leads the rest of the spear, so the craftsworkers who "spearheaded" this movement led it.

8. ❸ This is a Factual Information question asking for specific information that can be found in paragraph 5. The correct answer is choice 3, "It was slow to improve conditions for workers." The paragraph states, "More than a decade of agitation did finally bring a workday shortened to 10 hours to most industries by the 1850's, and the courts also recognized workers' right to strike, but these gains had little immediate impact." This statement explicitly supports choice 3. All three other choices are contradicted by the paragraph.

9. ❷ This is a Factual Information question asking for specific information about a particular phrase in the passage. The phrase in question is highlighted in the passage. The correct answer is choice 2, "created divisions among workers." The paragraph states (emphasis added): " . . . they (workers) were divided by ethnic and racial antagonisms, gender, conflicting religious perspectives, occupational differences, political party loyalties, and disagreements over tactics." So "political party loyalties and disagreements over tactics" are explicitly stated as two causes of division among workers. The other choices are not stated and are incorrect.

10. ❶ This is a Reference question. The word being tested is *them*. It is highlighted in the passage. This is a simple pronoun-referent item. The word *them* in this sentence refers to those people to whom "the factory and industrialism were not agents of opportunity but reminders of their loss of independence and a measure of control over their lives." Choice 1, "Workers," is the only choice that refers to this type of person, so it is the correct answer.

11. ❹ This is an Insert Text question. You can see the four black squares in paragraph 1 that represent the possible answer choices here.

Before 1815 manufacturing in the United States had been done in homes or shops by skilled artisans. ■ As master craftworkers, they imparted the knowledge of their trades to apprentices and journeymen. ■ In addition, women often worked in their homes part-time, making finished articles from raw material supplied by merchant capitalists. ■ After 1815 this older form of manufacturing began to give way to factories with machinery tended by unskilled or semiskilled laborers. ■ Cheap transportation networks, the rise of cities, and the availability of capital and credit all stimulated the shift to factory production.

The sentence provided, "This new form of manufacturing depended on the movement of goods to distant locations and a centralized source of laborers," is best inserted at square 4. The inserted sentence refers explicitly to "a new form of manufacturing." This "new form of manufacturing" is the one mentioned in the sentence preceding square 4, "factories with machinery tended by unskilled or semiskilled laborers." The inserted sentence then explains that this new system depended on "the movement of goods to distant locations and a centralized source of laborers." The sentence that follows square 4 goes on to say, "Cheap transportation networks, the rise of cities, and the availability of capital and credit all stimulated the shift to factory production." Thus the inserted sentence contains references to both the sentence before square 4 and the sentence after square 4. This is not true of any of the other possible insert points, so square 4 is the correct answer.

12. This is a Fill in a Table question. It is completed correctly below. The correct choices for the "Before 1815" column are 2 and 6. Choices 3, 5, and 7 belong in the "1815–1850" column. Choices 1 and 4 should not be used in either column.

Directions: Complete the table below by indicating which of the answer choices describe characteristics of the period before 1815 and which describe characteristics of the 1815–1860 period. ***This question is worth 3 points.***

BEFORE 1815	1815–1850
➤ Workers took pride in their workmanship.	➤ The income gap between the rich and the poor increased greatly.
➤ Workers went through an extensive period of training.	➤ Emphasis was placed on following schedules.
	➤ Few workers expected to own their own businesses.

Answer Choices

1. A united, highly successful labor movement took shape.

2. Workers took pride in their workmanship.

3. The income gap between the rich and the poor increased greatly.

4. Transportation networks began to decline.

5. Emphasis was placed on following schedules.

6. Workers went through an extensive period of training.

7. Few workers expected to own their own businesses.

Correct Choices

Choice 2: "Workers took pride in their workmanship" belongs in the "Before 1815" column because it is mentioned in the passage as one of the characteristics of labor before 1815.

Choice 3: "The income gap between the rich and the poor increased greatly" belongs in the "1815–1850" column because it is mentioned in the passage as one of the characteristics of society that emerged in the period between 1815 and 1850.

Choice 5: "Emphasis was placed on following schedules" belongs in the "1815–1850" column because it is mentioned in the passage as one of the characteristics of labor in the factory system that emerged between 1815 and 1850.

Choice 6: "Workers went through an extensive period of training" belongs in the "Before 1815" column because it is mentioned in the passage as one of the characteristics of labor before 1815.

Choice 7: "Few workers expected to own their own businesses" belongs in the "1815–1850" column because it is mentioned in the passage as one of the characteristics of society that emerged in the period between 1815 and 1850.

Incorrect Choices

Choice 1: "A united, highly successful labor movement took shape" does not belong in the table because it contradicts the passage.

Choice 4: "Transportation networks began to decline" does not belong in the table because it is not mentioned in the passage in connection with either the period before 1815 or the period between 1815 and 1850.

Practice Set 6

SWIMMING MACHINES

Tunas, mackerels, and billfishes (marlins, sailfishes, and swordfish) swim continuously. Feeding, courtship, reproduction, and even "rest" are carried out while in constant motion. As a result, practically every aspect of the body form and function of these swimming "machines" is adapted to enhance their ability to swim.

Many of the adaptations of these fishes serve to reduce water resistance (drag). Interestingly enough, several of these hydrodynamic adaptations resemble features designed to improve the aerodynamics of high-speed aircraft. Though human engineers are new to the game, tunas and their relatives evolved their "high-tech" designs long ago.

Tunas, mackerels, and billfishes have made streamlining into an art form. Their bodies are sleek and compact. The body shapes of tunas, in fact, are nearly ideal from an engineering point of view. Most species lack scales over most of the body, making it smooth and slippery. The eyes lie flush with the body and do not protrude at all. They are also covered with a slick, transparent lid that reduces drag. The fins are stiff, smooth, and narrow, qualities that also help cut drag. When not in use, the fins are tucked into special grooves or depressions so that they lie flush with the body and do not break up its smooth contours. Airplanes retract their landing gear while in flight for the same reason.

Tunas, mackerels, and billfishes have even more sophisticated adaptations than these to improve their hydrodynamics. The long bill of marlins, sailfishes, and swordfish probably helps them slip through the water. Many supersonic aircraft have a similar needle at the nose.

Most tunas and billfishes have a series of keels and finlets near the tail. Although most of their scales have been lost, tunas and mackerels retain a patch of coarse scales near the head called the corselet. The keels, finlets, and corselet help direct the flow of water over the body surface in such as way as to reduce resistance (see the figure). Again, supersonic jets have similar features.

Because they are always swimming, tunas simply have to open their mouths and water is forced in and over their gills. Accordingly, they have lost most of the muscles that other fishes use to suck in water and push it past the gills. In fact, tunas must swim to breathe. They must also keep swimming to keep from sinking, since most have largely or completely lost the swim bladder, the gas-filled sac that helps most other fish remain buoyant.

One potential problem is that opening the mouth to breathe detracts from the streamlining of these fishes and tends to slow them down. Some species of tuna have specialized grooves in their tongue. It is thought that these grooves help to channel water through the mouth and out the gill slits, thereby reducing water resistance.

There are adaptations that increase the amount of forward thrust as well as those that reduce drag. Again, these fishes are the envy of engineers. Their high, narrow tails with swept-back tips are almost perfectly adapted to provide propulsion with the least possible effort. Perhaps most important of all to these and other fast swimmers is their ability to sense and make use of swirls and eddies (circular currents) in the water. They can glide past eddies that would slow them down and then gain extra thrust by "pushing off" the eddies. Scientists and engineers are beginning to study this ability of fishes in the hope of designing more efficient propulsion systems for ships.

The muscles of these fishes and the mechanism that maintains a warm body temperature are also highly efficient. A bluefin tuna in water of 7°C (45°F) can maintain a core temperature of over 25°C (77°F). This warm body temperature may help not only the muscles to work better, but also the brain and the eyes. The billfishes have gone one step further. They have evolved special "heaters" of modified muscle tissue that warm the eyes and brain, maintaining peak performance of these critical organs.

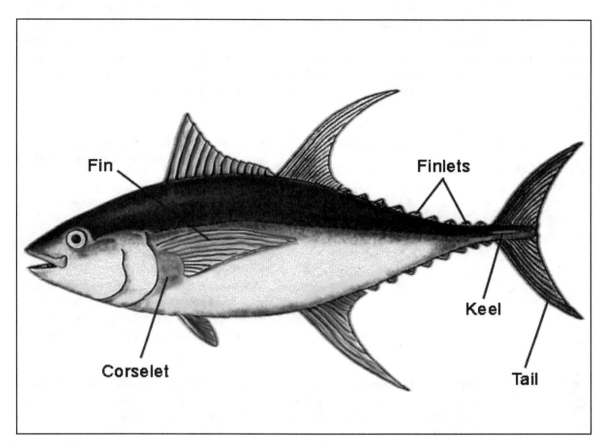

PARAGRAPH 1

Tunas, mackerels, and billfishes (marlins, sailfishes, and swordfish) swim continuously. Feeding, courtship, reproduction, and even "rest" are carried out while in constant motion. As a result, practically every aspect of the body form and function of these swimming "machines" is adapted to enhance their ability to swim.

Directions: Mark your answer by filling in the oval next to your choice.

1. The word enhance in the passage is closest in meaning to

○ use
○ improve
○ counteract
○ balance

PARAGRAPH 3

Tunas, mackerels, and billfishes have made streamlining into an art form. Their bodies are sleek and compact. The body shapes of tunas, in fact, are nearly ideal from an engineering point of view. Most species lack scales over most of the body, making it smooth and slippery. The eyes lie flush with the body and do not protrude at all. They are also covered with a slick, transparent lid that reduces drag. The fins are stiff, smooth, and narrow, qualities that also help cut drag. When not in use, the fins are tucked into special grooves or depressions so that they lie flush with the body and do not break up its smooth contours. Airplanes retract their landing gear while in flight for the same reason.

2. The word they in the passage refers to

  ○ qualities
  ○ fins
  ○ grooves
  ○ depressions

3. Why does the author mention that Airplanes retract their landing gear while in flight?

  ○ To show that air resistance and water resistance work differently from each other
  ○ To argue that some fishes are better designed than airplanes are
  ○ To provide evidence that airplane engineers have studied the design of fish bodies
  ○ To demonstrate a similarity in design between certain fishes and airplanes

PARAGRAPH 4

Tunas, mackerels, and billfishes have even more sophisticated adaptations than these to improve their hydrodynamics. The long bill of marlins, sailfishes, and swordfish probably helps them slip through the water. Many supersonic aircraft have a similar needle at the nose.

4. The word sophisticated in the passage is closest in meaning to

  ○ complex
  ○ amazing
  ○ creative
  ○ practical

5. According to paragraph 4, the long bills of marlins, sailfish, and swordfish probably help these fishes by

  ○ increasing their ability to defend themselves
  ○ allowing them to change direction easily
  ○ increasing their ability to detect odors
  ○ reducing water resistance as they swim

PARAGRAPH 6

Because they are always swimming, tunas simply have to open their mouths and water is forced in and over their gills. Accordingly, they have lost most of the muscles that other fishes use to suck in water and push it past the gills. In fact, tunas must swim to breathe. They must also keep swimming to keep from sinking, since most have largely or completely lost the swim bladder, the gas-filled sac that helps most other fish remain buoyant.

6. According to the passage, which of the following is one of the reasons that tunas are in constant motion?

○ They lack a swim bladder.
○ They need to suck in more water than other fishes do.
○ They have large muscles for breathing.
○ They cannot open their mouths unless they are in motion.

PARAGRAPH 7

One potential problem is that opening the mouth to breathe detracts from the stream-lining of these fishes and tends to slow them down. Some species of tuna have specialized grooves in their tongue. It is thought that these grooves help to channel water through the mouth and out the gill slits, thereby reducing water resistance.

7. Which of the sentences below best expresses the essential information in the highlighted sentence in the passage? *Incorrect* answer choices change the meaning in important ways or leave out essential information.

○ These fishes often have a problem opening their mouths while swimming.
○ The streamlining of these fishes prevents them from slowing down.
○ The streamlining of these fishes tends to slow down their breathing.
○ Opening the mouth to breathe can reduce the speed of these fishes.

8. The word channel in the passage is closest in meaning to

○ reduce
○ remove
○ direct
○ provide

There are adaptations that increase the amount of forward thrust as well as those that reduce drag. Again, these fishes are the envy of engineers. Their high, narrow tails with swept-back tips are almost perfectly adapted to provide propulsion with the least possible effort. Perhaps most important of all to these and other fast swimmers is their ability to sense and make use of swirls and eddies (circular currents) in the water. They can glide past eddies that would slow them down and then gain extra thrust by "pushing off" the eddies. Scientists and engineers are beginning to study this ability of fishes in the hope of designing more efficient propulsion systems for ships.

9. According to the passage, one of the adaptations of fast-swimming fishes that might be used to improve the performance of ships is these fishes' ability to

○ cover great distances without stopping
○ gain speed by forcing water past their gills

○ swim directly through eddies
○ make efficient use of water currents

The muscles of these fishes and the mechanism that maintains a warm body temperature are also highly efficient. A bluefin tuna in water of 7°C (45°F) can maintain a core temperature of over 25°C (77°F). This warm body temperature may help not only the muscles to work better, but also the brain and the eyes. The billfishes have gone one step further. They have evolved special "heaters" of modified muscle tissue that warm the eyes and brain, maintaining peak performance of these critical organs.

10. According to paragraph 9, which of the following is true of bluefin tunas?

○ Their eyes and brain are more efficient than those of any other fish.
○ Their body temperature can change greatly depending on the water temperature.
○ They can swim in waters that are much colder than their own bodies.
○ They have special muscle tissue that warms their eyes and brain.

Again, supersonic jets have similar features.
■ Because they are always swimming, tunas simply have to open their mouths and water is forced in and over their gills. ■ Accordingly, they have lost most of the muscles that other fishes use to suck in water and push it past the gills. ■ In fact, tunas must swim to breathe. ■ They must also keep swimming to keep from sinking, since most have largely or completely lost the swim bladder, the gas-filled sac that helps most other fish remain buoyant.

11. Look at the four squares [■] that indicate where the following sentence can be added to the passage.

Consequently, tunas do not need to suck in water.

Where would the sentence best fit?

○ Again, supersonic jets have similar features.
Consequently, tunas do not need to suck in water. Because they are always swimming, tunas simply have to open their mouths and water is forced in and over their gills. ■ Accordingly, they have lost most of the muscles that other fishes use to suck in water and push it past the gills. ■ In fact, tunas must swim to breathe. ■ They must also keep swimming to keep from sinking, since most have largely or completely lost the swim bladder, the gas-filled sac that helps most other fish remain buoyant.

○ Again, supersonic jets have similar features.
■ Because they are always swimming, tunas simply have to open their mouths and water is forced in and over their gills. **Consequently, tunas do not need to suck in water.** Accordingly, they have lost most of the muscles that other fishes use to suck in water and push it past the gills. ■ In fact, tunas must swim to breathe. ■ They must also keep swimming to keep from sinking, since most have largely or completely lost the swim bladder, the gas-filled sac that helps most other fish remain buoyant.

○ Again, supersonic jets have similar features.
■ Because they are always swimming, tunas simply have to open their mouths and water is forced in and over their gills. ■ Accordingly, they have lost most of the muscles that other fishes use to suck in water and push it past the gills. **Consequently, tunas do not need to suck in water.** In fact, tunas must swim to breathe. ■ They must also keep swimming to keep from sinking, since most have largely or completely lost the swim bladder, the gas-filled sac that helps most other fish remain buoyant.

○ Again, supersonic jets have similar features.
■ Because they are always swimming, tunas simply have to open their mouths and water is forced in and over their gills. ■ Accordingly, they have lost most of the muscles that other fishes use to suck in water and push it past the gills. ■ In fact, tunas must swim to breathe.
Consequently, tunas do not need to suck in water. They must also keep swimming to keep from sinking, since most have largely or completely lost the swim bladder, the gas-filled sac that helps most other fish remain buoyant.

12. **Directions:** Complete the table below by indicating which features of fishes are associated in the passage with reducing water resistance and which are associated with increasing thrust. **_This question is worth 3 points._**

REDUCING WATER RESISTANCE	INCREASING THRUST
➤	➤
➤	➤
➤	

Features of Fishes

1. The absence of scales from most of the body

2. The ability to take advantage of eddies

3. The ability to feed and reproduce while swimming

4. Eyes that do not protrude

5. Fins that are stiff, narrow, and smooth

6. The habit of swimming with the mouth open

7. A high, narrow tail with swept-back tips

Answers and Explanations

1. **❷** This is a Vocabulary question. The word being tested is *enhance*. It is high-lighted in the passage. The correct answer is choice 2, "improve." To *enhance* something means to "make it better." If something has been "improved," it has been made better.

2. **❷** This is a Reference question. The word being tested is *they*. It is highlighted in the passage. Choice 2, "fins," is the correct answer. This is a simple pronoun-ref-erent item. The word *they* refers to something that lies flush with the body when not in use. This is true only of "fins."

3. **❹** This is a Rhetorical Purpose question. It asks why the author mentions that "Airplanes retract their landing gear while in flight." The phrase being tested is highlighted in the passage. The correct answer is choice 4, "To demonstrate a sim-ilarity in design between certain fishes and airplanes." The paragraph in which the highlighted phrase appears describes how certain fish use their fins. The high-lighted phrase is used to provide a more familiar example (airplanes) of the prin-ciple involved to help the reader visualize how fins work. The paragraph does not discuss airplanes in any other context, so choices 2 and 3 are incorrect. Air and water resistance are not mentioned in this paragraph, so choice 1 is incorrect.

4. **❶** This is a Vocabulary question. The word being tested is *sophisticated*. It is high-lighted in the passage. The correct answer is choice 1, "complex." If something is *sophisticated*, it is "not simple," so it must be "complex."

5. **❹** This is a Factual Information question asking for specific information that can be found in paragraph 4. The correct answer is choice 4, "reducing water resist-ance as they swim." The overall theme of the passage is how certain fish swim so efficiently. Paragraphs 1 and 2 make the general statement that "practically every aspect of the body form and function of these swimming 'machines' is adapted to enhance their ability to swim. Many of the adaptations of these fishes serve to reduce water resistance (drag)."

   Paragraph 4 explicitly states (emphasis added) that "Tunas, mackerels, and billfishes have even more sophisticated *adaptations than these to improve their hydrodynamics. The long bill* of marlins, sailfishes, and swordfish probably helps them slip through the water." This is a specific example of one adaptation that these fish have made to increase their swimming efficiency. None of the other choices is mentioned in the paragraph.

6. **❶** This is a Factual Information question asking for specific information that can be found in the passage. The correct answer is choice 1, "They lack a swim bladder."

   Paragraph 6 explicitly states ". . . tunas must swim to breathe. They must also keep swimming to keep from sinking, since most have largely or completely lost the swim bladder . . ." The other choices are not supported by the passage.

7. ❹ This is a Sentence Simplification question. As with all of these items, a single sentence in the passage is highlighted:

> One potential problem is that opening the mouth to breathe detracts from the streamlining of these fishes and tends to slow them down.

The correct answer is choice 4. That choice contains all of the *essential* ideas in the highlighted sentence. It is also the only choice that does not change the meaning of the sentence. It omits the fact that this is "a problem" and also "that it detracts from streamlining" because that information is not essential to the meaning.

Choice 1 says that these fish have trouble opening their mouths while swimming, which is not true. Choice 2, that streamlining prevents fish from slowing down, may be true, but it is not mentioned in this sentence. The fish are slowed down when they open their mouths, which reduces streamlining. Choice 3, that streamlining slows the fishes' breathing, is also not mentioned.

8. ❸ This is a Vocabulary question. The word being tested is *channel*. It is highlighted in the passage. The correct answer is choice 3, "direct." *Channel* here is used as a verb, meaning to "move" or "push."

9. ❷ This is a Factual Information question asking for specific information that can be found in the passage. The correct answer is choice 2, "make efficient use of water currents." Paragraph 8 explicitly states: "Perhaps most important of all to these and other fast swimmers is their ability to sense and make use of swirls and eddies (circular currents) in the water. They can glide past eddies that would slow them down and then gain extra thrust by "pushing off" the eddies. Scientists and engineers are beginning to study this ability of fishes in the hope of designing more efficient propulsion systems for ships." The other choices are not mentioned in connection with the performance of ships.

10. ❸ This is a Factual Information question asking for specific information that can be found in paragraph 9. The correct answer is choice 3, "They can swim in waters that are much colder than their own bodies." That paragraph says, "A bluefin tuna in water of 7°C (45°F) can maintain a core temperature of over 25°C (77°F)." So it is clear that choice C is correct. Choice 1 is not stated in the paragraph. Choice 2 is contradicted by the paragraph. Choice 4 is true of billfish, not bluefin tuna.

11. ❷ This is an Insert Text question. You can see the four black squares in paragraph 6 that represent the possible answer choices here. The last sentence of paragraph 5 is also reproduced below.

Again, supersonic jets have similar features.
■ Because they are always swimming, tunas simply have to open their mouths and water is forced in and over their gills. ■ Accordingly, they have lost most of the muscles that other fishes use to suck in water and push it past the gills. ■ In fact, tunas must swim to breathe. ■ They must

also keep swimming to keep from sinking, since most have largely or completely lost the swim bladder, the gas-filled sac that helps most other fish remain buoyant.

The sentence provided, "Consequently, tunas do not need to suck in water," is best inserted at square 2. The sentence provides an explanation for the muscle loss described in the sentence that follows square 2 and is a result of the fact described in the preceding sentence, which says that because the fish are always swimming, they only have to open their mouths to suck in water. Thus if the provided sentence is inserted at square 2, it provides a logical bridge between cause and effect. The sentence makes no logical sense anywhere else.

12. This is a Fill in a Table question. It is completed correctly below. The correct choices for the "Reducing water resistance" column are 1, 4, and 5. Choices 2 and 7 belong in the "Increasing thrust" column. Choices 3 and 6 should not be used in either column.

Directions: Complete the table below by indicating which features of fishes are associated in the passage with reducing water resistance and which are associated with increasing thrust. ***This question is worth 3 points.***

REDUCING WATER RESISTANCE	INCREASING THRUST
➤ The absence of scales from most of the body	➤ The ability to take advantage of eddies
➤ Eyes that do not protrude	➤ A high, narrow tail with swept-back tips
➤ Fins that are stiff, narrow and smooth	

Features of Fishes

1. The absence of scales from most of the body
2. The ability to take advantage of eddies
3. The ability to feed and reproduce while swimming
4. Eyes that do not protrude
5. Fins that are stiff, narrow and smooth
6. The habit of swimming with the mouth open
7. A high, narrow tail with swept-back tips

Keys: Reducing Water Resistance (1, 4, 5); Increasing Thrust (2, 7)

Correct Choices

Choice 1: "The absence of scales from most of the body" belongs in the "Reducing water resistance" column because it is mentioned in paragraphs 3 and 5 as a factor that reduces water resistance.

Choice 2: "The ability to take advantage of eddies" belongs in the "Increasing thrust" column because it is mentioned in paragraph 8 as a characteristic that helps increase thrust.

Choice 4: "Eyes that do not protrude" belongs in the "Reducing water resistance" column because it is mentioned in paragraph 3 as a factor that reduces water resistance.

Choice 5: "Fins that are stiff, narrow and smooth" belongs in the "Reducing water resistance" column because it is mentioned in paragraph 3 as a factor that reduces water resistance.

Choice 7: "A high, narrow tail with swept-back tips" belongs in the "Increasing thrust" column because it is mentioned in paragraph 8 as a characteristic that helps increase thrust.

Incorrect Choices

Choice 3: "The ability to feed and reproduce while swimming" does not belong in the table because it is not mentioned in the passage in connection with either reducing water resistance or increasing thrust.

Choice 6: "The habit of swimming with the mouth open" does not belong in the table because it is not mentioned in the passage in connection with either reducing water resistance or increasing thrust.

PRACTICE TOEFL iBT READING SECTION

DIRECTIONS

This section measures your ability to understand academic passages in English.

The Reading section is divided into separately timed parts.

Most questions are worth 1 point, but the last question for each passage is worth more than 1 point. The directions for the last question indicate how many points you may receive.

You will now begin the Reading section. There are three passages in the section. You should allow **20 Minutes** to read each passage and answer the questions about it. You should allow **60 Minutes** to complete the entire section.

NINETEENTH-CENTURY POLITICS IN THE UNITED STATES

The development of the modern presidency in the United States began with Andrew Jackson who swept to power in 1829 at the head of the Democratic Party and served until 1837. During his administration he immeasurably enlarged the power of the presidency. "The President is the direct representative of the American people," he lectured the Senate when it opposed him. "He was elected by the people, and is responsible to them." With this declaration, Jackson redefined the character of the presidential office and its relationship to the people.

During Jackson's second term, his opponents had gradually come together to form the Whig party. Whigs and Democrats held different attitudes toward the changes brought about by the market, banks, and commerce. The Democrats tended to view society as a continuing conflict between "the people"—farmers, planters, and workers—and a set of greedy aristocrats. This "paper money aristocracy" of bankers and investors manipulated the banking system for their own profit, Democrats claimed, and sapped the nation's virtue by encouraging speculation and the desire for sudden, unearned wealth. The Democrats wanted the rewards of the market without sacrificing the features of a simple agrarian republic. They wanted the wealth that the market offered without the competitive, changing society; the complex dealing; the dominance of urban centers; and the loss of independence that came with it.

Whigs, on the other hand, were more comfortable with the market. For them, commerce and economic development were agents of civilization. Nor did the Whigs envision any conflict in society between farmers and workers on the one hand and businesspeople and bankers on the other. Economic growth would benefit everyone by raising national income and expanding opportunity. The government's responsibility was to provide a well-regulated economy that guaranteed opportunity for citizens of ability.

Whigs and Democrats differed not only in their attitudes toward the market but also about how active the central government should be in people's lives. Despite Andrew Jackson's inclination to be a strong President, Democrats as a rule believed in limited government. Government's role in the economy was to promote competition by destroying monopolies[1] and special privileges. In keeping with this philosophy of limited government, Democrats also rejected the idea that moral beliefs were the proper sphere of government action. Religion and politics, they believed, should be kept clearly separate, and they generally opposed humanitarian legislation.

---

[1]Monopolies—Companies or individuals that exclusively own or control commercial enterprises with no competitors

The Whigs, in contrast, viewed government power positively. They believed that it should be used to protect individual rights and public liberty, and that it had a special role where individual effort was ineffective. By regulating the economy and competition, the government could ensure equal opportunity. Indeed, for Whigs the concept of government promoting the general welfare went beyond the economy. In particular, Whigs in the northern sections of the United States also believed that government power should be used to foster the moral welfare of the country. They were much more likely to favor social-reform legislation and aid to education.

In some ways the social makeup of the two parties was similar. To be competitive in winning votes, Whigs and Democrats both had to have significant support among farmers, the largest group in society, and workers. Neither party could win an election by appealing exclusively to the rich or the poor. The Whigs, however, enjoyed disproportionate strength among the business and commercial classes. Whigs appealed to planters who needed credit to finance their cotton and rice trade in the world market, to farmers who were eager to sell their surpluses, and to workers who wished to improve themselves. Democrats attracted farmers isolated from the market or uncomfortable with it, workers alienated from the emerging industrial system, and rising entrepreneurs who wanted to break monopolies and open the economy to newcomers like themselves. The Whigs were strongest in the towns, cities, and those rural areas that were fully integrated into the market economy, whereas Democrats dominated areas of semisubsistence farming that were more isolated and languishing economically.

PARAGRAPH 1

The development of the modern presidency in the United States began with Andrew Jackson who swept to power in 1829 at the head of the Democratic Party and served until 1837. During his administration he immeasurably enlarged the power of the presidency. "The President is the direct representative of the American people," he lectured the Senate when it opposed him. "He was elected by the people, and is responsible to them." With this declaration, Jackson redefined the character of the presidential office and its relationship to the people.

Directions: Mark your answer by filling in the oval next to your choice.

1. The word immeasurably in the passage is closest in meaning to

   ○ frequently
   ○ greatly
   ○ rapidly
   ○ reportedly

2. According to paragraph 1, the presidency of Andrew Jackson was especially significant for which of the following reasons?

   ○ The President granted a portion of his power to the Senate.
   ○ The President began to address the Senate on a regular basis.
   ○ It was the beginning of the modern presidency in the United States.
   ○ It was the first time that the Senate had been known to oppose the President.

During Jackson's second term, his opponents had gradually come together to form the Whig party. Whigs and Democrats held different attitudes toward the changes brought about by the market, banks, and commerce. The Democrats tended to view society as a continuing conflict between "the people"—farmers, planters, and workers—and a set of greedy aristocrats. This "paper money aristocracy" of bankers and investors manipulated the banking system for their own profit, Democrats claimed, and sapped the nation's virtue by encouraging speculation and the desire for sudden, unearned wealth. The Democrats wanted the rewards of the market without sacrificing the features of a simple agrarian republic. They wanted the wealth that the market offered without the competitive, changing society; the complex dealing; the dominance of urban centers; and the loss of independence that came with it.

3. The author mentions bankers and investors in the passage as an example of which of the following?

○ The Democratic Party's main source of support

○ The people that Democrats claimed were unfairly becoming rich

○ The people most interested in a return to a simple agrarian republic

○ One of the groups in favor of Andrew Jackson's presidency

Whigs, on the other hand, were more comfortable with the market. For them, commerce and economic development were agents of civilization. Nor did the Whigs envision any conflict in society between farmers and workers on the one hand and businesspeople and bankers on the other. Economic growth would benefit everyone by raising national income and expanding opportunity. The government's responsibility was to provide a well-regulated economy that guaranteed opportunity for citizens of ability.

4. According to paragraph 3, Whigs believed that commerce and economic development would have which of the following effects on society?

○ They would promote the advancement of society as a whole.

○ They would cause disagreements between Whigs and Democrats.

○ They would supply new positions for Whig Party members.

○ They would prevent conflict between farmers and workers.

5. According to paragraph 3, which of the following describes the Whig Party's view of the role of government?

○ To regulate the continuing conflict between farmers and businesspeople

○ To restrict the changes brought about by the market

○ To maintain an economy that allowed all capable citizens to benefit

○ To reduce the emphasis on economic development

PARAGRAPH 4

Whigs and Democrats differed not only in their attitudes toward the market but also about how active the central government should be in people's lives. Despite Andrew Jackson's inclination to be a strong President, Democrats as a rule believed in limited government. Government's role in the economy was to promote competition by destroying monopolies[1] and special privileges. In keeping with this philosophy of limited government, Democrats also rejected the idea that moral beliefs were the proper sphere of government action. Religion and politics, they believed, should be kept clearly separate, and they generally opposed humanitarian legislation.

6. The word inclination in the passage is closest in meaning to

◯ argument
◯ tendency
◯ example
◯ warning

7. According to paragraph 4, a Democrat would be most likely to support government action in which of the following areas?

◯ Creating a state religion
◯ Supporting humanitarian legislation
◯ Destroying monopolies
◯ Recommending particular moral beliefs

---

[1]Monopolies—Companies or individuals that exclusively own or control commercial enterprises with no competitors

The Whigs, in contrast, viewed government power positively. They believed that it should be used to protect individual rights and public liberty, and that it had a special role where individual effort was ineffective. By regulating the economy and competition, the government could ensure equal opportunity. Indeed, for Whigs the concept of government promoting the general welfare went beyond the economy. In particular, Whigs in the northern sections of the United States also believed that government power should be used to foster the moral welfare of the country. They were much more likely to favor social-reform legislation and aid to education.

8. The word concept in the passage is closest in meaning to

- ⟡ power
- ⟡ reality
- ⟡ difficulty
- ⟡ idea

9. Which of the following can be inferred from paragraph 5 about variations in political beliefs within the Whig Party?

- ⟡ They were focused on issues of public liberty.
- ⟡ They caused some members to leave the Whig party.
- ⟡ They were unimportant to most Whigs.
- ⟡ They reflected regional interests.

In some ways the social makeup of the two parties was similar. To be competitive in winning votes, Whigs and Democrats both had to have significant support among farmers, the largest group in society, and workers. Neither party could win an election by appealing exclusively to the rich or the poor. The Whigs, however, enjoyed disproportionate strength among the business and commercial classes. Whigs appealed to planters who needed credit to finance their cotton and rice trade in the world market, to farmers who were eager to sell their surpluses, and to workers who wished to improve themselves. Democrats attracted farmers isolated from the market or uncomfortable with it, workers alienated from the emerging industrial system, and rising entrepreneurs who wanted to break monopolies and open the economy to newcomers like themselves. The Whigs were strongest in the towns, cities, and those rural areas that were fully integrated into the market economy, whereas Democrats dominated areas of semisubsistence farming that were more isolated and languishing economically.

10. According to paragraph 6, the Democrats were supported by all of the following groups EXCEPT

○ workers unhappy with the new industrial system
○ planters involved in international trade
○ rising entrepreneurs
○ individuals seeking to open the economy to newcomers

11. Which of the sentences below best expresses the essential information in the highlighted sentence in the passage? *Incorrect* choices change the meaning in important ways or leave out essential information.

○ Whigs were able to attract support only in the wealthiest parts of the economy because Democrats dominated in other areas.
○ Whig and Democratic areas of influence were naturally split between urban and rural areas, respectively.
○ The semisubsistence farming areas dominated by Democrats became increasingly isolated by the Whigs' control of the market economy.
○ The Democrats' power was greatest in poorer areas while the Whigs were strongest in those areas where the market was already fully operating.

PARAGRAPH 2

During Jackson's second term, his opponents had gradually come together to form the Whig party. ■ Whigs and Democrats held different attitudes toward the changes brought about by the market, banks, and commerce. ■ The Democrats tended to view society as a continuing conflict between "the people"—farmers, planters, and workers—and a set of greedy aristocrats. ■ This "paper money aristocracy" of bankers and investors manipulated the banking system for their own profit, Democrats claimed, and sapped the nation's virtue by encouraging speculation and the desire for sudden, unearned wealth. ■ The Democrats wanted the rewards of the market without sacrificing the features of a simple agrarian republic. They wanted the wealth that the market offered without the competitive, changing society; the complex dealing; the dominance of urban centers; and the loss of independence that came with it.

12. Look at the four squares ■ that indicate where the following sentence can be added to the passage.

This new party argued against the policies of Jackson and his party in a number of important areas, beginning with the economy.

Where would the sentence best fit?

◯ During Jackson's second term, his opponents had gradually come together to form the Whig party. **This new party argued against the policies of Jackson and his party in a number of important areas, beginning with the economy.** Whigs and Democrats held different attitudes toward the changes brought about by the market, banks, and commerce. ■ The Democrats tended to view society as a continuing conflict between "the people"— farmers, planters, and workers—and a set of greedy aristocrats. ■ This "paper money aristocracy" of bankers and investors manipulated the banking system for their own profit, Democrats claimed, and sapped the nation's virtue by encouraging speculation and the desire for sudden, unearned wealth. ■ The Democrats wanted the rewards of the market without sacrificing the features of a simple agrarian republic. They wanted the wealth that the market offered without the competitive, changing society; the complex dealing; the dominance of urban centers; and the loss of independence that came with it.

◯ During Jackson's second term, his opponents had gradually come together to form the Whig party. ■ Whigs and Democrats held different attitudes toward the changes brought about by the market, banks, and commerce. **This new party argued against the policies of Jackson and his party in a number of important areas, beginning with the economy.** The Democrats tended to view society as a continuing conflict between "the people"— farmers, planters, and workers—and a set of greedy aristocrats. ■ This "paper money aristocracy" of bankers and investors manipulated the banking system for their own profit, Democrats claimed, and sapped the nation's virtue by encouraging speculation and the desire for sudden, unearned wealth. ■ The Democrats wanted the rewards of the market without sacrificing the features of a simple agrarian republic. They wanted the wealth that the market offered without the competitive, changing society; the complex dealing; the dominance of urban centers; and the loss of independence that came with it.

◯ During Jackson's second term, his opponents had gradually come together to form the Whig party. ■ Whigs and Democrats held different attitudes toward the changes brought about by the market, banks, and commerce. ■ The Democrats tended to view society as a continuing conflict between "the people"—farmers, planters, and workers—and a set of greedy aristocrats.

This new party argued against the policies of Jackson and his party in a number of important areas, beginning with the economy. This "paper money aristocracy" of bankers and investors manipulated the banking system for their own profit, Democrats claimed, and sapped the nation's virtue by encouraging speculation and the desire for sudden, unearned wealth. ■ The Democrats wanted the rewards of the market without sacrificing the features of a simple agrarian republic. They wanted the wealth that the market offered without the competitive, changing society; the complex dealing; the dominance of urban centers; and the loss of independence that came with it.

⬭ During Jackson's second term, his opponents had gradually come together to form the Whig party. ■ Whigs and Democrats held different attitudes toward the changes brought about by the market, banks, and commerce. ■ The Democrats tended to view society as a continuing conflict between "the people"—farmers, planters, and workers—and a set of greedy aristocrats. ■ This "paper money aristocracy" of bankers and investors manipulated the banking system for their own profit, Democrats claimed, and sapped the nation's virtue by encouraging speculation and the desire for sudden, unearned wealth. **This new party argued against the policies of Jackson and his party in a number of important areas, beginning with the economy.** The Democrats wanted the rewards of the market without sacrificing the features of a simple agrarian republic. They wanted the wealth that the market offered without the competitive, changing society; the complex dealing; the dominance of urban centers; and the loss of independence that came with it.

13. Directions: An introductory sentence for a brief summary of the passage is provided below. Complete the summary by selecting the THREE answer choices that express the most important ideas in the passage. Some answer choices do not belong in the summary because they express ideas that are not presented in the passage or are minor ideas in the passage. *This question is worth 2 points.*

The political system of the United States in the mid-nineteenth century was strongly influenced by the social and economic circumstances of the time.

-
-
-

Answer Choices

1. The Democratic and Whig Parties developed in response to the needs of competing economic and political constituencies.

2. During Andrew Jackson's two terms as President, he served as leader of both the Democratic and Whig Parties.

3. The Democratic Party primarily represented the interests of the market, banks, and commerce.

4. In contrast to the Democrats, the Whigs favored government aid for education.

5. A fundamental difference between Whigs and Democrats involved the importance of the market in society.

6. The role of government in the lives of the people was an important political distinction between the two parties.

THE EXPRESSION OF EMOTIONS

Joy and sadness are experienced by people in all cultures around the world, but how can we tell when other people are happy or despondent? It turns out that the expression of many emotions may be universal. Smiling is apparently a universal sign of friendliness and approval. Baring the teeth in a hostile way, as noted by Charles Darwin in the nineteenth century, may be a universal sign of anger. As the originator of the theory of evolution, Darwin believed that the universal recognition of facial expressions would have survival value. For example, facial expressions could signal the approach of enemies (or friends) in the absence of language.

Most investigators concur that certain facial expressions suggest the same emotions in all people. Moreover, people in diverse cultures recognize the emotions manifested by the facial expressions. In classic research Paul Ekman took photographs of people exhibiting the emotions of anger, disgust, fear, happiness, and sadness. He then asked people around the world to indicate what emotions were being depicted in them. Those queried ranged from European college students to members of the Fore, a tribe that dwells in the New Guinea highlands. All groups, including the Fore, who had almost no contact with Western culture, agreed on the portrayed emotions. The Fore also displayed familiar facial expressions when asked how they would respond if they were the characters in stories that called for basic emotional responses. Ekman and his colleagues more recently obtained similar results in a study of ten cultures in which participants were permitted to report that multiple emotions were shown by facial expressions. The participants generally agreed on which two emotions were being shown and which emotion was more intense.

Psychological researchers generally recognize that facial expressions reflect emotional states. In fact, various emotional states give rise to certain patterns of electrical activity in the facial muscles and in the brain. The facial-feedback hypothesis argues, however, that the causal relationship between emotions and facial expressions can also work in the opposite direction. According to this hypothesis, signals from the facial muscles ("feedback") are sent back to emotion centers of the brain, and so a person's facial expression can influence that person's emotional state. Consider Darwin's words: "The free expression by outward signs of an emotion intensifies it. On the other hand, the repression, as far as possible, of all outward signs softens our emotions." Can smiling give rise to feelings of good will, for example, and frowning to anger?

Psychological research has given rise to some interesting findings concerning the facial-feedback hypothesis. Causing participants in experiments to smile, for example, leads them to report more positive feelings and to rate cartoons (humorous drawings of people or situations) as being more humorous. When they are caused to frown, they rate cartoons as being more aggressive.

What are the possible links between facial expressions and emotion? One link is arousal, which is the level of activity or preparedness for activity in an organism. Intense contraction of facial muscles, such as those used in signifying fear, heightens arousal. Self-perception of heightened arousal then leads to heightened emotional activity. Other links may involve changes in brain temperature and the release of neurotransmitters (substances that transmit nerve impulses.) The contraction of facial muscles both influences the internal emotional state and reflects it. Ekman has found that the so-called Duchenne smile, which is characterized by "crow's feet" wrinkles around the eyes and a subtle drop in the eye cover fold so that the skin above the eye moves down slightly toward the eyeball, can lead to pleasant feelings.

"keep a stiff upper lip": Avoid showing emotions in difficult situations

Ekman's observation may be relevant to the British expression "<u>keep a stiff upper lip</u>" as a recommendation for handling stress. It might be that a "stiff" lip suppresses emotional response—as long as the lip is not quivering with fear or tension. But when the emotion that leads to stiffening the lip is more intense, and involves strong muscle tension, facial feedback may heighten emotional response.

PARAGRAPH 1

Joy and sadness are experienced by people in all cultures around the world, but how can we tell when other people are happy or despondent? It turns out that the expression of many emotions may be universal. Smiling is apparently a universal sign of friendliness and approval. Baring the teeth in a hostile way, as noted by Charles Darwin in the nineteenth century, may be a universal sign of anger. As the originator of the theory of evolution, Darwin believed that the universal recognition of facial expressions would have survival value. For example, facial expressions could signal the approach of enemies (or friends) in the absence of language.

Directions: Mark your answer by filling in the oval next to your choice.

1. The word despondent in the passage is closest in meaning to

- ○ curious
- ○ unhappy
- ○ thoughtful
- ○ uncertain

2. The author mentions "Baring the teeth in a hostile way" in order to

- ○ differentiate one possible meaning of a particular facial expression from other meanings of it
- ○ support Darwin's theory of evolution
- ○ provide an example of a facial expression whose meaning is widely understood
- ○ contrast a facial expression that is easily understood with other facial expressions

PARAGRAPH 2

Most investigators concur that certain facial expressions suggest the same emotions in all people. Moreover, people in diverse cultures recognize the emotions manifested by the facial expressions. In classic research Paul Ekman took photographs of people exhibiting the emotions of anger, disgust, fear, happiness, and sadness. He then asked people around the world to indicate what emotions were being depicted in them. Those queried ranged from European college students to members of the Fore, a tribe that dwells in the New Guinea highlands. All groups, including the Fore, who had almost no contact with Western culture, agreed on the portrayed emotions. The Fore also displayed familiar facial expressions when asked how they would respond if they were the characters in stories that called for basic emotional responses. Ekman and his colleagues more recently obtained similar results in a study of ten cultures in which participants were permitted to report that multiple emotions were shown by facial expressions. The participants generally agreed on which two emotions were being shown and which emotion was more intense.

3. The word concur in the passage is closest in meaning to

○ estimate
○ agree
○ expect
○ understand

4. The word them in the passage refers to

○ emotions
○ people
○ photographs
○ cultures

5. According to paragraph 2, which of the following was true of the Fore people of New Guinea?

○ They did not want to be shown photographs.
○ They were famous for their story-telling skills.
○ They knew very little about Western culture.
○ They did not encourage the expression of emotions.

6. Which of the sentences below best expresses the essential information in the highlighted sentence in the passage? *Incorrect* choices change the meaning in important ways or leave out essential information.

○ The Fore's facial expressions indicated their unwillingness to pretend to be story characters.
○ The Fore were asked to display familiar facial expressions when they told their stories.
○ The Fore exhibited the same relationship of facial expressions and basic emotions that is seen in Western culture when they acted out stories.
○ The Fore were familiar with the facial expressions and basic emotions of characters in stories.

PARAGRAPH 3

Psychological researchers generally recognize that facial expressions reflect emotional states. In fact, various emotional states give rise to certain patterns of electrical activity in the facial muscles and in the brain. The facial-feedback hypothesis argues, however, that the causal relationship between emotions and facial expressions can also work in the opposite direction. According to this hypothesis, signals from the facial muscles ("feedback") are sent back to emotion centers of the brain, and so a person's facial expression can influence that person's emotional state. Consider Darwin's words: "The free expression by outward signs of an emotion intensifies it. On the other hand, the repression, as far as possible, of all outward signs softens our emotions." Can smiling give rise to feelings of good will, for example, and frowning to anger?

7. According to the passage, what did Darwin believe would happen to human emotions that were not expressed?

○ They would become less intense.
○ They would last longer than usual.
○ They would cause problems later.
○ They would become more negative.

PARAGRAPH 4

Psychological research has given rise to some interesting findings concerning the facial-feedback hypothesis. Causing participants in experiments to smile, for example, leads them to report more positive feelings and to rate cartoons (humorous drawings of people or situations) as being more humorous. When they are caused to frown, they rate cartoons as being more aggressive.

8. According to the passage, research involving which of the following supported the facial-feedback hypothesis?

○ The reactions of people in experiments to cartoons

○ The tendency of people in experiments to cooperate

○ The release of neurotransmitters by people during experiments

○ The long-term effects of repressing emotions

9. The word rate in the passage is closest in meaning to

○ judge
○ reject
○ draw
○ want

PARAGRAPH 6

Ekman's observation may be relevant to the British expression "keep a stiff upper lip" as a recommendation for handling stress. It might be that a "stiff" lip suppresses emotional response—as long as the lip is not quivering with fear or tension. But when the emotion that leads to stiffening the lip is more intense, and involves strong muscle tension, facial feedback may heighten emotional response.

10. The word relevant in the passage is closest in meaning to

○ contradictory
○ confusing
○ dependent
○ applicable

11. According to the passage, stiffening the upper lip may have which of the following effects?

○ It first suppresses stress, then intensifies it.

○ It may cause fear and tension in those who see it.

○ It can damage the lip muscles.

○ It may either heighten or reduce emotional response.

■ Most investigators concur that certain facial expressions suggest the same emotions in all people. ■ Moreover, people in diverse cultures recognize the emotions manifested by the facial expressions. ■ In classic research Paul Ekman took photographs of people exhibiting the emotions of anger, disgust, fear, happiness, and sadness. ■ He then asked people around the world to indicate what emotions were being depicted in them. Those queried ranged from European college students to members of the Fore, a tribe that dwells in the New Guinea highlands. All groups, including the Fore, who had almost no contact with Western culture, agreed on the portrayed emotions. The Fore also displayed familiar facial expressions when asked how they would respond if they were the characters in stories that called for basic emotional responses. Ekman and his colleagues more recently obtained similar results in a study of ten cultures in which participants were permitted to report that multiple emotions were shown by facial expressions. The participants generally agreed on which two emotions were being shown and which emotion was more intense.

12. Look at the four squares ■ that indicate where the following sentence could be added to the passage.

This universality in the recognition of emotions was demonstrated by using rather simple methods.

Where would the sentence best fit?

○ **This universality in the recognition of emotions was demonstrated by using rather simple methods.** Most investigators concur that certain facial expressions suggest the same emotions in all people. ■ Moreover, people in diverse cultures recognize the emotions manifested by the facial expressions. ■ In classic research Paul Ekman took photographs of people exhibiting the emotions of anger, disgust, fear, happiness, and sadness. ■ He then asked people around the world to indicate what emotions were being depicted in them. Those queried ranged from European college students to members of the Fore, a tribe that dwells in the New Guinea highlands. All groups, including the Fore, who had almost no contact with Western culture, agreed on the portrayed emotions. The Fore also displayed familiar facial expressions when asked how they would respond if they were the characters in stories that called for basic emotional responses. Ekman and his colleagues more recently obtained similar results in a study of ten cultures in which participants were permitted to report that multiple emotions were shown by facial expressions. The participants generally agreed on which two emotions were being shown and which emotion was more intense.

○ ■ Most investigators concur that certain facial expressions suggest the same emotions in all people. **This universality in the recognition of emotions was demonstrated by using rather simple methods.** Moreover, people in diverse cultures recognize the emotions manifested by the facial expressions. ■ In classic research Paul Ekman took photographs of people exhibiting the emotions of anger, disgust, fear, happiness, and sadness. ■ He then asked people around the world to indicate what emotions were being depicted in them. Those queried ranged from European college students to members of the Fore, a tribe that dwells in the New Guinea highlands. All groups, including the Fore, who had almost no contact with Western culture, agreed on the portrayed emotions. The Fore also displayed familiar facial expressions when asked how they would respond if they were the characters in stories that called for basic emotional responses. Ekman and his colleagues more recently obtained similar results in a study of ten cultures in which participants were permitted to report that multiple emotions were shown by facial expressions. The participants generally agreed on which two emotions were being shown and which emotion was more intense.

○ ■ Most investigators concur that certain facial expressions suggest the same emotions in all people. ■ Moreover, people in diverse cultures recognize the emotions manifested by the facial expressions. **This universality in the recognition of emotions was demonstrated by using rather simple methods.** In classic research Paul Ekman took photographs of people exhibiting the emotions of anger, disgust, fear, happiness, and sadness. ■ He then asked people around the world to indicate what emotions were being depicted in them. Those queried ranged from European college students to members of the Fore, a tribe that dwells in the New Guinea highlands. All groups, including the Fore, who had almost no contact with Western culture, agreed on the portrayed emotions. The Fore also displayed familiar facial expressions when asked how they would respond if they were the characters in stories that called for basic emotional responses. Ekman and his colleagues more recently obtained similar results in a study of ten cultures in which participants were permitted to report that multiple emotions were shown by facial expressions. The participants generally agreed on which two emotions were being shown and which emotion was more intense.

○ ■ Most investigators concur that certain facial expressions suggest the same emotions in all people. ■ Moreover, people in diverse cultures recognize the emotions manifested by the facial expressions. ■ In classic research Paul Ekman took photographs of people exhibiting the emotions of anger, disgust, fear, happiness, and sadness. **This universality in the recognition of emotions was demonstrated by using rather simple methods.** He then asked people around the world to indicate what emotions were being depicted in them. Those queried ranged from European college students to members of the Fore, a tribe that dwells in the New Guinea highlands. All groups, including the Fore, who had almost no contact with Western culture, agreed on the portrayed emotions. The Fore also displayed familiar facial expressions when asked how they would respond if they were the characters in stories that called for basic emotional responses. Ekman and his colleagues more recently obtained similar results in a study of ten cultures in which participants were permitted to report that multiple emotions were shown by facial expressions. The participants generally agreed on which two emotions were being shown and which emotion was more intense.

13. **Directions:** An introductory sentence for a brief summary of the passage is provided below. Complete the summary by selecting the THREE answer choices that express the most important ideas in the passage. Some sentences do not belong in the summary because they express ideas that are not presented in the passage or are minor ideas in the passage. *This question is worth 2 points.*

Psychological research seems to confirm that people associate particular facial expressions with the same emotions across cultures.

- ◆

- ◆

- ◆

Answer Choices

1. Artificially producing the Duchenne smile can cause a person to have pleasant feelings.

2. Facial expressions and emotional states interact with each other through a variety of feedback mechanisms.

3. People commonly believe that they can control their facial expressions so that their true emotions remain hidden.

4. A person's facial expression may reflect the person's emotional state.

5. Ekman argued that the ability to accurately recognize the emotional content of facial expressions was valuable for human beings.

6. Facial expressions that occur as a result of an individual's emotional state may themselves feed back information that influences the person's emotions.

GEOLOGY AND LANDSCAPE

Most people consider the landscape to be unchanging, but Earth is a dynamic body, and its surface is continually altering—slowly on the human time scale, but relatively rapidly when compared to the great age of Earth (about 4,500 billion years). There are two principal influences that shape the terrain: constructive processes such as uplift, which create new landscape features, and destructive forces such as erosion, which gradually wear away exposed landforms.

Hills and mountains are often regarded as the epitome of permanence, successfully resisting the destructive forces of nature, but in fact they tend to be relatively short-lived in geological terms. As a general rule, the higher a mountain is, the more recently it was formed; for example, the high mountains of the Himalayas are only about 50 million years old. Lower mountains tend to be older, and are often the eroded relics of much higher mountain chains. About 400 million years ago, when the present-day continents of North America and Europe were joined, the Caledonian mountain chain was the same size as the modern Himalayas. Today, however, the relics of the Caledonian orogeny (mountain-building period) exist as the comparatively low mountains of Greenland, the northern Appalachians in the United States, the Scottish Highlands, and the Norwegian coastal plateau.

The Earth's crust is thought to be divided into huge, movable segments, called plates, which float on a soft plastic layer of rock. Some mountains were formed as a result of these plates crashing into each other and forcing up the rock at the plate margins. In this process, sedimentary rocks that originally formed on the seabed may be folded upwards to altitudes of more than 26,000 feet. Other mountains may be raised by earthquakes, which fracture the Earth's crust and can displace enough rock to produce block mountains. A third type of mountain may be formed as a result of volcanic activity which occurs in regions of active fold mountain belts, such as in the Cascade Range of western North America. The Cascades are made up of lavas and volcanic materials. Many of the peaks are extinct volcanoes.

Whatever the reason for mountain formation, as soon as land rises above sea level it is subjected to destructive forces. The exposed rocks are attacked by the various weather processes and gradually broken down into fragments, which are then carried away and later deposited as sediments. Thus, any landscape represents only a temporary stage in the continuous battle between the forces of uplift and those of erosion.

The weather, in its many forms, is the main agent of erosion. Rain washes away loose soil and penetrates cracks in the rocks. Carbon dioxide in the air reacts with the rainwater, forming a weak acid (carbonic acid) that may chemically attack the rocks. The rain seeps underground and the water may reappear later as springs. These springs are the sources of streams and rivers, which cut through the rocks and carry away debris from the mountains to the lowlands.

Under very cold conditions, rocks can be shattered by ice and frost. Glaciers may form in permanently cold areas, and these slowly moving masses of ice cut out valleys, carrying with them huge quantities of eroded rock debris. In dry areas the wind is the principal agent of erosion. It carries fine particles of sand, which bombard exposed rock surfaces, thereby wearing them into yet more sand. Even living things contribute to the formation of landscapes. Tree roots force their way into cracks in rocks and, in so doing, speed their splitting. In contrast, the roots of grasses and other small plants may help to hold loose soil fragments together, thereby helping to prevent erosion by the wind.

Most people consider the landscape to be unchanging, but Earth is a dynamic body, and its surface is continually altering—slowly on the human time scale, but relatively rapidly when compared to the great age of Earth (about 4,500 billion years). There are two principal influences that shape the terrain: constructive processes such as uplift, which create new landscape features, and destructive forces such as erosion, which gradually wear away exposed landforms.

Directions: Mark your answer by filling in the oval next to your choice.

1. According to paragraph 1, which of the following statements is true of changes in Earth's landscape?

   ○ They occur more often by uplift than by erosion.
   ○ They occur only at special times.
   ○ They occur less frequently now than they once did.
   ○ They occur quickly in geological terms.

2. The word relatively in the passage is closest in meaning to

   ○ unusually
   ○ comparatively
   ○ occasionally
   ○ naturally

Hills and mountains are often regarded as the epitome of permanence, successfully resisting the destructive forces of nature, but in fact they tend to be relatively short-lived in geological terms. As a general rule, the higher a mountain is, the more recently it was formed; for example, the high mountains of the Himalayas are only about 50 million years old. Lower mountains tend to be older, and are often the eroded relics of much higher mountain chains. About 400 million years ago, when the present-day continents of North America and Europe were joined, the Caledonian mountain chain was the same size as the modern Himalayas. Today, however, the relics of the Caledonian orogeny (mountain-building period) exist as the comparatively low mountains of Greenland, the northern Appalachians in the United States, the Scottish Highlands, and the Norwegian coastal plateau.

3. Which of the following can be inferred from paragraph 2 about the mountains of the Himalayas?

   ○ Their current height is not an indication of their age.
   ○ At present, they are much higher than the mountains of the Caledonian range.
   ○ They were a uniform height about 400 million years ago.
   ○ They are not as high as the Caledonian mountains were 400 million years ago.

4. The word relics in the passage is closest in meaning to

   ○ resemblances
   ○ regions
   ○ remains
   ○ restorations

The Earth's crust is thought to be divided into huge, movable segments, called plates, which float on a soft plastic layer of rock. Some mountains were formed as a result of these plates crashing into each other and forcing up the rock at the plate margins. In this process, sedimentary rocks that originally formed on the seabed may be folded upwards to altitudes of more than 26,000 feet. Other mountains may be raised by earthquakes, which fracture the Earth's crust and can displace enough rock to produce block mountains. A third type of mountain may be formed as a result of volcanic activity which occurs in regions of active fold mountain belts, such as in the Cascade Range of western North America. The Cascades are made up of lavas and volcanic materials. Many of the peaks are extinct volcanoes.

5. According to paragraph 3, one cause of mountain formation is the

○ effect of climatic change on sea level
○ slowing down of volcanic activity
○ force of Earth's crustal plates hitting each other
○ replacement of sedimentary rock with volcanic rock

The weather, in its many forms, is the main agent of erosion. Rain washes away loose soil and penetrates cracks in the rocks. Carbon dioxide in the air reacts with the rainwater, forming a weak acid (carbonic acid) that may chemically attack the rocks. The rain seeps underground and the water may reappear later as springs. These springs are the sources of streams and rivers, which cut through the rocks and carry away debris from the mountains to the lowlands.

6. Why does the author mention Carbon dioxide in the passage?

○ To explain the origin of a chemical that can erode rocks
○ To contrast carbon dioxide with carbonic acid
○ To give an example of how rainwater penetrates soil
○ To argue for the desirability of preventing erosion

7. The word seeps in the passage is closest in meaning to

○ dries gradually
○ flows slowly
○ freezes quickly
○ warms slightly

PARAGRAPH 6

Under very cold conditions, rocks can be shattered by ice and frost. Glaciers may form in permanently cold areas, and these slowly moving masses of ice cut out valleys, carrying with them huge quantities of eroded rock debris. In dry areas the wind is the principal agent of erosion. It carries fine particles of sand, which bombard exposed rock surfaces, thereby wearing them into yet more sand. Even living things contribute to the formation of landscapes. Tree roots force their way into cracks in rocks and, in so doing, speed their splitting. In contrast, the roots of grasses and other small plants may help to hold loose soil fragments together, thereby helping to prevent erosion by the wind.

8. The word them in the passage refers to

- ○ cold areas
- ○ masses of ice
- ○ valleys
- ○ rock debris

PARAGRAPH 2

Hills and mountains are often regarded as the epitome of permanence, successfully resisting the destructive forces of nature, but in fact they tend to be relatively short-lived in geological terms. As a general rule, the higher a mountain is, the more recently it was formed; for example, the high mountains of the Himalayas are only about 50 million years old. Lower mountains tend to be older, and are often the eroded relics of much higher mountain chains. About 400 million years ago, when the present-day continents of North America and Europe were joined, the Caledonian mountain chain was the same size as the modern Himalayas. Today, however, the relics of the Caledonian orogeny (mountain-building period) exist as the comparatively low mountains of Greenland, the northern Appalachians in the United States, the Scottish Highlands, and the Norwegian coastal plateau.

9. Which of the sentences below best expresses the essential information in the highlighted sentence in the passage? *Incorrect* choices change the meaning in important ways or leave out essential information.

- ○ When they are relatively young, hills and mountains successfully resist the destructive forces of nature.
- ○ Although they seem permanent, hills and mountains exist for a relatively short period of geological time.
- ○ Hills and mountains successfully resist the destructive forces of nature, but only for a short time.
- ○ Hills and mountains resist the destructive forces of nature better than other types of landforms.

Under very cold conditions, rocks can be shattered by ice and frost. Glaciers may form in permanently cold areas, and these slowly moving masses of ice cut out valleys, carrying with them huge quantities of eroded rock debris. ■ In dry areas the wind is the principal agent of erosion. ■ It carries fine particles of sand, which bombard exposed rock surfaces, thereby wearing them into yet more sand. ■ Even living things contribute to the formation of landscapes. ■ Tree roots force their way into cracks in rocks and, in so doing, speed their splitting. In contrast, the roots of grasses and other small plants may help to hold loose soil fragments together, thereby helping to prevent erosion by the wind.

10. According to paragraph 6, which of the following is both a cause and result of erosion?

○ Glacial activity
○ Rock debris
○ Tree roots
○ Sand

11. Look at the four squares ■ that indicate where the following sentence could be added to the passage.

Under different climatic conditions, another type of destructive force contributes to erosion.

Where would the sentence best fit?

○ Under very cold conditions, rocks can be shattered by ice and frost. Glaciers may form in permanently cold areas, and these slowly moving masses of ice scour out valleys, carrying with them huge quantities of eroded rock debris. **Under different climatic conditions, another type of destructive force contributes to erosion.** In dry areas the wind is the principal agent of erosion. ■ It carries fine particles of sand, which bombard the exposed rock surfaces, thereby wearing them into yet more sand. ■ Even living things contribute to the formation of landscapes. ■ Tree roots force their way into cracks in rocks and, in so doing, speed their splitting. In contrast, the roots of grasses and other small plants may help to hold loose soil fragments together, thereby helping to prevent erosion by the wind.

○ Under very cold conditions, rocks can be shattered by ice and frost. Glaciers may form in permanently cold areas, and these slowly moving masses of ice scour out valleys, carrying with them huge quantities of eroded rock debris. ■ In dry areas the wind is the principal agent of erosion. **Under different climatic conditions, another type of destructive force contributes to erosion.** It carries fine particles of sand, which bombard the exposed rock surfaces, thereby wearing them into yet more sand. ■ Even living things contribute to the formation of landscapes. ■ Tree roots force their way into cracks in rocks and, in so doing, speed their splitting. In contrast, the roots of grasses and other small plants may help to hold loose soil fragments together, thereby helping to prevent erosion by the wind.

○ Under very cold conditions, rocks can be shattered by ice and frost. Glaciers may form in permanently cold areas, and these slowly moving masses of ice scour out valleys, carrying with them huge quantities of eroded rock debris. ■ In dry areas the wind is the principal agent of erosion. ■ It carries fine particles of sand, which bombard the exposed rock surfaces, thereby wearing them into yet more sand. **Under different climatic conditions, another type of destructive force contributes to erosion.** Even living things contribute to the formation of landscapes. ■ Tree roots force their way into cracks in rocks and, in so doing, speed their splitting. In contrast, the roots of grasses and other small plants may help to hold loose soil fragments together, thereby helping to prevent erosion by the wind.

○ Under very cold conditions, rocks can be shattered by ice and frost. Glaciers may form in permanently cold areas, and these slowly moving masses of ice scour out valleys, carrying with them huge quantities of eroded rock debris. ■ In dry areas the wind is the principal agent of erosion. ■ It carries fine particles of sand, which bombard the exposed rock surfaces, thereby wearing them into yet more sand. ■ Even living things contribute to the formation of landscapes. **Under different climatic conditions, another type of destructive force contributes to erosion.** Tree roots force their way into cracks in rocks and, in so doing, speed their splitting. In contrast, the roots of grasses and other small plants may help to hold loose soil fragments together, thereby helping to prevent erosion by the wind.

12. **Directions:** Three of the answer choices below are used in the passage to illustrate constructive processes and two are used to illustrate destructive processes. Complete the table by matching appropriate answer choices to the processes they are used to illustrate. ***This question is worth 3 points.***

CONSTRUCTIVE PROCESSES	DESTRUCTIVE PROCESSES
➤	➤
➤	➤
➤	

Answer Choices

1. Collision of Earth's crustal plates

2. Separation of continents

3. Wind-driven sand

4. Formation of grass roots in soil

5. Earthquakes

6. Volcanic activity

7. Weather processes

ANSWER KEY AND EXPLANATIONS

Answer Key and Self-Scoring Chart

Directions. Check your answers against the Answer Key below. Write the number 1 on the line to the right of each question if you picked the correct answer. (For questions worth more than one point, follow the directions given.) Total your points at the bottom of the chart.

Question Number   Correct Answer

Nineteenth-Century Politics in the United States

1.	2	_____
2.	3	_____
3.	2	_____
4.	1	_____
5.	3	_____
6.	2	_____
7.	3	_____
8.	4	_____
9.	4	_____
10.	2	_____
11.	4	_____
12.	1	_____

For question 13, write 2 if you picked all three correct answers. Write 1 if you picked two correct answers.

13.	1, 5, 6	_____

The Expression of Emotions

1.	2	_____
2.	3	_____
3.	2	_____
4.	3	_____
5.	3	_____
6.	3	_____
7.	1	_____
8.	1	_____
9.	1	_____
10.	4	_____
11.	4	_____
12.	3	_____

For question 13, write 2 if you picked all three correct answers. Write 1 if you picked two correct answers.

13.	2, 4, 6	_____

Question Number   Correct Answer

Geology and Landscape

Question	Answer	
1.	4	_____
2.	2	_____
3.	2	_____
4.	3	_____
5.	3	_____
6.	1	_____
7.	2	_____
8.	2	_____
9.	2	_____
10.	4	_____
11.	1	_____

For question 12, write 3 if you placed five answer choices correctly. Write 2 if you placed 4 choices correctly. Write 1 if you placed 3 choices correctly.

12. Constructive: 1, 5, 6
    Destructive: 3, 7   _____
    TOTAL: _____

On the opposite page is a table that converts your Reading Practice section answers into a TOEFL iBT Reading Scaled Score. Take the number of correct answers from your Answer Key table and find that number in the left-hand column of the table. On the right-hand side of the table is a range of TOEFL iBT Reading scores for that number of correct answers. For example, if the total of points from your answer key is 26, the table estimates a scaled score of 19 to 21. Your scaled score is given as a range instead of a single number for the following reasons:

➤ The estimates of scores are based on the performance of students who participated in a field study for these Reading Comprehension questions. Those students took the test on computer; you used a book. Although the two experiences are comparable, the differences make exact comparisons impossible.
➤ The students who participated in the field study were volunteers and may have differed in average ability from the actual TOEFL test-taking population.
➤ The conversion of scores from the field study in which these questions were administered to the current TOEFL iBT scale involved two scale conversions. Converting from one scale to another always involves some statistical error.

You should use your score estimate as a general guide only. Your actual score on TOEFL iBT may be higher or lower than your score on the practice version. A free practice version of TOEFL iBT, which you can take on computer, is available at toeflpractice.ets.org.

Reading Comprehension

RAW POINT TOTAL	SCALE SCORE
42–41	30
40–39	27–30
38	28
37–36	26–28
35–33	25–27
32	23–25
31–30	22–24
29	20–22
28–27	19–22
26	19–21
25–24	18–21
23	16–18
22–21	15–18
20	14–16
19–17	12–16
16–15	9–15
14	9–13
13–12	5–13
11	3–13
10–9	0–13
8	0–11
7–1	0–4

Answers and Explanations

Nineteenth-Century Politics in the United States

1. ❷ This is a Vocabulary question. The word being tested is *immeasurably*. It is highlighted in the passage. *Immeasurably* means "in a manner too big to be measured." So if Jackson enlarged the president's powers so much that the results can't be measured, he enlarged them "greatly."

2. ❸ This is a Factual Information question asking for specific information that can be found in paragraph 1. The correct answer is choice 3 because the first sentence of the paragraph explicitly states that this was when the development of the modern presidency began. The remainder of the paragraph is devoted to explaining the significant changes in government that this development involved. The result, as stated in sentence 5, was that the nature of the presidency itself was redefined. Choice 1 is contradicted by the paragraph; Jackson didn't give presidential power away, he increased it. Choice 2 is not mentioned in the paragraph: it says Jackson addressed the Senate, but not that this was the beginning of regular addresses. Choice 4, which says that this was the first time the Senate opposed the President, is not stated in the passage.

3. ❷ This is a Rhetorical Purpose question. It is asking you why the author mentions "bankers and investors" in the passage. The phrase being tested is highlighted in the passage. The correct answer is choice 2. The author is using bankers and investors as examples of people that the Democrats claimed were "manipulating" the banking system for their own profit. That means that they were unfairly becoming rich. Choices 1, 3, and 4 are all incorrect because, based upon the passage, they seem unlikely to be true. Therefore, the author would not use them as examples.

4. ❶ This is a Factual Information question asking for specific information that can be found in paragraph 3. Choice 1 is the correct answer. The paragraph says that Whigs believed commerce and economic development "would benefit everyone." That means essentially the same thing as choice 1, which says that Whigs believed economic growth would "promote the advancement of society as a whole." "Society as a whole" is another way of saying "everyone." Choices 2 and 3 are not mentioned in the paragraph. Choice 4, about conflict between groups, is mentioned but in a different context, so it is not a belief held by Whigs.

5. ❸ This is a Factual Information question asking for specific information that can be found in paragraph 3. The correct answer is choice 3: the Whigs viewed government as responsible for maintaining an economy that allowed all capable citizens to benefit. This is a restatement of paragraph 3, sentence 5. The paragraph states that Whigs did not envision continuing conflict between farmers and business people, so choice 1 is wrong. Whigs favored changes brought about by the market, so choice 2 is wrong. Whigs were in favor of increased emphasis on economic development, so choice 4 is incorrect.

6. ❷ This is a Vocabulary question. The word being tested is *inclination*. It is highlighted in the passage. The fact that Jackson had an *inclination* to be a strong President means that he preferred being strong to having limited powers. In other words, his "tendency" was to favor a strong presidency, so choice 2 is the correct answer.

7. ❸ This is a Factual Information question asking for specific information that can be found in paragraph 4. The correct answer is choice 3, which is explicitly stated in sentence 3 of the paragraph. Sentences 4 and 5 explicitly refute the other choices.

8. ❹ This is a Vocabulary question. The word being tested is *concept*. It is highlighted in the passage. The passage says that "for Whigs the concept of government was . . ." In other words, "the way Whigs thought about government was." That process of thinking represents ideas, so choice 4 is the correct answer here.

9. ❹ This is an Inference question asking for an inference that can be supported by paragraph 5. The correct answer is choice 4: variations in Whigs' political beliefs reflected regional differences. This is supported by sentence 5 of the paragraph, which says that certain beliefs "particularly" reflected the views of northern Whigs. That suggests that Whigs in other regions of the country had beliefs that varied from this view and implies that such differences were regional. The other three choices are not mentioned in the passage in connection with "variations" in Whig beliefs, so there is no basis for inferring any of them.

10. ❷ This is a Negative Factual Information question asking for specific information that can be found in paragraph 6. Choice 2 is the correct answer. Sentence 5 says that it was Whigs, not Democrats, who had the support of planters involved in international trade. The next sentence, sentence 6, says that in contrast, Democrats had the support of the groups mentioned in choices 1, 3, and 4 ("workers," "entrepreneurs," and certain other "individuals"). Therefore, all of the groups described in the answer choices, EXCEPT the planters of choice 2, did support the Democrats.

11. ❹ This is a Sentence Simplification question. As with all of these items, a single sentence in the passage is highlighted:

The Whigs were strongest in the towns, cities, and those rural areas that were fully integrated into the market economy, whereas Democrats dominated areas of semisubsistence farming that were more isolated and languishing economically.

The correct answer is choice 4. Choice 4 contains all of the essential information in the tested sentence but the order in which it is presented is reversed. The highlighted sentence describes areas of Whig strength first, and then the areas where Democrats were strong. The correct answer, choice 4, describes Democrat strongholds first, and then Whig areas. No meaning has been changed, and no information has been left out.

Choice 1 is incorrect because it states that Whigs were able to attract support only in the wealthiest areas. The highlighted sentence does not say that; it says their support came from places integrated into the market, which can include areas of all economic levels.

Choice 2 is incorrect because it says that the two parties were split between rural and urban areas. However, the highlighted sentence says that Whigs were strong in rural areas that were integrated into the market economy. In other words, the split between the parties was based on the degree to which an area was integrated into the market, not whether it was urban or rural.

Choice 3 is incorrect because the highlighted sentence makes no mention of how (or if) the Whigs' control of the market economy affected the areas dominated by the Democrats.

12. ❶ This is an Insert Text question. You can see the four black squares in paragraph 2 that represent the possible answer choices here.

During Jackson's second term, his opponents had gradually come together to form the Whig party. ■ Whigs and Democrats held different attitudes toward the changes brought about by the market, banks, and commerce. ■ The Democrats tended to view society as a continuing conflict between "the people"—farmers, planters, and workers—and a set of greedy aristocrats. ■ This "paper money aristocracy" of bankers and investors manipulated the banking system for their own profit, Democrats claimed, and sapped the nation's virtue by encouraging speculation and the desire for sudden, unearned wealth. ■ The Democrats wanted the rewards of the market without sacrificing the features of a simple agrarian republic. They wanted the wealth that the market offered without the competitive, changing society; the complex dealing; the dominance of urban centers; and the loss of independence that came with it.

The sentence provided, "This new party argued against the policies of Jackson and his party in a number of important areas, beginning with the economy," is best inserted at square 1.

Square 1 is correct because the phrase "This new party" refers directly and only to the Whigs, who are first mentioned (as a recently formed party) in sentence 1 of this paragraph.

Square 2 is incorrect because the sentence before is not limited to the new Whig party. It discusses both Whigs and Democrats.

Squares 3 and 4 are both incorrect because the sentences preceding them refer to the Democrats (the old party), not the Whigs.

13. ❶ ❺ ❻ This is a Prose Summary question. It is completed correctly below. The correct choices are 1, 5, and 6. Choices 2, 3, and 4 are therefore incorrect.

Directions: An introductory sentence for a brief summary of the passage is provided below. Complete the summary by selecting the THREE answer choices that express the most important ideas in the passage. Some answer choices do not belong in the summary because they express ideas that are not presented in the passage or are minor ideas in the passage. *This question is worth 2 points.*

The political system of the United States in the mid-nineteenth century was strongly influenced by the social and economic circumstances of the time.

- The Democratic and Whig Parties developed in response to the needs of competing economic and political constituencies.
- A fundamental difference between Whigs and Democrats involved the importance of the market in society.
- The role of government in the lives of the people was an important political distinction between the two parties.

Answer Choices

1. The Democratic and Whig Parties developed in response to the needs of competing economic and political constituencies.

2. During Andrew Jackson's two terms as President, he served as leader of both the Democratic and Whig Parties.

3. The Democratic Party primarily represented the interests of the market, banks, and commerce.

4. In contrast to the Democrats, the Whigs favored government aid for education.

5. A fundamental difference between Whigs and Democrats involved the importance of the market in society.

6. The role of government in the lives of the people was an important political distinction between the two parties.

Correct Choices

Choice 1, "The Democratic and Whig Parties developed in response to the needs of competing economic and political constituencies," is correct because it is a recurring theme throughout the entire passage. It is a broad general statement about the development of the Whigs and Democrats. Paragraphs 2, 3, 4, 5, and 6 all provide support for this statement with examples of the nature of the competing constituencies in the United States at that time and the ways in which these two parties responded to them.

Choice 5, "A fundamental difference between Whigs and Democrats involved the importance of the market in society," is correct because it is a broad general statement about the differences between the Whigs and Democrats. Paragraphs 2, 3, 4, and 6 all provide support for this statement with examples of the differences in the ways that the two parties viewed the market and society.

Choice 6, "The role of government in the lives of the people was an important political distinction between the two parties," is correct because it is another broad general statement about the differences between the Whigs and Democrats. Paragraphs 2, 3, 4, and 5 all explicitly explore this distinction between Whigs and Democrats.

Incorrect Choices

Choice 2, "During Andrew Jackson's two terms as President, he served as leader of both the Democratic and Whig Parties," is incorrect because it contradicts the passage. Jackson was head of the Democratic Party.

Choice 3, "The Democratic Party primarily represented the interests of the market, banks, and commerce," is incorrect because it is not true. The Whigs primarily represented these groups, as stated in paragraphs 3 and 6.

Choice 4, "In contrast to the Democrats, the Whigs favored government aid for education," is incorrect because the passage states only that "Whigs in the north were likely to favor aid to education. It is not clearly stated how other Whigs or Democrats felt on this issue.

The Expression of Emotions

1. ❷ This is a Vocabulary question. The word being tested is *despondent*. It is highlighted in the passage. The correct answer is choice 2, "*unhappy*." The sentence in which the highlighted word appears uses *despondent* as a contrast to *happy*. Since *unhappy* is the opposite of *happy*, it provides the fullest possible contrast and is equivalent to the contrast between *Joy* and *sadness* at the beginning of the sentence.

2. ❸ This is a Rhetorical Purpose question. It is asking you why the author mentions "baring the teeth in a hostile way" in the passage. This phrase is highlighted in the passage. The correct answer is choice 3; baring the teeth is an example of a facial expression whose meaning is widely understood. The central theme of paragraph 1 of the passage is facial expressions that are universal. The author provides various examples of such expressions, and baring the teeth is mentioned as a universal sign of anger. The other choices are all mentioned in the passage, but not in conjunction with baring the teeth, so they are all incorrect.

3. ❷ This is a Vocabulary question. The word being tested is *concur*. It is highlighted in the passage. The correct answer is choice 2, "agree." *Concur* means to agree, so if investigators concur about the meaning of certain facial expressions, they agree on their meaning.

4. ❸ This is a Reference question. The word being tested is *them*, and it is highlighted in the passage. This is a simple pronoun-referent item. The word *them* refers to the photographs that Paul Eckman showed to people from diverse cultures, so the correct answer is choice 3, "photographs."

5. ❸ This is a Factual Information question asking for specific information that can be found in paragraph 2. The correct answer is choice 3, which states that the Fore people of New Zealand knew very little about Western culture. The paragraph explicitly says that the Fore had almost no contact with Western culture. None of the other three choices is mentioned in connection with the Fore, so none of them is correct.

6. ❸ This is a Sentence Simplification question. As with all of these items, a single sentence in the passage is highlighted:

> The Fore also displayed familiar facial expressions when asked how they would respond if they were the characters in stories that called for basic emotional responses.

The correct answer is choice 3. It contains all of the essential ideas in the highlighted sentence without changing the meaning. This choice says that the Fore "exhibited the same relationship of facial and basic emotions that is seen in Western culture when they acted out stories." The sentence that precedes the highlighted sentence states that in a survey, the Fore agreed with Westerners on how various emotions are portrayed. Then the highlighted sentence says that in a different situation (story-telling) the Fores' expressions were also familiar; that is, these expressions were the same as those exhibited by Westerners in this situation.

Choices 1 and 2 are incorrect because each one changes the highlighted sentence into a statement that is not true.

Choice 4 is incorrect because it says that the Fore were familiar with the facial expressions of characters in stories. The highlighted sentence says that it was the investigators who were familiar with the Fores' expressions. This is a change in meaning, so it is incorrect.

7. ❶ This is a Factual Information question asking for specific information that can be found in the passage. The correct answer is choice 1, emotions that are not expressed become less intense. This is correct based on the direct quotation of Darwin in paragraph 3. In that quotation, Darwin says that emotions that are freely expressed become more intense, while "on the other hand" those that are not freely expressed are "softened," meaning that they become less intense.

Choices 2, 3, and 4 are all incorrect because there is nothing in the passage that indicates Darwin ever believed these things about expressing emotions. Some or all of them may actually be true, but there is nothing in this passage that supports them.

8. ❶ This is a Factual Information question asking for specific information that can be found in the passage. You can see that the phrase "The facial-feedback hypothesis" is highlighted where it first appears in the passage in paragraph 3. The correct answer is choice 1, research supporting this hypothesis came from studying experiments of the reactions of people to cartoons. This idea is found in paragraph 4, which uses these experiments as an example of how facial feedback works.

Choice 3, the release of neurotransmitters, is mentioned in paragraph 5 but not in connection with the facial-feedback hypothesis, so it is incorrect.

Choices 2 and 4 are not explicitly mentioned at all in the passage.

9. **❶** This is a Vocabulary question. The word being tested is *rate*, and it is highlighted in the passage. The correct answer is choice 1, "judge." *Rate* in this context means "to judge."

10. **❹** This is a Vocabulary question. The word being tested is *relevant*, and it is highlighted in the passage. The correct answer is choice 4, "applicable. "*Relevant* means that Ekman's observation applies ("is applicable") to an expression.

11. **❹** This is a Factual Information question asking for specific information that can be found in the passage. The correct answer is choice 4; stiffening the upper lip may either heighten or reduce emotional response. This is stated explicitly in paragraph 6 of the passage as a possible paradox in the relationship between facial expressions and emotions.

   Choice 1 is incorrect because paragraph 6 contradicts it.

   Choice 2 is incorrect because the passage mentions only the fear and tension of a person trying to keep a stiff upper lip, not any fear or tension that expression may cause in others.

   Choice 3 is incorrect because there is no suggestion anywhere in the passage that stiffening the upper lip may damage lip muscles.

12. **❸** This is an Insert Text question. You can see the four black squares in paragraph 2 that represent the possible answer choices here.

   ■ Most investigators concur that certain facial expressions suggest the same emotions in all people. ■ Moreover, people in diverse cultures recognize the emotions manifested by the facial expressions. ■ In classic research Paul Ekman took photographs of people exhibiting the emotions of anger, disgust, fear, happiness, and sadness. ■ He then asked people around the world to indicate what emotions were being depicted in them. Those queried ranged from European college students to members of the Fore, a tribe that dwells in the New Guinea highlands. All groups, including the Fore, who had almost no contact with Western culture, agreed on the portrayed emotions. The Fore also displayed familiar facial expressions when asked how they would respond if they were the characters in stories that called for basic emotional responses. Ekman and his colleagues more recently obtained similar results in a study of ten cultures in which participants were permitted to report that multiple emotions were shown by facial expressions. The participants generally agreed on which two emotions were being shown and which emotion was more intense.

   The sentence provided, "This universality in the recognition of emotions was demonstrated by using rather simple methods," is best inserted at square 3.
   Square 3 is correct because the inserted sentence begins with the phrase "This universality." The universality being referred to is the fact, stated in the second sentence, that "people in diverse cultures recognize the emotions manifested by the facial expressions."

None of the other answer choices follows a sentence that contains a universal statement. Sentence 1 mentions that "Most investigators concur," which means that some do not. Therefore this is not a universal statement.

Squares 2 and 4 are incorrect because there is nothing in either sentence to which "This universality" could refer.

13. **❷ ❹ ❻** This is a Prose Summary question. It is completed correctly below. The correct choices are 2, 4, and 6. Choices 1, 3, and 5 are therefore incorrect.

Directions: An introductory sentence for a brief summary of the passage is provided below. Complete the summary by selecting the THREE answer choices that express the most important ideas in the passage. Some answer choices do not belong in the summary because they express ideas that are not presented in the passage or are minor ideas in the passage. *This question is worth 2 points.*

Psychological research seems to confirm that people associate particular facial expressions with the same emotions across cultures.

- Facial expressions and emotional states interact with each other through a variety of feedback mechanisms.
- A person's facial expression may reflect the person's emotional state.
- Facial expressions that occur as a result of an individual's emotional state may themselves feed back information that influences the person's emotions.

Answer Choices

1. Artificially producing the Duchenne smile can cause a person to have pleasant feelings.

2. Facial expressions and emotional states interact with each other through a variety of feedback mechanisms.

3. People commonly believe that they can control their facial expressions so that their true emotions remain hidden.

4. A person's facial expression may reflect the person's emotional state.

5. Ekman argued that the ability to accurately recognize the emotional content of facial expressions was valuable for human beings.

6. Facial expressions that occur as a result of an individual's emotional state may themselves feed back information that influences the person's emotions.

Correct Choices

Choice 2, "Facial expressions and emotional states interact with each other through a variety of feedback mechanisms," is correct because it is a broad, general statement that is developed throughout the passage. Questions about the nature of this interaction and details of research on this issue are discussed in every paragraph, so it is clearly a "main idea."

Choice 4, "A person's facial expression may reflect the person's emotional state," is correct because, like choice 2, it is a major idea that the passage explores in detail. Paragraphs 3, 4, 5, and 6 are devoted to discussing attempts to understand whether and how facial expressions may reflect a person's emotional state.

Choice 6, "Facial expressions that occur as a result of an individual's emotional state may themselves feed back information that influences the person's emotions," is correct because it is the main tenet of the "facial-feedback theory" that is extensively discussed in paragraphs 3, 4, 5, and 6.

Incorrect Choices

Choice 1, "Artificially producing the Duchenne smile can cause a person to have pleasant feelings," is incorrect because it is a minor, supporting detail mentioned in paragraph 5 as an example of a more general, and important, statement about the links between facial expressions and emotion (see choice 6, above).

Choice 3, "People commonly believe that they can control their facial expressions so that their true emotions remain hidden," is incorrect because while it may be true, the passage does not make this claim.

Choice 5, "Ekman argued that the ability to accurately recognize the emotional content of facial expressions was valuable for human beings," is incorrect because according to the passage, Ekman did not make this argument; Charles Darwin did. Ekman's research was directed toward determining the universality of certain facial expressions, not the "value" of people's ability to recognize those expressions.

Geology and Landscape

1. **❹** This is a Factual Information question asking for specific information that can be found in paragraph 1. The correct answer is choice 4. Sentence 1 of the paragraph explicitly states that Earth's landscape changes relatively rapidly compared to Earth's overall age. Choice 1, on the frequency of landscape changes, is contradicted by the paragraph. Choice 2, that landscape changes occur only at special times, is also contradicted by the paragraph. Choice 3, the frequency of landscape changes, is not mentioned.

2. **❷** This is a Vocabulary question. The word being tested is *relatively*, and it is highlighted in the passage. The correct answer is choice 2. The sentence in which *relatively* appears is comparing Earth's time scale to the human time scale, so "comparatively" is the correct answer.

3. **❷** This is an Inference question asking for an inference that can be supported by paragraph 2. The correct answer is choice 2, the Himalayas are higher than the Caledonian mountains. The paragraph states that younger mountains are generally higher than older mountains. It also states that the Himalayas are much younger than the Caledonians. Since the Himalayas are the younger range and younger mountain ranges are higher than older ranges, we can infer that the younger Himalayas are higher than the older Caledonians.

   Choices 1 and 4 are incorrect because they explicitly contradict the passage. The height of the Himalayas is an indication of their age, and the Himalayas are about the same height that the Caledonians were 400 million years ago.

Choice 3 is incorrect because nothing there is nothing in the paragraph about "uniform height."

4. ❸ This is a Vocabulary question. The word being tested is *relics*, and it is highlighted in the passage. Choice 3 is the correct answer. The *relics* of the Caledonian range are what is left of them. "Remains" means what is left of something, so it is the correct answer.

5. ❸ This is a Factual Information question asking for specific information that can be found in paragraph 3. The correct answer is choice 3, mountains are formed by crustal plates hitting each other. The paragraph states that mountains are formed in three ways: by, crustal plates hitting each other, by earthquakes, and by volcanoes. Choices 1, 2, and 4 are not among these causes of mountain formation, so they are therefore incorrect.

6. ❶ This is a Rhetorical Purpose question. It asks why the author mentions "carbon dioxide" in the passage. This term is highlighted in the passage. The correct answer is choice 1; carbon dioxide is mentioned to explain the origin of a chemical that can erode rocks. The author is describing a particular cause of erosion, and the starting point of that process is carbon dioxide.

7. ❷ This is a Vocabulary question. The word being tested is *seeps*, and it is highlighted in the passage. Choice 2, "flows slowly," is the correct answer. The sentence is describing the way in which rain moves underground from Earth's surface. It cannot do this by "drying" (choice 1), "freezing" (choice 3), or "warming" (choice 4).

8. ❷ This is a Reference question. The word being tested is *them*, and it is highlighted in the passage. Choice 2, "masses of ice" is the correct answer. This is a simple pronoun-referent item. The word *them* refers to the glaciers that are carrying eroded rock. Notice that in this case, a whole series of words separates the pronoun from its referent.

9. ❷ This is a Sentence Simplification question. As with all of these items, a single sentence in the passage is highlighted:

Hills and mountains are often regarded as the epitome of permanence, successfully resisting the destructive forces of nature, but in fact they tend to be relatively short-lived in geological terms.

The correct answer is choice 2. That choice contains all of the essential information in the highlighted sentence. It omits the information in the second clause of the highlighted sentence ("successfully resisting the destructive forces of nature") because that information is not essential to the meaning.

Choices 1, 3, and 4 are all incorrect because they change the meaning of the highlighted sentence. Choice 1 adds information on the age of a mountain that is not mentioned in the highlighted sentence.

Choice 3 introduces information about how long mountains resist forces of nature in absolute terms; the highlighted sentence says that the resistance is relatively short in geological terms, which is an entirely different meaning.

Choice 4 compares mountains to other land forms. The highlighted sentence does not make any such comparison.

10. ❹ This is a Factual Information question asking for specific information that can be found in paragraph 6. The correct answer is choice 4, "sand." Sentences 3 and 4 of that paragraph describe erosion in dry areas. Sand is carried by wind and bombards rock; this bombardment breaks down the rock, and, as a result, more sand is created. Thus sand is both the cause and the result of erosion, so choice 4 is correct. Glacial activity (choice 1) and tree roots (choice 3) are both mentioned only as causes of erosion. Rock debris (choice 2) is mentioned only as a result of erosion.

11. ❶ This is an Insert Text question. You can see the four black squares in paragraph 6 that represent the possible answer choices here.

Under very cold conditions, rocks can be shattered by ice and frost. Glaciers may form in permanently cold areas, and these slowly moving masses of ice cut out valleys, carrying with them huge quantities of eroded rock debris. ■ In dry areas the wind is the principal agent of erosion. ■ It carries fine particles of sand, which bombard exposed rock surfaces, thereby wearing them into yet more sand. ■ Even living things contribute to the formation of landscapes.■ Tree roots force their way into cracks in rocks and, in so doing, speed their splitting. In contrast, the roots of grasses and other small plants may help to hold loose soil fragments together, thereby helping to prevent erosion by the wind.

The sentence provided, "Under different climatic conditions, another type of destructive force contributes to erosion," is best inserted at square 1.
Square 1 is correct because the inserted sentence is a transitional sentence, moving the discussion away from one set of climatic conditions (cold) to another set of climatic conditions (dryness). It is at square 1 that the transition between topics takes place.

Squares 2, 3, and 4 all precede sentences that provide details of dry climatic conditions. No transition is taking place at any of those places, so the inserted sentence is not needed.

12. This is a Fill in a Table question. It is completed correctly below. The correct choices for the "constructive processes" column are 1, 5, and 6. Choices 3 and 7 are the correct choices for the "destructive processes" column. Choices 2 and 4 should not be used in either column.

Directions: Three of the answer choices below are used in the passage to illustrate constructive processes and two are used to illustrate destructive processes. Complete the table by matching appropriate answer choices to the processes they are used to illustrate. ***This question is worth 3 points.***

CONSTRUCTIVE PROCESSES	DESTRUCTIVE PROCESSES
➤ Collision of Earth's crustal plates	➤ Wind-driven sand
➤ Earthquakes	➤ Weather processes
➤ Volcanic activity	

Answer Choices

1. Collision of Earth's crustal plates

2. Separation of continents

3. Wind-driven sand

4. Formation of grass roots in soil

5. Earthquakes

6. Volcanic activity

7. Weather processes

Correct Choices

Choice 1: "Collision of Earth's crustal plates (constructive process)" belongs in this column because it is mentioned in the passage as one of the constructive processes by which mountains are formed.

Choice 3: "Wind-driven sand (destructive process)" belongs in this column because it is mentioned in the passage as one of the destructive forces that wear away the land.

Choice 5: "Earthquakes (constructive process)" belongs in this column because it is mentioned in the passage as one of the constructive forces by which mountains are formed.

Choice 6: "Volcanic activity (constructive process)" belongs in this column because it is mentioned in the passage as one of the constructive forces by which mountains are formed.

Choice 7: "Weather processes (destructive process)" belongs in this column because it is mentioned in the passage as one of the destructive forces that wear away the land.

Incorrect Choices

Choice 2: "Separation of continents" does not belong in the table because it not mentioned in the passage as either a constructive or destructive process.

Choice 4: "Formation of grass roots in soil" does not belong in the table because it not mentioned in the passage as either a constructive or destructive process.

CHAPTER 3

TOEFL iBT Listening

I n the TOEFL iBT Listening section you will listen to four to six lectures and two to three conversations. There will be six questions per lecture and five questions per conversation. You will have a total of 60 to 90 minutes to answer all of the Listening questions.

> **READ THIS CHAPTER TO FIND OUT**
>
> ➤ **the 9 types of TOEFL iBT Listening questions**
>
> ➤ **how to recognize each Listening question type**
>
> ➤ **tips for answering each Listening question type**
>
> ➤ **strategies for raising your TOEFL Listening score**

TOEFL iBT Listening Materials

There are two types of Listening materials on the TOEFL iBT, conversations and lectures. Both are based on the actual speech that is used in North American colleges and universities.

Each lecture or conversation is four to six minutes long and, as far as possible, represents authentic academic language. For example, a professor giving a lecture may digress somewhat from the main topic, interactions between students and the professor can be extensive, and explanations of content can be elaborate. Features of oral language such as false starts, misspeaks with self-corrections, and repetitions are included. The speakers who record the texts are encouraged to use their own speech patterns (e.g., pauses, hesitations), as long as they preserve the content of the text. You should take notes during the lectures and conversations. This material is not meant to challenge your memory.

CONVERSATIONS

There are two types of conversations in TOEFL:

➤ office hours
➤ service encounters

These conversations are typical of those that occur on North American university campuses. Office hours are interactions that take place in a professor's office. The content may be academic or related to course requirements. For example, in an office conversation a student could request an extension on a due date (non-academic content), or a student could ask for clarification about the content of a lecture (academic content). Service encounters are interactions that take place on a university campus and have non-academic content. Examples include inquiring about a payment for housing or registering for class. Each conversation is followed by five questions.

LECTURES

Lectures in TOEFL iBT represent the kind of language used when teachers teach in a classroom. The lecture excerpt may be just a teacher speaking, a student asking the teacher a question, or the teacher asking the students a question and calling on one student for a response. Each lecture is approximately 5 minutes in length and is followed by six questions.

The content of the lectures reflects the content that is presented in introductory-level academic settings. Lecture topics cover a broad range of subjects. You will not be expected to have any prior knowledge of the subject matter. All the information you need to answer the questions will be contained in the Listening passage. The lists below are provided to give you an idea of the topics that typically appear in the Listening section. In general these topics are divided into four major categories:

➤ Arts
➤ Life Science
➤ Physical Science
➤ Social Science

Arts lectures may be on topics such as:

➤ Architecture
➤ Industrial design/art
➤ City planning
➤ Crafts: weaving, knitting, fabrics, furniture, carving, mosaics, ceramics, etc; folk and tribal art
➤ Cave/rock art
➤ Music and music history
➤ Photography
➤ Literature and authors
➤ Books, newspapers, magazines, journals

Life Science lectures may be on topics such as:

➤ Extinction of or conservation efforts for animals and plants
➤ Fish and other aquatic organisms
➤ Bacteria and other one-celled organisms
➤ Viruses
➤ Medical techniques
➤ Public health
➤ Physiology of sensory organs

- Biochemistry
- Animal behavior, e.g., migration, food foraging, defensive behavior
- Habitats and the adaptation of animals and plants to them
- Nutrition and its impact on the body
- Animal communication

Physical Science lectures may be on topics such as:

- Weather and atmosphere
- Oceanography
- Glaciers, glacial landforms, ice ages
- Deserts and other extreme environments
- Pollution, alternative energy, environmental policy
- Other planets' atmospheres
- Astronomy and cosmology
- Properties of light, optics
- Properties of sound
- Electromagnetic radiation
- Particle physics
- Technology of TV, radio, radar
- Math
- Chemistry of inorganic things
- Computer science
- Seismology (plate structure, earthquakes, tectonics, continental drift, structure of volcanoes)

Social Science lectures may be on topics such as:

- Anthropology of non-industrialized civilizations
- Early writing systems
- Historical linguistics
- Business, management
- TV/radio as mass communication
- Social behavior of groups, community dynamics, communal behavior
- Child development
- Education
- Modern history (including the history of urbanization and industrialization and their economic and social effects)

TOEFL iBT Listening Questions

Most of the TOEFL iBT Listening questions that follow the lectures and conversations are traditional multiple-choice questions with four answer choices and a single correct answer. There are, however, some other types of questions:

- Multiple-choice questions with more than one answer (for example, two answers out of four or more choices)
- Questions that require you to put in order events or steps in a process
- Questions that require you to match objects or text to categories in a table

At least one of the questions following most lectures and conversations will be a replay question. In replay questions you will hear a portion of the lecture or conversation again. You will then be asked a multiple-choice question about what you have just heard.

There are nine types of questions in the Listening section. These types are divided into three categories as follows:

TOEFL LISTENING QUESTION TYPES

Basic Comprehension Questions

1. Gist-Content
2. Gist-Purpose
3. Detail

Pragmatic Understanding Questions

4. Understanding the Function of What Is Said
5. Understanding the Speaker's Attitude

Connecting Information Questions

6. Understanding Organization
7. Connecting Content
8. Making Inferences

The following sections will explain each of these question types one by one. You'll find out how to recognize each type, and you'll see examples of each type with explanations. You'll also find tips that can help you answer each TOEFL Listening question type.

BASIC COMPREHENSION QUESTIONS

Basic comprehension of the listening passage is tested in three ways: with Gist-Content, Gist-Purpose, and Detail questions.

Type 1: Gist-Content Questions

Understanding the *gist* of a lecture or conversation means understanding the general topic or main idea. The gist of the lecture or conversation may be expressed explicitly or implicitly. Questions that test understanding the gist may require you to generalize or synthesize information in what you hear.

How to Recognize Gist-Content Questions

Gist-Content questions are typically phrased as follows:

➤ What problem does the man have?
➤ What are the speakers mainly discussing?
➤ What is the main topic of the lecture?
➤ What is the lecture mainly about?
➤ What aspect of X does the professor mainly discuss?

Tips for Gist-Content Questions

➤ Gist-Content questions ask about the *overall* content of the listening. Eliminate choices that refer to only small portions of the listening passage.

➤ Use your notes. Decide what overall theme ties the details in your notes together. Choose the answer that comes closest to describing this overall theme.

Example

Excerpt from a longer listening passage:

Professor

. . . So the Earth's surface is made up of these huge segments, these tectonic plates. And these plates move, right? But how can, uh, motion of plates, do you think, influence climate on the Earth? Again, all of you probably read this section in the book, I hope, but, uh, uh, how—how can just motion of the plates impact the climate?

. . . when a plate moves, if there's landmass on the plate, then the landmass moves too, okay? That's why continents shift their positions, because the plates they're on move. So as a landmass moves away from the equator, its climate would get colder. So, right now we have a continent—the landmass Antarctica—that's on a pole.

So that's dramatically influencing the climate in Antarctica. Um, there was a time when most of the landmasses were closer to a pole; they weren't so close to the Equator. Uh, maybe 200 million years ago Antarctica was attached to the South American continent, oh and Africa was attached too and the three of them began moving away from the equator together.

. . . in the Himalayas. That was where two continental plates collided. Two continents on separate plates. Um, when this, uh, Indian, uh, uh, plate collided with the Asian plate, it wasn't until then that we created the Himalayas. When we did that, then we started creating the type of cold climate that we see there now. Wasn't there until this area was uplifted.

So again, that's something else that plate tectonics plays a critical role in. Now these processes are relatively slow; the, uh, Himalayas are still rising, but on the order of millimeters per year. So they're not dramatically influencing climate on your—the time scale of your lifetime. But over the last few thousands of—tens of thousands of years, uh—hundreds of thousands of years—yes, they've dramatically influenced it.

Uh, another important thing—number three—on how plate tectonics have influenced climate is how they've influenced—we talked about how changing landmasses can affect atmospheric circulation patterns, but if you alter where the landmasses are connected, it can impact oceanic, uh, uh, uh, circulation patterns.

. . . Um, so, uh, these other processes, if—if we were to disconnect North and South America right through the middle, say, through Panama that would dramatically influence climate in North and South America—probably the whole globe. So suddenly now as the two continents gradually move apart, you can have different circulation patterns in the ocean between the two. So, uh, that might cause a dramatic change in climate if that were to happen, just as we've had happen here in Antarctica to separate, uh, from South America.

What is the main topic of the talk?

⬭ The differences in climate that occur in different countries
⬭ How movement of the earth's plates can affect climate

○ Why the ocean has less affect on climate than previously thought
○ The history of the climate of the region where the college is located

Explanation

Choice 2 is the answer that best represents the main topic of the passage. The professor uses Antarctica and the Himalayas as examples to make his general point that climate is affected by plate tectonics, the movement of Earth's plates.

Note that for Gist-Content questions the correct answer and the incorrect choices can sometimes be worded more abstractly.

Example

The following Gist-Content question refers to the same lecture:

What is the main topic of the talk?

○ A climate experiment and its results
○ A geologic process and its effect
○ How a theory was disproved
○ How land movement is measured

Explanation

Once again, the correct answer is choice 2. Even though the wording is very different, it basically says the same thing as choice 2 in the previous example: A geologic process (movement of the earth's plates) has an effect (changes in climate).

Type 2: Gist-Purpose Questions

Some gist questions focus on the purpose of the conversation rather than on the content. This type of question will more likely occur with conversations, but Gist-Purpose questions may also occasionally be found with lectures.

How to Recognize Gist-Purpose Questions

Gist-Purpose questions are typically phrased as follows:

➤ Why does the student visit the professor?
➤ Why does the student visit the registrar's office?
➤ Why did the professor ask to see the student?
➤ Why does the professor explain X?

Tips for Gist-Purpose Questions

➤ Listen for the unifying theme of the conversation. For example, during a professor's office hours, a student asks the professor for help with a paper on glaciers. Their conversation includes facts about glaciers, but the unifying theme of the conversation is that the student needs help writing his paper. In this conversation the speakers are not attempting to convey a main idea about glaciers.
➤ In Service Encounter conversations, the student is often trying to solve a problem. Understanding what the student's problem is and how it will be solved will help you answer the Gist-Purpose question.

Example

Narrator

Listen to a conversation between a professor and a student.

Student

I was hoping you could look over my notecards for my presentation . . . just to see what you think of it.

Professor

Okay, so refresh my memory: what's your presentation about?

Student

Two models of decision making . . .

Professor

Oh, yes—the classical and the administrative model.

Student

Yeah, that's it.

Professor

And what's the point of your talk?

Student

I'm gonna talk about the advantages and disadvantages of both models.

Professor

But what's the point of your talk? Are you going to say that one's better than the other?

Student

Well I think the administrative model's definitely more realistic. But I don't think it's complete. It's kind of a tool . . . a tool to see what can go wrong.

Professor

Okay, so what's the point of your talk? What are you trying to convince me to believe?

Student

Well, uh, the classical model—you shouldn't use it by itself. A lot of companies just try to follow the classical model, but they should really use both models together.

Professor

Okay, good. So let me take a look at your notes here . . . . Oh typed notes . . . . Wow you've got a lot packed in here. Are you sure you're going to be able to follow this during your talk?

Student

Oh, sure that's why I typed them, because otherwise . . . well my handwriting's not very clear.

Why does the student visit the professor?

○ To get some notecards for his presentation
○ To show her some examples of common errors in research
○ To review the notes for his presentation with her
○ To ask for help in finding a topic for his presentation

Explanation

While much of the conversation is concerned with the content of the man's presentation, the best answer to the question "Why does the man visit the professor?" is choice 3: To review the notes for his presentation with her.

Type 3: Detail Questions

Detail questions require you to understand and remember explicit details or facts from a lecture or conversation. These details are typically related, directly or indirectly, to the gist of the text, by providing elaboration, examples, or other support. In some cases where there is a long digression that is not clearly related to the main idea, you may be asked about some details of the digression.

How to Recognize Detail Questions

Detail questions are typically phrased as follows:

➤ According to the professor, what is one way that X can affect Y?
➤ What are X?
➤ What resulted from the invention of the X?
➤ According to the professor, what is the main problem with the X theory?

Tips for Detail Questions

➤ Refer to your notes as you answer. Remember, you will not be asked about minor points. Your notes should contain the major details from the conversation or lecture.
➤ Do not choose an answer only because it contains some of the words that were used in the conversation or lecture. Incorrect responses will often contain words and phrases from the listening.
➤ If you are unsure of the correct response, decide which one of the choices is most consistent with the main idea of the conversation or lecture.

Examples

Professor

Uh, other things that glaciers can do is, uh, as they retreat, instead of depositing some till, uh, scraped up soil, in the area, they might leave a big ice block and it breaks off and as the ice block melts it leaves a depression which can become a lake. These are called kettle lakes. These are very critical ecosystems in this region, um because uh uh they support some unique biological diversity, these kettle lakes do.

The Great Lakes are like this, they were left over from the Pleist—from the Pleistocene glaciers, uh, the Great Lakes used to be a lot bigger as the glaciers were retreating, some of the lakes were as much as a hundred feet higher in elevation. The beach of a former higher stage of Lake Erie was about fifty miles away from where the beach—the current beach of Lake Erie is right now. So I just wanted to tell you a little bit more about glaciers and some positive things uh that we get from climate change, like the ecosystems that develop in these kettle lakes, and how we can look at them in an environmental perspective . . .

What are kettle lakes?

- ⬭ Lakes that form in the center of a volcano
- ⬭ Lakes that have been damaged by the greenhouse effect
- ⬭ Lakes formed by unusually large amounts of precipitation
- ⬭ Lakes formed when pieces of glaciers melt

How did the glaciers affect the Great Lakes?

- ⬭ They made the Great lakes smaller.
- ⬭ They made the Great Lakes deeper.
- ⬭ They reduced the biodiversity of the Great Lakes.
- ⬭ They widened the beaches around the Great Lakes.

Explanation

The answer to the first question is found in the beginning of the lecture when the professor explains what a kettle lake is. Remember that new terminology is often tested in Detail questions. The answer to the second question is found later in the lecture where the professor says, ". . . the Great Lakes used to be a lot bigger as the glaciers were retreating . . . "

PRAGMATIC UNDERSTANDING QUESTIONS

Pragmatic Understanding questions test understanding of certain features of spoken English that go beyond basic comprehension. Generally speaking, these types of questions test how well you understand the function of an utterance or the stance that the speaker expresses. In most instances, Pragmatic Understanding questions will test parts of the conversation or lecture where a speaker's purpose or stance is not expressed directly. In these cases, what is directly stated—the surface expression—will not be an exact match of the speaker's function or purpose.

What people say is often intended to be understood on a level that lies beyond or beneath the surface expression. To use an often-cited example, the sentence "It sure is cold in here" can be understood literally as a statement of fact about the temperature of a room. But suppose the speaker is, say, a guest in your home, who is also shivering and glancing at an open window. In that case, what your guest may really mean is that he wants you to close the open window. In this example, the function of the speaker's statement—getting you to close the window—lies beneath the surface expression. Other functions that often lie beneath surface expression include directing, recommending, complaining, accepting, agreeing, narrating, questioning, and so on.

Understanding meaning within the context of an entire lecture or conversation is critical in instances where the speaker's stance is involved. Is a given statement intended to be taken as fact or opinion? How certain is the speaker of the information she is reporting? Is the speaker conveying certain feelings or attitudes about some person or thing or event? As above, these feelings or attitudes may lie beneath the surface expression. Thus they can easily go unrecognized or be misunderstood by non-native speakers.

Pragmatic Understanding questions typically involve a replay of a small portion of the listening passage in order to focus your attention on the relevant portion of the spoken text. Two question types test pragmatic understanding: Understanding the

Function of What Is Said questions and Understanding the Speaker's Attitude questions.

Type 4: Understanding the Function of What Is Said Questions

The first type of Pragmatic Understanding question tests whether you can understand the **function** of what is said. This question type often involves replaying a portion of the listening passage.

How to Recognize Understanding the Function of What Is Said Questions

Understanding the Function of What Is Said questions are typically phrased as follows:

➤ What does the professor imply when he says this: (replay)
➤ What can be inferred from the professor's response to the student? (replay)
➤ What is the purpose of the woman's response? (replay)
➤ Why does the student say this: (replay)

Tip for Understanding the Function of What Is Said Questions

➤ Remember that the function of what is said may not match what the speaker directly states. In the following example, a secretary asks a student if he knows where the housing office is. She is not, however, doing this to get information about the housing office's location.

Example

Excerpt from a conversation between a male student and a female housing office secretary. They are discussing his dorm fees.

Narrator
Listen again to a part of the conversation. Then answer the question.

Student
Okay. I'll just pay with a credit card. [pause] And where do I do that at?

Secretary
At, um, the housing office.

Student
Housing office, all right.

Secretary
Do you know where they are?

Narrator
What is the woman trying to find out from the man?

⭘ Where the housing office is
⭘ Approximately how far away the housing office is
⭘ Whether she needs to tell him where the housing office is
⭘ Whether he has been to the housing office already

Explanation
The pragmatic function of the woman's question is to ask the man whether or not he needs to be told the location of the housing office. The best answer for this question is choice 3.

Type 5: Understanding the Speaker's Attitude Questions
The second type of Pragmatic Understanding question tests whether you understand a speaker's attitude or opinion. You may be asked a question about the speaker's feelings, likes and dislikes, or reason for anxiety or amusement. Also included in this category are questions about a speaker's degree of certainty: Is the speaker referencing a source or giving a personal opinion? Are the facts presented generally accepted or are they disputed?

How to Recognize Understanding the Speaker's Attitude Questions
Understanding the Speaker's Attitude questions are typically phrased as follows:

➤ What can be inferred about the student?
➤ What is the professor's attitude toward X?
➤ What is the professor's opinion of X?
➤ What can be inferred about the student when she says this: (replay)
➤ What does the woman mean when she says this: (replay)

Tip for Understanding the Speaker's Attitude Questions
➤ Learn to pay attention to the speaker's tone of voice. Does the speaker sound apologetic? Confused? Enthusiastic? The speaker's tone can help you answer this kind of question.

Example
Excerpt from a conversation between a male student and his female advisor. In this part of a longer conversation, they are discussing the student's job.

Advisor
Well, good. So, bookstore isn't working out?

Student
Oh, bookstore's working out fine. I just I—this pays almost double what the bookstore does.

Advisor
Oh wow!

Student
Yeah. Plus credit.

Advisor
Plus credit.

Student
And it's more hours, which . . . . The bookstore's-I mean it's a decent job 'n all. Everybody I work with . . . that part's great; it's just . . . I mean I'm shelving books and kind of hanging out and not doing much else . . . if it weren't for the people, it'd be totally boring.

Narrator

What is the student's attitude toward the people he currently works with?

- ◯ He finds them boring.
- ◯ He likes them.
- ◯ He is annoyed by them.
- ◯ He does not have much in common with them.

Explanation

In this example it may be easy to confuse the student's attitude toward his job with his attitude toward the people he works with. The correct answer is choice 2. The student is bored with the job, not the people he works with.

CONNECTING INFORMATION QUESTIONS

Connecting Information questions require you to make connections between or among pieces of information in the text. Your ability to integrate information from different parts of the listening passage, to make inferences, to draw conclusions, to form generalizations, and to make predictions is tested. To choose the right answer, you will need to be able to identify and explain relationships among ideas and details in a text. These relationships may be explicit or implicit.

There are three types of Connecting Information questions.

Type 6: Understanding Organization Questions

In Understanding Organization questions you may be asked about the overall organization of the listening passage, or you may be asked about the relationship between two portions of the listening passage. Here are two examples:

(i) How does the professor organize the information that she presents to the class?
  - ◯ In the order in which the events occurred
(ii) How does the professor clarify the points he makes about Mexico?
  - ◯ By comparing Mexico to a neighboring country

The first of these questions asks about the overall organization of information, testing understanding of connections throughout the whole listening passage. The second asks about a portion of the passage, testing understanding of the relationship between two different ideas.

Some Understanding Organization questions may ask you to identify or recognize how one statement functions with respect to surrounding text. Functions may include indicating or signaling a topic shift, connecting a main topic to a subtopic, providing an introduction or a conclusion, giving an example, starting a digression, or even making a joke.

Example

Narrator

Listen again to a statement made by the professor. Then answer the question.

Professor

"There's this committee I'm on . . . Th-the name of the thing and it's probably, well, you don't have to take notes about this, um, the name of the thing is academic standards."

Narrator

Why does the professor tell the students that they do not have to take notes?

- The information is in their books.
- The information may not be accurate.
- She is going to tell a personal story.
- They already know what she is going to talk about.

The listening text preceding the replayed statement is about how bureaucracies work. What follows the replayed statement is a personal story about bureaucracies. The key lies in recognizing that the portion of the lecture following the replayed statement is a personal story. The correct answer is choice 3. With the replayed statement the professor indicates to the class that what she is about to say does not have the same status as what she was talking about previously.

How to Recognize Understanding Organization Questions

Understanding Organization questions are typically phrased as follows:

➤ How does the professor organize the information about X that he presents to the class?

➤ How is the discussion organized?

➤ Why does the professor discuss X?

➤ Why does the professor mention X?

Tips for Understanding Organization Questions

➤ Questions that ask about the overall organization of the passage are more likely to be found after lectures than after conversations. Refer to your notes to answer these questions. It may not have been apparent from the start that the professor organized the information (for example) chronologically, or from least to most complex, or in some other way.

➤ Pay attention to comparisons made by the professor. In the following example the professor is discussing the structure of plants. He uses steel and the steel girders in a new building to make a point. When the professor mentions something that is seemingly off-topic, you should ask yourself what point the professor is making.

Examples

Professor

So, we have reproductive parts—the seeds, the fruit-walls—we have leaf parts, but the great majority of plant fibers come from vasculature within the stem . . . fibers that occur in stem material. And what we do is consider these fibers [false start]—basically they're what are called <u>bast</u> fibers. Bast fibers. Now basically bast fibers are parts of the plant that the plant uses to maintain vertical structure.

Think about it this way: what's the first thing you see when you see a building being built . . . uh what's the first thing they put up? besides the foundation of course? The metal-work, right? They put all those steel girders up there, the framework. OK, well, think of [false start]—bast fibers basically constitute the structural framework to support the stem of the plant. OK? So as the plant grows, it basically builds a girder system within that plant, like steel, so to speak.

So suppose you cut across the stem of one of these plants, take a look at how the bast fibers are arranged, so you're looking at a cross-section . . . you'll see that the fibers run vertically side-by-side. Up and down next to each other, forming a kind of <u>tube</u>, which is significant . . . 'cause, which is physically stronger—a solid rod or a tube? The tube—physics tells you that. What's essentially happening—well, the plant is forming a structural ring of these bast fibers all around the stem, and that shape allows for structural rigidity, but also allows for bending and motion.

Why does the professor talk about steel?

- ⬭ To identify the substance that has replaced fiber products.
- ⬭ To explain a method for separating fibers from a plant.
- ⬭ To compare the chemical structure of fibers to metals.
- ⬭ To illustrate the function of fibers in a plant's stem.

Why does the professor mention a tube?

- ⬭ To explain how some fibers are arranged in a plant.
- ⬭ To show how plants carry water to growing fibers.
- ⬭ To describe an experiment involving plant fibers.
- ⬭ To explain why some plant stems cannot bend.

Explanation

The lecture is about plants and plant fibers, not steel girders. The professor mentions steel girders only to compare them to the structural framework of fibers in a plant. The best answer to the first question is choice 4. Likewise, the second question also concerns the professor's attempts to help the students visualize a plant's structure. The best answer to the second question is choice 1.

Type 7: Connecting Content Questions

Connecting Content questions measure your understanding of the relationships among ideas in a text. These relationships may be explicitly stated, or you may have to infer them from the words you hear.

The questions may ask you to organize information in a different way from the way it was presented in the listening passage. You might be asked to identify comparisons, cause and effect, or contradiction and agreement. You may also be asked to classify items in categories, identify a sequence of events or steps in a process, or specify relationships among objects along some dimension.

Example

Narrator

What type of symmetry do these animals have? Place a checkmark in the correct box.

	Asymmetry	Radial Symmetry	Bilateral Symmetry
Earthworm			✔
Human			✔
Sponge	✔		
Sea Anemone	✔	✔	

In this question you are asked to present information in a different format from that in which it was presented in a lecture.

Other Connecting Content questions will require you to make inferences about the relationships among things mentioned in the listening passage. You may have to predict an outcome, draw a logical conclusion, extrapolate some additional information, infer a cause-and-effect relationship, or specify some particular sequence of events.

How to Recognize Connecting Content Questions
Connecting Content questions are typically phrased as follows:

➤ What is the likely outcome of doing procedure X before procedure Y?
➤ What can be inferred about X?
➤ What does the professor imply about X?

Tip for Connecting Content Questions

➤ Questions that require you to fill in a chart or table or put events in order fall into this category. As you listen to the lectures on the CD accompanying this study guide, pay attention to the way you format your notes. Clearly identifying terms and their definitions as well as steps in a process will help you answer questions of this type.

Example

Professor
OK, Neptune and its moons. Neptune has several moons, but there's only . . . we'll probably only worry about two of them, the two fairly interesting ones. The first one's Triton. So you have this little struggle with the word Titan which is the big moon of Saturn and the name <u>Triton</u> which is the big moon of <u>Neptune</u>. Triton it's it's the only <u>large moon</u> in the solar system to go backwards, to go around its what we call its <u>parent planet</u>, in this case Neptune, the wrong way. OK? Every other large moon orbits the parent planet in the same counterclockwise direction . . . same as most of the other bodies in the solar system. But this moon. . . the reverse direction, which is perfectly OK as far as the laws of gravity are concerned. But it indicates some sort of peculiar event in the early solar system that gave this moon a motion in contrast to the general spin of the raw material that it was formed from.

The other moon orbiting Neptune that I want to talk about is Nereid [NEER ee ihd]. Nereid is, Nereid has the most eccentric orbit, the most lopsided elliptical type orbit for a large moon in the solar system. The others tend more like circular orbits.

. . . Does it mean that the planets Pluto and Neptune might have been related somehow in the past and then drifted slowly into their present orbits. If Pluto . . . did Pluto ever belong to the Neptune system? Do Neptune's moons represent Pluto type bodies that have been captured by Neptune? Was some sort of . . . was Pluto the object that disrupted the Neptune system at some point in the past?

It's really hard to prove any of those things. But now we're starting to appreciate that there's quite a few junior Plutos out there. Not big enough to really call a planet, but large enough that they're significant in history of the early solar system. So we'll come back to those when we talk about comets and other small bodies in the fringes of the outer solar system.

What does the professor imply about the orbits of Triton and Nereid?

- ◯ They used to be closer together.
- ◯ They might provide evidence of an undiscovered planet.
- ◯ They might reverse directions in the future.
- ◯ They might have been changed by some unusual event.

Explanation

In Connecting Content questions you will have to use information from more than one place in the listening passage. In this example, the professor describes the orbits of Triton and Nereid. In both cases he refers to events in the early solar system that might have changed or disrupted their orbits. The best answer for this question is choice 4, "They might have been changed by some unusual event."

Type 8: Making Inferences Questions

The final type of connecting information question is Making Inferences questions. In this kind of question you usually have to reach a conclusion based on facts presented in the listening passage.

How to Recognize Making Inferences Questions

Making Inferences questions are typically phrased as follows:

- ➤ What does the professor imply about X?
- ➤ What will the student probably do next?
- ➤ What can be inferred about X?
- ➤ What does the professor imply when he says this: (replay)

Tip for Making Inferences Questions

- ➤ In some cases, answering this kind of question correctly means adding up details from the passage to reach a conclusion. In other cases, the professor may imply something without directly stating it. In most cases the answer you choose will use vocabulary not found in the listening passage.

Example

Professor

Dada is often considered under the broader category of Fantasy. It's one of the early directions in the Fantasy style. The term "Dada" itself is a nonsense word—it has no meaning . . . and where the word originated isn't known. The "philosophy" behind the "Dada" movement was to create works that conveyed the concept of <u>absurdity</u>—the artwork was meant to shock the public by presenting the ridiculous absurd concepts. Dada artists rejected reason—or rational thought. They did not believe that rational thought would help solve social problems . . .

. . . When he turned to Dada, he quit painting and devoted himself to making a type of sculpture he referred to as a "ready-made" . . . probably because they were constructed of readily available objects . . . . At the time, many people reacted to Dadaism by saying that the works were not art at all . . . and in fact, that's exactly how Duchamp and others conceived of it—as a form of "NON-art" . . . or ANTI-art.

Duchamp also took a reproduction of DaVinci's famous painting, the Mona Lisa, and he drew a mustache and goatee on the subject's face. Treating this masterpiece with such disrespect was another way. Duchamp was challenging the established cultural standards of his day.

What does the professor imply about the philosophy of the Dada movement?

⬭ It was not taken seriously by most artists.
⬭ It varied from one country to another.
⬭ It challenged people's concept of what art is.
⬭ It was based on a realistic style of art.

Explanation

Note the highlighted portions of the listening passage. You can see that Dadaism was meant to challenge the public's conception of what art was meant to be. The best answer to the question is choice 3.

BASIC STRATEGIES FOR THE TOEFL iBT LISTENING SECTION

➤ Take notes while you listen. Only the major points will be tested, so do not try to write down every detail. After testing, notes are collected and shredded before you leave the test center.
➤ When listening to a lecture, pay attention to the new words or concepts introduced by the professor. These will often be tested.
➤ When listening to a lecture, pay attention to the way the lecture is structured and the way the ideas in the lecture are connected.
➤ Listening questions must be answered in order. Once you mark an answer, you cannot go back and change it.
➤ Choose the best answer. The computer will ask you to confirm your choice. After clicking *yes*, you automatically go on to the next question.

How to Sharpen Your Listening Skills

Listening is one of the most important skills necessary for success on TOEFL iBT and in academics in general. The ability to listen and understand is tested in three out of four sections of TOEFL iBT.

The best way to improve your listening skills is to listen frequently to many different types of material in various subject areas (sciences, social sciences, arts, business, etc.). Of course, watching movies and TV and listening to radio is an excellent way to practice listening. Audio tapes and CDs of talks are available in libraries and bookstores; those with transcripts of the listening material are particularly helpful. The Internet is also a great resource for listening material.

Here are some ways you can strengthen skills for the three listening purposes tested on the TOEFL iBT.

Listening for Basic Comprehension

➤ Increase your vocabulary knowledge, perhaps by using flashcards.
➤ Focus on the content and flow of material. Do not be distracted by the speaker's style and delivery.
➤ Anticipate what the speaker is going to say as a way to stay focused.
➤ Stay active by asking yourself questions (e.g., What main idea is the professor communicating?).

➤ Copy the words "main idea," "major points," and "important details" on different lines of paper. Listen carefully and write these things down while listening. Listen again until all important points and details are written down.

➤ Listen to a portion of a lecture or talk and write a brief summary of important points. Gradually increase the amount you listen to and summarize. Note: Summarizing skills are not tested in the Listening section, but they are useful for the integrated tasks in the Writing and Speaking sections.

Listening for Pragmatic Understanding

➤ Think about what each speaker hopes to accomplish; that is, what is the purpose of the speech or conversation? Is the speaker apologizing, complaining, making suggestions?

➤ Notice the way each speaker talks. Is the level of language formal or casual? How certain does each speaker sound? Is the speaker's voice calm or emotional? What does the speaker's tone of voice tell you?

➤ Notice the degree of certainty of the speaker. How sure is the speaker about the information? Does the speaker's tone of voice indicate something about his or her degree of certainty?

➤ Listen for changes in topic or side comments in which the speaker briefly moves away from the main topic and then returns (digressions).

➤ Watch television or movie comedies and pay attention to stress and intonation patterns used to convey meaning.

Listening to Connect Ideas

➤ Think about how the lecture is organized. Listen for the signal words that indicate the introduction, major steps or ideas, examples, and the conclusion or summary.

➤ Identify the relationships between ideas in the information being discussed. Possible relationships include: cause-and-effect, compare-and-contrast, steps in a process.

➤ Listen for words that show connections and relationships between ideas.

➤ When you listen to recorded material, stop the recording at various points and try to predict what information or idea will be expressed next.

➤ Create an outline of the information discussed while listening or after listening.

LISTENING PRACTICE SETS

PRACTICE SET 1

Now listen to Track 1 on the CD.

Questions

Directions: Mark your answer by filling in the oval next to your choice.

1. Why does the man go to see his professor?

◯ To borrow some charts and graphs from her
◯ To ask her to explain some statistical procedures
◯ To talk about a report he is writing
◯ To discuss a grade he got on a paper

2. *Listen again to part of the conversation by playing track 2.*
   Then answer the question.

◯ To question the length of the paper
◯ To offer encouragement
◯ To dispute the data sources
◯ To explain a theory

3. What information will the man include in his report?

For each phrase below, place a checkmark in the "Include" column or the "Not include" column.

	Include in Report	Not Include in Report
Climate charts		
Interviews with meteorologists		
Journal notes		
Statistical tests		

4. Why does the professor tell the man about the appointment at the doctor's office?

- ⬭ To demonstrate a way of remembering things
- ⬭ To explain why she needs to leave soon
- ⬭ To illustrate a point that appears in his report
- ⬭ To emphasize the importance of good health

5. What does the professor offer to do for the man?

- ⬭ Help him collect more data in other areas of the state
- ⬭ Submit his research findings for publication
- ⬭ Give him the doctor's telephone number
- ⬭ Review the first version of his report

Listening Script

Narrator
Listen to a conversation between a student and a professor.

Student
Uh, excuse me, Professor Thompson. I know your office hours are tomorrow, but I was wondering if you had a few minutes free now to discuss something.

Professor
Sure, John. What did you want to talk about?

Student
Well, I have some quick questions about how to write up the research project I did this semester— about climate variations.

Professor
Oh, yes. You were looking at variations in climate in the Grant City area, right? How far along have you gotten?

Student
I've got all my data, so I'm starting to summarize it now, preparing graphs and stuff. But I'm just . . . I'm looking at it and I'm afraid that it's not enough, but I'm not sure what else to put in the report.

Professor

I hear the same thing from every student. You know, you have to remember now that you're the expert on what you've done. So, think about what you'd need to include if you were going to explain your research project to someone with general or casual knowledge about the subject, like . . . like your parents. That's usually my rule of thumb: would my parents understand this?

Student

OK. I get it.

Professor

I hope you can recognize by my saying that how much you do know about the subject.

Student

Right. I understand. I was wondering if I should also include the notes from the research journal you suggested I keep?

Professor

Yes, definitely. You should use them to indicate what your evolution in thought was through time. So, just set up, you know, what was the purpose of what you were doing—to try to understand the climate variability of this area—and what you did, and what your approach was.

Student

OK. So, for example, I studied meteorological records; I looked at climate charts; I used different methods for analyzing the data, like certain statistical tests; and then I discuss the results. Is that what you mean?

Professor

Yes, that's right. You should include all of that. The statistical tests are especially important. And also be sure you include a good reference section where all your published and unpublished data came from, 'cause you have a lot of unpublished climate data.

Student

Hmm . . . something just came into my mind and went out the other side.

Professor

That happens to me a lot, so I've come up with a pretty good memory management tool. I carry a little pad with me all the time and jot down questions or ideas that I don't want to forget. For example, I went to the doctor with my daughter and her baby son last week and we knew we wouldn't remember everything we wanted to ask the doctor, so we actually made a list of five things we wanted answers to.

Student

A notepad is a good idea. Since I'm so busy now at the end of the semester, I'm getting pretty forgetful these days. OK. I just remembered what I was trying to say before.

Professor

Good. I was hoping you'd come up with it.

Student

Yes. It ends up that I have data on more than just the immediate Grant City area, so I also included some regional data in the report. With everything else it should be a pretty good indicator of the climate in this part of the state.

Professor

Sounds good. I'd be happy to look over a draft version before you hand in the final copy, if you wish.

Student

Great. I'll plan to get you a draft of the paper by next Friday. Thanks very much. Well, see ya.

Professor

OK.

Answers and Explanations

1. ❸ You should recognize that this is a Gist-Purpose question. The man says, "I have some quick questions about how to write up the research project I did this semester." He is going to write a report about his project and is unsure of what to include. Choice 3 is the correct answer.

2. ❷ You should recognize that this is an Understanding the Function of What Is Said question. The question asks you to re-listen to this part of the conversation:

Professor

You know, you have to remember now that you're the expert on what you've done. So, think about what you'd need to include if you were going to explain your research project to someone with general or casual knowledge about the subject, like . . . like your parents. That's usually my rule of thumb: would my parents understand this?

Student

OK. I get it.

Professor

I hope you can recognize by my saying that how much you do know about the subject.

Then you are asked specifically about this sentence:

Why does the professor say this:

Professor

I hope you can recognize by my saying that how much you do know about the subject.

The student is unsure of how to present the information in his report. The professor is trying to give the student confidence in his own judgment. Therefore, the correct answer is choice B, "To offer encouragement."

3. This question is easy to recognize as a Connecting Content question. The student and the professor discuss several sources of information that the student used to investigate climate variation. They do not discuss interviewing meteorologists, even though they mention other kinds of conversations, like the professor's discussion with her child's doctor. The chart correctly filled out looks like this:

For each phrase below, click in the "Include" column or the "Not Include" column.

	Include in Report	Not Include in Report
Climate charts	X	
Interviews with meteorologists		X
Journal notes	X	
Statistical tests	X	

4. ❶ This is an Understanding the Function of What Is Said question. The correct answer is choice 1. The professor's purpose in mentioning the doctor's office is to show the man how writing down questions as they occur can be useful. The man has forgotten a question he wanted to ask the professor. The professor, when she spoke to the doctor, wrote down her questions beforehand, so she would not forget. She mentions the doctor's office in order to demonstrate a strategy for remembering.

5. ❹ This is a Detail question. The discussion ends with the professor offering to "look over a draft version" of the man's paper.

PRACTICE SET 2

Now listen to Track 3 on the CD. Play Audio

Questions

Directions: Mark your answer by filling in the oval next to your choice.

1. What is the main purpose of the lecture?

   ⬭ To illustrate the importance of extrinsic values
   ⬭ To explain Aristotle's views about the importance of teaching
   ⬭ To explain why people change what they value
   ⬭ To discuss Aristotle's views about human happiness

2. The professor gives examples of things that have value for her. Indicate for each example what type of value it has for her.

   Place a checkmark in the correct box. This question is worth 2 points.

	Only Extrinsic Value	Only Intrinsic Value	Both Extrinsic and Intrinsic Value
Teaching			
Exercise			
Health			
Playing a musical instrument			

3. Why is happiness central to Aristotle's theory?

○ Because it is so difficult for people to attain
○ Because it is valued for its own sake by all people
○ Because it is a means to a productive life
○ Because most people agree about what happiness is

4. According to the professor, why does Aristotle think that fame cannot provide true happiness?

○ Fame cannot be obtained without help from other people.
○ Fame cannot be obtained by all people.
○ Fame does not last forever.
○ People cannot share their fame with other people.

5. *Listen again to part of the lecture by playing track 4. Then answer the question.* 🎧 **Play Audio**

○ Teaching is not a highly valued profession in society.
○ She may change professions in order to earn more money.
○ The reason she is a teacher has little to do with her salary.
○ More people would become teachers if the salary were higher.

Listening Script

Narrator

Listen to part of a lecture in a philosophy class.

Professor

OK. Another ancient Greek philosopher we need to discuss is Aristotle—Aristotle's ethical theory. What Aristotle's ethical theory is all about is this: he's trying to show you how to be happy—what true happiness is.

Now, why is he interested in human happiness? It's not just because it's something that all people want or aim for. It's more than that. But to get there we need to first make a very important distinction. Let me introduce a couple of technical terms: extrinsic value and intrinsic value.

To understand Aristotle's interest in happiness, you need to understand this distinction.

Some things we aim for and value, not for themselves but for what they bring about in addition to themselves. If I value something as a means to something else, then it has what we will call "extrinsic value." Other things we desire and hold to be valuable for themselves alone. If we value something not as a means to something else, but for its own sake, let us say that it has "intrinsic value."

Exercise. There may be some people who value exercise for itself, but I don't. I value exercise because if I exercise, I tend to stay healthier than I would if I didn't. So I desire to engage in exercise and I value exercise extrinsically . . . not for its own sake, but as a means to something beyond it. It brings me good health.

Health. Why do I value good health? Well, here it gets a little more complicated for me. Um, health is important for me because I can't . . . do other things I want to do—play music, teach philosophy—if I'm ill. So health is important to me—has value to me—as a means to a productive life. But health is also important to me because I just kind of like to be healthy—it feels good. It's pleasant to be healthy, unpleasant not to be. So to some degree I value health both for itself and as a means to something else: productivity. It's got extrinsic and intrinsic value for me.

Then there's some things that are just valued for themselves. I'm a musician, not a professional musician; I just play a musical instrument for fun. Why do I value playing music? Well, like most amateur musicians, I only play because, well, I just enjoy it. It's something that's an end in itself.

Now, something else I value is teaching. Why? Well, it brings in a modest income, but I could make more money doing other things. I'd do it even if they didn't pay me. I just enjoy teaching. In that sense it's an end to itself.

But teaching's not something that has intrinsic value for all people—and that's true generally. Most things that are enjoyed in and of themselves vary from person to person. Some people value teaching intrinsically, but others don't.

So how does all this relate to human happiness? Well, Aristotle asks: is there something that all human beings value . . . and value only intrinsically, for its own sake and only for its own sake? If you could find such a thing, that would be the universal final good, or truly the ultimate purpose or goal for all human beings. Aristotle thought the answer was yes. What is it? Happiness. Everyone will agree, he argues, that happiness is the ultimate end to be valued for itself and really only for itself. For what other purpose is there in being happy? What does it yield? The attainment of happiness becomes the ultimate or highest good for Aristotle.

The next question that Aristotle raises is: what is happiness? We all want it; we all desire it; we all seek it. It's the goal we have in life. But what is it? How do we find it? Here he notes, with some frustration, people disagree.

But he does give us a couple of criteria, or features, to keep in mind as we look for what true human happiness is. True human happiness should be, as he puts it, complete. Complete in that it's all we require. Well, true human happiness . . . if you had that, what else do you need? Nothing.

And, second, true happiness should be something that I can obtain on my own. I shouldn't have to rely on other people for it. Many people value fame and seek fame. Fame for them becomes the goal. But, according to Aristotle, this won't work either, because fame depends altogether too much on other people. I can't get it on my own, without help from other people.

In the end, Aristotle says that true happiness is the exercise of reason—a life of intellectual contemplation . . . of thinking. So let's see how he comes to that.

Answers and Explanations

1. ❹ You should recognize that this is a Gist-Purpose question. The professor discusses the difference between extrinsic and intrinsic value, but what is her purpose in doing this? "To understand Aristotle's interest in happiness, you need to understand this distinction (extrinsic and intrinsic)." The professor's purpose is choice 4: "To discuss Aristotle's views about human happiness."

2. This question is easy to recognize as a Connecting Content question. The professor gives examples of some activities and discusses whether they have intrinsic value, extrinsic value, or both. Her explanations of why she values exercise, health, and playing a musical instrument are fairly clear and explicit. For teaching, it is clear that for her it has intrinsic value, but she admits this may be different for others.

The question is about "what type of value it has for her." The chart correctly filled out looks like this:

	Only Extrinsic Value	Only Intrinsic Value	Both Extrinsic and Intrinsic Value
Teaching		X	
Exercise	X		
Health			X
Playing a musical instrument		X	

3. ❷ This is a Detail question. The question is answered by the professor when she says, "Everyone will agree, he [Aristotle] argues, that happiness is the ultimate end . . . to be valued for itself and really only for itself." The best answer for this question is choice 2. Note that this detail question is directly related to the main idea or gist of the passage.

4. ❶ This is another Detail question. It is not as closely related to the gist as the previous question. At the end of the passage the professor compares happiness and fame. She says, "according to Aristotle, this won't work either, because fame depends altogether too much on other people. I can't get it on my own . . . ." The correct answer is choice 1.

5. ❸ This is an Understanding the Function of What Is Said question. The professor discusses teaching to stress its <u>intrinsic</u> value for her. Therefore, the best answer is choice 3. The reason she is a teacher has little to do with money. Salary would be an <u>extrinsic</u> value, but she does not value teaching because of the salary.

PRACTICE SET 3

Now listen to Track 5 on the CD.

Questions

Directions: Mark your answer by filling in the oval next to your choice.

1. What is the professor mainly discussing?

⬭ The development of motor skills in children
⬭ How psychologists measure muscle activity in the throat
⬭ A theory about the relationship between muscle activity and thinking
⬭ A study on deaf people's problem-solving techniques

2. *Listen again to part of the lecture by playing track 6. Then answer the question.*

⬭ To give an example of a laryngeal habit
⬭ To explain the meaning of a term
⬭ To explain why he is discussing laryngeal habits
⬭ To remind students of a point he had discussed previously

THE OFFICIAL GUIDE TO THE NEW TOEFL iBT

3. What does the professor say about people who use sign language?

- ⬭ It is not possible to study their thinking habits.
- ⬭ They exhibit laryngeal habits.
- ⬭ The muscles in their hands move when they solve problems.
- ⬭ They do not exhibit ideomotor action.

4. What point does the professor make when he refers to the university library?

- ⬭ A study on problem solving took place there.
- ⬭ Students should go there to read more about behaviorism.
- ⬭ Students' eyes will turn toward it if they think about it.
- ⬭ He learned about William James's concept of thinking there.

5. The professor describes a magic trick to the class. What does the magic trick demonstrate?

- ⬭ An action people make that they are not aware of
- ⬭ That behaviorists are not really scientists
- ⬭ How psychologists study children
- ⬭ A method for remembering locations

6. What is the professor's opinion of the motor theory of thinking?

- ⬭ Most of the evidence he has collected contradicts it.
- ⬭ It explains adult behavior better than it explains child behavior.
- ⬭ It is the most valid theory of thinking at the present time.
- ⬭ It cannot be completely proved or disproved.

Listening Script

Narrator

Listen to part of a psychology lecture. The professor is discussing behaviorism.

Professor

Now, many people consider John Watson to be the founder of behaviorism. And like other behaviorists, he believed that psychologists should study only the behaviors they can observe and measure. They're not interested in mental processes. While a person could describe his thoughts, no one else can see or hear them to verify the accuracy of his report. But one thing you can observe is muscular habits. What Watson did was to observe muscular habits because he viewed them as a manifestation of thinking. One kind of habit that he studied are laryngeal habits.

Watson thought laryngeal habits . . . you know, from larynx, in other words, related to the voice box . . . he thought those habits were an expression of thinking. He argued that for very young children, thinking is really talking out loud to oneself because they talk out loud even if they're not trying to communicate with someone in particular. As the individual matures, that overt talking to oneself becomes covert talking to oneself, but thinking still shows up as a laryngeal habit. One of the bits of evidence that supports this is that when people are trying to solve a problem, they, um, typically have increased muscular activity in the throat region. That is, if you put electrodes on the throat and measure muscle potential—muscle activity—you discover that when people are thinking, like if they're diligently trying to solve a problem, that there is muscular activity in the throat region.

So, Watson made the argument that problem solving, or thinking, can be defined as a set of behaviors—a set of responses—and in this case the response he observed was the throat activity.

That's what he means when he calls it a laryngeal habit. Now, as I am thinking about what I am going to be saying, my muscles in my throat are responding. So, thinking can be measured as muscle activity. Now, the motor theory . . . yes?

Student
Professor Blake, um, did he happen to look at people who sign? I mean deaf people?

Professor
Uh, he did indeed, um, and to jump ahead, what one finds in deaf individuals who use sign language when they're given problems of various kinds, they have muscular changes in their hands when they are trying to solve a problem . . . muscle changes in the hand, just like the muscular changes going on in the throat region for speaking individuals.

So, for Watson, thinking is identical with the activity of muscles. A related concept of thinking was developed by William James. It's called ideomotor action.

Ideomotor action is an activity that occurs without our noticing it, without our being aware of it. I'll give you one simple example. If you think of locations, there tends to be eye movement that occurs with your thinking about that location. In particular, from where we're sitting, imagine that you're asked to think of our university library. Well, if you close your eyes and think of the library, and if you're sitting directly facing me, then according to this notion, your eyeballs will move slightly to the left, to your left, 'cause the library's in that general direction.

James and others said that this is an idea leading to a motor action, and that's why it's called "ideomotor action"—an idea leads to motor activity. If you wish to impress your friends and relatives, you can change this simple process into a magic trick. Ask people to do something such as I've just described: think of something on their left; think of something on their right. You get them to think about two things on either side with their eyes closed, and you watch their eyes very carefully. And if you do that, you'll discover that you can see rather clearly the eye movement—that is, you can see the movement of the eyeballs. Now, then you say, think of either one and I'll tell which you're thinking of.

OK. Well, Watson makes the assumption that muscular activity is equivalent to thinking. But given everything we've been talking about here, one has to ask: are there alternatives to this motor theory—this claim that muscular activities are equivalent to thinking? Is there anything else that might account for this change in muscular activity, other than saying that it is thinking? And the answer is clearly yes. Is there any way to answer the question definitively? I think the answer is no.

Answers and Explanations

1. ❸ This is a Gist-Content question. The professor discusses two types of muscular activities: laryngeal habits and ideomotor activity, and how they are related to thinking. The best answer is choice 3, a theory about the relationship between muscle activity and thinking. The other choices are mentioned by the professor, but are not the main topic of the discussion.

2. ❷ This is an Understanding the Function of What Is Said question. The professor introduces an unusual term, "laryngeal habits." He then says, " . . . you know, from larynx, in other words, related to the voice box . . . ". His brief explanation is meant to help the students understand the term "laryngeal habits." Choice 2 is the best answer to this question.

3. ❸ This is a Detail question. The professor responds to a student who asks a ques-

tion about people who use sign language. He says that they "have muscular changes in their hands . . . just like the muscular changes going on in the throat region for speaking individuals." The best answer is choice 3. This Detail question is related to the main idea of the passage as both are concerned with the relationship between muscular changes and thinking.

4. ❸ This is an Understanding Organization question. The professor talks about muscular activity in the eyes that will occur if the students think about the location of the library. The question asks for the conclusion of that example. The best answer is choice 3. Students' eyes will turn toward it if they think about it.

5. ❶ This is a Connecting Content question. Answering the question correctly requires you to understand that the magic trick the professor is describing is an "ideomotor activity" and that these types of activities occur "without our noticing it, without our being aware of it." The best answer to this question is choice 1.

6. ❹ Question like this one that ask for the professor's opinion are Understanding the Speaker's Attitude questions. The professor's opinion can be found at the end of the listening passage. He says that there may be alternative theories, but there is no way to answer the question definitively. The best answer to this question is choice 4. It cannot be completely proved or disproved.

PRACTICE SET 4

Now listen to Track 7 on the CD. Play Audio

Questions

Directions: Mark your answer by filling in the oval next to your choice.

1. What is Bode's Law?

○ A law of gravitation
○ An estimate of the distance between Mars and Jupiter
○ A prediction of how many asteroids there are
○ A pattern in the spacing of the planets

2. Why does the professor explain Bode's Law to the class?

○ To describe the size of the asteroids
○ To explain how the asteroid belt was discovered
○ To explain how gravitational forces influence the planets
○ To describe the impact of telescopes on astronomy

3. How does the professor introduce Bode's Law?

○ By demonstrating how it is derived mathematically
○ By describing the discovery of Uranus
○ By drawing attention to the inaccuracy of a certain pattern
○ By telling the names of several of the asteroids

4. *Listen again to part of the lecture by playing track 8.* [Play Audio] *Then answer the question.*

○ To introduce an alternative application of Bode's Law
○ To give an example of what Bode's Law cannot explain
○ To describe the limitations of gravitational theory
○ To contrast Bode's Law with a real scientific law

5. According to the professor, what two factors contributed to the discovery of the asteroid Ceres?
   Choose 2 answers.

☐ Improved telescopes
☐ Advances in mathematics
☐ The discovery of a new star
☐ The position of Uranus in a pattern

6. What does the professor imply about the asteroid belt?

○ It is farther from the Sun than Uranus.
○ Bode believed it was made up of small stars.
○ It is located where people expected to find a planet.
○ Ceres is the only one of the asteroids that can be seen without a telescope.

Listening Script

Narrator
Listen to part of a lecture in an astronomy class. You will not need to remember the numbers the professor mentions.

Professor
OK. Let's get going. Today I'm going to talk about how the asteroid belt was discovered. And . . . I'm going to start by writing some numbers on the board. Here they are:
We'll start with zero, then 3,. . . 6, . . . 12. Uh, tell me what I'm doing.

Female student
Multiplying by 2?

Professor
Right. I'm doubling the numbers, so 2 times 12 is 24, and the next one I'm going to write after 24 would be . . .

Female student
48.

Professor

48. Then 96. We'll stop there for now. Uh, now I'll write another row of numbers under that. Tell me what I'm doing.

    4, 7, 10 . . . How am I getting this second row?

Male student

Adding 4 to the numbers in the first row.

Professor

I'm adding 4 to each number in the first row to give you a second row. So the last two will be 52, 100, and now tell me what I'm doing.

Female student

Putting in a decimal?

Professor

Yes, I divided all those numbers by 10 by putting in a decimal point. Now I'm going to write the names of the planets under the numbers. Mercury . . . Venus. . . Earth. . . Mars.

    So, what do the numbers mean? Do you remember from the reading?

Male student

Is it the distance of the planets from the Sun?

Professor

Right. In astronomical units—not perfect, but tantalizingly close. The value for Mars is off by . . . 6 or 7 percent or so. It's . . . but it's within 10 percent of the average distance to Mars from the Sun. But I kind of have to skip the one after Mars for now. Then Jupiter's right there at 5-point something, and then Saturn is about 10 astronomical units from the Sun. Um, well, this pattern is known as Bode's Law.

    Um, it isn't really a scientific law, not in the sense of predicting gravitation mathematically or something, but it's attempting a pattern in the spacing of the planets, and it was noticed by Bode hundreds of years ago. Well, you can imagine that there was some interest in why the 2.8 spot in the pattern was skipped, and um . . . but there wasn't anything obvious there, in the early telescopes. Then what happened in the late 1700s? The discovery of . . . ?

Female student

Another planet?

Professor

The next planet out, Uranus—after Saturn.

    And look, Uranus fits in the next spot in the pattern pretty nicely, um, not perfectly, but close. And so then people got really excited about the validity of this thing and finding the missing object between Mars and Jupiter. And telescopes, remember, were getting better. So people went to work on finding objects that would be at that missing distance from the Sun, and then in 1801, the object Ceres was discovered.

    And Ceres was in the right place—the missing spot. Uh, but it was way too faint to be a planet. It looked like a little star. Uh, and because of its starlike appearance, um, it was called an "asteroid."

OK? "Aster" is Greek for "star," as in "astronomy." Um, and so, Ceres was the first and is the largest of what became many objects discovered at that same distance. Not just one thing, but all the objects found at that distance form the asteroid belt. So the asteroid belt is the most famous success of this Bode's Law. That's how the asteroid belt was discovered.

Answers and Explanations

1. ❹ This is a Detail question. Although the entire passage is concerned with answering "What is Bode's Law?" the professor specifically answers the question when he says, " . . . it's attempting a pattern in the spacing of the planets . . . . " The best answer to this question is choice 4.

2. ❷ This is a Gist-Purpose question. Gist questions are not usually answered very explicitly in the passage, but in this case the professor addresses the purpose of the discussion twice. At one point he says, "I'm going to talk about how the asteroid belt was discovered," and later he states, "That's how the asteroid belt was discovered." The best answer to this question is choice 2.

3. ❶ This is an Understanding Organization question. The professor first demonstrates the pattern of numbers before explaining Bode's Law and what the pattern means. The best answer to this question is choice 1.

4. ❹ This is an Understanding the Function of What Is Said replay question. The pattern the professor describes is called Bode's Law. The professor is pointing out how Bode's Law differs from other scientific laws. The best answer to this question is choice 4.

5. ❶ ❹ This is a Detail question. Note that for this question there are two correct answers. The professor explains that "Uranus fits in the next spot in the pattern pretty nicely . . . and telescopes were getting better . . . and then in 1801, the object Ceres was discovered." Choices 1 and 4 are the correct answers. Advances in mathematics and the discovery of a new star are not mentioned by the professor.

6. ❸ This is a Making Inferences question. Starting at the point in the passage where the professor says, " . . . there was some interest in why the 2.8 spot in the pattern was skipped . . . there wasn't anything obvious there," it's clear that what the astronomers are looking for is a planet. He later says, "Ceres was in the right place . . . but way too faint to be a planet." The clear implication is that astronomers were expecting to find a planet. The best answer to the question is choice 3.

PRACTICE SET 5

Now listen to Track 9 on the CD.

Questions

Directions: Mark your answer by filling in the oval next to your choice.

1. What aspect of Manila hemp fibers does the professor mainly discuss in the lecture?

⬭ Similarities between cotton fibers and Manila hemp fibers
⬭ Various types of Manila hemp fibers
⬭ The economic importance of Manila hemp fibers
⬭ A use of Manila hemp fibers

2. *Listen again to part of the lecture by playing track 10. Then answer the question.*

⬭ To tell the class a joke
⬭ To apologize for not completing some work
⬭ To introduce the topic of the lecture
⬭ To encourage students to ask about her trip

3. What does the professor imply about the name "Manila hemp"?

◯ It is a commercial brand name.
◯ Part of the name is inappropriate.
◯ The name has recently changed.
◯ The name was first used in the 1940's.

4. Why does the professor mention the Golden Gate Bridge?

◯ To demonstrate a disadvantage of steel cables
◯ To give an example of the creative use of color
◯ To show that steel cables are able to resist salt water
◯ To give an example of a use of Manila hemp

5. According to the professor, what was the main reason that many ships used Manila hemp ropes instead of steel cables?

◯ Manila hemp was cheaper.
◯ Manila hemp was easier to produce.
◯ Manila hemp is more resistant to salt water.
◯ Manila hemp is lighter in weight.

6. According to the lecture, what are two ways to increase the strength of rope made from Manila hemp fibers?
Choose 2 answers.

☐ Coat the fibers with zinc-based paint
☐ Combine the fibers into bundles
☐ Soak bundles of fibers in salt water
☐ Twist bundles of fibers

Listening Script

Narrator
Listen to part of a lecture from a Botany class.

Professor
Hi, everyone. Good to see you all today. Actually, I expected the population to be a lot lower today. It typically runs between 50 and 60 percent on the day the research paper is due. Um, I was hoping to have your exams back today, but, uh, the situation was that I went away for the weekend, and I was supposed to get in yesterday at five, and I expected to fully complete all the exams by midnight or so, which is the time that I usually go to bed, but my flight was delayed, and I ended up not getting in until one o'clock in the morning. Anyway, I'll do my best to have them finished by the next time we meet.

OK. In the last class, we started talking about useful plant fibers. In particular, we talked about cotton fibers, which we said were very useful, not only in the textile industry, but also in the chemical industry, and in the production of many products, such as plastics, paper, explosives, and so on. Today we'll continue talking about useful fibers, and we'll begin with a fiber that's commonly known as "Manila hemp."

Now, for some strange reason, many people believe that Manila hemp is a hemp plant. But Manila hemp is not really hemp. It's actually a member of the banana family—it even bears little banana-shaped fruits. The "Manila" part of the name makes sense, because Manila hemp is produced chiefly in the Philippine Islands and, of course, the capital city of the Philippines is Manila.

Now, as fibers go, Manila hemp fibers are very long. They can easily be several feet in length and they're also very strong, very flexible. They have one more characteristic that's very important, and that is that they are exceptionally resistant to salt water. And this combination of characteristics—long, strong, flexible, resistant to salt water—makes Manila hemp a great material for ropes, especially for ropes that are gonna be used on ocean-going ships. In fact, by the early 1940's, even though steel cables were available, most ships in the United States Navy were not moored with steel cables; they were moored with Manila hemp ropes.

Now, why was that? Well, the main reason was that steel cables degrade very, very quickly in contact with salt water. If you've ever been to San Francisco, you know that the Golden Gate Bridge is red. And it's red because of the zinc paint that goes on those stainless steel cables. That, if they start at one end of the bridge and they work to the other end, by the time they finish, it's already time to go back and start painting the beginning of the bridge again, because the bridge was built with steel cables, and steel cables can't take the salt air unless they're treated repeatedly with a zinc–based paint.

On the other hand, plant products like Manila hemp, you can drag through the ocean for weeks on end. If you wanna tie your anchor to it and drop it right into the ocean, that's no problem, because plant fibers can stand up for months, even years, in direct contact with salt water. OK. So how do you take plant fibers that individually you could break with your hands and turn them into a rope that's strong enough to moor a ship that weighs thousands of tons? Well, what you do is you extract these long fibers from the Manila hemp plant, and then you take several of these fibers, and you group them into a bundle, because by grouping the fibers you greatly increase their breaking strength–that bundle of fibers is much stronger than any of the individual fibers that compose it. And then you take that bundle of fibers and you twist it a little bit, because by twisting it, you increase its breaking strength even more. And then you take several of these little bundles, and you group and twist them into bigger bundles, which you then group and twist into even bigger bundles, and so on, until eventually, you end up with a very, very strong rope.

Answers and Explanations

1. ❹ Questions like this one that ask about what the professor mainly discusses are Gist-Content questions. This question asks what aspect of Manila hemp fibers are mainly discussed, so it has a narrower focus than other Gist-Content questions. The professor mainly discusses characteristics of Manila hemp and how these characteristics make Manila hemp useful to the shipping industry. The best answer to this question is choice 4.

2. ❷ This is an Understanding the Function of What Is Said replay question. The professor mentions that she went away for the weekend and because a flight was delayed, she was late returning. She tells this story in order to apologize for not completing marking exams. The best answer to this question is choice 2.

3. ❷ This is a Making Inferences question. The professor explains that Manila hemp is produced chiefly in the area near Manila, so the word *Manila* in the name is appropriate. However, Manila hemp is not a type of hemp plant, so the word *hemp* in the name is not appropriate. The best answer to this question is choice 2.

4. ❶ This is an Understanding Organization question. The professor mentions the Golden Gate Bridge in order to make a comparison between the steel cables of the bridge and Manila hemp ropes. The fact that the steel cables must be constantly repainted is a disadvantage. The best answer to the question is choice 1.

5. ❸ This is a Detail question. It is related to the professor's main point about Manila hemp. The professor says that Manila hemp is "exceptionally resistant to salt water." Much of the listening passage deals with the professor's reinforcing and exemplifying this point. The best answer to this question is choice 3.

6. ❷ ❹ Near the end of the listening passage, the professor describes how Manila hemp ropes are made. The answer to this Detail question can be found there. The professor talks about grouping fibers into bundles and then twisting the bundles to make them stronger. Note that this question requires two answers. The best answers to this question are choices 2 and 4.

PRACTICE TOEFL iBT LISTENING SECTION

This section measures your ability to understand conversations and lectures in English.

You should listen to each conversation and lecture only **one** time.

After each conversation or lecture, you will answer some questions about it. The questions typically ask about the main idea and supporting details. Some questions ask about a speaker's purpose or attitude. Answer the questions based on what is stated or implied by the speakers.

You may take notes while you listen. You may use your notes to help you answer the questions. Your notes will **not** be scored.

In some questions, you will see this icon: 🎧**Play Audio** This means that you will hear, but not see, part of the question.

Most questions are worth 1 point. If a question is worth more than 1 point, it will have special directions that indicate how many points you can receive.

You will have **55 Minutes** to listen to the Conversations and Lectures and to answer the questions. You should answer each question, even if you must guess the answer.

Listen to Track 11 on the CD. 🎧**Play Audio**

Questions

Directions: Mark your answer by filling in the oval next to your choice.

1. Why does the student go to see the professor?

   ○ To prepare for her graduate school interview
   ○ To get advice about her graduate school application
   ○ To give the professor her graduate school application
   ○ To find out if she was accepted into graduate school

2. According to the professor, what information should the student include in her statement of purpose?
   Choose 2 answers.

   ☐ Her academic motivation
   ☐ Her background in medicine
   ☐ Some personal information
   ☐ The ways her teachers have influenced her

3. What does the professor consider unusual about the student's background?

   ○ Her work experience
   ○ Her creative writing experience
   ○ Her athletic achievements
   ○ Her music training

4. Why does the professor tell a story about his friend who went to medical school?

   ○ To warn the student about how difficult graduate school can be
   ○ To illustrate a point he is making

○ To help the student relax
○ To change the subject

5. What does the professor imply about the people who admit students to graduate school?

○ They often lack expertise in the fields of the applicants.
○ They do not usually read the statement of purpose.
○ They are influenced by the appearance of an application.
○ They remember most of the applications they receive.

Listen to Track 12 on the CD. [Play Audio]

Questions

6. What are the students mainly discussing?

○ Drugs that are harmful to the human body
○ Bacteria that produce antibiotics
○ DNA that is related to athletic performance
○ Genes that protect bacteria from antibiotics

7. *Listen again to part of the conversation by playing track 13.* [Play Audio]
   Then answer the question.

○ To find out if the man has done his assignment
○ To ask the man to find out if the library is open
○ To let the man know that she cannot study much longer
○ To ask if the man has ever met her roommate

8. According to the conversation, why are transposes sometimes called "jumping genes"?

○ They are able to move from one bacteria cell to another.
○ They are found in people with exceptional jumping ability.
○ They occur in every other generation of bacteria.
○ Their movements are rapid and unpredictable.

9. According to the conversation, what are two ways in which bacteria cells get resistance genes?
   Choose 2 answers.

☐ The resistance genes are carried from nearby cells.
☐ The resistance genes are carried by white blood cells.
☐ The resistance genes are inherited from the parent cell.
☐ The resistance genes are carried by antibiotics.

10. What can be inferred about the resistance genes discussed in the conversation?

○ They are found in all bacteria cells.
○ They are not able to resist antibiotics.
○ They make the treatment of bacterial diseases more difficult.
○ They are essential to the body's defenses against bacteria.

Listen to Track 14 on the CD.

Questions

11. What is the talk mainly about?

- ⃝ A common method of managing water supplies
- ⃝ The formation of underground water systems
- ⃝ Natural processes that renew water supplies
- ⃝ Maintaining the purity of underground water systems

12. What is the professor's point of view concerning the method of "safe yield"?

- ⃝ It has helped to preserve the environment.
- ⃝ It should be researched in states other than Arizona.
- ⃝ It is not an effective resource policy.
- ⃝ It ignores the different ways people use water.

13. According to the professor, what are two problems associated with removing water from an underground system?
Choose 2 answers.

- ☐ Pollutants can enter the water more quickly.
- ☐ The surface area can dry and crack.
- ☐ The amount of water stored in the system can drop.
- ☐ Dependent streams and springs can dry up.

14. *Listen again to part of the lecture by playing track 15. Then answer the question.*

- ⃝ To find out whether the students are familiar with the issue
- ⃝ To introduce a new problem for discussion
- ⃝ To respond to a student's question
- ⃝ To encourage the students to care about the topic

15. What is a key feature of a sustainable water system?

- ⃝ It is able to satisfy short-term and long-term needs.
- ⃝ It is not affected by changing environmental conditions.
- ⃝ It usually originates in lakes, springs, or streams.
- ⃝ It is not used to supply human needs.

16. What does the professor imply about water systems managed by the "safe yield" method?

- ⃝ They recharge at a rapid rate.
- ⃝ They are not sustainable.
- ⃝ They must have large storage areas.
- ⃝ They provide a poor quality of water.

Listen to Track 16 on the CD.

Questions

17. Why does the professor talk about Plato's description of society?

⭕ To explain why societies face certain problems
⭕ To point out problems with Plato's ethical theory
⭕ To introduce students to the political structure of ancient Greece
⭕ To help explain Plato's view about the nature of the human soul

18. *Listen again to part of the lecture by playing track 17.*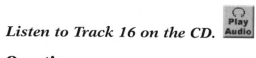
    Then answer the question.

⭕ It may be familiar to some of the students.
⭕ It will be discussed in more detail in a later class.
⭕ It is not an interesting theory.
⭕ It is not a very complicated theory.

19. *Listen again to part of the lecture by playing track 18.*
    Then answer the question.

⭕ To find out if students have understood what she just said
⭕ To suggest an answer to a question that she just asked
⭕ To express disagreement with a point made by Plato
⭕ To explain why harmony is difficult for a society to achieve

20. What are two points that reflect Plato's views about education?
    Choose 2 answers.

☐ All people can be trained to become leaders.
☐ All people should learn to use their intellect.
☐ Leaders should be responsible for the education of workers and soldiers.
☐ All people should learn about the nature of the human soul.

21. Based on information in the lecture, indicate whether the statements below about human emotion reflect beliefs held by Plato.
    For each sentence, put a checkmark in the YES or NO column.

	YES	NO
Emotion is usually controlled by the faculty of desire.		
Emotion ought to be controlled by the faculty of intellect.		
Emotion is what motivates soldiers.		

22. According to Plato, what is the main characteristic of a good or just person?

◯ The parts of the person's soul exist in harmony.
◯ The person does not try to control other people.
◯ The person's relationships with other people are harmonious.
◯ The person does not act in an emotional manner.

Listen to track 19 on the CD. 🎧 **Play Audio**

Questions

23. What is the main topic of the lecture?

◯ The size of root systems
◯ Various types of root systems
◯ The nutrients required by rye plants
◯ Improving two types of plant species

24. According to the professor, why did one scientist grow a rye plant in water?

◯ To expose the roots to sunlight
◯ To be able to fertilize it with gas
◯ To be able to see its entire root system
◯ To see how minerals penetrate its roots

25. *Listen again to part of the lecture by playing track 20.* 🎧 **Play Audio** *Then answer the question.*

◯ She wanted to correct the wording of a previous statement.
◯ She wishes she did not have to bubble gas through it.
◯ She realized the odor of gas could be unpleasant.
◯ She forgot to tell the students about a step in the experiment.

26. The professor mentions houseplants that receive too much water. Why does she mention them?

◯ To show that many different types of plants can grow in water
◯ To explain why plants grown in water should have a gas bubbled through them
◯ To remind the students of the importance of their next experiment
◯ To make a point about the length of houseplants' roots

27. *Listen again to part of the lecture by playing track 21.* 🎧 **Play Audio** *Then answer the question.*

◯ Why a mistake made in textbooks was never corrected
◯ Why she does not believe that the roots of rye plants extend to 1,000 km
◯ How the roots of rye plants develop to such a great length
◯ How plants grown in water make use of fertilizer

28. According to the professor, what similarity is there between crabgrass and rye plants?

○ Both start growing in the month of May.
○ Both have root systems that require a lot of water.
○ Both have more shoot surface than root surface.
○ Both produce many shoots from a single seed.

Listen to track 22 on the CD. 🎧 **Play Audio**

Questions

29. What is the lecture mainly about?

○ Technological innovations in the automobile industry
○ The organizational structure of companies
○ Ways to improve efficiency in an engineering department
○ Methods of resolving conflicts in organizations

30. Why does the professor talk about a construction company that has work in different cities?

○ To give an example of functional organization
○ To give an example of organization around projects
○ To illustrate problems with functional organization
○ To illustrate the types of conflict that can arise in companies

31. *Listen again to part of the lecture by playing track 23.* 🎧 **Play Audio**
Then answer the question.

○ He does not understand why the student is talking about engineers.
○ He wants to know how the engineers will communicate with their coworkers.
○ The student has not provided a complete answer to his question.
○ He wants the student to do more research on the topic.

32. What is an example of a violation of the "unity of command" principle?

○ More than one person supervises the same employee.
○ A company decides not to standardize its products.
○ Several project managers are responsible for designing a new product.
○ An employee does not follow a supervisor's instructions.

33. According to the professor, where might there be a conflict in an organizational structure based on both projects and function?

○ Between architects and finance experts
○ Between the need to specialize and the need to standardize
○ Between two engineers who work on the same project
○ Between the needs of projects in different cities

34. Indicate whether each sentence below describes functional organization or project organization. Place a checkmark in the correct box.

	Functional Organization	Project Organization
It encourages people with similar expertise to work closely together.		
It helps the company to adapt quickly and meet changing needs.		
It helps to achieve uniformity in projects.		

ANSWER KEY, LISTENING SCRIPTS, AND EXPLANATIONS

Answer Key and Self-Scoring Chart

Directions: Check your answers against the Answer Key below. Write the number 1 on the line to the right of each question if you picked the correct answer. (For questions worth more than one point, follow the directions given.) Total your points at the bottom of the chart.

Question Number	Correct Answer	
1.	2	_____
2.	1, 3	_____
3.	3	_____
4.	2	_____
5.	3	_____
6.	4	_____
7.	3	_____
8.	1	_____
9.	1, 3	_____
10.	3	_____
11.	1	_____
12.	3	_____
13.	3, 4	_____
14.	4	_____
15.	1	_____
16.	2	_____
17.	4	_____
18.	1	_____
19.	2	_____
20.	2, 3	_____

For question 21, write 2 if you placed three answer choices correctly. Write 1 if you placed two choices correctly.

21.	Yes: 2, 3	
	No: 1	_____
22.	1	_____
23.	1	_____
24.	2	_____
25.	1	_____
26.	2	_____
27.	3	_____
28.	4	_____
29.	2	_____
30.	2	_____
31.	3	_____
32.	1	_____
33.	2	_____

34.   Functional: 1, 3
                             Project: 2   _____
                             TOTAL: _____

Below is a table that converts your Listening Practice section answers into a TOEFL iBT Scaled Score. Take the number of correct answers from your Answer Key table and find that number in the left-hand column of the table. On the right-hand side of the table is a range of TOEFL iBT Listening scores for that number of correct answers. For example, if the total of points from your answer key is 27, the table says your estimated TOEFL iBT Listening section scaled score is in the range of 22 to 24. Your scaled score is given as a range instead of a single number for the following reasons:

➤ The estimates of scores are based on the performance of students who participated in a field study for these listening comprehension questions. Those students took the test on computer. You took your practice test by listening to a CD and answering questions in a book. Although the two experiences are comparable, the differences make it impossible to give an exact prediction of your score.

➤ The students who participated in the field study were volunteers and may have differed in average ability from the actual TOEFL test-taking population.

➤ The conversion of scores from the field study in which these questions were administered to the current TOEFL iBT scale involved two scale conversions. Converting from one scale to another always involves some statistical error.

You should use your score estimate as a general guide only. Your actual score on TOEFL iBT may be higher or lower than your score on the practice section. A free practice version of TOEFL iBT, which you can take on computer, is available at www.toeflpractice.ets.org.

Listening

Raw Point Total	Scale Score
34	28–30
33	28–30
32	27–29
31	26–29
30	25–27
29	25–27
28	24–26
27	22–24
26	21–23
25	21–23
24	17–22
23	16–21
22	16–21
21	16–18

Continued

Listening—cont'd

Raw Point Total	Scale Score
20	14–18
19	13–17
18	13–17
17	11–16
16	10–15
15	10–15
14	9–13
13	8–12
12	6–12
11	4–10
10	3–10
9	0–9
8	0–9
7	0–7
6	0–5
5	0–3
4	0–3
3	0–3
2	0–3
1	0–3
0	0–3

Answer Explanations

Questions 1–5

Listening Script

Narrator
Listen to a conversation between a student and a professor.

Professor
Hey, Ellen. How are you doing?

Student
Oh, pretty good, thanks. How are you?

Professor
OK.

Student
Did you, um, have a chance to look at my grad school application . . . you know, the statement of purpose I wrote.

Professor
Well, yeah. In fact, here it is. I just read it.

Student

Oh, great! What did you think?

Professor

Basically, it's good. What you might actually do is take some of these different points here, and actually break them out into separate paragraphs. So, um, one: your purpose for applying for graduate study; uh, why do you want to go to graduate school, and an area of specialty; and, uh, why you want to do the area you're specifying; um, and what you want to do with your degree once you get it.

Student

OK.

Professor

So those are . . . they're pretty clear on those four points they want.

Student

Right.

Professor

So, you might just break them out into uh . . . you know, separate paragraphs and expand on each point some. But really what's critical with these is that, um, you've gotta let yourself come through. See, you gotta let them see you in these statements. Expand some more on what's happened in your own life and what shows your . . . your motivation and interest in this area—in geology. Let 'em see what really, what . . . what captures your imagination about this field.

Student

OK. So make it a little more . . . personal? That's OK?

Professor

That's fine. They look for that stuff. You don't wanna go overboard . . .

Student

Right.

Professor

. . . but it's critical that . . . that somebody sees what your passion is—your personal motivation for doing this.

Student

OK.

Professor

And that's gotta come out in here. Um, and let's see, uh, you might also give a little, uh–since this is your only chance to do it, you might give a little more explanation about your unique undergraduate background. So, you know, how you went through, you know, the music program; what you got from that; why you decided to change. I mean, it's kind of unusual to go from music to geology, right?

Student

Yeah. I was . . . I was afraid that, you know, maybe the personal type stuff wouldn't be what they wanted but . . .

Professor

No, in fact it's . . . um, give an example: I . . . I had a friend, when I was an undergrad, um, went to medical school. And he put on his med school application–and he could actually tell if somebody actually read it 'cause, um, he had asthma and the reason that he wanted to go to med school was he said he wanted to do sports medicine because he, you know, he had this real interest. He was an athlete too, and . . . and wanted to help athletes who had this physical problem. And he could always tell if somebody actually read his letter because they would always ask him about that.

Student

. . . Mmm . . . so something unique.

Professor

Yeah. So see, you know, that's what's good and and I think for you probably, you know, your music background's the most unique thing that you've got in your record.

Student

Right.

Professor

. . . Mmm . . . so you see, you gotta make yourself stand out from a coupla hundred applications. Does that help any?

Student

Yeah, it does. It gives me some good ideas.

Professor

And . . . what you might also do too is, you know, uh, you might get a friend to proof it or something at some point.

Student

Oh, sure . . . sure.

Professor

Also, think about presentation—how the application looks. In a way you're actually showing some other skills here, like organization. A lot of stuff that's . . . that they're not . . . they're not formally asking for, they're looking at. So your presentation format, your grammar, all that stuff, they're look- ing at in your materials at the same time.

Student

Right. OK.

Answers and Explanations

1. ❷ For Listening conversations that take place in a professor's office hours, it is very likely that the first question will be a Gist-Purpose question. That is the case here. This discussion is about how the woman should write her graduate school

application, not about an interview or whether or not she had been admitted. The professor already has her application and has reviewed it, so the purpose cannot be for her to give him the application. Thus choice 2 is the correct answer; she wants advice about the application.

2. **❶ ❸** When you are taking the TOEFL iBT on computer, whenever you see squares in front of the question choices instead of ovals, you should recognize that the question calls for you to select two or more answers from among the choices. In this case, the professor stresses the following two items that the woman needs to include in her application letter:

1. How her college career has made her interested in graduate school
2. How she stands out as an individual

Thus the correct answers are choices 1 and 3. She does not have a background in medicine (choice 2), and the professor does not mention her teachers (choice 4).

3. **❹** This is a Detail question. The professor mentions twice that the woman's decision to go from studying music to geology is unusual.

4. **❷** This is an Understanding the Function of What Is Said question. Clearly the professor is illustrating his point that a good application should individualize the writer. His friend who went to medical school is an example.

5. **❸** This is a Making Inferences question. The last thing the professor mentions to the student is that she should think about the format of her application and the statement of purpose. He says that the format of the application can demonstrate her organizational skills and strongly implies that avoiding any writing errors shows thoroughness. By making these points, he is implying that the readers of the application will be influenced by its appearance, even if the influence is unconscious. He says nothing about the readers' expertise (choice 1); he implies that sometimes they may not read the application carefully, but he does not imply that this is what usually happens (choice 2); and he says the opposite of choice 4. The correct answer is choice 3.

Questions 6–10

Listening Script

Narrator
Listen to part of a conversation between two students. The woman is helping the man review for a biology examination.

Male student
OK, so . . . what do you think we should go over next?

Female student
How about if we go over this stuff about how bacteria become resistant to antibiotics.

Male student

OK.

Female student

Um, but first of all, though, how many pages do we have left? I told my roommate I'd meet her at the library at seven o'clock.

Male student

Ummm . . . There's only a few pages left. We should be finished in a few minutes.

Female student

OK. So, ummm . . .

Male student

About how bacteria become resistant to antibiotics.

Female student

Oh yeah, OK. So you know that some bacteria cells are able to resist the drugs we use against them, and that's because they have these special genes that, like, protect them from the drugs.

Male student

Right. If I remember correctly, I think the genes like . . . weaken the antibiotics, or like . . . stop the antibiotics from getting into the bacteria cell, something like that?

Female student

Exactly. So when bacteria have these genes, it's very difficult for the antibiotics to kill the bacteria.

Male student

Right.

Female student

So, do you remember what those genes are called?

Male student

Umm . . .

Female student

Resistance genes.

Male student

Resistance genes. Right. Resistance genes. OK.

Female student

And that makes sense, right? Because they help the bacteria resist the antibiotics.

Male student

Yeah, that makes sense. OK.

Female student

OK. But the question is: how do bacteria get the resistance genes?

Male student

How do they get the resistance genes? They just inherit them from the parent cell, right?

Female student

OK, yeah, that's true. They can inherit them from the parent cell, but that's not what I'm talking about.

Male student

OK.

Female student

I'm talking about how they get resistance genes from other cells in their environment, you know, from the other cells around them.

Male student

Oh, I see what you mean. Umm, is that that stuff about "hopping genes," or something like that?

Female student

Right. Although actually they're called "jumping genes," not "hopping genes."

Male student

Oh, OK. Jumping genes.

Female student

Yeah, but they have another name, too, that I can't think of. Umm . . . lemme see if I can find it here in the book . . .

Male student

I think it's probably on . . .

Female student

Oh, OK. Here it is. Transposons. That's what they're called.

Male student

Lemme see. OK. Trans . . . po . . . sons . . . trans . . . posons. So "transposon" is another name for a jumping gene?

Female student

Right. And these transposons are, you know, like, little bits of DNA that are able to move from one cell to another. That's why they're called "jumping genes." They kind of, you know, "jump" from one cell to another.

Male student

OK.

Female student

And these transposons are how resistance genes are able to get from one bacteria cell to another bacteria cell. What happens is that a resistance gene from one cell attaches itself to a transposon and then, when the transposon jumps to another cell . . .

Male student

The other cell gets the resistance gene and . . .

Female student

Right.

Male student

That's how it becomes resistant to antibiotics.

Female student

Right.

Male student

Wow. That's really cool. So that's how it happens.

Female student

That's how it happens.

Answers and Explanations

This question set, from an early version of TOEFL iBT, does not exactly fit the rules for TOEFL conversations given earlier in this chapter. Instead of being between a student and a university employee, it is between two students who are studying for an exam. We have included it here because it is good practice and it closely resembles an office hours conversation on an academic topic. It has also been field-tested with actual test takers, providing data on the difficulty level of the items.

6. ❹ This conversation is about academic content in the area of Life Science. The man is trying to learn something for his biology test. It makes sense, then, that the first question is a Gist-Content question: "What are the students mainly discussing?" The students discuss drugs, but they are drugs that fight bacteria, so choice 1 is eliminated. They are not discussing how antibiotics are produced, but how they are resisted, so choice 2 is eliminated. If all you heard was "jumping" and "hopping," you might think they were discussing athletics, but that is not how those words are being used, so choice 3 is eliminated. Choice 4 is the correct answer: the man is learning how some bacteria acquire genes that make them resistant to antibiotics.

7. ❸ This replay item is an Understanding the Function of What Is Said question. You are asked why the woman says the following:

"Um, but first of all, though, how many pages do we have left? I told my roommate I'd meet her at the library at seven o'clock."

Her statement about meeting her roommate is part of the context in which the main discussion takes place. The man is trying to learn about bacteria, but she is saying they have only a limited amount of time to spend on the discussion. The function of her statement is to tell the man that she must keep her appointment with her roommate and therefore they must finish soon.

8. ❶ This is a Detail question. When you hear a new term defined, in either a lecture or a conversation, you should note it. Here the students spend a large part of the conversation discussing why the "transposons" are called "jumping genes." The woman says twice that the reason is that the genes can migrate, or "jump" from one cell to another. The correct answer is choice 1.

9. ❶ ❸ This is another Detail question. It asks you to identify two ways that bacteria acquire the resistance gene. Both students mention that the gene can be inherited from a parent cell. They then have a longer discussion about the "jumping gene" and how a "jumping gene" can carry the resistance gene to a new cell. Nothing is mentioned about "white blood cells," and "resistance genes being carried by antibiotics" is directly contradicted by the discussion. The correct answers are choices are 1 and 3.

10. ❸ The question uses the verb *inferred*, so you know this is a Making Inferences question. The students say repeatedly that some bacteria resist "the drugs we use against them." From this you can infer that an antibiotic is a medicine used against some bacteria. The students say the resistance genes "weaken the antibiotics" and "stop the antibiotics." From these clues you should infer that choice 3, "the resistance genes make the treatment of bacterial diseases more difficult," is the correct answer.

Questions 11–16

Listening Script

Narrator
Listen to part of a talk in an Environmental Science class.

Professor
So, I wanted to discuss a few other terms here . . . actually, some, uh some ideas about how we manage our resources.

Let's talk about what that . . . what that means. If we take a resource like water . . . well, maybe we should get a little bit more specific here—back up from the more general case–and talk about underground water in particular.

So, hydrogeologists have tried to figure out . . . how much water can you take out from underground sources? This has been an important question. Let me ask you guys: how much water, based on what you know so far, could you take out of, say, an aquifer . . . under the city?

Male student
As . . . as much as would get re-charged?

Professor

OK. So, we wouldn't want to take out any more than naturally comes into it. The implication is that, uh, well, if you only take as much out as comes in, you're not gonna deplete the amount of water that's stored in there, right?

Wrong, but that's the principle. That's the idea behind how we manage our water supplies. It's called "safe yield." Basically what this method says is that you can pump as much water out of a system as naturally recharges . . . as naturally flows back in.

So, this principle of safe yield—it's based on balancing what we take out with what gets recharged. But what it does is, it ignores how much water naturally comes out of the system.

In a natural system, a certain amount of recharge comes in and a certain amount of water naturally flows out through springs, streams, and lakes. And over the long term the amount that's stored in the aquifer doesn't really change much. It's balanced. Now humans come in . . . and start taking water out of the system. How have we changed the equation?

Female student

It's not balanced anymore?

Professor

Right. We take water out, but water also naturally flows out. And the recharge rate doesn't change, so the result is we've reduced the amount of water that's stored in the underground system.

If you keep doing that long enough—if you pump as much water out as naturally comes in—gradually the underground water levels drop. And when that happens, that can affect surface water. How? Well, in underground systems there are natural discharge points—places where the water flows out of the underground systems, out to lakes and streams. Well, a drop in the water level can mean those discharge points will eventually dry up. That means water's not getting to lakes and streams that depend on it. So we've ended up reducing the surface water supply, too.

You know, in the state of Arizona we're managing some major water supplies with this principle of safe yield, under a method that will eventually dry up the natural discharge points of those aquifer systems.

Now, why is this an issue? Well, aren't some of you going to want to live in this state for a while? Want your kids to grow up here, and your kids' kids? You might be concerned with . . . does Arizona have a water supply which is sustainable—key word here? What that means . . . the general definition of sustainable is will there be enough to meet the needs of the present without compromising the ability of the future to have the availability . . . to have the same resources?

Now, I hope you see that these two ideas are incompatible: sustainability and safe yield. Because what sustainability means is that it's sustainable for all systems dependent on the water–for the people that use it and for . . . uh, for supplying water to the dependent lakes and streams.

So, I'm gonna repeat this: so, if we're using a safe-yield method, if we're only balancing what we take out with what gets recharged, but—don't forget, water's also flowing out naturally—then the amount stored underground is gonna gradually get reduced and that's gonna lead to another problem. These discharge points—where the water flows out to the lakes and streams—they're gonna dry up. OK.

Answers and Explanations

11. ❶ The first question in this set is a Gist-Content question, as is usually the case in a lecture set. It's important to remember that you are hearing only part of the lecture. The beginning of this excerpt shows that the professor is talking about

different ways to manage natural resources. He chooses underground water as an example of a natural resource, and then goes on to discuss one particular way of managing the underground water supply called "safe yield." His focus is on the "safe yield" approach to managing underground water supplies. Thus the correct answer is choice 1. The other choices are aspects of underground water that an environmental scientist might discuss, but they are not the focus of this excerpt.

12. ❸ The lecture makes clear that the professor does not think the "safe yield" approach is appropriate. He communicates this indirectly in several ways, particularly when he says, "we're managing some major water supplies with this principle of safe yield, under a method that will eventually dry up the natural discharge points of those aquifer systems." Although the term "safe yield" indicates that it is safe, the professor is saying that it is, in reality, not safe, because it does not take into account the other ways that water can leave the system besides pumping water out for people's use. The correct answer is choice 3.

13. ❸ ❹ This is a Detail question. All four choices are possible results of removing water from an underground system, but the professor discusses only 3 and 4.

14. ❹ This is an Understanding the Function of What Is Said question. The professor asks these questions:

"Now, why is this an issue? Well, aren't some of you going to want to live in this state for a while? Want your kids to grow up here, and your kids' kids?"

The purpose is to point out to the students that, over time, there will be serious consequences to depleting the underground water supply. He thinks the students should consider the future of the state of Arizona. Therefore, the correct answer is choice 4.

15. ❶ This is a Detail question. The professor defines sustainability as the ability to meet present and future needs. Since his main criticism of "safe yield" management is that it is not sustainable, knowing the meaning of *sustainable* is key to understanding the lecture. "Short-term and long-term needs" are the same as "present and future needs," so choice 1 is the correct answer.

16. ❷ Because the question uses the word *imply*, we expect this to be a Making Inferences question. It is, however, a very easy inference. The professor says, "these two ideas are incompatible: sustainability and safe yield." If the "safe yield" method is incompatible with sustainability, then water supplies managed by "safe yield" are not sustainable. The correct answer is choice 2.

Questions 17–22

Listening Script

Narrator
Listen to part of a lecture in a philosophy class. The professor has been talking about ethics.

Professor

OK. If we're going to discuss goodness and justice—what makes an individual good or a society just or virtuous—then we need to start with the ancient Greeks. So we'll start with Plato—Plato's philosophy.

Now, some of you may have studied Plato's philosophy in some other course, so this might be easy. OK. At the risk of boring you, let me give you just an overview of Plato's ethical theory. Plato says the soul has—and by "soul" he simply means that which animates the body, gives it life—anyway, he says that the soul has three separate parts . . . called, um, "faculties," which I'll come back to. He believed that goodness in an individual was to be found when the three parts of the soul worked together, when they weren't in conflict, but existed in harmony. A good or just person will have a soul in which the three faculties work well together.

So, how does he arrive at that analysis? Well, he starts out in his very famous work, *The Republic,* um, he starts out by saying it's very difficult to get a grasp on what the individual's soul looks like. So, to get some idea of what the individual human soul is like, he says we should study the structure of society—what kinds of people and activities every society has to have. He argues that every society has to have three groups of people: workers, soldiers, and leaders. And each has a sort of defining characteristic.

Every society has to have workers like farmers or, um, people who work in factories, producing all the things that we need for everyday life. And according to Plato, the key feature of workers is that they're focused on their own desires or appetites—interested in satisfying the needs of the body. So workers are associated with desire . . . OK?

Now, if you live in a society that has a good amount of wealth—um, good agriculture, good industry—other societies are probably going to try to take it. So you need a class of soldiers, who are supposed to protect the state from external threats. Well, these soldiers, well, they're going to be in dangerous situations quite frequently, so you need people with, um, a . . . a lot of high spirit—uh, an emotional type of individual. Emotion is what characterizes this group.

And then, Plato says, the third group you need is leaders. Their main role will be to think rationally, to use their reason or intellect to make decisions. As decision makers, leaders determine what the state is to do, how the affairs of the citizens are to be run.

Plato then asks himself: OK, assume we've got such a society with these three groups. When will this society be a good, um, a . . . a just society? Well, you can only have a good society when its three parts are working well together—each doing its proper thing. And Plato believes this can only happen if workers and soldiers learn moderation or self-control.

But why? Why do workers and soldiers have to learn self-control? Well, how can a society flourish if the workers and soldiers don't control their desires and emotions? Plato thinks that if they aren't under control, workers will sleep too much and play too much, so they're not going to get their jobs done. And soldiers need to channel their high spiritedness in a certain direction, precisely by being courageous.

But you're not going to get that automatically. You need to teach them this kind of moderation. So you need an educational system that first of all will train the leaders, so that they'll make good decisions, so they'll know what's wise. Then make leaders responsible—um, uh, turn over to them the education of the other two groups. And through education, build a society so that the workers and soldiers learn to use their intellect to control their desires and emotions. If you had all that, then, for Plato, you'd have a good or just society.

Now, take that picture—that social, political picture—and apply it to the individual person. You remember about the soul? That it consists of three separate parts, or faculties? Can you guess what they are? Desires, emotions, and intellect—the characteristics associated with the three groups of society. And can you guess how Plato defines a good or just person? Well, it's parallel to how he characterizes a good or just society. The three parts have to be in harmony.

In each of us, our desires and emotions often get the better of us, and lead us to do foolish things. They're in conflict with the intellect. So, to get them to all work together, to co-exist in harmony, every person needs to be shaped in the same way that we've shaped society–through the educational system. Individuals must be educated to use their intellect to control their emotions and desires. That's harmony in the soul.

Answers and Explanations

17. ❹ This is a Gist-Purpose question. Most of the excerpt that you listened to was about Plato's theory that society is made up of three groups. However, the beginning and the end of the excerpt set the context for this discussion. Plato discusses society because he thinks a society is similar to an individual person. The speaker is describing Plato's ideas, and does not say whether they are true or not, so neither choice 1 nor choice 2 can be correct. Again, the speaker is not concerned with the real, historical societies, so choice 3 cannot be correct. Only choice 4 is possible.

18. ❶ This question asks you to listen again to this statement:

   "Now, some of you may have studied Plato's philosophy in some other course, so this might be easy. OK. At the risk of boring you, let me give you just an overview of Plato's ethical theory."

   You are then asked a Making Inferences question. The professor is anticipating that some students may have already studied *The Republic* in another class and be familiar with the basics of Plato's theory. He says that the review may be "easy" or "boring" to students already familiar with the theory, but he is talking about his review, not the theory itself. So choices 2, 3, and 4 are not implied. Choice 1, that some students might be familiar with the theory, is implied.

19. ❷ This question asks you to listen again to this part of the lecture:

   "But why? Why do workers and soldiers have to learn self-control? Well, how can a society flourish if the workers and soldiers don't control their desires and emotions?"

   Then you are asked why the professor says this:

   "Well, how can a society flourish if the workers and soldiers don't control their desires and emotions?"

   You are asked the purpose of a question, so this is an Understanding the Function of What Is Said item. The quote is an example of a rhetorical question and is really an answer to the previous question, "Why do workers and soldiers have to learn self-control?" The question "How can a society flourish . . ." is a way of saying "A society cannot flourish if workers and soldiers do not exercise self-control." The correct answer is choice 2.

20. ❷ ❸ This is a Detail question that asks you to identify two points the professor makes about Plato's view of education. Since the lecture has been about both

Plato's theoretical model of society and about a model of human nature, you might anticipate that one point will be about society and one about the individual. According to the professor's summary, for individuals, the intellect must be strengthened through education. For the model society, the leaders must educate the other two groups. The correct answers are choices 2 and 3.

21. This question is easy to recognize as a Connecting Content question. Based on information in the lecture, you must indicate whether or not certain statements about human emotion reflect beliefs held by Plato. The chart correctly filled out looks like this:

For each sentence, put a checkmark in the YES or NO column.

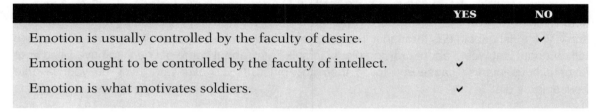

	YES	NO
Emotion is usually controlled by the faculty of desire.		✔
Emotion ought to be controlled by the faculty of intellect.	✔	
Emotion is what motivates soldiers.	✔	

The professor discusses emotions and desires as being controlled by the intellect, but he says nothing about them being related to one another, so statement 1 is not supported by the lecture. According to the professor, Plato does believe that for people to be happy, the intellect must control emotions, so statement 2 is supported. The professor says about Plato's soldiers "Emotion is what characterizes this group." So statement 3 is also supported by the lecture.

22. ❶ This is a Detail question. In the last two paragraphs of the lecture, when the professor returns to discussing individuals, he says three times that in Plato's theory the parts of the individual must be in harmony. When the lecturer repeats a point two or three times, that is a good clue that it is one of the main points of the excerpt and you should be prepared to answer a question about it. The correct answer is choice 1.

Questions 23–28

Listening Script

Narrator
Listen to part of a talk in a botany class.

Professor
OK. So we've talked about some different types of root systems of plants, and I've shown you some pretty cool slides, but now I want to talk about the extent of the root system—the overall size of the root system . . . the depth. I want to tell you about one particular experiment. I think you're going to find this pretty amazing. OK. So there was this scientist . . . this very meticulous scientist decided that the best place to see a whole root system—to actually see how big the entire system got–the best place would be to grow it . . . where?

Female student

Um, water?

Professor

In water. So he took rye plants—it was rye plants—and he started growing them in water. Now, you've all heard of growing stuff in water before, right?

Male student

It's done commercially, right? Uh, like to grow vegetables and flowers?

Professor

Right. They grow all kinds of commercial crops in water. So, if you're growing things in water, you can add the fertilizer. What do you need to do to that water besides put fertilizer in it? Anyone ever actually tried to grow plants in water? You must bubble water through it. Bubble gas through it. I'm sorry, you must bubble gas through it. So, gas, you have to bubble through. Think about the soil we talked about last week, about growing plants in soil. Think about some of you who have killed your favorite houseplants, 'cause you loved them too much. If you overwater, why do your favorite houseplants die?

Female student

Oh, no oxygen.

Professor

Not enough oxygen for the roots . . . which do what twenty-four hours a day in all seasons?

Female student

Respiration?

Professor

Respire . . . respiration . . . they breathe. So, if you just stick rye plants in water, it doesn't make a difference how much fertilizer you add, you also need to bubble gas through the water, so they have access to that oxygen. If they don't have that, they're in big trouble. OK. So this guy–this scientist—grew a rye plant in water so he could see the root system how big it got—its surface area. I read about this and the book said one thousand kilometers of roots. I kept thinking: this has to be a mistake. It just doesn't make any sense to me that . . . that . . . that could be right. But that's what all the books have, and no one's ever corrected it. So, let me explain to you about this rye plant. If you take a little seed of many grasses–and remember rye is a grass; if you take a tiny little seed and you germinate it—actually, take one of my least favorite grasses that starts growing about May. What's my least favorite grass that starts growing about May?

Male student

Crabgrass.

Professor

Crabgrass.

Remember how I showed you in the lab, one little seed starts out producing one little shoot. Then at a week or so later you've got about six shoots, and then, three weeks later you've got about fifteen shoots coming out all directions like this—all those little shoots up there?

Well, that's what they did with the rye. And the little seedling started and pretty soon there were several shoots, and then more shoots. In the end, that one single seed produced eighty shoots, with an average of fifty centimeters of height . . . from one seed. Eighty shoots coming out, average fifty centimeters high. When they looked at the shoot versus the root surface, they found that the shoot surface, with all of its leaves, had a total surface area of about five square meters. Now, here's the biggie, when they looked at the root surface area, you would expect that the root and the shoot would be in balance, right? So, they should be pretty close in terms of surface area, right?

Male student

Uh-un.

Professor

What's that? Did somebody say "no"? Well, you're absolutely correct. Instead of five square meters, the root system was found to have more than two hundred square meters of surface area. Where did all of that extra surface area come from? Who did it? Who was responsible for all those extra square meters of surface area? What did roots do to increase their surface area?

Female student

Root hairs.

Professor

Root hairs, that's exactly it. So those root hairs were responsible for an incredible chunk of surface area. They constantly have to be spread out in the water so they can absorb minerals from the fertilizer, and of course they need oxygen access as well.

Answers and Explanations

23. ❶ This is a Gist-Content question. This lecture is not highly organized and includes interaction from the students. However, despite the short digressions, the lecturer at the beginning and at the end repeats that the point of the talk is to explain how big root systems can be compared to the other parts of the plant. She mentions nutrients and different kinds of grasses, but they are subordinate to her main point. The correct answer is choice 1.

24. ❸ This is a Detail question. The professor says that the scientist in the experiment wanted "to actually see how big the entire system got . . ." "Entire system" refers to root system, so the correct answer is choice 3.

25. ❶ This is an Understanding the Function of What Is Said question. You are asked to listen to this part of the lecture again:

What do you need to do to that water besides put fertilizer in it? Anyone ever actually tried to grow plants in water? You must bubble water through it. Bubble gas through it. I'm sorry, you must bubble gas through it. So, gas, you have to bubble through.

Then you are asked specifically why the professor says: "I'm sorry, you must bubble gas through it."

In real speech, people sometimes misspeak; that is, they say a word that is different from the one they intended. This happens more often in informal speech, and this discussion is informal. As you can see from the script, in the previous sentence the professor said, "You must bubble water through it." *It* refers to water. So she has said, "You must bubble water through water," which does not make sense. The professor immediately corrects herself and repeats the correction twice, so the students know she meant to say "gas." Her purpose is to correct her previous words, so choice 1 is the correct answer.

26. ❷ This is an Understanding Organization question. Although this might seem to be a digression, the professor is using an example to explain why plants that are grown in water must have gas bubbled through the water. When people give houseplants too much water, they are, in effect, "growing the plants in water" unintentionally. The plants die because the roots are deprived of oxygen. The purpose of the discussion of houseplants is to explain why in the experiment, gas was bubbled though the water. The correct answer is choice 2.

27. ❸ You are asked to listen again to this part of the lecture:

> I read about this and the book said one thousand kilometers of roots. I kept thinking: this has to be a mistake. It just doesn't make any sense to me that . . . that . . . that could be right. But that's what all the books have, and no one's ever corrected it. So, let me explain to you about this rye plant.

Like most replay questions, this is an Understanding the Function of What Is Said item. The lecturer says that "one thousand kilometers of roots" did not make any sense to her. She seems to be expressing doubt. But her next sentence makes clear that the "one thousand kilometers" figure is accurate. She intends to explain why such a surprising, or unbelievable, fact is true. The correct answer is choice 3.

28. ❹ This is a Detail question. The professor mentions crabgrass because it is more familiar to her students than rye. She is making the point that many different kinds of grasses produce many roots from a single seed. She mentions that crabgrass begins growing in May, but that is not her point (choice 1). She does not say anything about how much water it requires (choice 2). Choice 3 is the opposite of what she says. Choice 4 is the correct answer.

Questions 29–34

Listening Script

Narrator
Listen to part of a lecture in a business management class.

Professor
OK. Uh, let's talk about organization and structure in a company. How are companies typically structured?

Female student
Functionally.

Professor

And . . . ?

Female student

By projects.

Professor

Right. By function . . . and by projects. Twenty years ago companies were organized in function groups, where people with a certain expertise worked together as a unit—the, uh, architects in one unit, the finance people in another unit. Well, nowadays a lot of companies are organized around projects—like a construction company could be building an office building in one city and an apartment house somewhere else, and each project has its own architects and engineers.

Now, the good thing about project organization is that it's easier to change to adapt to the needs of the project—it's a small group, a dedicated team, not the whole company.

Now, with that in mind, here's a question for you: Why do we continue to organize ourselves by function, even now, when in fact we admit that projects are the lifeblood of a lot of organizations? Why do some companies maintain a functional organization instead of organizing around projects? Yes?

Female student

Because, um, if you don't have that functional structure within your organization, chances are you'd have a harder time meeting the goals of the projects.

Professor

Why?

Female student

Why?

Professor

Listen, let's say we got four new cars we want to design. Why do we need a functional organization? Why not just organize the company around the four projects–these people make car number one, these other people make car number two . . .

Female student

Yeah, but who's gonna be responsible for what? You know, the way you tell who's . . .

Professor

Well . . . well, we'll appoint a manager: new car number one manager, car number two manager–they're completely responsible. Why should we have a single engineering department that has all four cars passing through it?

Female student

When you design a car, you need the expertise of all the engineers in the company. Each engineer needs to be in touch with the entire engineering department.

Professor

Yeah, but I keep . . . I keep asking why? I wanna know why. Yes.

Male student

Well, to eliminate redundancy's probably one of the biggest factors in an organization. So that uh . . . so that there's there's . . . standards of . . . for uniformity and efficiency in the organization.

Professor

OK. And . . . and that's probably the primary reason for functional organization right there—is that we want some engineering consistency. We want the same kind of technology used in all four cars. If we disperse those four engineers into four parts of the organization and they work by themselves, there's a lot less chance that the technology's gonna be the same from car to car. So instead we maintain the functional organization—that means the engineers work together in one part of the building. And their offices are next to each other because we want them to talk to each other. When an engineer works on a project, they bring the expertise of their whole functional group with them.

But there's a downside of that though, isn't there? I mean, organizing a company into functional groups is not all positive. Where's the allegiance of those engineers? It's to their coordinator, right? It's to that chief engineer. But we really want our one engineer, the engineer that's working on car number one, we want that person's loyalty to be to that project as well as to the head of the engineering group. We . . . we really want both, don't we? We want to maintain the functional organization, so we can maintain uniformity and technology transfer, and expertise. We want the cutting edge expertise in every group. But at the same time we also want the engineer to be totally dedicated to the needs of the project. Ideally, we have a . . . a hybrid, a combination of both functional and project organization.

But there's a problem with this kind of hybrid structure. When you have both functional and project organization, well, what does that violate in terms of basic management principles?

Female student

Unity of command.

Professor

Unity of command. That's exactly right. So this . . . this is a vicious violation of unity of command, isn't it? It says that this engineer working on a project seems to have two bosses. We . . . we got the engineering boss, and we got the project manager boss. But the project manager is responsible for the project, and is not the official manager of the engineer who works on the project. And we try to maintain peace in the organizations and sometimes it's disrupted and we have conflicts, don't we? The project manager for car one wants a car part to fit in a particular way, for a specific situation, a specialized case. Well, the, uh, engineering director says no, we gotta have standardization. We gotta have all the cars done this way. We can't make a special mold for that particular part for that particular car. We're not gonna do that. So we got a conflict.

Answers and Explanations

29. ❷ This is a Gist-Content question. Although the lecture includes exchanges between the professor and the students, it is clearly organized around a comparison of the strengths and weaknesses of two different organizational principles. It is not about the automobile industry; that is just an example (choice 1). It is not even about engineering; that is a function that is used as an example (choice 3). It does not offer a resolution of the conflict it describes (choice 4). The correct choice is 2; it is about two alternative organizational structures.

30. ❷ This is an Understanding Organization question. The professor discusses the construction company as an example of the kind of company that could be organized around project teams. Choice 2 is correct. The other choices are about functional organizations, the opposite organizing principle.

31. ❸ In this replay question you listen again to a question from the professor, an answer by a student, and another question by the professor. It is an Understanding the Function of What Is Said question. In order to understand the professor's second question, you must recognize that it is a repetition of the previous question. By repeating his question after the student's answer, the professor is signaling that it has not been satisfactorily answered. He is also signaling that the answer to his question is an important point. The correct answer is choice 3; the student's answer does not include a point the professor wants to make.

32. ❶ This is a Detail question. In this lecture, the professor does not explicitly define "unity of command." But in the last part of the talk he gives an example of the absence of unity of command: "this engineer working on a project seems to have two bosses." Choice 1 is the correct response.

33. ❷ To answer this question you need to recognize the difference between the examples the professor uses in the lecture and the principle that the lecture is actually about. The question asks about a "conflict" discussed in the lecture. Choices 1, 3, and 4 are about specific conflicts that might occur in one of the organizations the professor uses as examples. Only choice 2 is about the general principle of a conflict between two equally important goals. Choice 2 is the correct answer.

34. This question is easy to recognize as a Connecting Content question. Based on information in the lecture, you must indicate whether or not certain statements describe functional organization of project organization. The chart correctly filled out looks like this:

	Functional Organization	Project Organization
It encourages people with similar expertise to work closely together.	✔	
It helps the company to adapt quickly and meet changing needs.		✔
It helps to achieve uniformity in projects.	✔	

TOEFL iBT Speaking

Introduction to the Speaking Section

The TOEFL iBT Speaking section is designed to evaluate the English speaking proficiency of students like you whose native language is not English but who want to pursue undergraduate or graduate study in an English-speaking context. Like all the other sections of the TOEFL iBT, the Speaking section is delivered via computer.

In the Speaking section you will be asked to speak on a variety of topics that draw on personal experience, campus-based situations, and academic-type content material. There are six questions. The first two questions are called Independent Speaking Tasks because they require you to draw entirely on your own ideas, opinions, and experiences when responding. The other four questions are Integrated Speaking Tasks. In these tasks you will listen to a conversation or to an excerpt from a lecture, or read a passage and then listen to a brief discussion or lecture excerpt, before you are asked the question. These questions are called Integrated Tasks because they require that you integrate your English-language skills—listening and speaking, or listening, reading, and speaking. In responding to these questions, you will be asked to base your spoken response on the listening passage or on both the listening passage and the reading passage together.

The Speaking section takes approximately 20 minutes. Response time allowed for each question ranges from 45 to 60 seconds. For Speaking questions that involve listening, you will hear short spoken passages or conversations on head-phones. For Speaking questions that involve reading, you will read short written pas-sages on your computer screen. You can take notes throughout the Speaking section and use your notes when responding to the Speaking questions. For each of the six questions, you will be given a short time to prepare a response. You will answer each of the questions by speaking into a microphone. Your spoken responses will be recorded and sent to a scoring cen-ter, and they will be scored by experienced raters.

TIP:
For all the questions in the test you are given between 45 to 60 seconds to respond. So, when practicing, time your speech accordingly.

Your responses will be scored holistically. This means that the rater will lis-ten for various features in your response and assign a single score based on the overall skill you display in your answer. Although the scoring criteria vary somewhat depending on the question, the raters will generally be listening for the following features in your answer:

TIP:
Familiarize yourself with the scoring rubric; it will help you understand how responses are evaluated.

➤ *Delivery:* How clear your speech is. Good responses are those in which the speech is fluid and clear, with good pronunciation, natural pacing, and natural-sounding intonation patterns.
➤ *Language Use:* How effectively you use grammar and vocabulary to convey your ideas. Raters will be looking to see how well you can control both basic and more complex language structures and use appropriate vocabulary.
➤ *Topic Development:* How fully you answer the question and how coherently you present your ideas. Good responses generally use all or most of the time allotted, and the relationship between ideas and the progression from one idea to the next is clear and easy to follow.

It is important to note that raters do not expect your response to be perfect, and high scoring responses may contain occasional errors and minor lapses in any of the three areas described above.

Use the sample Independent and Integrated Speaking rubrics on pages 242 to 248 to see how responses are scored.

Speaking Question Types

INDEPENDENT: QUESTIONS 1 AND 2

Question 1

For this task, you will be asked to speak about a person, place, object, or event that is familiar to you. You will be given 45 seconds for your response. The topics for this question will vary, but you will always be asked to base your response on personal experience or a familiar topic. You might, for example, be asked about a place you like to visit, an important event in your life, a person who influenced you, or an activity that you enjoy.

This question will always ask you both to *describe* something (for example, an important event, a favorite activity, an influential person) and to *give reasons*—to explain why the event was important, why the activity is one of your favorites, how the person influenced you, etc. Be sure to respond to all parts of the question. Your response should include specific details and/or examples because they will make your description informative and your reasons comprehensible.

> TIP:
> Make a list of familiar topics, and practice speaking about them. You may want to begin by describing a familiar place or recounting a personal experience.

After you are presented with the question, you will have 15 seconds to prepare an answer. You may want to jot down a few brief notes about what you will want to say, but you should not try to write out a full and complete answer. There will not be enough time for you to do that, and raters want to know how well you can *speak* in response to a question, not how well you can *read aloud* from something you have written. If you do jot down notes during the preparation time, you should not rely on them too much in giving your answer.

> TIP:
> When giving descriptions, try to avoid presenting long lists since this will reduce the time you have available to elaborate on the rest of your response.

The question will be read aloud by a narrator and will remain on the screen throughout the time you are giving your response.

Example

The following example shows how a question of this type will appear on your computer screen.

1. Choose a teacher you admire and explain why you admire him or her. Please include specific examples and details in your explanation.

Preparation Time: 15 Seconds

Response Time: 45 Seconds

You will be told when to begin to prepare your response and when to begin speaking. After the question is read, a "Preparation Time" clock will appear below the question and begin to count down from 15 seconds (00:00:15). At the end of 15 seconds you will hear a short beep. After the beep, the clock will change to read "Response Time" and will begin to count down from 45 seconds (00:00:45). When the response time has ended, recording will stop and a new screen will appear alerting you that the response time has ended.

To answer a question like the one above, you would probably begin by briefly identifying the teacher you are going to speak about—not necessarily by name, of course, but by giving just enough relevant information so that someone listening to your response can make sense of your explanation. For example, what subject did the teacher teach? How old were you when you had him or her as a teacher? After briefly describing the teacher in whatever way is useful, you could then proceed to explain what it was about the teacher that made you admire him or her. Perhaps it was something specific that he or she did. If so, you should describe what the teacher did and provide details that illustrate why the action was admirable. Maybe the teacher displayed a special personal quality or had a special character trait. If so, you would want to describe it and give details that provide evidence of it—occasions when you noticed it, the effect it had on you, and so forth. There are many, many ways to answer this question, and of course there is no "right" or "wrong" answer. The important thing, if you were to receive this particular question, is that you communicate enough information about the person to help the rater understand why you find that person admirable.

TIP:
Record your own voice and listen to make sure that your pronunciation and fluency of speech are clear. Then take the recording to an English teacher or tutor who can evaluate your response using the TOEFL iBT Speaking rubric.

Question 2

In this second Independent Speaking Task, you will be presented with two possible actions, situations, or opinions. Then you will be asked to say which of the actions or situations you think is preferable or which opinion you think is more justified and then explain your choice by providing reasons and details. As with question 1, you will have 45 seconds to give your response.

Topics for this question include everyday issues of general interest to a student. You may be asked, for example, whether you think it is better to study at home or at the library, or whether you think students should take courses from a wide variety of fields or else focus on a single subject area, or whether first-year college students should be required to live in the dormitory or be allowed to live off campus in apartments of their own. You could also be presented with two opposing opinions about a familiar topic—for example, about whether or not television has been a benefit for humanity—and you would then be asked which of the two opinions you agree with.

This question will always ask you to state what your choice or preference or opinion is and to explain why—in other words, to support your answer with reasons, explanations, details, and/or examples. It is important that you respond to all parts of the question, and that you are clear about what your opinion is and give reasons that will communicate why you

TIP:
One good exercise would be to state an opinion or a preference and then present supporting reasons clearly and with detail.

have made the choice you did. It does not matter which of the two actions, situations, or opinions you choose, and, as with Question 1, there is no "right" or "wrong" answer. Your response will be rated not on which of the alternatives you choose but rather on how well you explain your choice by supporting it with reasons and details.

Like Question 1, this question will appear on your computer screen and be read aloud at the same time by the narrator, and you will be given 15 seconds to prepare an answer. You should use this time to think about what you want to say, organize your thoughts, and jot down some notes if you feel this will be helpful. But remember, you should not try to write out

TIP:
Study and practice words and expressions commonly used to express opinions, such as:
In my opinion . . .
I believe . . .

a full answer—just a few words or phrases that may help remind you of the direction you want to take in giving your response.

Example

The following example shows how a question of this type will appear on your computer screen.

---

2. Some students study for classes individually. Others study in groups. Which method of studying do you think is better for students and why.

Preparation Time: 15 Seconds
Response Time: 45 Seconds

After you hear the question, you will be told when to begin to prepare your response and when to begin speaking. As with question 1, a "Preparation Time" clock will appear below the question and begin to count down from 15 seconds (00:00:15). At the end of 15 seconds you will hear a short beep. After the beep, the clock will change to read "Response Time" and will begin to count down from 45 seconds (00:00:45). When the response time has ended, recording will stop and a new screen will appear alerting you that the response time has ended.

In answering a question like this one, it is important that you begin by clearly stating what your opinion is: do you think it is better for students to study for classes individually or do you think it is better for them to study in groups? If you do not begin by stating your opinion, it may be difficult for someone listening to your response to understand your reasons for holding that opinion. As for the reasons you give in support of your opinion, they can vary widely and may be based on your own experience and observations. For example, if the position you take is that it is better for students to study alone, you might say that when students meet to study in groups, they often waste time discussing matters that have nothing to do with their class work. You might continue this explanation by contrasting the inefficiency of studying in a group with the kind of

> **TIP:**
> Practice making a recommendation and explaining why it is your preferred course of action.

productivity a student can achieve when studying alone. If you have personal experiences that help illustrate your point, you might want to include them in your explanation. If so, you should be clear about how they illustrate your point. Or perhaps you want to take the opposite position, that it is better for students to study in groups. In that case, you would explain the advantages of group study and the disadvantages of studying alone. Perhaps you think that the more capable students can help the less capable students when students study together. Or perhaps you have found that students who study in groups often share each other's lecture notes and this way they can make sure everyone understands all the material that has been covered in a course. There are any number of good reasons for either choice. In fact, it may be your opinion that in some cases it is better to study in groups and in other cases it is better to study alone. If that is the opinion you would like to express, you should explain—with reasons, examples, and/or specific details—why group study is better in some cases and individual study is better in others. Here again, there is no "right" or "wrong" answer to a question like this. The important thing is to clearly communicate to the person who will be listening to your response what your opinion is and explain the reasons you have for holding it.

INTEGRATED LISTENING/READING/SPEAKING: QUESTIONS 3 AND 4

Question 3

Question 3 is the first of the four Integrated Tasks in the Speaking section. For this question, you will read a short reading passage on your computer screen about a topic of campus-related interest. You will then listen to two people (or in some cases, one person) discussing that topic and expressing an opinion about the topic from the reading. Then you will be asked a question based on what you have read and what you have heard. You will have 60 seconds to speak your response. The general areas from which these topics are typically drawn include university policies, rules or procedures; university plans; campus facilities or quality of life on campus. The topics are designed to be accessible to all test takers and will be presented to you in a way that does not require that you have prior firsthand experience of college or university life in North America.

The reading passage could take various forms. For example, it could be a bulletin from the administration of a university regarding a new parking rule, or a letter to the editor of a campus newspaper responding to a new university policy restricting the use of radios in dormitory rooms, or an article from the campus newspaper discussing a proposal to build a new football stadium. In addition to describing the proposal, the reading passage will usually present two reasons either for or against the proposal. The reading passage is brief, usually between 75 and 100 words long. You will be given sufficient time to read the passage.

In the dialogue (or monologue) that will be played after you have read the reading passage, you will hear one or two speakers—usually students—speaking about the same article (or letter or announcement) that you have just read. If there are two speakers, one of them will have a strong opinion about the the proposed change—either in favor of it or against it—and will give reasons to support that opinion. The discussion is brief and typically lasts between 60 and 80 seconds.

After you have read the passage and then listened to the discussion, you will be asked a question about what you have read and heard. For example, there may be a reading passage that describes plans to make a new university rule and a conversation in which a professor and a student are discussing the rule. If in the conversation the student thinks the new rule is a bad idea, you would be asked to state what the student's opinion is and to explain the reasons the student gives for holding that opinion using information from both the reading and the listening.

This task tests your ability to integrate information from two sources—the reading passage and the listening—and to summarize some aspect of what you have heard. The reading passage provides the context that allows you to understand what the speakers are talking about. The speakers will generally refer to the reading passage only indirectly. Therefore, as you read the reading passage, you should pay attention to a number of things: the description of the proposal (*what* has been proposed, planned, changed, etc.), and the reasons that are given for or against the proposal.

This will help you understand what it is that the two speakers are discussing as you listen to their conversation.

In some cases, a speaker will object to the position taken in the reading and will give information that challenges the reasons offered in the reading for that position. In other cases, a speaker will agree with the position from the reading and will give information that supports those reasons. It is therefore important, as you listen to the discussion, to determine the speaker's opinions toward the proposal and to understand the relationship between what the speakers say and what you have learned from the reading passage.

To answer question 3, it is important to understand not only what the question asks you to do, but also what the question does *not* ask you to do. This type of Integrated Speaking task does not ask for your own opinion; rather, it asks you to state the opinion of one of the speakers and to summarize the speaker's reasons for having that opinion.

You will be given between 40 and 45 seconds to read the passage, depending on its length, after which you will listen to the discussion. Then you will be given 30 seconds to prepare your answer and 60 seconds to respond. As with all the other questions, you may take notes while reading, listening, and preparing your answer, and you may refer to your notes while answering the question.

TIP:
Remember that taking notes on the reading and listening material in the integrated Speaking tasks on the TOEFL iBT test is allowed.

Example

The following sample question consists of an announcement of a university's decision to increase tuition and a discussion between students about whether the increase is justified. This example shows how a question of this type will be presented to you on your computer.

You will hear:

Narrator

In this question you will read a short passage about a campus situation and then listen to a talk on the same topic. You will then answer a question using information from both the reading passage and the talk. After you hear the question, you will have 30 seconds to prepare your response and 60 seconds to speak.

Then you will hear this:

Narrator

City University is planning to increase tuition and fees. Read the announcement about the increase from the president of City University. You will have 45 seconds to read the announcement. Begin reading now.

Announcement from the President

The university has decided to increase tuition and fees for all students by approximately 8% next semester. For the past 5 years, the tuition and fees have remained the same, but it is necessary to increase them now for several reasons. The university has many more students than we had five years ago, and we must hire additional professors to teach these students. We have also made a new commitment to research and technology and will be renovating and upgrading our laboratory facilities to better meet our students' needs.

The reading passage will appear on the screen:
When the passage appears, a clock at the top of your computer screen will begin counting down the time you have to read. When reading time has ended, the passage will disappear from the screen and will be replaced by a picture of two students engaged in conversation.

You will then hear:

Narrator

Now listen to two students as they discuss the announcement.

Then the dialogue will begin.

Man

Oh great, now we have to come up with more money for next semester.

Woman

Yeah, I know, but I can see why. When I first started here, classes were so much smaller than they are now. With this many students, it's hard to get the personal attention you need . . .

Man

Yeah, I guess you're right. You know, in some classes I can't even get a seat. And I couldn't take the math course I wanted to because it was already full when I signed up.

Woman

And the other thing is, well, I am kind of worried about not being able to get a job after I graduate.

Man

Why? I mean you're doing really well in your classes, aren't you?

Woman

I'm doing ok, but the facilities here are so limited. There are some great new experiments in microbiology that we can't even do here . . . there isn't enough equipment in the laboratories, and the equipment they have is out of date. How am I going to compete for jobs with people who have practical research experience? I think the extra tuition will be a good investment.

When the dialogue has ended, the picture of the students will be replaced by the following:

Now get ready to answer the question.

The question will then appear on your computer screen and will also be read aloud by the narrator.

---

3. The woman expresses her opinion of the announcement by the university president. State her opinion and explain the reasons she gives for holding that opinion.

Preparation Time: 30 Seconds

Response Time: 60 Seconds

After you hear the question, you will be told when to begin to prepare your response and when to begin speaking. A "Preparation Time" clock will appear below the question and begin to count down from 30 seconds (00:00:30). At the end of 30 seconds you will hear a short beep. After the beep, the clock will change to read "Response Time" and will begin counting down from 60 seconds (00:00:60). When the response time has ended, recording will stop and a new screen will appear alerting you that the response time has ended.

In giving your response to this question, you should state what the woman's opinion about the tuition increase is, and then explain her reasons for holding that opinion. You will probably have noticed as you listened to the conversation that the woman's reasons are essentially the same as those of the university president but are drawn from her own experience as a student, so in your answer you would probably want to connect information from the two sources. You could perhaps begin by saying that the woman agrees with the announcement and thinks that the university is right to increase its fees. In describing her reasons, you might say that she thinks the tuition increase is necessary because the university can then hire more teachers. She feels that classes are getting too crowded and more teachers are needed. You might also want to mention that she has found it hard to get personal attention from her professors. You could also point out that she agrees that the money should be spent to improve laboratory facilities because they are out of date, and that this has made it hard for her to get the practical laboratory experience she feels she needs to get a good job. Your response should be complete enough that someone listening to your response who has not read the announcement or heard the conversation would understand what the new policy is, what the woman's opinion about it is, and the reasons she has for her opinion. There is a great deal of information in the reading passage and the conversation, and you are not expected to summarize all of the information in giving your response.

> TIP:
> Recognize the attitude of the speaker through intonation, stress, and word choice. This helps you understand his or her point of view and plan an appropriate response.

Question 4

Question 4 is the second of the Integrated Speaking Tasks. For this task you will read a short passage about an academic subject and listen to a professor give a brief excerpt from a lecture on that subject. You will then be asked a question which you will answer based on what you have read and heard. You will have 60 seconds in which to give your spoken response.

The topics for this question are drawn from a variety of fields: life science, social science, physical science, and the humanities. Although the topics are are academic in nature, none of the written passages, lectures, or the questions themselves requires prior knowledge of any academic field in particular. The language and concepts used are designed to be accessible to you no matter what your academic specialization may be.

The reading passage is usually between 75 and 100 words in length. It provides background or context to help you understand the lecture that will follow. The reading passage will usually treat the topic in somewhat general and abstract terms, and the lecture will treat the topic more specifically and concretely, often by providing an extended example, counterexample, or application of the concept presented in the reading. To answer the question that follows the lecture, you will need to draw on the reading as well as the lecture, and integrate and convey key information from both these sources.

> **TIP:**
> Find listening and reading material on a topic that you like. The reading and the listening material can provide similar or different views. Take notes on what you listen to and read and create outlines. Use your notes and outlines to orally summarize the information and ideas from the listening and reading materials. Try to paraphrase what you have heard and read by using different words and grammatical structures.

For example, some tasks will contain a reading passage that gives the definition of a general principle or process and a lecture that discusses a specific instance and/or counterexample of the principle or process. For a pairing like this, you might be asked to explain the principle or process using the specific information from the listening. Or another pairing might include a reading passage that describes a problem and a lecture that presents the success, failure, or unintended consequences of an attempt to solve the problem, together with a question that asks you to explain the attempt to solve the problem and account for its results.

The sample question 4 task presented below is a typical example. It begins with a reading passage discussing a general concept—the domestication of animal species—by describing two characteristics that make an animal species suitable for domestication. This passage is coupled with a lecture in which the professor talks about the behavior of two species of animals—a familiar domesticated animal that has both of the characteristics and a common, undomesticated species that lacks these characteristics. The question asks you to apply the more general information you have learned in the reading to the examples discussed in the lecture, and explain how the behavior of the two species of animals is related to their suitability for domestication.

Example

The following example shows how a question of this type will be presented to you on your computer. Question 4 will be presented visually in the same way as Question 3.

First you will hear the narrator say this:

Narrator

In this question you will read a short passage on an academic subject and then listen to a talk on the same topic. You will then answer a question using information from both the reading passage and the talk. After you hear the question, you will have 30 seconds to prepare your response and 60 seconds to speak.

Then you will hear this:

Narrator
Now read the passage about animal domestication. You have 45 seconds to read the passage. Begin reading now.

The reading passage will then appear on the screen:

Animal Domestication

For thousands of years, humans have been able to domesticate, or tame, many large mammals that in the wild live together in herds. Once tamed, these mammals are used for agricultural work and transportation. Yet some herd mammals are not easily domesticated.

A good indicator of an animal's suitability for domestication is how protective the animal is of its territory. Non-territorial animals are more easily domesticated than territorial animals because they can live close together with animals from other herds. A second indicator is that animals with a hierarchical social structure, in which herd members follow a leader, are easy to domesticate, since a human can function as the "leader."

A clock at the top of your computer screen will count down the time you have to read. When reading time has ended, a picture of a professor in front of a class will appear on the screen:

And you will hear this:

Narrator
Now listen to a lecture on this topic in an ecology class.

Then you will hear the lecture:

Professor
So we've been discussing the suitability of animals for domestication . . . particularly animals that live together in herds. Now, if we take horses, for example . . . in the wild, horses live in herds that consist of one male and several females and their young. When a herd moves, the dominant male leads, with the dominant female and her young immediately behind him. The dominant female and her young are then followed immediately by the second most important female and her young, and so on. This is why domesticated horses can be harnessed one after the other in a row. They're "programmed" to follow the lead of another horse. On top of that, you often find different herds of horses in the wild occupying overlapping areas—they don't fight off other herds that enter the same territory.

But it's exactly the opposite with an animal like the uh, the antelope . . . which . . . well, antelopes are herd animals too. But unlike horses, a male antelope will fight fiercely to prevent another male from entering its territory during the breeding season, OK—very different from the behavior of horses. Try keeping a couple of male antelopes together in a small space and see what happens. Also, antelopes don't have a social hierarchy—they don't instinctively follow any leader. That makes it harder for humans to control their behavior.

When the lecture has ended, the picture of the professor will be replaced by a screen instructing you to get ready to answer the question. Then the question will appear on the screen and will be read aloud by a narrator as well.

---

4. The professor describes the behavior of horses and antelope in herds. Explain how their behavior is related to their suitability for domestication.

Preparation Time: 30 Seconds

Response Time: 60 Seconds

After you hear the question, you will be told when to begin to prepare your response and when to begin speaking. A "Preparation Time" clock will appear below the question and begin to count down from 30 seconds (00:00:30). At the end of 30 seconds you will hear a short beep. After the beep, the clock will change to read "Response Time" and will begin to count down from 60 seconds (00:00:60). When the response time has ended, recording will stop and a new screen will appear alerting you that the response time has ended.

To answer this question, you would use information from both the reading passage and the lecture, linking the specific information the professor provides in the lecture with the more general concepts introduced in the reading. For example, you could begin your response by saying that herd animals can be easily domesticated if they have a hierarchical social structure and are not territorial, and that this is why it is easier to domesticate horses than antelopes. You would want to provide some details about the behavior of horses, pointing out that their hierarchical social structure makes them willing to follow one another and thus allows a human being to act as their

TIP:
Read a short article. Make an outline that includes only the major points of the article. Use the outline to orally summarize the information. Then add detail to the outline and orally summarize it again.

leader. You could also say that because horses are not territorial, they can be harnessed together without fighting. You would probably want to contrast horses' behavior with that of antelopes, which are territorial. You could explain that unlike horses, male antelopes fight if they are together, and that because antelopes do not have a social hierarchy, humans can't control them by acting as their leader. Notice that you are not asked to summarize all the information in the reading and in the lecture about animal domestication and horses and antelopes. But you should provide enough information so that even a listener who had not read the passage or listened to the lecture would be able to understand your explanation.

Other question 4 tasks include such pairings as a reading passage about malaria that discusses, in general terms, what is now known about the casues of this disease, how it is spread, and how it can be prevented, coupled with a lecture about the history of malaria research that describes the work of one particular doctor in the 1800s. The question that follows this lecture asks you to describe the doctor's beliefs about the cause of malaria and the recommendations he made to prevent its spread, and then to explain why his recommendations were effective. To answer this question, you would tell how the doctor's recommendations were in line with what is now known to be true about the disease. Here, as in all speaking questions that are based on academic content, you are provided with all the facts necessary to give your response, and no outside knowledge is assumed.

INTEGRATED LISTENING/SPEAKING: QUESTIONS 5 AND 6

Question 5

The Integrated Listening/Speaking tasks in questions 5 and 6 do not have a reading passage associated with them. For question 5, you will listen to a short conversation about a campus-related situation and respond to a question based on what you have heard. In the conversation, two people will typically discuss a problem and two possible solutions. The problem is one that concerns one of them or both of them directly. After you listen to the conversation, you will be asked to briefly describe the situation that was discussed in the conversation and to give your own opinion about solutions to the problem. You will have 60 seconds in which to give your spoken response. The topics for this task are based on common, everyday situations or problems that might arise at a college or university.

Typically, the speakers in the conversation will be two students, or a student and a professor, or a student and a university staff member (e.g., a teaching assistant, librarian, administrator, etc.). The problems may involve such issues as scheduling conflicts, unavoidable absences, unavailable resources, student elections, financial difficulties, and so forth. In some cases, the problem is one that affects both speakers equally, and they must decide on a single, common solution. In other cases, the problem may involve only one of the speakers, and in this situation that speaker will present his or her problem and the other speaker (or both of them) will propose the two possible solutions. The conversations are usually between 60 and 90 seconds long.

TIP:
It is very important to practice your conversational speaking skills as often as possible. One way of doing this might be joining an English language conversation club. If such clubs do not exist in your area, you may want to start your own and, if possible, invite native speakers to join in.

The question you are asked when the conversation has ended has several parts: you are asked first to describe the problem that the speakers are discussing, then to state which of the two solutions you prefer, and finally to explain why you prefer that solution. The reasons you give for your preference can include information provided by the speakers in their discussion as well as your own experiences. For example, if your own experience with a similar or related problem is relevant to your choice of one solution over the other, you may draw on that experience when explaining your reasons. Here, as in other Speaking tasks in which you are asked to choose between two alternatives and give reasons for your choice, it does not matter which of the two proposed solutions you choose, and there is no "right" solution or "wrong" solution. Your response will be rated not on which solution you choose but rather on how well you describe the problem, state the solution you prefer, and explain the reasons for your preference.

The types of problems discussed by the speakers in these conversations will vary. The problem could be that one of the speakers needs to arrange transportation for a class field trip and does not know whom to ask. Or the problem could be that a student has a doctor's appointment scheduled at the same time as a meeting with job recruiters. Another could be about a student who is not getting along with other members of his or her study group. In the following sample question, the speakers are discussing a problem that you may find very familiar: too much schoolwork and not enough time to do it.

Example

The following example shows how you would hear and see this task on your computer:

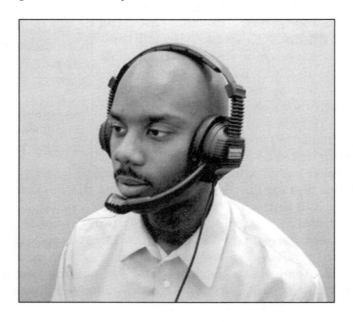

You will hear:

Narrator

In this question, you will listen to a conversation. You will then be asked to talk about the information in the conversation and to give your opinion about the ideas presented. After you hear the question, you will have 20 seconds to prepare your response and 60 seconds to speak.

Then a picture of two students will appear on the screen.

Then you will hear the conversation:

Man

Hey Lisa, how's it going?

Woman

Hi Mark. Uh, I'm OK, I guess, but my schoolwork is really stressing me out.

Man *[sympathetically]*

Yeah? What's wrong?

Woman

Well, I've got a paper to write and two exams to study for. And a bunch of math problems to finish. It's just so much that I can't concentrate on any of it. I start concentrating on studying for one of my exams, and then I'm like, how long's it gonna take to finish that problem set?

Man

Wow. Sounds like you've got a lot more work than you can handle right now. *[Not wanting to sound too pushy]* Look, have you talked to some of your professors . . . mean, you know, try to explain the problem. Look, you could probably get an extension on your paper, or on the math assignment . . .

Woman

You think? It would give me a little more time to prepare for my exams right now.

Man

Well, I mean another thing that you might do . . . I mean have you tried making yourself a schedule? I mean that's what I do when I'm feeling overwhelmed.

Woman

What does that do for you?

Man

Well, I mean it helps you to focus your energies. You know, you make yourself a chart that shows the next few days and the time till your stuff is due and . . .

Woman

Uh-huh . . . *[meaning "I'm listening"]*

Man

I mean think about what you need to do and when you have to do it by. You know then start filling in your schedule—like, all right 9:00 [nine] to 11:30 [eleven-thirty] A.M., study for exam. 12:00 [twelve] to 3:00 [three], work on problem set. But I mean don't make the time periods too long. Like, don't put in eight hours of studying—you know, you'll get tired, or start worrying about your other work again. But if you keep to your schedule, you know you'll just have to worry about one thing at a time.

Woman

Yeah, that might work. *[somewhat noncommittally]*

When the conversation has ended, the picture of the two students will be replaced by a screen instructing you to get ready to answer the question. Then the question will appear on the screen and will be read aloud by the narrator.

---

5. The students discuss two possible solutions to the woman's problem. Describe the problem. Then state which of the two solutions you prefer and explain why.

> Preparation Time: 20 Seconds
>
> Response Time: 60 Seconds

After you hear the question, you will be told when to begin to prepare your response and when to begin speaking. A "Preparation Time" clock will appear below the question and begin to count down from 20 seconds (00:00:20). At the end of 20 seconds you will hear a short beep. After the beep, the clock will change to read "Response Time" and will begin to count down from 60 seconds (00:00:60). When the response time has ended, recording will stop and a new screen will appear alerting you that the response time has ended.

To answer this question, you should begin by briefly describing the woman's problem, giving just enough details so that someone listening to your response but who has not heard the conversation would know what you are talking about. Then you would state which solution you prefer, and explain why. If you believe the second solution is preferable, you would probably begin by saying that you think it would be better if the woman prepared a schedule, and then you would proceed to explain why. There are any number of reasons you can give: you might say, for example, that the problem of too much work to do is something that the woman is going to confront in the future as well, and that if she learns how to organize a schedule now, this will help her throughout her academic career. You could also speak about the disadvantages of the other solution: for example, even though her professors might be willing to give her an extension, they might somehow penalize her for it by grading her assignments more severely. If your own personal experiences are relevant to your reasons for choosing one solution over the other, you may wish to mention those experiences, but you should keep in mind that the focus of the question is the problem faced by the speaker or speakers, not your own situation. Remember, too, a question like this can be answered in many different ways, and there is no "right" or "wrong" choice.

Question 6

This integrated task, the last of the six Speaking tasks, is based on academic content. For this task you will first listen to a professor present a brief excerpt from a lecture on an academic subject and then you will be asked a question about what you have heard. You will have 60 seconds in which to give your spoken response.

As with Question 4 (the other Speaking task that is based on academic content), the topics for this question are drawn from a variety of fields within the life sciences, social sciences, physical sciences, and the humanities. Here too, no prior knowledge of any academic field in particular is required for you to understand the lecture or answer the question.

The lecture excerpt is between 60 and 90 seconds long, and focuses on a single topic. Usually the professor will begin the lecture by defining a concept, by highlighting an issue, or by introducing a phenomenon, and will then go on to discuss important aspects of it or perspectives relating to it. The lecture will contain illustrative examples that help explain or clarify the main concept or issue. The question you are asked after you have heard the lecture will typically ask that you explain the main concept or issue of the lecture, using points and examples that were given in the lecture.

The lectures can be about processes, methods, theories, ideas, or phenomena of any type—natural, social, psychological, etc. If a lecture is about a process, the professor might explain the process by describing some of its functions. In a lecture about a theory, the professor might explain the theory by describing its applications. In a lecture about a phenomenon, the professor might explain it through examples that illustrate its causes or its effects.

> **TIP:**
> Find a textbook that includes questions about the material at the end of chapters, etc. Practice answering the questions orally.

In the sample Question 6 given below, the lecture is about a social phenomenon—the emergence of a national culture in the United States in the early twentieth century. The professor illustrates this phenomenon by describing two of its causes—radio and the automobile—and how they contributed to it. After you hear the lecture, you are asked to use information from the lecture to explain how the two causes contributed to the formation of a national culture.

Example

The following example shows how a question of this type will be presented to you on your computer.

First you will hear the narrator say this:

Narrator

In this question, you will listen to part of a lecture. You will then be asked to summarize important information from the lecture. After you hear the question, you will have 20 seconds to prepare your response and 60 seconds to speak.

Then a picture of a professor standing in front of a class of students will appear on your screen, and you will hear the narrator say:

Narrator

Now listen to part of a talk in a United States history class.

The professor will then begin the lecture.

Professor

Because the United States is such a large country, it took time for a common national culture to emerge. One hundred years ago there was very little communication among the different regions of the United States. One result of this lack of communication was that people around the United States had very little in common with one another. People in different parts of the country spoke differently, dressed differently, and behaved differently. But connections among Americans began to increase thanks to two technological innovations: the automobile and the radio.

Automobiles began to be mass produced in the 1920's, which meant they became less expensive and more widely available. Americans in small towns and rural communities now had the ability to travel with ease to nearby cities. They could even take vacations to other parts of the country. The increased mobility provided by automobiles changed people's attitudes and created links that had not existed before. For example, people in small towns began to adopt behaviors, clothes, and speech that were popular in big cities or in other parts of the country.

As more Americans were purchasing cars, radio ownership was also increasing dramatically. Americans in different regions of the country began to listen to the same popular radio programs and musical artists. People repeated things they heard on the radio—some phrases and speech patterns heard in songs and radio programs began to be used by people all over the United States. People also listened to news reports on the radio. They heard the same news throughout the country, whereas in newspapers much news tended to be local. Radio brought Americans together by offering them shared experiences and information about events around the country.

When the lecture has ended, the picture of the professor will be replaced by a screen instructing you to get ready to answer the question. Then the question will appear on the screen and be read aloud at the same time by the narrator.

---

6. Using points and examples from the talk, explain how the automobile and the radio contributed to a common culture in the United States.

Preparation Time: 20 Seconds

Response Time: 60 Seconds

After you hear the question, you will be told when to begin preparing your response and when to begin speaking. A "Preparation Time" clock will appear below the question and begin to count down from 20 seconds (00:00:20). At the end of 20 seconds you will hear a short beep. After the beep, the clock will change to read "Response Time" and will begin to count down from 60 seconds (00:00:60). When the response time has ended, recording will stop and a new screen will appear alerting you that the response time has ended.

To answer this question, you might begin with a little background and mention that the United States did not have a common culture 100 years ago because people in different regions of the country did not communicate much with each other. Then you could say that the automobile and the radio changed this situation, and go on to summarize the information from the lecture that explains how they caused this change. For example, you could say that when automobiles became inexpensive, people from small towns could travel easily to cities or to other parts of the country, and that when they began to do this, they started acting like people from those other regions and started to dress and speak in the same way. As for the role that radio played in the emergence of a national culture, you could point out that when radio became popular, people from different parts of the country began listening to the same programs and the same news reports and began to speak alike and have similar experiences and ideas. If you have time, you could conclude by saying that these similar ways of speaking and dressing and thinking became the national culture of the United States. You should remember that you do not need to repeat all of the details provided in the lecture. There is simply too much information in the lecture to allow you to do that. You should, however, convey enough information so that someone who has not heard the lecture would be able to form a good idea of what the professor was explaining to the class.

Other lectures for question 6 could include such topics as how people learn, and the central concept might be that learning occurs when two events are associated in the brain. The professor would illustrate that concept by describing two different ways that events can be associated in the brain, and you would be asked to use points and examples from the lecture to explain how these two ways of associating events result in learning. Or in a lecture about money, the professor might provide two different definitions of the concept and illustrate them with two examples, and you would be asked in your response to explain the two definitions, using the two examples. The question that follows a lecture like this would typically ask you to use points and examples that you heard in the lecture to explain how people learn or what the definitions of money are.

Strategies for Raising Your TOEFL Speaking Score

➤ When you take the Practice TOEFL Speaking section in this chapter, listen carefully to each of your recorded responses. Create a set of guiding questions to help you evaluate your performance. Here are some examples of the kind of questions you may want to include:

◆ Did I complete the task?
◆ Did I speak clearly?
◆ Did I make grammatical errors?
◆ Did I use words correctly?
◆ Did I organize my ideas clearly and appropriately?
◆ Did I provide a complete response?
◆ Did I use the time effectively?

Once you have completed your evaluation, decide what changes you want to make to your response. Then try again, making a new recording. Compare the two recordings and determine if any further revisions are necessary.

➤ Try to periodically analyze your strengths and weaknesses. Try to understand what you are and are not able to do well and why.

➤ When you monitor your speaking practice, try to evaluate the pace of your speech. After each practice ask yourself the following questions:

◆ Did I speak too fast?
◆ Did I speak too slowly?
◆ Did I pause too often?

➤ You may want to monitor your own progress by keeping an audio journal, which entails keeping samples of your speaking activities or practices. You can also ask for feedback from one or more friends, tutors, or teachers.

TIPS FOR THE DAY OF THE TEST

➤ Remember that taking notes on the reading and listening material in the integrated Speaking tasks on the TOEFL iBT test is allowed.

➤ Listen to the item directions carefully to understand exactly what you are being asked to do.

➤ Use your preparation time as effectively as possible. Plan your response by thinking about the important ideas you want to convey in a simple, organized fashion.

➤ Do not begin speaking until you are told to do so.

➤ Answer each question as completely as possible in the time allowed.

➤ Make sure to adjust your microphone and volume carefully.

➤ Speak into the microphone at an appropriate volume. Do not put your mouth directly onto the microphone. If you touch your mouth to the microphone, scorers may find it difficult to understand what you are saying.

➤ Avoid whispering. If you whisper, scorers may find it difficult to understand what you are saying.

PRACTICE TOEFL iBT SPEAKING SECTION

INSTRUCTIONS

The following Speaking section of the test will last approximately 20 minutes. To complete it, you will need a CD player, as well as a tape recorder and a blank cassette tape.

During the test, you will answer 6 speaking questions. Two of the questions ask about familiar topics. Four questions ask about short conversations, lectures, and reading passages. You may take notes as you listen to the conversations and lectures. The questions and the reading passages are printed in this test book. The time you will have to prepare your response and to speak is printed below each question. You should answer all of the questions as completely as possible in the time allowed. The preparation time begins immediately after you hear the question. You will be told when to begin to prepare and when to begin speaking.

Play the CD tracks listed in the test instructions. Record each of your responses.

When you are finished, go on to the next section. It contains explanations of the answers and will help you determine your score.

PRACTICE TOEFL iBT SPEAKING SECTION

1.

You will now be asked a question about a familiar topic. After you hear the question, you will have 15 seconds to prepare your response and 45 seconds to speak.

Now play track #24 on the CD to hear Question 1.

Choose a place you go to often that is important to you and explain why it is important. Please include specific details in your explanation.

Preparation time: 15 seconds
Response time: 45 seconds

2.

You will now be asked to give your opinion about a familiar topic. After you hear the question, you will have 15 seconds to prepare your response and 45 seconds to speak.

Now play track #25 on the CD to hear Question 2.

Some college students choose to take courses in a variety of subject areas in order to get a broad education. Others choose to focus on a single subject area in order to have a deeper understanding of that area. Which approach to course selection do you think is better for students and why?

Preparation time: 15 seconds
Response time: 45 seconds

3.

You will now read a short passage and then listen to a talk on the same topic. You will then be asked a question about them. After you hear the question, you will have 30 seconds to prepare your response and 60 seconds to speak.

Now play track #26 on the CD to hear Question 3.

Reading time: 45 seconds

Bus Service Elimination Planned

The university has decided to discontinue its free bus service for students. The reason given for this decision is that few students ride the buses and the buses are expensive to operate. Currently, the buses run from the center of campus past university buildings and through some of the neighborhoods surrounding the campus. The money saved by eliminating the bus service will be used to expand the overcrowded student parking lots.

The man expresses his opinion of the university's plan to eliminate the bus service. State his opinion and explain the reasons he gives for holding that opinion.

Preparation time: 30 seconds
Response time: 60 seconds

4.

You will now read a short passage and then listen to a talk on the same academic topic. You will then be asked a question about them. After you hear the question, you will have 30 seconds to prepare your response and 60 seconds to speak.

Now play track #27 on the CD to hear Question 4.

Reading Time: 45 seconds

Social Interaction

People deal with each other every day. This interaction is at the heart of social life. The study of social interaction is concerned with the influence people have over one another's behavior. People take each other into account in their daily behavior and in fact, the very presence of others can affect behavior. For example, one principle of social interaction, audience effects, suggests that individuals' work is affected by their knowledge that they are visible to others, that the presence of others tends to alter the way people behave or perform an activity.

Explain how the examples of tying shoes and learning to type demonstrate the principle of audience effects.

Preparation time: 30 seconds
Response time: 60 seconds

5.

You will now listen to a conversation. You will then be asked a question about it. After you hear the question, you will have 20 seconds to prepare your response and 60 seconds to speak.

Now play track #28 on the CD to hear Question 5.

The speakers discuss two possible solutions to the woman's problem. Describe the problem and the two solutions. Then explain what you think the woman should do and why.

Preparation time: 20 seconds
Response time: 60 seconds

6.

You will now listen to part of a lecture. You will then be asked a question about it. After you hear the question, you will have 20 seconds to prepare your response and 60 seconds to speak.

Now play track #29 on the CD to hear Question 6 .

Using points and examples from the talk, explain the two definitions of money presented by the professor.

Preparation time: 20 seconds
Response Time: 60 seconds

This is the end of the Speaking section of the TOEFL iBT test.

LISTENING SCRIPTS AND SAMPLE RESPONSES WITH RATERS' COMMENTS

The raters who listen to your response will analyze it in three general categories. These categories are Delivery, Language Use, and Topic Development. All three categories have equal importance. Use the sample Independent and Integrated Speaking rubrics on pages 242 to 246 to see how responses are scored.

This section includes important points that should be covered when answering each question. All of these points must be present in a response in order for it to receive the highest score in the Topic Development category. These important points are guides to the kind of information raters expect to hear in a high-level response.

This section also refers to example responses on the accompanying CD. Some responses were scored at the highest level, while others were not. The responses are followed by explanations for their scores.

Question 1

Listening Script

Narrator

Choose a place you go to often that is important to you and explain why it is important. Please include specific details in your explanation.

Preparation time: 15 seconds
Response time: 45 seconds

Important Points

In this question, you are asked to talk about a place you like to go often and explain why it is important to you. People who listen to your response should be able to easily follow the progression of your ideas. Responses scored at the highest level contain ideas supported with details and elaboration that go beyond simple structures. For example, the response, *"I like this place because it is nice"* does not have enough detail. Why is this place nice? Developing this idea more might look like this: *"I like this place because it is quiet and peaceful. Listening to the ocean waves on the beach relaxes me and helps me to relieve stress."*

Sample Responses

Play track #30 on the CD to hear a high-level response for Question 1.

Rater's Comments

The speaker continues speaking throughout the entire 45 seconds. She speaks clearly using a variety of vocabulary and a wide range of grammar. Her reasons are well developed. She uses specific details about why France is an important place for her. Instead of just saying, *"I'm interested in French culture because it is interesting,"* she elaborates by talking about her friend, her interest in French history and culture from a young age, and the food. There is a logical progression of ideas that make the response easy to understand.

Play track #31 on the CD to hear a mid-level response for Question 1.

Rater's Comments

This response is sustained and the speech is generally understandable. At times, though, the speaker's pronunciation makes it difficult to understand the meaning of her ideas. She really gives only one reason why she likes shopping. This reason is used repetitively without much elaboration. Shopping is something she likes very much and makes her feel better. She could have added complexity to her ideas by saying something like "*When I go shopping, I usually go with friends and we have a good time together without thinking about jobs, or schoolwork.*" She also makes some basic grammatical errors and uses a limited range of vocabulary.

Question 2

Listening Script

Narrator

Some college students choose to take courses in a variety of subject areas in order to get a broad education. Others choose to focus on a single subject area in order to have a deeper understanding of that area. Which approach to course selection do you think is better for students and why?

Preparation time: 15 seconds
Response time: 45 seconds

Important Points

In this question, you are asked to make a choice between two given options. In a complete, well-developed response, you should clearly state your choice/preference. You may choose both options, but you must support both of them with reasons that are detailed. If you think taking a variety of courses is better, make sure you explain in detail what your reasons are for having that opinion. Here is an example: "Taking a variety of courses is better because it gives you an opportunity to learn about subjects outside of your field of study. Because so many fields of study are related, you never know when knowledge from one area will be helpful in another." This kind of response clearly shows which option was chosen and includes a detailed reason why it was chosen.

Sample Responses

Play track #32 on the CD to hear a high-level response for Question 2.

Rater's Comments

The speaker gives a thoughtful, sustained answer with ideas and reasons that progress logically. He speaks fluently and demonstrates good control of grammar and vocabulary, with only minor errors that do not obscure the meaning of his ideas. The speaker very clearly states his opinion that the answer depends on whether you are an undergraduate or graduate student. He continues by giving a detailed reason that supports each perspective.

Play track #33 on the CD to hear a low-level response for Question 2.

Rater's Comments

Although the speaker's pronunciation is clear, his pace is slow and irregular. The clearest parts of his speech are words that he has taken from the prompt of the question. He demonstrates very limited vocabulary. His thoughts are understandable at the sentence level, but there are very few connections between sentences. Such connections would help listeners to understand what is being said or enable them to predict what will likely come next. The opinion is stated in the beginning. However, he frequently uses words from the prompt and repeats the same idea throughout the response.

Question 3

Listening Script

Narrator

The university is planning to eliminate its bus service. Read the article from the university newspaper about the plan. You will have 45 seconds to read the article. Begin reading now.

Reading time: 45 seconds

Bus Service Elimination Planned

The university has decided to discontinue its free bus service for students. The reason given for this decision is that few students ride the buses and the buses are expensive to operate. Currently, the buses run from the center of campus past university buildings and through some of the neighborhoods surrounding the campus. The money saved by eliminating the bus service will be used to expand the overcrowded student parking lots.

Narrator

Now listen to two students discussing the article.

Man

I don't like the university's plan.

Woman

Really? I've ridden those buses, and sometimes there were only a few people on the bus. It <u>did</u> seem like kind of a waste.

Man

I see your point. But I think the problem is the route's out-of-date. It only goes through the neighborhoods that've gotten too expensive for students to live in. It's ridiculous that they haven't already changed the route—you know, so it goes where most off-campus students live <u>now</u>. I bet if they did that, they'd get plenty of students riding those buses.

Woman

Well, at least they're adding more parking. It's gotten really tough to find a space.

Man

That's the other part I don't like, actually. Cutting back the bus service and adding parking's just gonna encourage more students to drive on campus. And that'll just add to the noise around campus and create more traffic . . . and that'll increase the need for <u>more</u> parking spaces . . .

Woman

Yeah, I guess I can see your point. Maybe it would be better if more students used the buses instead of driving.

Man

Right. And the university should make it easier to do that, not harder.

Narrator

The man expresses his opinion of the university's plan to eliminate the bus service. State his opinion and explain the reasons he gives for holding that opinion.

Preparation time: 30 seconds
Response time: 60 seconds

Important Points

The university plans to eliminate the bus service because it is too expensive to run and too few students use it. The man disagrees with the university plan. He believes the reason few students take the bus is that the route goes to neighborhoods where students do not live. If the routes were changed, many more students would ride the bus.

The man disagrees with the way the university plans to use the money it saves on the bus service. Building more parking lots on campus will encourage more students to drive on campus. This would increase noise and traffic on campus.

Sample Responses

Play track #34 on the CD to hear a high-level response for Question 3.

Rater's Comments

The speaker gives a clear and coherent response that is detailed and accurate. He speaks quickly, but this does not prevent him from being understood. He very clearly states the man's opinion and summarizes the man's reasons for having that opinion. He uses complex grammatical structures and a wide variety of appropriate vocabulary. As a result, his speech seems to flow automatically.

Play track #35 on the CD to hear a mid-level response for Question 3.

Rater's Comments

The speaker's first language moderately influences her pronunciation, intonation, and pacing. This creates some listener effort. She provides content that is relevant to the task, but her limitations in language use hinder her ability to accurately convey relevant details. She fills the entire time with understandable speech. However, she incorrectly repeats throughout the response time that students cannot afford to ride the bus. She also says that few students will drive cars and overcrowd the parking lots. This creates confusion for the listener. The speaker never mentions the man's concern about increased noise and traffic on campus.

Question 4
Listening Script

Narrator
Now read the passage about the nature of social interaction. You will have 45 seconds to read the passage. Begin reading now.

Reading Time: 45 seconds

Social Interaction

People deal with each other every day. This interaction is at the heart of social life. The study of social interaction is concerned with the influence people have over one another's behavior. People take each other into account in their daily behavior and in fact, the very presence of others can affect behavior. For example, one principle of social interaction, audience effects, suggests that individuals' work is affected by their knowledge that they are visible to others, that the presence of others tends to alter the way people behave or perform an activity.

Narrator
Now listen to part of a talk in a sociology class. The professor is discussing <u>audience</u> <u>effects</u>.

Professor
OK, so we said that the way we interact with others has an impact on our behavior . . .

In fact, there's some interesting research to suggest that in one type of interaction—when we're being observed specifically, when we <u>know</u> we're being watched as we perform some activity— we tend to <u>increase the speed </u>at which we perform that activity.

In one study, college students were asked to each put on a pair of shoes—shoes with laces they would have to tie. Now one group of students was told that they would be observed. The second group, however, didn't <u>know</u> they were being observed. The students who were aware that they were being watched actually tied their shoes much faster than the students who thought they were alone.

Other studies confirm the same is true even when we're learning new activities. Let's say someone is learning a new task—for example, learning how to type. When they're conscious of being observed, they'll likely begin typing at a much faster rate than they would if they were alone.

But, and this is interesting, the study also showed that certain common behavior—things people typically do, like . . . making mistakes when you're learning something new that behavior pattern will also increase. So in other words, when we're learning to type, and we know we're being watched, we'll type faster but we'll also make more mistakes.

Narrator

Explain how the examples of tying shoes and learning to type demonstrate the principle of audience effects.

Preparation time: 30 seconds
Response time: 60 seconds

Important Points

The principle of audience effects suggests that when people are aware of being observed, their behavior changes. Specifically, in the two studies described, people worked faster when they were aware of being observed. In one study, two groups were told to put on shoes that tied. One group was told it would be observed and the other was not. The group that knew it was being observed tied shoes much faster than the other group. In learning to type, those being observed type faster, but they also make more mistakes than those not aware of being observed.

Sample Responses

Play track #36 on the CD to hear a high-level response for Question 4.

Rater's Comments

The speaker speaks clearly. She identifies the concept of audience effects and the two examples from the listening. She organizes her response in a logical way that leads the listener from one sentence to the next. She supports her response with accurate details and demonstrates a sophisticated level of both grammatical structures and vocabulary. This is evident in the way she smoothly transitions from one idea to the next and the efficient use of language to accurately summarize the examples from the listening. There are only very minor errors in language use, but they do not prevent her response from being understood.

Play track #37 on the CD to hear a mid-level response for Question 4.

Rater's Comments

The speaker sustains his response throughout. His pronunciation and intonation is affected by the speaker's first language. These pronunciation errors make it hard to know what he means. The speaker identifies the concept and the two examples, but with inaccuracies. Instead of summarizing each experiment, he combines the summary of both experiments. This causes him to incorrectly conclude that you make more mistakes when you are being watched while tying your shoes. Additionally, the speaker sometimes stumbles when trying to form basic words (*slowlier*), which shows a moderate control of grammar and vocabulary.

Question 5
Listening Script

Narrator

Listen to a conversation between a student and her geology professor.

Man

Mary, I'm so glad I ran into you.

Woman

Oh hello, Professor Jensen.

Man

Listen, I know it's short notice . . . and maybe you've already made plans for spring break . . . but . . . one of my students just dropped out of the field trip to the Smithson River Caves. You're next on the waiting list, so now there's room for you to come along.

Woman

You're kidding! [*disappointed*] I didn't think there was a chance . . . and . . . well, it's a three-day trip, right? I agreed to spend next week helping Professor Clark set up the new museum exhibition. I think she's really counting on me.

Man

Yeah, three days. But you know . . . if you'd rather come on the field trip, why not speak with her and see if she has anyone to replace you?

Woman

Yeah, I'd hate to miss out on the caves. I'll definitely ask Professor Clark if there's someone else who could help her.

Man

You know . . . we don't leave until Wednesday. If you still have to help out, any chance you could get the museum setup done before then?

Woman

Oh yeah . . . not until Wednesday . . . so then yeah . . . maybe that's possible too.

Narrator

The speakers discuss two possible solutions to the woman's problem. Describe the problem and the two solutions. Then explain what you think the woman should do and why.

Preparation time: 20 seconds
Response time: 60 seconds

Important Points

The problem the student faces is a conflict between an earlier commitment to help with a museum exhibition setup and a more recent opportunity to go on a field trip led by one of her professors. She could talk to Dr. Clark about finding a replacement to help with setting up the museum exhibition. As an alternative, since the field trip doesn't start until later in the week, the student could try to finish setting up the exhibit before the field trip.

After summarizing the problem and solutions, you should choose the solution you think is best and give a detailed reason. For example, you could say that you think the student should stay to set up the museum exhibit because she should honor the commitment she made to Dr. Clark.

Sample Responses

Play track #38 on the CD to hear a high-level response for Question 5.

Rater's Comments

There are minor pronunciation and intonation errors, but they do not prevent the speaker's response from being understood. She uses connecting words to mark the progression of ideas. Her control of grammar and vocabulary are evident in the way she efficiently summarizes the situation from the listening. The speaker clearly identifies the problem and both solutions. She organizes her response, so it is easy to follow her ideas from one to the next. She indicates her opinion of what the student should do. Although she runs out of time before she can explain why she holds that opinion, it is clear that she understands the task.

Play track #39 on the CD to hear a mid-level response for Question 5.

Rater's Comments

The response is generally understandable. The speaker sustains speech throughout the response time. However, the sense of hesitation in the way the response is delivered requires some listener effort. The choppy delivery sometimes makes it difficult to know when one sentence or idea ends and when others begin. The speaker makes a number of errors with simple grammatical structures (*very like to, let her to take, make somebody to replace her*). Overall meaning, though, is not greatly affected by these errors. The speaker identifies the problem and describes the two solutions. A higher-level vocabulary would have been helpful to more efficiently summarize the situation. The problems and two solutions are summarized with too much detail, which prevents the speaker from having time to state her preferred solution and give a reason for it.

Question 6
Listening Script

Narrator
Now listen to a part of a talk in an economics class.

Professor
So, let's talk about <u>money</u>. What <u>is</u> money? Well, typically people think of coins and paper "bills" as money . . . but that's using a somewhat narrow definition of the term. A <u>broad</u> definition is this: [slowly] money is anything that people can use to make purchases with. Since many things can be used to make purchases, money can have many different forms. Certainly, coins and bills are <u>one</u> form of money. People exchange goods and services for coins or paper bills, and they use this money . . . these bills . . . to obtain other goods and services. For example, you might give a taxi driver five dollars to purchase a ride in his taxi. And he in turn gives the five dollars to a farmer to buy some vegetables . . .

But, as I said, coins and bills aren't the only form of money under this broad definition. Some societies make use of a barter system. Basically, in a barter system people exchange goods and services directly for other goods and services. The taxi driver, for example, might give a ride to a farmer in exchange for some vegetables. Since the vegetables are used to pay for a service, by our broad definition the vegetables are used in barter as a form of <u>money</u>.

Now, as I mentioned, there's also a second . . . a narrower definition of money. In the United States only coins and bills are <u>legal tender</u>—meaning that by law, a seller <u>must</u> accept them as payment. The taxi driver <u>must</u> accept coins or bills as payment for a taxi ride. OK? But in the U.S., the taxi driver is <u>not</u> required to accept vegetables in exchange for a ride. So a narrower definition of money might be whatever is legal tender in a society, whatever <u>has</u> to be accepted as payment.

Narrator
Using points and examples from the talk, explain the two definitions of money presented by the professor.

Preparation time: 20 seconds
Response Time: 60 seconds

Important Points
Under the broad definition, money is anything that can be used as payment (as a medium of exchange), e.g., coins/bills and barter. If you take a taxi ride, you could use vegetables as payment for the cab ride. Under a narrower definition, money is anything that <u>must be</u> accepted as payment (legal tender). In the United States, coins and bills are legal tender. A taxi driver must accept coins and bills as payment for the taxi ride. Vegetables and credit cards are not legal tender in the United States, so the taxi driver does not have to accept these as payment.

Sample Responses

Play track # 40 on the CD to hear a high-level response for Question 6.

Rater's Comments
The speaker's pronunciation and intonation are highly intelligible. She speaks a little too quickly at times, but the overall meaning is not lost. Her words and ideas flow easily from one idea to the next. She uses complex grammatical structures and a wide range of vocabulary. The speaker fluently summarizes the stimulus accurately recounting the broad and narrow definition. Her response is detailed and sustained. She spends too much time summarizing the first definition and example, so she does not fully explain the second definition and example. However, it is obvious from the apparent ease in which she speaks that she understands the concept and is able to talk about it.

Play track #41 on the CD to hear a mid-level response for Question 6.

Rater's Comments
The speaker's pronunciation is generally clear. She sustains speech and continues to try to elaborate her ideas. The hesitance and choppiness indicates a lack of control of vocabulary and grammar. This significantly affects the overall intelligibility of the response. She conveys some relevant details including an almost accurate summary of both definitions of money. However, her response is clearly incomplete. The speaker's struggle to find the right words to convey her ideas prevents her from efficiently using her time. Neither of the examples is included in the response. Most of her ideas are underdeveloped.

Score	General Description	Delivery	Language Use	Topic Development
4	The response fulfills the demands of the task, with at most minor lapses in completeness. It is highly intelligible and exhibits sustained, coherent discourse. A response at this level is characterized by all of the following:	Generally well-paced flow (fluid expression). Speech is clear. It may include minor lapses, or minor difficulties with pronunciation or intonation patterns, which do not affect overall intelligibility.	The response demonstrates effective use of grammar and vocabulary. It exhibits a fairly high degree of automaticity with good control of basic and complex structures (as appropriate). Some minor (or systematic) errors are noticeable but do not obscure meaning.	Response is sustained and sufficient to the task. It is generally well developed and coherent; relationships between ideas are clear (or clear progression of ideas).
3	The response addresses the task appropriately, but may fall short of being fully developed. It is generally intelligible and coherent, with some fluidity of expression though it exhibits some noticeable lapses in the expression of ideas. A response at this level is characterized by at least two of the following:	Speech is generally clear, with some fluidity of expression, though minor difficulties with pronunciation, intonation, or pacing are noticeable and may require listener effort at times (though overall intelligibility is not significantly affected).	The response demonstrates fairly automatic and effective use of grammar and vocabulary, and fairly coherent expression of relevant ideas. Response may exhibit some imprecise or inaccurate use of vocabulary or grammatical structures used. This may affect overall fluency, but it does not seriously interfere with the communication of the message.	Response is mostly coherent and sustained and conveys relevant ideas/information. Overall development is somewhat limited, usually lacks elaboration or specificity. Relationships between ideas may at times not be immediately clear.

Score	General Description	Delivery	Language Use	Topic Development
2	The response addresses the task, but development of the topic is limited. It contains intelligible speech, although problems with delivery and/or overall coherence occur; meaning may be obscured in places. A response at this level is characterized by at least two of the following:	Speech is basically intelligible, though listener effort is needed because of unclear articulation, awkward intonation, or choppy rhythm/pace; meaning may be obscured in places.	The response demonstrates limited range and control of grammar and vocabulary. These limitations often prevent full expression of ideas. For the most part, only basic sentence structures are used successfully and spoken with fluidity. Structures and vocabulary may express mainly simple (short) and/or general propositions, with simple or unclear connections made among them (serial listing, conjunction, juxtaposition).	The response is connected to the task, though the number of ideas presented or the development of ideas is limited. Mostly basic ideas are expressed with limited elaboration (details and support). At times relevant substance may be vaguely expressed or repetitious. Connections of ideas may be unclear.
1	The response is very limited in content and/or coherence or is only minimally connected to the task, or speech is largely unintelligible. A response at this level is characterized by at least two of the following:	Consistent pronuciation, stress, and intonation difficulties cause considerable listener effort; delivery is choppy fragmented, or telegraphic; frequent pauses and hesitations.	Range and control of grammar and vocabulary severely limit (or prevent expression of) ideas and connections among ideas. Some low-level responses may rely heavily on practiced or formulaic expressions.	Limited relevant content expressed. The response generally lacks substance beyond expression of very basic ideas. Speaker may be unable to sustain speech to complete task and may rely heavily on repetition of the prompt.
0	Speaker makes no attempt to respond OR response is unrelated to the topic.			

TOEFL iBT Speaking Scoring Rubric

Integrated Tasks (Questions 3, 4, 5 & 6)

Score	General Description	Delivery	Language Use	Topic Development
4	The response fulfills the demands of the task, with at most minor lapses in completeness. It is highly intelligible and exhibits sustained, coherent discourse. A response at this level is characterized by all of the following:	Speech is generally clear, fluid and sustained. It may include minor lapses or minor difficulties with pronunciation or intonation. Pace may vary at times as speaker attempts to recall information. Overall intelligibility remains high.	The response demonstrates good control of basic and complex grammatical structures that allow for coherent, efficient (automatic) expression of relevant ideas. Contains generally effective word choice. Though some minor (or systematic) errors or imprecise use may be noticeable, they do not require listener effort (or obscure meaning).	The response presents a clear progression of ideas and conveys the relevant information required by the task. It includes appropriate detail, though it may have minor errors or minor omissions.
3	The response addresses the task appropriately, but may fall short of being fully developed. It is generally intelligible and coherent, with some fluidity of expression, though it exhibits some noticeable lapses in the expression of ideas. A response at this level is characterized by at least two of the following:	Speech is generally clear, with some fluidity of expression, but it exhibits minor difficulties with pronunciation, intonation, or pacing and may require some listener effort at times. Overall intelligibility remains good, however.	The response demonstrates fairly automatic and effective use of grammar and vocabulary, and fairly coherent expression of relevant idea. Response may exhibit some imprecise or inaccurate use of vocabulary or grammatical structures or be somewhat limited in the range of structures used. Such limitations do no seriously	The response is sustained and conveys relevant information required by the task. However, it exhibits some incompleteness inaccuracy, lack of specificity with respect to content, or choppiness in the progrssion of ideas.

TOEFL iBT Speaking Scoring Rubric

Integrated Tasks (Questions 3, 4, 5 & 6)

Score	General Description	Delivery	Language Use	Topic Development
			interfere with the communication of the message.	
2	The response is conected to the task, though it may be missing some relevant information or contain inaccuracies. It contains some intelligible speech, but at times problems with intelligibility and/or overall coherance may obscure meaning. A response at this level is characterized by at least two of the following:	Speech is clear at times, though it exhibits problems with pronunciation, intonation, or pacing and so may require significant listener effort. Speech may not be sustained at a consistent level throughout. Problems with intelligibility may obscure meaning in places (but not throughout).	The response is limited in the range and control of vocabulary and grammar demonstrated (some complex structures may be used, but typically contain errors). This results in limited or inaccurate connections. Automaticity of expression may be evident only at the phrasal level.	The response conveys some relevant information but is clearly incomplete of inaccurate. It is incomplete if it omits key ideas, makes vague reference to key ideas, or demonstrates limited development of important information. An inaccurate response demonstrates misunderstanding of key ideas from the stimulus. Typically, ideas expressed may not be well connected or cohesive so that familiarity with the stimulus is necessary in order to follow what is being discussed.
1	The response is very limited in content or coherence or is only minimally connected to the task. Speech may be largely unintelligible. A response at this level is characterized by at least two of the following:	Consistent pronunciation and intonation problems cause considerable listener effort and frequently obscure meaning. Delivery is choppy; fragmented, or telegraphic, Speech contains frequent	Range and control of grammar and vocabulary severely limits (or prevents) expression of ideas and connections among ideas. Some very	The response fails to provide much relevant content. Ideas that are expressed are often inaccurate, or limited to vague utterances or repetitions (including repetition of prompt).

TOEFL iBT Speaking Scoring Rubric
Integrated Tasks (Questions 3, 4, 5 & 6)

Score	General Description	Delivery	Language Use	Topic Development
		pauses and hesitations.	low-level responses may rely on isolated words or short utterances to communicate ideas.	
0	Speaker makes no attempt to respond OR response is unrelated to the topic.			

Frequently Asked Questions about TOEFL Speaking

1. Why does the TOEFL iBT include a Speaking section?

The focus of the TOEFL iBT is on communicative competence and tests your ability to use English to communicate effectively in an academic setting. Speaking is a key communication skill, along with listening, reading, and writing, and has an important place in the TOEFL iBT assessment.

2. Why are the answers for some of the questions in the TOEFL iBT Speaking section based on reading and/or listening passages?

Speaking tasks that combine reading and/or listening passages with speaking are called integrated tasks. They are included in the TOEFL iBT in recognition of the fact that to succeed academically in English-speaking colleges and universities, students need to be able to combine all their English-language skills—in reading, listening, and speaking, as well as writing—inside and outside the classroom.

3. How much reading and listening will I have to do for the TOEFL iBT Speaking section?

The reading and listening passages that are associated with the integrated tasks vary in length but are all quite brief. Reading passages range from approximately 75 to 100 words, and the listening passages are generally between 60 and 90 seconds long. In addition to being short, the listening and reading passages are not intended to be difficult. They are designed to provide you with clear and accessible information to use in answering the speaking questions.

4. May I take notes at all times during the Speaking section?

Yes. You may take notes at any time during the Speaking section—while reading the written passages, listening to the spoken dialogues or lectures, and preparing your responses. While you listen to the dialogues or lectures and take notes, you should not try to write down word for word everything you hear. If you try to do this, you will probably miss hearing important information. Similarly, while preparing your spoken response, do not try to write out an answer that you will then try to speak. You will not have enough time to write out a full response, and raters will be rating you on your ability to speak, not on your ability to read aloud from a text that you have written. Instead, you should use your preparation to review whatever notes you have taken and to organize your ideas.

5. How will my responses be rated?

Each of the six tasks on the TOEFL iBT is rated by human scorers who will assign ratings ranging from 0 to 4 for each response. The scorers will evaluate your responses for the ability they display in topic development, delivery, and language use, and assign an overall score for each response, based on these three factors.

6. How will the total Speaking score be determined?

The scores on your individual speaking tasks are added up, with each individual task score carrying the same weight. The sum of these individual scores is converted into a scaled score of 0 to 30, and that is the Speaking score that will be reported to the institutions you request.

7. How will mistakes affect my score?

Raters will not focus on the number of errors you make. They will score the response based on the overall performance. A response that contains minor or occasional errors may still be scored at the highest level.

8. What happens if I do not have time to finish my answer?

You may find that for some tasks, you are not able to include in your answer all the information you would like to. The time allotted for each speaking response is considered sufficient for you to give a complete answer, and you should try to give as thorough an answer as possible. However, the raters who evaluate your responses recognize that it may not always be possible for you to anticipate precisely how much of what you want to say will fit into the amount of time provided. Keep in mind that how clearly and coherently you convey information is as important as *how much* information you convey. Therefore, you should avoid speaking at an unnaturally rapid pace if you see that time is going to run out before you say everything you have planned to say. You may find it useful to time yourself when practicing the speaking tasks. This will help you get an idea of how much can be said in the allotted time.

9. What happens if I finish my response before time runs out?

If you finish your answer before time runs out, you may want to consider what additional information you could add that make your answer more complete. If you find yourself with extra time, it may not be a good idea for you to merely repeat what you have already said. Rather, ask yourself what else you could say to clarify, elaborate on, or otherwise develop your response more fully. Timing yourself when practicing the speaking tasks should help you get accustomed to the time allowances.

10. May I go back and change an answer?

No. Each of your spoken responses is recorded, and it is not possible to go back and re-record what you have said. For each question, you will be given some time to prepare your answer, and this should help you plan ahead of time what you want to say.

You should also remember that your speaking responses are not expected to be perfect. If in the course of giving your spoken response, you realize that you should have said something differently, you should feel free to correct your mistake if you wish, just as you would if you had made a mistake while speaking in your native language and wanted to correct it. Otherwise you may want to simply ignore an error and continue with your response, making sure that the remainder of what you say is as intelligible, coherent, and accurate as possible.

11. How will my accent and pronunciation affect my score?

All TOEFL iBT test takers will have speech that is accented to some degree or another, and your score will not be affected by your accent, unless your accent interferes with the intelligibility of your response. Minor and/or occasional pronunciation mistakes are also expected, even among the most proficient test takers, and, here again, as long as pronunciation mistakes do not interfere with the intelligibility of your response, they will not count against your score.

TOEFL iBT Writing

Introduction to the Writing Section

There are two tasks in the Writing section of the TOEFL iBT: an Integrated Writing Task and an Independent Writing Task.

The Integrated Writing task comes first because it involves some listening, and when you are taking the real TOEFL iBT you will wear your headphones. When you are finished with the Integrated Writing Task, which takes about 20 minutes, you will be free to take your headphones off to work on the Independent Writing Task. You will have 30 minutes to complete the Independent Writing Task.

This chapter discusses each of the writing tasks in detail and the scoring criteria that readers will use to evaluate your writing. It includes samples of each task, sample responses to each task, and specific advice on how to approach writing your own response.

For both the writing tasks on the TOEFL iBT, the people evaluating your writing recognize that your response is a first draft. You are not expected to produce a well-researched, comprehensive essay about a highly specific, specialized topic. You can earn a high score with an essay that contains some errors.

The Integrated Writing Task

You will read a passage about an academic topic for three minutes, and then you will hear a lecture related to the topic. Then you will be asked to summarize the points in the listening passage and explain how they relate to specific points in the reading passage.

This task gives you the opportunity to demonstrate your ability to show that you can communicate in writing about academic information you have read and listened to.

Example

A reading passage like the following will appear on your computer screen. You will have 3 minutes to read the passage.

In many organizations, perhaps the best way to approach certain new projects is to assemble a group of people into a team. Having a team of people attack a project offers several advantages. First of all, a group of people has a wider range of knowledge, expertise, and skills than any single individual is likely to possess. Also, because of the numbers of people involved and the greater resources they possess, a group can work more quickly in response to the task assigned to it and can come up with highly creative solutions to problems and issues. Sometimes these creative solutions come about because a group is more likely to make risky decisions that an individual might not undertake. This is because the group spreads responsibility for a decision to all the members and thus no single individual can be held accountable if the decision turns out to be wrong.

Taking part in a group process can be very rewarding for members of the team. Team members who have a voice in making a decision will no doubt feel better about carrying out the work that is entailed by that decision than they might doing work that is imposed on them by others. Also, the individual team member has a much better chance to "shine," to get his or her contributions and ideas not only recognized but recognized as highly significant, because a team's overall results can be more far-reaching and have greater impact than what might have otherwise been possible for the person to accomplish or contribute working alone.

Then you will hear:

Narrator
Now listen to part of a lecture on the topic you just read about.

Professor
Now I want to tell you about what one company found when it decided that it would turn over some of its new projects to teams of people, and make the team responsible for planning the projects and getting the work done. After about six months, the company took a look at how well the teams performed.

On virtually every team, some members got almost a "free ride" . . . they didn't contribute much at all, but if their team did a good job, they nevertheless benefited from the recognition the team got. And what about group members who worked especially well and who provided a lot of insight on problems and issues? Well . . . the recognition for a job well done went to the group as a whole, no names were named. So it won't surprise you to learn that when the real contributors were asked how they felt about the group process, their attitude was just the opposite of what the reading predicts.

Another finding was that some projects just didn't move very quickly. Why? Because it took so long to reach consensus; it took many, many meetings to build the agreement among group members about how they would move the project along. On the other hand, there were other instances where one or two people managed to become very influential over what their group did. Sometimes when those influencers said "That will never work" about an idea the group was developing, the idea was quickly dropped instead of being further discussed. And then there was another occasion when a couple influencers convinced the group that a plan of theirs was "highly creative." And even though some members tried to warn the rest of the group that the project was moving in directions that might not work, they were basically ignored by other group members. Can you guess the ending to *this* story? When the project failed, the blame was placed on all the members of the group.

The reading passage will then reappear on your computer screen, along with the following directions and writing task:

You have **20 minutes** to plan and write your response. Your response will be judged on the basis of the quality of your writing and on how well your response presents the points in the lecture and their relationship to the reading passage. Typically, an effective response will be 150 to 225 words.

Summarize the points made in the lecture you just heard, explaining how they cast doubt on points made in the reading.

The writing clock will then start a countdown for 20 minutes of writing time.

HOW THE TASK IS PHRASED

If the lecture challenges the information in the reading passage, the writing task will usually be phrased in one of the following ways:

➤ Summarize the points made in the lecture, being sure to explain how they cast doubt on specific points made in the reading passage.
➤ Summarize the points made in the lecture, being sure to explain how they challenge specific claims/arguments made in the reading passage.
➤ Summarize the points made in the lecture, being sure to specifically explain how they answer the problems raised in the reading passage.

If the lecture supports or strengthens the information in the reading passage, the writing task will usually be phrased in one of the following ways:

➤ Summarize the points made in the lecture, being sure to specifically explain how they support the explanations in the reading passage.
➤ Summarize the points made in the lecture, being sure to specifically explain how they strengthen specific points made in the reading passage.

STRATEGIES FOR RAISING YOUR SCORE ON THE INTEGRATED WRITING TASK

As you read:

➤ Take notes on your scratch paper.

➤ Look for the main idea of the reading passage. The main idea often has to do with some policy or practice or some position on an issue. Or it may have to do with proposing some overall hypothesis about the way some process or procedure works or should work or how some natural phenomenon is believed to work.

➤ See how this main idea is evaluated or developed. Usually it will be developed in one of two ways:

1. Arguments or explanations are presented that support the main position, for example, why there are good reasons to believe that some policy or practice will be beneficial or prove useful or advisable or perhaps why it has been a good thing in the past.

2. Arguments or explanations or problems are brought up concerning why some policy or practice or position or hypothesis will not or does not work or will not be useful or advisable.

➤ Don't worry about forgetting the reading passage. It will reappear on your computer screen when it is time to write.

➤ Note points in the passage that either support the main idea or provide reasons to doubt the main idea. Typically the main idea will be developed with three points.

As you listen:

➤ Take notes on your scratch paper.

➤ Listen for information, examples, or explanations that make points in the reading passage seem wrong or less convincing or even untrue. For instance, in the example just given, the reading passage says that working in teams is a good thing because it gives individuals a chance to stand out. But the lecture says that often everyone gets equal credit for the work of a team, even if some people do not do any work at all. The reading says that work proceeds quickly on a team because there are more people involved who each brings his or her expertise. But the lecture completely contradicts this claim by stating that it may take a long time for the group to reach consensus. The lecture brings up the idea that the whole team can be blamed for a failure when the fault lies with only a few team members. This casts doubt on the claim in the reading that teams can take risks and be creative because no one individual is held accountable.

As you write your response:

➤ You may take off your headset if you wish. You will not need your headset for the remainder of the TOEFL iBT test.

➤ Before you start writing, briefly reread the passage, consult your notes, and make a very brief outline of the points you wish to make. You can write this outline on your scratch paper or draw lines between the notes you took on the reading and the notes you took on the lecture. You can even type your outline and notes right into the answer area and then replace these by sentences and paragraphs as you compose your response.

➤ Remember that you are NOT being asked for your opinion. You ARE being asked to explain how the points in the listening relate to points in the reading.

➤ Write in full English sentences. You can write either one long paragraph or a series of short paragraphs listing the points of opposition between the reading and the lecture. Occasional language errors will not count against you as long as they do not cause you to misrepresent the meaning of points from the reading and the lecture.

➤ Remember that your job is to select the important information from the lecture and coherently and accurately present this information in relation to the relevant information from the reading. Your response should contain the following:

1. The specific ideas, explanations, and arguments in the lecture that oppose or challenge points in the reading

2. Coherent and accurate presentations of each point that you make; that is, the language you use should make sense and should accurately reflect the ideas presented in the lecture and the reading

3. A clear, coherent structure that enables the reader to understand what points in the lecture relate to what points in the reading.

➤ Suggested length is between 150 and 225 words. You will not be penalized if you write more, so long as what you write answers the question.

➤ CAUTION: You will receive a score of zero if all you do is copy words from the reading passage. You will receive a score of 1 if you write ONLY about the reading passage. *To respond successfully, you must do your best to write about the ways the points in the lecture are related to specific points in the reading.*

INTEGRATED WRITING SCORING RUBRIC

Here is the official Scoring Guide used by raters when they read the Integrated Writing Task.

SCORE	TASK DESCRIPTION
5	A response at this level successfully selects the important information from the lecture and coherently and accurately presents this information in relation to the relevant information presented in the reading. The response is well organized, and occasional language errors that are present do not result in inaccurate or imprecise presentation of content or connections.
4	A response at this level is generally good in selecting the important information from the lecture and in coherently and accurately presenting this information in relation to the relevant information in the reading, but it may have minor omission, inaccuracy, vagueness, or imprecision of some content from the lecture or in connection to points made in the reading. A response is also scored at this level if it has more frequent or noticeable minor language errors, as long as such usage and grammatical structures do not result in anything more than an occasional lapse of clarity or in the connection of ideas.

3	A response at this level contains some important information from the lecture and conveys some relevant connection to the reading, but it is marked by one or more of the following: ➤ Although the overall response is definitely oriented to the task, it conveys only vague, global, unclear, or somewhat imprecise connection of the points made in the lecture to points made in the reading. ➤ The response may omit one major key point made in the lecture. ➤ Some key points made in the lecture or the reading, or connections between the two, may be incomplete, inaccurate, or imprecise. ➤ Errors of usage and/or grammar may be more frequent or may result in noticeably vague expressions or obscured meanings in conveying ideas and connections.
2	A response at this level contains some relevant information from the lecture, but is marked by significant language difficulties or by significant omission or inaccuracy of important ideas from the lecture or in the connections between the lecture and the reading; a response at this level is marked by one or more of the following: ➤ The response significantly misrepresents or completely omits the overall connection between the lecture and the reading. ➤ The response significantly omits or significantly misrepresents important points made in the lecture. ➤ The response contains language errors or expressions that largely obscure connections or meaning at key junctures, or that would likely obscure understanding of key ideas for a reader not already familiar with the reading and the lecture.
1	A response at this level is marked by one or more of the following: ➤ The response provides little or no meaningful or relevant coherent content from the lecture. ➤ The language level of the response is so low that it is difficult to derive meaning.
0	A response at this level merely copies sentences from the reading, rejects the topic or is otherwise not connected to the topic, is written in a foreign language, consists of keystroke characters, or is blank.

SAMPLE SCORED RESPONSES FOR THE INTEGRATED WRITING TASK

The following were written in response to the task "Working in Teams" shown in the example above.

Score 5 Response

> The lecturer talks about research conducted by a firm that used the group system to handle their work. He says that the theory stated in the passage was very different and somewhat inaccurate when compared to what happened for real.
>
> First, some members got free rides. That is, some didn't work hard but gotrecognition for the success nonetheless. This also indicates that people who worked hard was not given recognition they should have got. In other words, they weren't given the oppotunity to "shine." This derectly contradicts what the passage indicates.
>
> Second, groups were slow in progress. The passage says that groups are nore responsive than individuals because of the number of people involved and their aggregated resources. However, the speaker talks about how the firm found out that groups were slower than individuals in dicision making. Groups needed more time for meetings, which are neccesary procceedures in decision making. This was another part where experience contradicted theory.
>
> Third, influetial people might emerge, and lead the group towards glory or failure. If the influent people are going in the right direction there would be no problem. But in cases where they go in the wrong direction, there is nobody that has enough influence to counter the decision made. In other words, the group might turn into a dictatorship, with the influential party as the leader, and might be less flexible in thinking. They might become one-sided, and thus fail to succeed.

Rater's Comments

There are several errors of spelling, word formation, and subject-verb agreement in this response; however, most of these errors seem to be the result of typing errors common to first drafts. This writer does an excellent job of presenting lecturer's points that contradict the arguments made in reading passage. The writer is very specific and has organized his points so that they are parallel with one another: in each of the supporting paragraphs, the lecturer's observation of what really happened is given first, then explicitly connected to a theoretical point from the reading. The final paragraph contains one noticeable error ("influent"), which is then used correctly two sentences later ("influential"). Overall, this is a successful response and earns a score of 5.

Score 4 Response

> The lecture that followed the paragraph on the team work in organizations, gave some negative views of the team work itself.
>
> Firstly, though it was said in the paragraph that the whole team idea would probably be faster than the individual work, it was said in the lecture just the opposite: it could actually

be a lot slower. That is because team members would sometimes take more time than needed just to reach the same conclussions, or just even to simply decide where to go from certain point to the next on.

Secondly, paragraph suggests that by doing work as a team might give you an "edge," the lecture suggests that that might also be a negative thing as well. The people who made themselves leaders in the group may just be wrong in certain decisions, or just simple thing something is so creative, when in reality it is not and it would not work, but the rest of the people would nevertheless still follow them, and end up not doing well at all.

And lastly, paragraph says that everyone feels responsible for their own part, and all together they are all more effective as a team. The lecture suggests quite the opposite in this case as well. It suggests that some team members are there only for the "free ride," and they don't do much of anything to contribute, but still get the credit as a whole.

Rater's Comments

The writer of this response is clearly attempting to interweave the points from the passage and lecture and does a good job of discussing what the lecturer says about group decision-making and the issue of some group members failing to contribute. The writer's second point, however, is not as clearly stated as the first and third points. The key sentence in this paragraph ("The people who made themselves leaders in the group may just be wrong in certain decisions, or just simple thing something is so creative, when in reality it is not and it would not work, but the rest of the people would nevertheless still follow them, and end up not doing well at all") is difficult to follow. This is what the Scoring Guide calls "an occasional lapse of clarity" in a response that earns a score of 4. Overall, this is still a very strong response that directly addresses the task and generally presents the relevant information from the lecture.

Score 3 Response

The lecturer provide the opposite opinion concerning what the article offered. The team work often bring negative effet. As we all know superficially, team work and team spirits are quite popular in today's business world and also the fashionable terms.

However, the lecturer find deeper and hiding results.

Firstly, the working results of team members can't be fully valued. For example, if a team member does nothing in the process of team discussion, decision making and final pratice, his or her work deliquency will not be recognized because we only emphasize team work. Also, the real excellent and creative member's work might be obliterated for the same reason.

Secondly, the team work might lose its value when team members are leading by several influential people in the group. One of the essential merits of team is to avoid the individule wrong. But one or two influential or persuasive people will make the team useless.

Thirdly, team work oftem become the excuse of taking responsibillity. All in charge, nobody care.

All in all, what we should do is the fully distinguish the advantages and disadvantages of a concept or widely used method. That is to keep the common sense.

Rater's Comments

This response frames the issue well. The first point is clearly stated and accurately conveys the lecturer's comments about team members who contribute very little and team members who contribute a great deal. However, the writer discusses the second point about influencers in somewhat error-prone or vague and non-idiomatic language ("hiding results," "working results" and "when team members are leading by . . . influential people"). The point about influencers drops off at making the team "useless" and does not fully explain the reason these influencers create problems. The final point beginning with the word "thirdly" is not fully related to the passage and lecture, and the meaning of it is unclear. This response illustrates many of the typical features that can cause a response to receive the score of 3.

Score 2 Response

> In a company's experement, some new projects were planed and acomplished by different teams. Some teams got very good results while some teams didn't. That is to say it's not nessesary for teams to achieve more than individuals do because some team members may only contribute a little in a team for they may relying on the others to do the majority.
>
> Another thing is the recognition for the achievement by the team is for the whole team, for everyone in the team. It's not only the dicision makers in the team feel good after successfully finishing the project, but also every member in the team.
>
> It is also showed in the lecture that in a team with one or two leaders, sometimes good ideas from some team member are dropped and ignored while sometimes they may be highly creative. In some teams decisions were made without collecting ideas from all team members. Then it would be hard to achieve creative solutions.
>
> For those failed projects, blames are always given to the whole team even though it's the leader or someone in the team who caught the unexpected result.

Rater's Comments

Although it has the appearance of a stronger response, on close reading, this example suffers from significant problems with connecting ideas and misrepresenting points. For instance, the third sentence of paragraph 1 seems to be getting at a point from the lecture ("some team members may contribute only a little . . . "). However, it is couched in such a way that makes it very unclear how it relates to the point of the task ("That is to say it's not necessary for teams to achieve more than individuals do because some team members may only contribute "). In addition, it is not clear where the information in paragraph 2 is coming from and what point the writer is trying to make. In paragraph 3 the writer tries to make a point about influencers, but again, it is not clear what information relates to what. For all these reasons, this response earns a score of 2.

Score 1 Response

> In this lecture, the example shows only one of the group succeed the project. Why the group will succeed on this project it is because of few factor.

> First of all,a group of people has a wider range of knowledge,expertise,and skills than any single individual is like to prossess, and easier to gather the information and resources to make the work effectively and the group will willingly to trey sometihing is risky decision to make the project for interesting and suceessful it is because all the member of the group carries the differnt responsibility for a decision, so once the decision turn wrong, no a any individual one will be blame for the whole responsiblity.
>
> On the other way, the groups which are fail the project is because they are lay on some more influence people in the group,so even the idea is come out. Once the inflenced people say that is no good, then the process of the idea will be drop down immediately instead taking more further discussion! So the idea will not be easy to settle down for a group.
>
> The form of the group is very important, and each of the member should be respect another and try out all the idea others had suggested, then it will develop a huge idea and the cooperate work environment for each other for effectively work!

Rater's Comments

The level of language used in this response is fairly low, and it is lowest in the second paragraph, which is the only reference to the lecture. Because the reader has difficulty gleaning meaning from that paragraph, the response contributes little coherent information and therefore earns a score of 1.

The Independent Writing Task

This second task in the Writing section of TOEFL iBT is the Independent Writing Task. You are presented with a question, and you have 30 minutes to write an essay in response. The question asks you to give your opinion on an issue. Here is how the question is typically phrased:

Do you agree or disagree with the following statement?

    [A sentence or sentences that present an issue appear here.]

Use specific reasons and examples to support your answer.

An effective response is typically about 300 words long. If you write fewer than 300 words, you may still receive a top score, but experience has shown that shorter responses typically do not demonstrate the development of ideas needed to earn a score of 5. There is no maximum word limit. You may write as much as you wish in the time allotted. But do not write just to be writing; write to respond to the topic. The number of ideas you express is important, but it is the quality of your ideas and the effeciveness with which you express them that will be most valued by the raters.

Example

Do you agree or disagree with the following statement?

> Always telling the truth is the most important consideration in any relationship.

Use specific reasons and examples to support your answer.

ESSAY-WRITING TIPS

➤ Think before you write. Make a brief outline or some notes on scratch paper to help you organize your thoughts. You can even type your outline and notes right in the answer area on the computer and then replace your outline with sentences and paragraphs.

➤ Keep track of your time. Try to finish writing your essay by the time the clock counts down to 4 or 5 minutes. Use the remaining time to check your work and make final changes. At the end of 30 minutes your essay will be automatically saved.

➤ ETS/TOEFL ScoreItNow is an excellent way to practice for the Independent Writing Task on TOEFL iBT. ScoreItNow is scored on a scale of 1 to 6, but to get an idea of how your essay would be scored on the TOEFL iBT 1–5 scale, you can just subtract 1 from the ScoreItNow score assigned by the software program. To find out how you can get your copy of ScoreItNow, visit the ETS Web site.

HOW ESSAYS ARE SCORED

Raters will judge the quality of your writing. They will consider how well you develop your ideas, how well you organize your essay, and how well you use language to express your ideas.

Development is the amount and kinds of support (examples, details, reasons) for your ideas that you present in your essay. To get a top score, your essay should be, according to the rater guidelines, "well developed, using clearly appropriate explanations, exemplifications, and/or details." The raters will judge whether you have addressed the topic and how well your details, examples, and reasons support your ideas.

Do not "memorize" long introductory and concluding paragraphs just to add words to your essay. Raters will not look favorably on wordy introductory and concluding paragraphs such as the following:

"The importance of the issue raised by the posed statement, namely creating a new holiday for people, cannot be underestimated as it concerns the very fabric of society. As it stands, the issue of creating a new holiday raises profound implications for the future. However, although the subject matter in general cannot be dismissed lightheartedly, the perspective of the issue as presented by the statement raises certain qualms regarding practical application."

"In conclusion, although I have to accept that it is imperative that something be done about creating a new holiday for people and find the underlying thrust of the implied proposal utterly convincing, I cannot help but feel wary of taking such irrevocable steps and personally feel that a more measured approach would be more rewarding."

Likewise, raters will not look favorably on paragraphs like the following, which uses a lot of words but fails to develop any real ideas:

"At the heart of any discussion regarding an issue pertaining to creating a new holiday, it has to borne in mind that a delicate line has to be trod when dealing with such matters. The human resources involved in such matters cannot be guaranteed regardless of all the good intentions that may be lavished. While it is true that creating a new holiday might be a viable and laudable remedy, it is transparently clear that applied wrongly such a course of action could be calamitous and compound the problem rather than provide a solution."

In your writing, make sure you develop some solid ideas about the given topic. Don't just use a lot of words saying that a certain issue exists. Your essay may be 300 or even 400 words long, but if it consists largely of the sorts of empty or content-free paragraphs shown above, you'll probably earn a score of just 1 or 2.

Organization is really something that raters notice—when you fail to organize. If an essay is organized, a reader will be able to read it from beginning to end without becoming confused. Writing in paragraphs and marking transitions from one idea to another in various ways usually helps the reader to follow your ideas. But be aware that just using transition words such as *first* or *second* does not guarantee that your essay is organized. The points you make must all relate to the topic of the essay and to the main idea you are presenting in response. In other words, your essay should be unified. The scoring guide mentions "unity" as well as "progression" and "coherence"—these are terms that all have to do with how well your essay is organized and how easy it is for the reader to follow your ideas. To earn a top score, you need to avoid redundancy (repetition of ideas), digression (points that are not related to your main point, that take away from the "unity" of your ideas), and unclear connections (places where it is hard for the reader to understand how two ideas or parts of your writing are related).

Language use is the third criterion on which your essay will be judged. To get a top score, an essay must display "consistent facility in the use of language." There should be a variety of sentence structures, and word choice should be appropriate. If your essay includes a few minor lexical or grammar errors, you can still get a high score. However, if you make a lot of grammar errors and if those errors make it hard to understand your meaning, you will get a lower score. Raters will also judge your essay based on the complexity of sentence structures and on the quality and complexity of your vocabulary. If you use very simple sentences and very basic vocabulary, you will probably not be able to express very complex ideas. If your language is hard to follow, your sentences are overly simple, and your vocabulary is limited, you may score no higher than a 3 no matter how impressive your ideas may be.

INDEPENDENT WRITING SCORING RUBRIC

SCORE	TASK DESCRIPTION
5	An essay at this level largely accomplishes all of the following: ➤ Effectively addresses the topic and task ➤ Is well organized and well developed, using clearly appropriate explanations, exemplifications, and/or details ➤ Displays unity, progression, and coherence ➤ Displays consistent facility in the use of language, demonstrating syntactic variety, appropriate word choice, and idiomaticity, though it may have minor lexical or grammatical errors
4	An essay at this level largely accomplishes all of the following: ➤ Addresses the topic and task well, though some points may not be fully elaborated ➤ Is generally well organized and well developed, using appropriate and sufficient explanations, exemplifications, and/or details ➤ Displays unity, progression, and coherence, though it may contain occasional redundancy, digression, or unclear connections ➤ Displays facility in the use of language, demonstrating syntactic variety and range of vocabulary, though it will probably have occasional noticeable minor errors in structure, word form, or use of idiomatic language that do not interfere with meaning
3	An essay at this level is marked by one or more of the following: ➤ Addresses the topic and task using somewhat developed explanations, exemplifications, and/or details ➤ Displays unity, progression, and coherence, though connection of ideas may be occasionally obscured ➤ May demonstrate inconsistent facility in sentence formation and word choice that may result in lack of clarity and occasionally obscure meaning ➤ May display accurate but limited range of syntactic structures and vocabulary
2	An essay at this level may reveal one or more of the following weaknesses: ➤ Limited development in response to the topic and task ➤ Inadequate organization or connection of ideas ➤ Inappropriate or insufficient exemplifications, explanations, or details to support or illustrate generalizations in response to the task ➤ A noticeably inappropriate choice of words or word forms ➤ An accumulation of errors in sentence structure and/or usage

An essay at this level is seriously flawed by one or more of the following weaknesses:

1

➤ Serious disorganization or underdevelopment
➤ Little or no detail, or irrelevant specifics, or questionable responsiveness to the task
➤ Serious and frequent errors in sentence structure or usage

0

An essay at this level merely copies words from the topic, rejects the topic, or is otherwise not connected to the topic, is written in a foreign language, consists of keystroke characters, or is blank.

SAMPLE SCORED RESPONSES FOR THE INDEPENDENT WRITING TASK

The following essays are responses to this Independent Writing Task:

Do you agree or disagree with the following statement?

Always telling the truth is the most important consideration in any relationship.

Use specific reasons and examples to support your answer.

This topic supports a variety of approaches. Some writers disagree with the statement and describe instances where to them it is appropriate to lie; typically these include white lies, lies to avoid hurting others, and lies in a business context (which often have more to do with not disclosing proprietary information than with outright lying). Others take the position that lies beget more lies and undermine trust. These writers present examples that support the statement. Still others look at both sides of the issue, often delineating or classifying situations where they consider lying appropriate and others where they consider lying inappropriate or more consequential. The telling of stories—real and hypothetical—is not inappropriate; it seems very reasonable to illustrate one's ideas on this topic with examples.

Score 5 Essay

DISHONESTY KILLS RELIABILITY

There are certain considerations or factors that everyone takes into account in a relationship. People may look for honesty, altruism, understanding, loyalty, being thoughtful etc! Everyone would more or less wish that the person s/he is dealing with, has some of these virtues above. Putting them in an order according to their importance, however can be very subjective and relative.

When someone asks him/herself the question "What do I consider to be the most important thing in my relationship?" the answer depends on a lot of factors such as how his/her earlier relationships were.

After stating that everyone's opinion can be different about this, for me honesty, in other words, always telling the truth is the most important consideration in a relationship. Opposite of this is inarguably lying and if someone needs to lie, either s/he is hiding something or is afraid of telling me something.

In any relationship of mine, I would wish that first of all, the person I'm dealing with is honest. Even though s/he thinks that s/he did something wrong that I wouldn't like, s/he'd better tell me the truth and not lie about it. Later on if I find out about a lie or hear the truth from someone else, that'd be much more unpleasant. In that case how can I ever believe or trust that person again? How can I ever believe that this person has enough confidence in me to forgive him/her and carry on with the relationship from there. So if I cannot trust a person anymore, if the person doesn't think I can handle the truth, there's no point to continuing that relationship.

Although I would like to see altruistic, understanding, thoughtful and loyal behavior from people, an instance of the opposite of these behaviors would not upset me as much as dishonesty would. Among all the possible behaviors, dishonesty is the only one for me that terminates how I feel about a person's reliability. Therefore honesty would be my first concern and the most important consideration in a relationship.

Rater's Comments

In this response the writer first approaches the topic by underscoring that a number of character traits are important to a relationship. The writer then effectively develops an argument that unlike other negative behaviors, dishonesty or unwillingness to fully disclose some bad action cannot be forgiven and can be the most important factor in destroying a relationship. The writer's language is fluent, accurate, and varied enough to effectively support the progression and connection of ideas. There is a variety of sentence structures, including rhetorical questions. The essay is not mechanically perfect, but as long as such errors are occasional, minor, and do not interfere with the reader's understanding, an essay like this one can still earn a top score.

Score 4 Essay

Always telling the truth in any relationship is really the most important consideration for many reasons. I could say that when you lie to someone, this person will not trust you anymore and what is a relationship based on? Trust, confidence, so the sense of relationship is being lost. Another point is that if the true is ommited once, it will surely appear sometime, somewhere and probably in the most unexpected way, causing lots of problems for the ones involved. So, the truth is the basis for everything.

First, confidence is the most important aspect of a friendship or a marriage, or anything like that, so, once it is lost, the whole thing goes down in a way that no one can bear it. To avoid losing confidence, there is only one way, telling the truth, lying will just help throwing it away. For example, a couple decided to go out on the weekend, but the man has a party to go with his friends to where he can not take his girlfriend and then he lies to her saying that he is sick and can not go to the date. She undertands him and they do not see each other in that weekend, but he goes to the party and has much fun. Suppose on monday, the girl talks to a friend that saw him at the party and asked why did not she go with him. She found out the true and all confidence was lost, the basis for their relation is now gone and what happens next is that they break up or if they do not, he will persist on lyes and someday it will end.

What happened to this couple is very common around here and many relationships, even friends and marriages end because of something like that. Some may argue that lying once or another will not interfere anything and it is part of a relation, but I strongly disagree, the most important thing is the true, even if it is to determine the end of a relation, it must be told. There are more chances to end something lying than saying what really happened

Rater's Comments

This essay earned a score of 4. It clearly develops reasons why lying is a bad thing, with a first paragraph that introduces the writer's position ("truth is the basis for everything"), a hypothetical story in paragraph 2, and a final paragraph that entertains and quickly dismisses a possible counterargument. All this amounts to solid development of the idea. The response displays facility in language use through a variety of sentence structures and the use of clear transitions between sentences. However, sometimes the writer's sentences include noticeable errors in word form ("if the true is ommited," "lying will just help throwing it away," "lying once or another," "persist on lyes"), and in some places the writer extends, or "runs on," a sentence to include many steps in the argument when using two or more sentences would make the relationships between ideas clearer. "Some may argue that lying once or another will not interfere anything and it is part of a relation, but I strongly disagree, the most important thing is the true, even if it is to determine the end of a relation, it must be told."

Score 3 Essay

Some people believe that it is one of the most important value in many relationships to tell the truth all the time. However, it cannot be always the best choice to tell the truth in many situatioins. Sometimes white lies are indispensable to keep relationships more lively and dilightly. There are some examples to support this idea.

Firstly, in the relationships between lovers, it is often essential to compliment their lovers on their appearance and their behavior. Even though they do not think that their boyfriend or girlfriend looks good on their new shoes and new clothes, it will probably diss them by telling the truth. On the other hand, little compliments will make them confident and happy making their relationship more tight.

Secondly, parents need to encourage their children by telling lies. Even if they are doing bad work on studying or exercising, telling the truth will hurt their hearts. What they need is a little encouraging words instead of truthful words.

Thirdly, for some patients telling them their current state of their desease will probably desperate them. It is accepted publically not to let the patients know the truth. They may be able to have hope to overcome their desease without knowing the truth.

In conclusion, it is not always better to tell the truth than lies. Some lies are acceptable in terms of making people's life more profusely. Not everybody has to know the truth, and it will lead them more happier not knowing it. In these cases, white lies are worth to be regarded as a virtue of people's relationships

Rater's Comments

This essay focuses on explaining why "white lies" are sometimes appropriate. The explanations here are "somewhat developed." Each example supports the writer's main point, but in every case, the writer does not say why the positive effect of the "white lie" outweighs any negative effect. There is inconsistent control of structure and vocabulary, with some errors in both structure and vocabulary obscuring meaning: "keep relationships . . . dilightly," "will probably desperate them," "making peoples life more profusely," "it will lead them more happier not knowing it." These weaknesses and errors earn this essay a score of 3.

Score 2 Essay

Recently, there is a big debate on the issue that telling the truth or not is the most important consideration in the relationship between people. For my experience, I think telling a truth is the most important consideration in people's relationship. In the following, I will illustrate my opinion by two reasons.

First of all, honest make the trust stronger between friends or colleages. As we know, if people tell a lie to others he will not be trusted. When he tell a truth, others will believe that he tells a lie. For example, a person who is honest to others, can get real help and get trust of others.

Secondly, telling a lie always makes things worse not only in work but also in family life. When somebody do something wrong in his job he should annouce his mistake to his manager. If he don't do that others may continue their jobs base on the mistake. Consequently, the work will be worse and worse.

> On the contrary, sometimes it is better to tell a lie to others, such as telling a lie to a patient. As we know, the sick become worse when a cancer patient know his illness. A good way to protect their life is to tell a lie. So that many doctors will not tell the truth to a dying patient.
>
> To sum up, people should tell the truth to maintain their relationship with other people, although sometimes people have to tell a lie. People can get trust when they are honest to others.

Rater's Comments

This essay is quite long; but even though it uses several examples, each idea is only partly developed, and the connections among ideas are weak or contradictory. For instance, in paragraph 2 the first sentence says, "honest make the trust stronger." The next two sentences present a contrast: "if people tell a lie to others he will not be trusted" then "when he tell a truth, others will believe that he tells a lie." Then the last sentence in the paragraph says, "For example, a person who is honest to others, can get real help and get trust of others." But that is not an example of the previous sentence and only confuses the reader. This last sentence does not advance the progression of ideas much beyond the first sentence and certainly is not an example of the point made by the second and third sentences. Thus connections throughout this paragraph are tenuous. Paragraph 3 begins by saying that telling a lie makes things worse at work and at home, but it doesn't follow through at all on the latter. The "On the contrary" paragraph comes as a surprise to the reader since paragraph 1 said that the writer was going to give two reasons why telling the truth was the most important consideration in human relationships. Because of all these weaknesses, this essay earns a score of 2.

Score 1 Essay

> Nowadays, many people think that the people who always telling the true is the most inportant consideration in any relationship between human. but another think that is necessary to tell some lies. It is seldom to reach the same issue.I agree with the first thinking because of the following reasons.
>
> First fo all, we all live in the realized world , people can respect you unless you want to use correct method to communicate with other people. It is very important ,especially in business , if you want to recieve the good resulit ,you must tell the ture about your own so that gain the considement.
>
> Secondly, if you are honest man/woman, many people may be want to make friend with you. You can have more chance to communate with other people . you may be gain more information from them.
>
> However,sometimes we must speak some lie.for examlpe, when our relatives have heavy illness such as cancer,we couldn't telling them the ture.because that not good for their health,and may be affect their life.
>
> In conclusion,tellingthe ture is the people good behavire .we must require most of people to tell the ture.thus,we can see the better world in our life unless we always tell the ture.

Rater's Comments

This essay contains serious and frequent errors in sentence structure and usage. Paragraph 2 beginning "First fo all" is nearly incomprehensible and contains vocabulary that is either vague at best or non-standard English ("realized world," "considement"). Paragraph 3 is completely vague, and paragraph 4 (actually one sentence), though it mentions a familiar example, is poorly expressed and certainly underdeveloped. For all these reasons, this essay rates a score of 1.

The Independent Writing Topics

The following is a list of the actual Independent Writing topics that were eligible for use on former versions of the TOEFL test. You will see topics very similar to these on the TOEFL iBT. Whatever the topic, you will be asked to give your opinion and to support your opinion with specific reasons and examples.

It does not matter whether you agree or disagree with the topic; the raters are trained to accept all varieties of opinions. What matters are the skills discussed in the previous section: your ability to respond directly to the question, to take a clear position, and to write an essay characterized by good organization, proper use of supporting examples, sentence variety, and correct sentence structures.

None of the topics requires specialized knowledge. Most topics are general and are based on the common experience of people in general and students in particular.

What should you do with this list of topics? To prepare for the Writing section of TOEFL iBT, you should choose topics from the list and practice writing essays in response. Make sure you time yourself, taking 30 minutes to read the question, plan your work, and write your essay. After completing the essay, read it over and compare it with the scoring guide. Or better yet, have a friend or teacher evaluate the essay against the scoring criteria and give you feedback.

TOPIC LIST

➤ People attend college or university for many different reasons (for example, new experiences, career preparation, increased knowledge). Why do **you** think people attend college or university? Use specific reasons and examples to support your answer.

➤ Do you agree or disagree with the following statement?
Parents are the best teachers.
Use specific reasons and examples to support your answer.

➤ Nowadays, food has become easier to prepare. Has this change improved the way people live? Use specific reasons and examples to support your answer.

➤ It has been said, "Not everything that is learned is contained in books." Compare and contrast knowledge gained from experience with knowledge gained from books. In your opinion, which source is more important? Why? Use specific reasons and examples to support your answer.

➤ A company has announced that it wishes to build a large factory near your community. Discuss the advantages and disadvantages of this new influence on your community. Do you support or oppose the factory? Explain your position.

➤ If you could change one important thing about your hometown, what would you change? Use reasons and specific examples to support your answer.

➤ How do movies or television influence people's behavior? Use reasons and specific examples to support your answer.

➤ Do you agree or disagree with the following statement?
Television has destroyed communication among friends and family.
Use specific reasons and examples to support your opinion.

➤ Some people prefer to live in a small town. Others prefer to live in a big city. Which place would you prefer to live in? Use specific reasons and details to support your answer.

➤ "When people succeed, it is because of hard work. Luck has nothing to do with success."
Do you agree or disagree with the quotation above?
Use specific reasons and examples to explain your position.

➤ Do you agree or disagree with the following statement?
Universities should give the same amount of money to their students' sports activities as they give to their university libraries.
Use specific reasons and examples to support your opinion.

➤ Many people visit museums when they travel to new places. Why do you think people visit museums? Use specific reasons and examples to support your answer.

➤ Some people prefer to eat at food stands or restaurants. Other people prefer to prepare and eat food at home. Which do you prefer? Use specific reasons and examples to support your answer.

➤ Some people believe that university students should be required to attend classes. Others believe that going to classes should be optional for students. Which point of view do you agree with? Use specific reasons and details to explain your answer.

➤ Neighbors are the people who live near us. In your opinion, what are the qualities of a good neighbor? Use specific details and examples in your answer.

➤ It has recently been announced that a new restaurant may be built in your neighborhood. Do you support or oppose this plan? Why? Use specific reasons and details to support your answer.

➤ Some people think that they can learn better by themselves than with a teacher. Others think that it is always better to have a teacher. Which do you prefer? Use specific reasons to develop your essay.

➤ What are some important qualities of a good supervisor (boss)? Use specific details and examples to explain why these qualities are important.

➤ Should governments spend more money on improving roads and highways, or should governments spend more money on improving public transportation (buses, trains, subways)? Why? Use specific reasons and details to develop your essay.

➤ It is better for children to grow up in the countryside than in a big city. Do you agree or disagree? Use specific reasons and examples to develop your essay.

➤ In general, people are living longer now. Discuss the causes of this phenomenon. Use specific reasons and details to develop your essay.

➤ We all work or will work in our jobs with many different kinds of people. In your opinion, what are some important characteristics of a co-worker (someone you work closely with)? Use reasons and specific examples to explain why these characteristics are important.

➤ In some countries, teenagers have jobs while they are still students. Do you think this is a good idea? Support your opinion by using specific reasons and details.

➤ A person you know is planning to move to your town or city. What do you think this person would like and dislike about living in your town or city? Why? Use specific reasons and details to develop your essay.

➤ It has recently been announced that a large shopping center may be built in your neighborhood. Do you support or oppose this plan? Why? Use specific reasons and details to support your answer.

➤ It has recently been announced that a new movie theater may be built in your neighborhood. Do you support or oppose this plan? Why? Use specific reasons and details to support your answer.

➤ Do you agree or disagree with the following statement?
People should sometimes do things that they do **not** enjoy doing.
Use specific reasons and examples to support your answer.

➤ Do you agree or disagree with the following statement?
Television, newspapers, magazines, and other media pay too much attention to the personal lives of famous people such as public figures and celebrities.
Use specific reasons and details to explain your opinion.

➤ Some people believe that the Earth is being harmed (damaged) by human activity. Others feel that human activity makes the Earth a better place to live. What is your opinion? Use specific reasons and examples to support your answer.

➤ It has recently been announced that a new high school may be built in your community. Do you support or oppose this plan? Why? Use specific reasons and details in your answer.

➤ Some people spend their entire lives in one place. Others move a number of times throughout their lives, looking for a better job, house, community, or even climate. Which do you prefer: staying in one place or moving in search of another place? Use reasons and specific examples to support your opinion.

➤ Is it better to enjoy your money when you earn it or is it better to save your money for some time in the future? Use specific reasons and examples to support your opinion.

➤ You have received a gift of money. The money is enough to buy either a piece of jewelry you like or tickets to a concert you want to attend. Which would you buy? Use specific reasons and details to support your answer.

➤ Businesses should hire employees for their entire lives. Do you agree or disagree? Use specific reasons and examples to support your answer.

➤ Do you agree or disagree with the following statement?
Attending a live performance (for example, a play, concert, or sporting event) is more enjoyable than watching the same event on television.
Use specific reasons and examples to support your opinion.

➤ Choose **one** of the following transportation vehicles and explain why you think it has changed people's lives.
◆ automobiles
◆ bicycles
◆ airplanes
Use specific reasons and examples to support your answer.

➤ Do you agree or disagree that progress is always good? Use specific reasons and examples to support your answer.

➤ Learning about the past has no value for those of us living in the present. Do you agree or disagree? Use specific reasons and examples to support your answer.

➤ Do you agree or disagree with the following statement?
With the help of technology, students nowadays can learn more information and learn it more quickly.
Use specific reasons and examples to support your answer.

➤ The expression "Never, never give up" means to keep trying and never stop working for your goals. Do you agree or disagree with this statement? Use specific reasons and examples to support your answer.

➤ Some people think that human needs for farmland, housing, and industry are more important than saving land for endangered animals. Do you agree or disagree with this point of view? Why or why not? Use specific reasons and examples to support your answer.

➤ What is a very important skill a person should learn in order to be successful in the world today? Choose **one** skill and use specific reasons and examples to support your choice.

➤ Why do you think some people are attracted to dangerous sports or other dangerous activities? Use specific reasons and examples to support your answer.

➤ Some people like to travel with a companion. Other people prefer to travel alone. Which do you prefer? Use specific reasons and examples to support your choice.

➤ Some people prefer to get up early in the morning and start the day's work. Others prefer to get up later in the day and work until late at night. Which do you prefer? Use specific reasons and examples to support your choice.

➤ What are the important qualities of a good son or daughter? Have these qualities changed or remained the same over time in your culture? Use specific reasons and examples to support your answer.

➤ Some people prefer to work for a large company. Others prefer to work for a small company. Which would you prefer? Use specific reasons and details to support your choice.

➤ People work because they need money to live. What are some **other** reasons that people work? Discuss one or more of these reasons. Use specific examples and details to support your answer.

➤ Do you agree or disagree with the following statement?
Face-to-face communication is better than other types of communication, such as letters, e-mail, or telephone calls.
Use specific reasons and details to support your answer.

➤ Some people like to do only what they already do well. Other people prefer to try new things and take risks. Which do you prefer? Use specific reasons and examples to support your choice.

➤ Some people believe that success in life comes from taking risks or chances. Others believe that success results from careful planning. In your opinion, what does success come from? Use specific reasons and examples to support your answer.

➤ What change would make your hometown more appealing to people your age? Use specific reasons and examples to support your opinion.

➤ Do you agree or disagree with the following statement?
The most important aspect of a job is the money a person earns.
Use specific reasons and examples to support your answer.

➤ Do you agree or disagree with the following statement?
One should never judge a person by external appearances.
Use specific reasons and details to support your answer.

➤ Do you agree or disagree with the following statement?
A person should never make an important decision alone.
Use specific reasons and examples to support your answer.

➤ A company is going to give some money either to support the arts or to protect the environment. Which do you think the company should choose? Use specific reasons and examples to support your answer.

➤ Some movies are serious, designed to make the audience think. Other movies are designed primarily to amuse and entertain. Which type of movie do you prefer? Use specific reasons and examples to support your answer.

➤ Do you agree or disagree with the following statement?
Businesses should do anything they can to make a profit.
Use specific reasons and examples to support your position.

➤ Some people are always in a hurry to go places and get things done. Other people prefer to take their time and live life at a slower pace. Which do you prefer? Use specific reasons and examples to support your answer.

➤ Do you agree or disagree with the following statement?
Games are as important for adults as they are for children.
Use specific reasons and examples to support your answer.

➤ Do you agree or disagree with the following statement?
Parents or other adult relatives should make important decisions for their older (15- to 18-year-old) teenage children.
Use specific reasons and examples to support your opinion.

➤ What do you want **most** in a friend—someone who is intelligent, someone who has a sense of humor, or someone who is reliable? Which **one** of these characteristics is most important to you? Use reasons and specific examples to explain your choice.

➤ Do you agree or disagree with the following statement?
Most experiences in our lives that seemed difficult at the time become valuable lessons for the future.
Use reasons and specific examples to support your answer.

➤ Some people prefer to work for themselves or own a business. Others prefer to work for an employer. Would you rather be self-employed, work for someone else, or own a business? Use specific reasons to explain your choice.

➤ Should a city try to preserve its old, historic buildings or destroy them and replace them with modern buildings? Use specific reasons and examples to support your opinion.

➤ Do you agree or disagree with the following statement?
Classmates are a more important influence than parents on a child's success in school.
Use specific reasons and examples to support your answer.

➤ If you were an employer, which kind of worker would you prefer to hire: an inexperienced worker at a lower salary or an experienced worker at a higher salary? Use specific reasons and details to support your answer.

➤ Many teachers assign homework to students every day. Do you think that daily homework is necessary for students? Use specific reasons and details to support your answer.

➤ If you could study a subject that you have never had the opportunity to study, what would you choose? Explain your choice, using specific reasons and details.

➤ Some people think that the automobile has improved modern life. Others think that the automobile has caused serious problems. What is your opinion? Use specific reasons and examples to support your answer.

➤ Which would you choose: a high-paying job with long hours that would give you little time with family and friends **or** a lower-paying job with shorter hours that would give you more time with family and friends? Explain your choice, using specific reasons and details.

➤ Do you agree or disagree with the following statement?
Grades (marks) encourage students to learn.
Use specific reasons and examples to support your opinion.

➤ Some people say that computers have made life easier and more convenient. Other people say that computers have made life more complex and stressful. What is your opinion? Use specific reasons and examples to support your answer.

➤ Do you agree or disagree with the following statement?
The best way to travel is in a group led by a tour guide.
Use specific reasons and examples to support your answer.

➤ Some universities require students to take classes in many subjects. Other universities require students to specialize in one subject. Which is better? Use specific reasons and examples to support your answer.

➤ Do you agree or disagree with the following statement?
Children should begin learning a foreign language as soon as they start school.
Use specific reasons and examples to support your position.

➤ Do you agree or disagree with the following statement?
Boys and girls should attend separate schools.
Use specific reasons and examples to support your answer.

➤ Is it more important to be able to work with a group of people on a team or to work independently? Use reasons and specific examples to support your answer.

➤ Your city has decided to build a statue or monument to honor a famous person in your country. Whom would you choose? Use reasons and specific examples to support your choice.

➤ Describe a custom from your country that you would like people from other countries to adopt. Explain your choice, using specific reasons and examples.

➤ Do you agree or disagree with the following statement?
Technology has made the world a better place to live.
Use specific reasons and examples to support your opinion.

➤ Do you agree or disagree with the following statement?
Advertising can tell you a lot about a country.
Use specific reasons and examples to support your answer.

➤ Do you agree or disagree with the following statement?
Modern technology is creating a single world culture.
Use specific reasons and examples to support your opinion.

➤ Some people say that the Internet provides people with a lot of valuable information. Others think access to so much information creates problems. Which view do you agree with? Use specific reasons and examples to support your opinion.

➤ A foreign visitor has only one day to spend in your country. Where should this visitor go on that day? Why? Use specific reasons and details to support your choice.

➤ If you could go back to some time and place in the past, when and where would you go? Why? Use specific reasons and details to support your choice.

➤ What discovery in the last 100 years has been most beneficial for people in your country? Use specific reasons and examples to support your choice.

➤ Do you agree or disagree with the following statement?
Telephones and e-mail have made communication between people less personal.
Use specific reasons and examples to support your opinion.

➤ If you could travel back in time to meet a famous person from history, what person would you like to meet? Use specific reasons and examples to support your choice.

- ➤ If you could meet a famous entertainer or athlete, who would that be, and why? Use specific reasons and examples to support your choice.

- ➤ If you could ask a famous person one question, what would you ask? Why? Use specific reasons and details to support your answer.

- ➤ Some people prefer to live in places that have the same weather or climate all year long. Others like to live in areas where the weather changes several times a year. Which do you prefer? Use specific reasons and examples to support your choice.

- ➤ Many students have to live with roommates while going to school or university. What are some of the important qualities of a good roommate? Use specific reasons and examples to explain why these qualities are important.

- ➤ Do you agree or disagree with the following statement?
  Dancing plays an important role in a culture.
  Use specific reasons and examples to support your answer.

- ➤ Some people think governments should spend as much money as possible exploring outer space (for example, traveling to the moon and to other planets). Other people disagree and think governments should spend this money on our basic needs on Earth. Which of these two opinions do you agree with? Use specific reasons and details to support your answer.

- ➤ People have different ways of escaping the stress and difficulties of modern life. Some read; some exercise; others work in their gardens. What do you think are the best ways of reducing stress? Use specific details and examples in your answer.

- ➤ Do you agree or disagree with the following statement?
  Teachers should be paid according to how much their students learn.
  Give specific reasons and examples to support your opinion.

- ➤ If you were asked to send one thing representing your country to an international exhibition, what would you choose? Why? Use specific reasons and details to explain your choice.

- ➤ You have been told that dormitory rooms at your university must be shared by two students. Would you rather have the university assign a student to share a room with you, or would you rather choose your own roommate? Use specific reasons and details to explain your answer.

- ➤ Some people think that governments should spend as much money as possible on developing or buying computer technology. Other people disagree and think that this money should be spent on more basic needs. Which one of these opinions do you agree with? Use specific reasons and details to support your answer.

- ➤ Some people like doing work by hand. Others prefer using machines. Which do you prefer? Use specific reasons and examples to support your answer.

- ➤ Schools should ask students to evaluate their teachers. Do you agree or disagree? Use specific reasons and examples to support your answer.

- ➤ In your opinion, what is the most important characteristic (for example, honesty, intelligence, a sense of humor) that a person can have to be successful in life? Use specific reasons and examples from your experience to explain your answer.

➤ It is generally agreed that society benefits from the work of its members. Compare the contributions of artists to society with the contributions of scientists to society. Which type of contribution do you think is valued more by your society? Give specific reasons to support your answer.

➤ Students at universities often have a choice of places to live. They may choose to live in university dormitories, or they may choose to live in apartments in the community. Compare the advantages of living in university housing with the advantages of living in an apartment in the community. Where would you prefer to live? Give reasons for your preference.

➤ You need to travel from your home to a place 40 miles (64 kilometers) away. Compare the different kinds of transportation you could use. Tell which method of travel you would choose. Give specific reasons for your choice.

➤ Some people believe that a college or university education should be available to all students. Others believe that higher education should be available only to good students. Discuss these views. Which view do you agree with? Explain why.

➤ Some people believe that the best way of learning about life is by listening to the advice of family and friends. Other people believe that the best way of learning about life is through personal experience. Compare the advantages of these two different ways of learning about life. Which do you think is preferable? Use specific examples to support your preference.

➤ When people move to another country, some of them decide to follow the customs of the new country. Others prefer to keep their own customs. Compare these two choices. Which one do you prefer? Support your answer with specific details.

➤ Some people prefer to spend most of their time alone. Others like to be with friends most of the time. Do you prefer to spend your time alone or with friends? Use specific reasons to support your answer.

➤ Some people prefer to spend time with one or two close friends. Others choose to spend time with a large number of friends. Compare the advantages of each choice. Which of these two ways of spending time do you prefer? Use specific reasons to support your answer.

➤ Some people think that children should begin their formal education at a very early age and should spend most of their time on school studies. Others believe that young children should spend most of their time playing. Compare these two views. Which view do you agree with? Why?

➤ The government has announced that it plans to build a new university. Some people think that your community would be a good place to locate the university. Compare the advantages and disadvantages of establishing a new university in your community. Use specific details in your discussion.

➤ Some people think that the family is the most important influence on young adults. Other people think that friends are the most important influence on young adults. Which view do you agree with? Use examples to support your position.

➤ Some people prefer to plan activities for their free time very carefully. Others choose not to make any plans at all for their free time. Compare the benefits of planning free-time activities with the benefits of not making plans. Which do you prefer—planning or not planning for your leisure time? Use specific reasons and examples to explain your choice.

➤ People learn in different ways. Some people learn by doing things; other people learn by reading about things; others learn by listening to people talk about things. Which of these methods of learning is best for you? Use specific examples to support your choice.

➤ Some people choose friends who are different from themselves. Others choose friends who are similar to themselves. Compare the advantages of having friends who are different from you with the advantages of having friends who are similar to you. Which kind of friend do you prefer for yourself? Why?

➤ Some people enjoy change, and they look forward to new experiences. Others like their lives to stay the same, and they do not change their usual habits. Compare these two approaches to life. Which approach do you prefer? Explain why.

➤ Do you agree or disagree with the following statement?
People behave differently when they wear different clothes.
Do you agree that different clothes influence the way people behave? Use specific examples to support your answer.

➤ Decisions can be made quickly, or they can be made after careful thought. Do you agree or disagree with the following statement?
The decisions that people make quickly are always wrong.
Use reasons and specific examples to support your opinion.

➤ Some people trust their first impressions about a person's character because they believe these judgments are generally correct. Other people do not judge a person's character quickly because they believe first impressions are often wrong. Compare these two attitudes. Which attitude do you agree with? Support your choice with specific examples.

➤ Do you agree or disagree with the following statement?
People are never satisfied with what they have; they always want something more or something different.
Use specific reasons to support your answer.

➤ Do you agree or disagree with the following statement?
People should read only those books that are about real events, real people, and established facts.
Use specific reasons and details to support your opinion.

➤ Do you agree or disagree with the following statement?
It is more important for students to study history and literature than it is for them to study science and mathematics.
Use specific reasons and examples to support your opinion.

➤ Do you agree or disagree with the following statement?
All students should be required to study art and music in secondary school.
Use specific reasons to support your answer.

➤ Do you agree or disagree with the following statement?
There is nothing that young people can teach older people.
Use specific reasons and examples to support your position.

➤ Do you agree or disagree with the following statement?
Reading fiction (such as novels and short stories) is more enjoyable than watching movies.
Use specific reasons and examples to explain your position.

➤ Some people say that physical exercise should be a required part of every school day. Other people believe that students should spend the whole school day on academic studies. Which opinion do you agree with? Use specific reasons and details to support your answer.

➤ A university plans to develop a new research center in your country. Some people want a center for business research. Other people want a center for research in agriculture (farming). Which of these two kinds of research centers do you recommend for your country? Use specific reasons in your recommendation.

➤ Some young children spend a great amount of their time participating in sports. Discuss the advantages and disadvantages of this. Use specific reasons and examples to support your answer.

➤ Do you agree or disagree with the following statement?
Only people who earn a lot of money are successful.
Use specific reasons and examples to support your answer.

➤ If you could invent something new, what product would you develop? Use specific details to explain why this invention is needed.

➤ Do you agree or disagree with the following statement?
A person's childhood years (the time from birth to twelve years of age) are the most important years of a person's life.
Use specific reasons and examples to support your answer.

➤ Do you agree or disagree with the following statement?
Children should be required to help with household tasks as soon as they are able to do so.
Use specific reasons and examples to support your answer.

➤ Some high schools require all students to wear school uniforms. Other high schools permit students to decide what to wear to school. Which of these two school policies do you think is better? Use specific reasons and examples to support your opinion.

➤ Do you agree or disagree with the following statement?
Playing a game is fun only when you win.
Use specific reasons and examples to support your answer.

➤ Do you agree or disagree with the following statement?
High schools should allow students to study the courses that students want to study.
Use specific reasons and examples to support your opinion.

➤ Do you agree or disagree with the following statement?
It is better to be a member of a group than to be the leader of a group.
Use specific reasons and examples to support your answer.

➤ What do you consider to be the most important room in a house? Why is this room more important to you than any other room? Use specific reasons and examples to support your opinion.

➤ Some items (such as clothes or furniture) can be made by hand or by machine. Which do you prefer—items made by hand or items made by machine? Use reasons and specific examples to explain your choice.

➤ If you could make one important change in a school that you attended, what change would you make? Use reasons and specific examples to support your answer.

➤ A gift (such as a camera, a soccer ball, or an animal) can contribute to a child's development. What gift would you give to help a child develop? Why? Use reasons and specific examples to support your choice.

➤ Some people believe that students should be given one long vacation each year. Others believe that students should have several short vacations throughout the year. Which viewpoint do you agree with? Use specific reasons and examples to support your choice.

➤ Would you prefer to live in a traditional house or in a modern apartment building? Use specific reasons and details to support your choice.

➤ Some people say that advertising encourages us to buy things we really do not need. Others say that advertisements tell us about new products that may improve our lives. Which viewpoint do you agree with? Use specific reasons and examples to support your answer.

➤ Some people prefer to spend their free time outdoors. Other people prefer to spend their leisure time indoors. Would you prefer to be outside, or would you prefer to be inside for your leisure activities? Use specific reasons and examples to explain your choice.

➤ Your school has received a gift of money. What do you think is the best way for your school to spend this money? Use specific reasons and details to support your choice.

➤ Do you agree or disagree with the following statement?
Playing games teaches us about life.
Use specific reasons and examples to support your answer.

➤ Imagine that you have received some land to use as you wish. How would you use this land? Use specific details to explain your answer.

➤ Do you agree or disagree with the following statement?
Watching television is bad for children.
Use specific details and examples to support your answer.

➤ What is the most important animal in your country? Why is the animal important? Use reasons and specific details to explain your answer.

➤ Many parts of the world are losing important natural resources, such as forests, animals, or clean water. Choose one resource that is disappearing and explain why it needs to be saved. Use specific reasons and examples to support your opinion.

➤ Do you agree or disagree with the following statement?
A zoo has no useful purpose.
Use specific reasons and examples to explain your answer.

➤ In some countries, people are no longer allowed to smoke in many public places and office buildings. Do you think this is a good rule or a bad rule? Use specific reasons and details to support your position.

➤ Plants can provide food, shelter, clothing, or medicine. What is one kind of plant that is important to you or the people in your country? Use specific reasons and details to explain your choice.

➤ You have the opportunity to visit a foreign country for two weeks. Which country would you like to visit? Use specific reasons and details to explain your choice.

➤ In the future, students may have the choice of studying at home by using technology such as computers or television or of studying at traditional schools. Which would you prefer? Use reasons and specific details to explain your choice.

➤ When famous people such as actors, athletes and rock stars give their opinions, many people listen. Do you think we should pay attention to these opinions? Use specific reasons and examples to support your answer.

➤ The twentieth century saw great change. In your opinion, what is one change that should be remembered about the twentieth century? Use specific reasons and details to explain your choice.

➤ When people need to complain about a product or poor service, some prefer to complain in writing and others prefer to complain in person. Which way do you prefer? Use specific reasons and examples to support your answer.

➤ People remember special gifts or presents that they have received. Why? Use specific reasons and examples to support your answer.

➤ Some famous athletes and entertainers earn millions of dollars every year. Do you think these people deserve such high salaries? Use specific reasons and examples to support your opinion.

➤ Is the ability to read and write more important today than in the past? Why or why not? Use specific reasons and examples to support your answer.

➤ People do many different things to stay healthy. What do you do for good health? Use specific reasons and examples to support your answer.

➤ You have decided to give several hours of your time each month to improve the community where you live. What is one thing you will do to improve your community? Why? Use specific reasons and details to explain your choice.

➤ People recognize a difference between children and adults. What events (experiences or ceremonies) make a person an adult? Use specific reasons and examples to explain your answer.

➤ Your school has enough money to purchase either computers for students or books for the library. Which should your school choose to buy—computers or books? Use specific reasons and examples to support your recommendation.

➤ Many students choose to attend schools or universities outside their home countries. Why do some students study abroad? Use specific reasons and details to explain your answer.

➤ People listen to music for different reasons and at different times. Why is music important to many people? Use specific reasons and examples to support your choice.

➤ Groups or organizations are an important part of some people's lives. Why are groups or organizations important to people? Use specific reasons and examples to explain your answer.

➤ Imagine that you are preparing for a trip. You plan to be away from your home for a year. In addition to clothing and personal care items, you can take one additional thing. What would you take and why? Use specific reasons and details to support your choice.

➤ When students move to a new school, they sometimes face problems. How can schools help these students with their problems? Use specific reasons and examples to explain your answer.

➤ It is sometimes said that borrowing money from a friend can harm or damage the friendship. Do you agree? Why or why not? Use reasons and specific examples to explain your answer.

➤ Every generation of people is different in important ways. How is your generation different from your parents' generation? Use specific reasons and examples to explain your answer.

➤ Some students like classes where teachers lecture (do all of the talking) in class. Other students prefer classes where the students do some of the talking. Which type of class do you prefer? Give specific reasons and details to support your choice.

➤ Holidays honor people or events. If you could create a new holiday, what person or event would it honor and how would you want people to celebrate it? Use specific reasons and details to support your answer.

➤ A friend of yours has received some money and plans to use all of it either
   ◆ to go on vacation
   ◆ to buy a car
Your friend has asked you for advice. Compare your friend's two choices and explain which one you think your friend should choose. Use specific reasons and details to support your choice.

➤ The twenty-first century has begun. What changes do you think this new century will bring? Use examples and details in your answer.

➤ What are some of the qualities of a good parent? Use specific details and examples to explain your answer.

➤ Movies are popular all over the world. Explain why movies are so popular. Use reasons and specific examples to support your answer.

➤ In your country, is there more need for land to be left in its natural condition or is there more need for land to be developed for housing and industry? Use specific reasons and examples to support your answer.

➤ Many people have a close relationship with their pets. These people treat their birds, cats, or other animals like members of their family. In your opinion, are such relationships good? Why or why not? Use specific reasons and examples to support your answer.

➤ Films can tell us a lot about the country in which they were made. What have you learned about a country from watching its movies? Use specific examples and details to support your response.

➤ Some students prefer to study alone. Others prefer to study with a group of students. Which do you prefer? Use specific reasons and examples to support your answer.

➤ You have enough money to purchase either a house or a business. Which would you choose to buy? Give specific reasons to explain your choice.

PRACTICE TOEFL iBT WRITING SECTION

DIRECTIONS

This section measures your ability to use writing to communicate in an academic environment. There will be two writing tasks.

For the first writing task, you will read a passage and listen to a lecture and then answer a question based on what you have read and heard. For the second task, you will answer a question based on your own knowledge and experience.

Now listen to the directions for the first writing task.

WRITING BASED ON READING AND LISTENING

Directions: For this task, you will read a passage about an academic topic and you will listen to a lecture about the same topic. You may take notes while you read and listen.

Then you will write a response to a question that asks you about the relationship between the lecture you heard and the reading passage. Try to answer the question as completely as possible using information from the reading passage and the lecture. The question does **not** ask you to express your personal opinion. You may refer to the reading passage again when you write. You may use your notes to help you answer the question.

Typically, an effective response will be 150 to 225 words. Your response will be judged on the quality of your writing and on the completeness and accuracy of the content.

You should allow **3 minutes** to read the passage. Then listen to the lecture. Then allow **20 minutes** to plan and write your response.

[Reading]

Altruism is a type of behavior in which an animal sacrifices its own interest for that of another animal or group of animals. Altruism is the opposite of selfishness; individuals performing altruistic acts gain nothing for themselves.

Examples of altruism abound, both among humans and among other mammals. Unselfish acts among humans range from the sharing of food with strangers to the donation of body organs to family members, and even to strangers. Such acts are altruistic in that they benefit another, yet provide little reward to the one performing the act.

In fact, many species of animals appear willing to sacrifice food, or even their life, to assist other members of their group. The meerkat, which is a mammal that dwells in burrows in grassland areas of Africa, is often cited as an example. In groups of meerkats, an individual acts as a sentinel, standing guard and looking out for predators while the others hunt for food or eat food they have obtained. If the sentinel meerkat sees a predator such as a hawk approaching the group, it gives an alarm cry alerting the other meerkats to run and seek shelter. By standing guard, the sentinel meerkat gains nothing—it goes without food while the others eat, and it places itself in grave danger. After it issues an alarm, it has to flee alone, which might make it more at risk to a predator, since animals in groups are often able to work together to fend off a predator. So the altruistic sentinel behavior helps ensure the survival of other members of the meerkat's group.

Now play Track 42 from the audio CD.

Summarize the points made in the lecture, being sure to specifically explain how they cast doubt on points made in the reading passage.

You must finish your answer in 20 minutes.

This task is available as FREE practice on the ETS TOEFL Practice online site (http://toeflpractice.ets.org). If you enter your essay online, you can receive a rating for your work.

WRITING BASED ON KNOWLEDGE AND EXPERIENCE

Directions: For this task, you will write an essay in response to a question that asks you to state, explain, and support your opinion on an issue.

Typically, an effective essay will contain a minimum of 300 words. Your essay will be judged on the quality of your writing. This includes the development of your ideas, the organization of your essay, and the quality and accuracy of the language you use to express your ideas.

You have 30 minutes to plan and complete your essay.

Some young adults want independence from their parents as soon as possible. Other young adults prefer to live with their families for a longer time. Which of these situations do you think is better? Use specific reasons and examples to support your opinion.

LISTENING SCRIPT, EXPLANATIONS, AND SAMPLE RESPONSES

Writing Based on Reading and Listening

Listening Script

The following is the script of the lecture that you heard and were asked to summarize.

You know, often in science, new findings force us to re-examine earlier beliefs and assumptions. And a recent study of meerkats is having exactly this effect. The study examined the meerkat's behavior quite closely, much more closely than had ever been done before. And some interesting things were found. . . like about eating habits . . . it showed that typically meerkats eat before they stand guard — so the ones standing guard had a full stomach! And the study also found that since the sentinel is the first to see a predator coming, it's the most likely to escape . . . because it often stands guard near a burrow, so it can run immediately into the burrow after giving the alarm. The other meerkats, the ones scattered about looking for food, are actually in greater danger.

And in fact, other studies have suggested that when an animal creates an alarm, the alarm call might cause the other group members either to gather together or else to move about very quickly, behaviors that might actually draw the predator's attention away from the caller, increasing that animal's own chances of survival.

And what about people—what about some human acts that might be considered altruistic? Let's take an extreme case, uh, suppose a person donates a kidney to a relative, or even to a complete stranger. A selfless act, right? But . . . doesn't the donor receive appreciation and approval from the stranger and from society? Doesn't the donor gain an increased sense of self-worth? Couldn't such non-material rewards be considered very valuable to some people?

Question

Summarize the points made in the lecture you just heard, being sure to specifically explain how they cast doubt on points made in the reading.

Topic Notes

You should understand the meaning of altruism and altruistic acts. The definitions are given in the reading: altruism describes behavior that is the opposite of selfishness; it is behavior that benefits another individual or the group with no reward. The lecturer questions whether the examples meet the definition.

A high-scoring response will include the following points made by the lecturer:

POINT MADE IN READING	CONTRASTING POINT FROM THE LECTURE
Human organ donors gain nothing from their action.	The donors receive appreciation and approval from the rest of society.
Sentinel meerkats go without food to stand guard.	Sentinels actually eat before the other meerkats.
Sentinel meerkats place themselves in danger from predators.	Sentinels are actually the first to escape the predators.

Responses scoring 4 and 5 discuss altruistic/non-altruistic aspects of the three points in the table: human organ donation, meerkat sentinel eating behavior, and meerkat sentinel ability to escape.

Sample Responses with Raters' Comments

Score 5 Essay

The lecture completely refutes the passage. It is said in the lecture that, the perceived acts of altruism are nothing more than sneaky methods of gaining advantage for one's self.Contrary to the belief in the passage that sentinels risk their lives for the cause of the whole group, the professor says that the meerkat sentinels are in fact less prone to outside threats. The alarm sentinels give off causes to group to move rashly which draws the predators attention towards them, thus drawing away the attention from the sentinels.
The lecture refutes the fact that these meerkats are altruistic in the sense that they gain nothing in exchange of their services. In fact, researches have shown that they have a full stomach as they perform this "altruistic" duty and have a better chance of escaping from danger because they witness it ifrst Proffesor also offers a different underlying motivation that causes people to believe that acts such as donating an organ or sharing food with someone in need are altruistic. She says that people gain appreciation as a result of such acts, which may be deemed by some much more important than materialistic gains.

Rater's Comments

This answer meets all the criteria for a Level 5 response to an integrated task. The writer does a good job of selecting, framing, and interweaving points from the lecture and reading, explicitly and fluently presenting accurate connections between the relevant points. All three points made by the lecturer are included. Language is used accurately and effectively, and the overall piece is well-organized.

Score 4 Essay

Baed on the lecture, meerkats actually do not sacrifice themself by becoming a sentinel. Firstly, the meerkats that become a sentinel usually eats before. Secondly, these meerkats usually standing guard near their burrows. As a result, when a predator is seen, they raise an alarm and reach a safe place before the other meerkats that hunt for food. This shows that these meerkats do not put themselves in danger. In fact, the lecturer warned that the the alarm raised by these meerkats could be harmfull for the other meerkats. One of the reason is that the responses of the other meerkats to the alarm might attract attention from the predator. Based on these reasons, meerkats can not be used as an example of a mammal that performs altruistic behavior.

The lecture also pointed out that, it is not always true that individuals performing altruistic acts gain nothings for themselves. For example, when a man give one of his/her kidney to a family member or even a stranger, his/her self-worth increase. He/she feels usefull for other people. Therefore, he/she gain something from his/her action.

In sum, altruism behavior in animal and human is questioned. It is difficult for individuals sacrifices its own interest without gain anything for themselves.

Rater's Comments

This response includes all the main points of the lecture. The first paragraph begins with a clear statement that sentinel meerkats do not sacrifice themselves. There are strong concluding statements in each of the first two paragraphs that are quite explicit about the import of the sentinel behavior and the organ donation. The connections to the reading could be stronger. The writer says that the sentinel meerkat eats "before," but does not make an explicit contrast to the passage which says that sentinel meerkats go without eating. The conclusion in the final paragraph is vague ("altruism . . . is questioned"). On balance then, this response is a level 4, with minor vagueness and omission. In terms of language, there are a number of minor errors: "themself," missing verb in the sentence beginning "Secondly," "one of the reason," "a man give," "It is difficult for individuals sacrificies."

Score 3 Essay

Acording to the lecture, examinig closely to the eating habits of meerkats, these animals are not altruistic, mainly because the sentinel before standing guard eats. So that it has a full stomach. Another fact is that the sentinel, being the first that sees the predator, is able to be the first in escape. Also the other meerkats that are hunting and looking for food are the ones in danger. Considering the altruistic human acts, the donation of body organs shouldn't be considered like that, mainly because when a person donates an organ he or she receives appreciation and recognition of society.

Because of this points the lecture might make the reader doubt, mainly because the eating habits of the meerkats have been studied closely, giving arguments in order to justify that meerkats aren't doing altruistic acts.

The other argument about human and their altruistic actions sounds logical and a situiation in which a person would donate organs just to get appreciation of society couls be probable.

Because of this both, reading and lecture, are completely opposite, might make the user doubt and reflect more about altruism.

Rater's Comments

This response is at level 3. On the positive side, the response includes all the facts of the sentinel meerkat from the lecture as well as organ donation. However it is very vague in how it relates (see the Level 3 description in the Scoring Guide) the various points in the lecture to the points in the reading. There is no clear reference to the claim in the reading that the sentinel is sacrificing food or any explanation of the other meerkats being in danger. The statement commenting on organ donation, "The other argument about human and their altruistic actions sounds logical and a situation in which a person would donate organs just to get appreciation of society could be probable," is not very clear.

Score 2 Essay

Alturism is considered an act of selfishness. A research has been made, that shows the difference of alturism between humans and a special kind of mammal which is the meerkat. There is one of the meerkat that acts as a sentinel (having eaten before going to his sentinel place), and when it it aware that a predator is coming, he instantly gives a loud cry, and makes the others to run away to protect themselves. They do not get anything for their profit (the sentinels profit but he just stays there to protect it specie.

The other example that is given, is with humans. A clear example was given to show how selfishless works in humas beings. When a person, wants to donate an organ to somebody who is part of the family or not, may be that person expects the tfamily of the person tha has received the organ to give him or her thanks because of that favour. So, in that sense they make clear that there is a sense of selfishness in human beings, because they expect someting back. However, meerkats, do not have a sense of alturism, they just do their job without expecting anything back from their community.

Rater's Comments

The best part of this response is the explanation of the lecturer's point that organ donation can be seen from a selfish point of view. However it misrepresents the concept of altruism and is confused about the meaning of the information from the lecture about the sentinel's having eaten. The response misrepresents the point of the lecture by saying that humans are selfish but meerkats are truly altruistic. Because of the significant inaccuracies about both the lecture and the reading, this response is at level 2.

Score 1 Essay

The lecture said about altruism. It happen both animal and human. First, the meerkat is a good example of altruism for animal. They have special eatting habit. The meerkat which guard and look out predator is full stomach. After finish standing guard they eat some food while other meerkat guard from predators. When they find predators then they alarm to others to hide into the shelter. Also, human is altruistic animal. People share their food with strangers or they donate food or clothing even body organs. It stated both human and animal are altruism.

This lecture make our easy to understand and organize this lecture in mind. It shows short summary about this reading, and also give us some detail information. That is outlind of this reading. In addition, every contents is related to the reading, and also offer some more information. For this reason we can make sure about this reading.

Rater's Comments

Even though this response seems to include some information from the lecture (the fact that the guard meerkat "is full stomach"), it does not show how the information undermines the notion of altruism in meerkats; if anything, it is somehow construed as supporting the concept of meerkat altruism. The second paragraph contains severe language problems and communicates nothing to fulfilling the task. For these reasons, this is a level 1 response.

Writing Based on Experience and Knowledge

Topic:

Some young adults want independence from their parents as soon as possible. Other young adults prefer to live with their families for a longer time. Which of these situations do you think is better? Use specific reasons and examples to support your opinion.

Topic Notes

This topic, in effect, equates independence with living apart from one's family. Both broader and narrower definitions of independence and "non- independence" are acceptable as possible responses to the given topic, even though a majority of writers will write to the dichotomy presented by the prompt. Some writers take a general overview and their choices and examples are general and "philosophical." Others use specific personal examples or personal narratives in their approach to the topic. Some writers take a specific side of the issue, and others approach the topic by discussing conditions under which it is better to move away and conditions under which a young adult might do better to stay longer with the family. All these approaches are valid, on-topic responses and are judged by the raters on their merits according to the scoring guidelines for this task type.

Score 5 Essay—Sample 1

Every young adults will grow and live apart from their parents to form their own families. The ages for those young adults to be independent depends on each person. Some people may have to live longer with their parents and some others may not. This essay will discuss the issue of independent life and living with their families for a longer time.

Most young adults prefer to have a seperate or independent life from their parents or families as soon as possible. This is because they have a strong urge for freedom in doing what they desire. But in fact many of them fail. This should not be surprising since often they are actually not ready mentally although they are physically ready. It is widely understood that to live independently requires a lot of energy and is not easy at all. In this twenty first century, people may need more and more preparation because competition is increasing rapidly. An observation shows that many University graduated students are unemployed. Therefore, they will not be able to support and fulfill their necessities.

So living independently at an early age is not suitable for all young adults, some young adults may need to take more time to prepare themselves before going out to struggle. Young adults need to be ready to support themselves. Taking time to get more education and living with their families for a longer time may lead them to a better independent life because they will be well prepared for the hard-life outside. Still, living with their families for *too* long will not be a good idea because they could get to used to it and tend to be less independent.

The time to live independently depends on the person himself. He or she must decide whether they are ready to leave their parents to have an independent life or not. The decision will vary from one person to another. A person should judge that he is capable of fulfilling his needs without being dependent on his parents; this indicates that he is ready for his independent life. Otherwise he might need to stay longer with his parents.

Rater's Comments

This well-developed essay meets all the criteria for earning a score of 5. The writer develops the topic through a detailed discussion of independence and of the suitability of living independently. The essay is unified and coherent. Sentence structure is varied, especially in paragraphs 2 and 3. The writer does not use high-level vocabulary, but word choice is correct throughout. There are minor errors ("University graduated students," "fulfill their necessities"), but these in no way interrupt the flow or meaning of the essay.

Score 5 Essay—Sample 2

Independence! Who doesn't want independece? But the bigger question is how much of an independence is being discussed here? Generally, when teenagers grow up, their needs and habit of living change. Some would like their parents to be in control of the major decisions of their lives, while on the other hand, some would not like their parents to be involved in any sort of decision making process of their lives. In my opinion, the young adults should always consult their parents as their guides. I will try to demonstrate my point in the following paragraphs.

Let's assume a teenager grows up into a young adult. Now a major decision that he/she might have had to make was to what college/university they were going to attend. If we assume that the person seek complete independence from the early age, then they are generally going to make the decision themselves. But even if they made this desicion by themself, what is the probability that this is the best desicion. We all would agree that the best lesson learned is from a mistake, but why even let that happen? This is the most important decision they would have to make so far, and if they don't ask around, if they don't look at the wider picture, how are they supposed to end up at their very best opportunity? This, is what is known as a making/breaking point because this decision of theirs can make or break a very powerful potential future.

Now, suppose they passed the first make/break point. Then comes another one when they are going to marry. Normally, in the western culture, the man and the woman choose their marriage partners themselves, so this is not much of an important issue here. But, what about the cultures that predominantly have arranged marriages? In that case, choosing a husband or a wife could be a huge decision, because generally the marriages are not as easily broken as in the western culture. So, when it comes to this point, one would definately want to know their parents thinking and their previous experiance. This could come in very handy when one has a choice to make.

To sum it up, it is very good idea to ask for parents guides, and is never a bad a idea to give up a part of independence for a better future.

Rater's Comments

This essay has a rather informal, conversational tone and an "argument" that is coherently and fully developed. Sentence structure is varied throughout, and the writer consistently demonstrates command of language and English idioms, especially by using various informal expressions ("Let's assume," "we would all agree," "can make or beak," "come in very handy"). The essay meets all the criteria for a score of 5.

Score 4 Essay—Sample 1

There are different opinion regarding how long young adults should live with their parents. Some argues that the sooner a young adults become independence is the better while other think that it will be beneficial if they can live with their parents longer. In my opinion both have positive and negative sides. This essay will provide arguments for each case.

Some young adults favor for leaving their parents soon. They want to live free, independence from their parents' supervision. The good thing about being independence as soon as possible is that they can learn how to live by themselves. They must think how to support their living, otherwise they will still need the help of their parents and can not be independence. Living in their own will teach them how to be tough in facing real difficulties. But, staying away from parents soon could also lead to negative behaviour if the young adults can not control themselves. They might think that they can do whatever they want with the friends they like. If their friends give bad influence on them, no one will warn them and they can have problems. Thus, I will agree for young adults to become independence as soon as possible if they are already mature enough and able to control themselves. Parents can help to judge this before they release them.

In the case of young adult is not mature enough, I believe that staying with parents will be better. Parents can provide guidance and help when their children need it. But, if the children is become too dependent on their parents, they will have difficulties in their older lives of becoming independece as the parents will not be available for them anymore.

So parents in some way should teach their children about independence, for example by giving them responsibilities that should be handled without supervision.

Based on those arguments, I would like to say that either way could be better that the other depending on the maturity of young adults themselves. If they are mature and have self-control then living independently is better, otherwise they better stay with their parents until ready.

Rater's Comments

The points made in this essay are thoroughly developed and concretely supported. The essay is well organized and coherent, with a nice flow. What keeps the response from scoring a 5 is the number of noticeable errors in structure and word choice: "Some argues," "favor for leaving," "living in their own," "become independence," "if the children is become too dependent." None of these errors interferes with meaning, but their quantity and effect earns the essay a score of 4.

Score 4 Essay—Sample 2

Independence from the family at early stages of life is a common phenomena exists in our society. moving out from the family house to live on your own in early ages of your adult life has an advantages and disadvantages. However, the disadvantages outweigh the advantages.

Independency is generally good and helpful for the individual, because it teaches individuals how to take care of different responsibilities, and how to handle things by yourself. people needs to know how to live independently of others, because eventually they will have to. So, the desire to get your independence from your family when you are young adult is good because it shows the some kind of individual maturity for being aware of the ultimate situation, when you have to move out and live on your own.

On the other hand, adults should consider moving out when they are sure that they are ready for it. Being ready includes being financially, physically, and psychologically ready. One major advantage for staying with your parents is financially advantage. Because one gets to save money between the residency and daily living issues.

Nowadays, life has become harder for the new generations to live and keep up with. And in order to do that, individualls needs to be fully equiped in terms of education, support, and maturity. And by staying with the family, one would not have to worry about alot of issues, instead, one will concerntrate more on getting equiped for the next step in his life, which is moving out and getting independent of others.

In conclusion, although moving out when you are still a young adult to live independently from the family has some good point, the disadvantages of it overcome these good points.

Rater's Comments

This essay is clearly organized and unified, though it does remain on a fairly abstract level. It is also generally well developed. Sentence structure is varied, but there are noticeable errors in syntax and expression ("is financially advantage," "has an advantages," "Because one gets to save money between the residency and daily living issues." "getting independent of others"). These errors earn this essay a score of 4.

Score 3 Essay—Sample 1

Right now adults have different points of view about live. Independent from their parents as soon as possible or continue to to live with their parents. Live with your parents have many differents advantage. First, some people dont want to have resposabilities, they want their parents still take the desicion. For example, house's responsablities or pays. Secound, When peoples live with their parents they dont expend a lot money for haouse or food. Third, they belief that their family is a great company. But in the other hand, when people live along have important advantage. For example, They live independient, they dont heve limitation in their own house. They dont need to negociate with other persons or family. Morover, they have a graet oportunity to learn about how administarte a house, amd what is the real value of the money. They can understand everytuhing about responsability in their house. Finally They have more freedom.

Both live independient and live with your parents have many different disadvantage. On the first points of view, live independient, the most important problem is money and expensive. For example, right now young adults need to find a good job for live in a good place because rents are expensive. It is the same with food and services. They need to have a excellent imcome to live in good conditions. Also, they need to work in the house along because dont have company. They need to clean, do the laundry, buy the food, and cook along. Although pepole think live independient have a huge sacrifies, also live with their parents it is difficult and have a lot of disadvantage. For example, when people live with thier parents have many different limitation with activities in the house, every time need to negociate with your family. In addition,

Rater's Comments

This essay is somewhat developed and is longer than the average essay with a score of 3. It has a coherent organization based on describing the pros and cons of living apart from one's parents and living with them, with supporting points. In some cases, however, this approach leads to redundancy, especially toward the end of the essay. Additionally, even discounting typographical mistakes, the various errors clearly reveal weakness in command of language ("Live with your parents have many differents advantage," "the most important problem is . . . expensive,"). Meaning is also sometimes obscured ("house's resonsabilities or pays," "They need to work in the house along because dont have company").

Score 3 Essay—Sample 2

Young adults show different patterns of behavior when they have to decide whether continuing to live with their family or not. For instance, in United States young adults prefer to live separated from they parents as soon as possible. This tendency reflects wises of freedom and independence. Altough these behavior has remarkable advantages and disadvantage, the advantage can overwhelm the negative effects.

It is important to recognize that by living separated from parents or family can be more risked than living with them. many young adults are victims of group pressure and gangs because of theirs parents absence.

However, a significant advantage of living by onself is that people develop ledearship skills. Individuals that live by themselves learn to do and sustain their own decisions. On the contrary, people who live with their parents are more shy and less confident. For instance, many of the greatest world leaders are or have been people that were separated from their parents when they were kids.

Another advantage of living indepntly is that peolpe can fully develop their creative potential. When people is forced to difficult situations, they can surprise us with outstanding abilities and values that otherwise remained hidden. A good example are blind people, these person show a remarkable ability for art and music. In a similar way, when parents are absent or too away for help, individuals manage to survive and be successful.

Rater's Comments

Though slightly stronger than the average essay with a score of 3, this essay fails to earn a score of 4 mainly because of errors that obscure meaning ("reflects wises of freedom and independence"). Also, connections among ideas are not always completely clear. For example, the details used to support the points made in paragraphs 3 and 4 are concrete but not well connected to each other or to the generalizations made by the writer.

Score 2 Essay—Sample 1

In my opinion,it is better when adults live with their families for a longer time. Some young adults make a big mistake going away from their families.They want independence,but sometimes it can cause a lot of problems.A lot of young adults in my country,depend of their parents.Ofcause they can do whatever they want.They can find a job,earn their own money,start a family,and so one,but they prefer to stay wiht their families and be depended.In my country parents allways care about their children.They support them by giving money,some advise.If you are young adults you can allways ask your parents about help,and they will s

Rater's Comments

Limited in development and lacking any organizing principle, this essay is squarely in the 2 range. The generalizations made are only barely supported. There are errors ("prefer to stay with their families and be depended," "ask your parents about help"), but it is the lack of development and extremely unclear connections between ideas ("A lot of young adults in my country, depend of their parents. Ofcause they can do whatever they want") that limit this essay to a score of 2.

Score 2 Essay—Sample 2

In my opoinion, young adults live with their families longer time is better than they become independent from their parents because they can recive living supports and advise from their parents.

> Some young adults want live by themselves eventhought they are not financialy independent. Therefore, their credit history is destoryed by irresponsible payments. Futhermore, when they have their own family, these credit dermages cause their worsest future.
>
> If they live with their family, they can get great advise from their family who know them very well. For example, when they are in great denger sutuation, only their family come to resucu them, so they can protect them self.
>
> For these resons, I think that young adults live with their families for long time is better than they become independent quickerly.

Rater's Comments

More developed that the average essay with a score of 2, this response fails to earn a 3 because it contains so many language errors ("receive living supports," "quickerly") and sentences that obscure meaning ("these credit dermages cause their worsest future," ". . . only their family come to resucu them, so they can protect them self"). These language weaknesses make it difficult for the reader to understand the ideas the writer tries to present.

Score 1 Essay—Sample 1

> These days most of the youngs adults wants to live independence from their parents. In my case I want to live independence only in my college years because I believ in hetrogeneous family.
>
> Nowadays young adults want to live independence because of privacy and second reasons is if they live independence then they will also learn take care of themself.

Rater's Comments

This essay essentially repeats the writing prompt twice and then briefly addresses the task. It is characterized by underdevelopment with very little elaboration. There are errors, but it is the lack of development that earns this essay a score of 1.

Score 1 Essay—Sample 2

> I have learnd a lot of tihng since I came to the U.S.A. It wasn't until I came here that I never seperated from my parents. In here, not only did I gain information everything, but I also felt love's value who i loved.
>
> That's why I insiste that young adults have to live without parents.

Rater's Comments

This essay fails to make any coherent points and is filled with errors of language and usage. These weaknesses earn it a score of 1.

CHAPTER 6

Writer's Handbook for English Language Learners

➤ **Grammar**—This section explains key grammar rules and gives examples.

➤ **Usage**—This section explains important usage rules and gives examples.

➤ **Mechanics**—This section describes the basic mechanics rules and gives examples. Mechanics includes spelling and punctuation.

➤ **Style**—This section discusses key aspects of effective style.

➤ **Organization and Development**—This section gives advice about the writing process and the development of all parts of an essay.

➤ **Advice to Writers**—This section discusses different types of essays.

➤ **Revising, Editing, and Proofreading**—This section explains what to do in each stage of improving your essay.

➤ **Glossary**—This section presents definitions for terms.

Grammar

This section provides information on the following grammar errors:

➤ Sentence Errors
➤ Word Errors
➤ Other Errors

SENTENCE ERRORS

Fragments

A fragment is an incomplete sentence. It does not express a complete thought, even though it starts with a capital letter and ends with a punctuation mark. It is missing either a subject or a verb or both.

Here are three examples of fragments:

Fragment: *Where there were mice and cockroaches.*
Fragment: *A movie that inspires deep emotions.*
Fragment: *Analyzing the characters' motives.*

These three groups of words cannot stand alone as complete sentences. They can be corrected in two ways. One way is to attach the fragment to a complete sentence:

Corrected sentence: *Peter left the apartment where there were mice and cockroaches.*
Corrected sentence: *I went to see "The Silver Star," a movie that inspires deep emotions.*
Corrected sentence: *Analyzing the characters' motives is central to understanding a novel.*

Another way to correct fragments is to add a complete subject, complete verb, or other words that express a complete thought:

Corrected sentence: *This is where there were mice and cockroaches.*
Corrected sentence: *A movie that inspires deep emotions is rare.*
Corrected sentence: *Analyzing the characters' motives is important.*

SUMMARY: Sentence fragments are incomplete sentences. Sometimes readers can figure out the meaning of a fragment by rereading the sentences that come before and after it. However, turning fragments into complete sentences will improve the connections between ideas.

Run-on Sentences

You may have a run-on sentence. Run-on sentences happen when we join two sentences together without a conjunction or the correct punctuation. Run-on sentences can be very confusing to read. Here is an example: *My sister loves to dance she is very good at it.*

There are several ways to correct run-on sentences:

1. Divide the run-on sentence into two separate sentences.

   Run-on sentence: *My sister loves to dance she is very good at it.*
   Corrected sentence: *My sister loves to dance. She is very good at it.*

   Run-on sentence: *Jim showed us his ticket someone gave it to him.*
   Corrected sentence: *Jim showed us his ticket. Someone gave it to him.*

2. Connect the parts of the run-on sentence with a coordinating conjunction and a comma. These are the most common coordinating conjunctions: *and, but, for, nor, or, so, yet.*

   Run-on sentence: *My sister loves to dance she is very good at it.*
   Corrected sentence: *My sister loves to dance, and she is very good at it.*

   Run-on sentence: *She agreed to chair the meeting she didn't come.*
   Corrected sentence: *She agreed to chair the meeting, but she didn't come.*

3. Connect the parts of the run-on sentence with a subordinating conjunction. These are the most common subordinating conjunctions: *after, although, as, because, before, if, since, unless, until, when, whereas, while.*

   Run-on sentence: *My sister loves to dance she is very good at it.*
   Corrected sentence: *My sister loves to dance because she is very good at it.*

Run-on sentence: *Maria and John like skiing Karen does not.*
Corrected sentence: <u>Although</u> *Maria and John like skiing<u>,</u> Karen does not.*

4. Connect the parts of the run-on sentence with a semicolon.

Run-on sentence: *Gordon laughed at Sandy's joke it was funny.*
Corrected sentence: *Gordon laughed at Sandy's joke<u>;</u> it was funny.*

Run-on sentence: *I thought he was here I was wrong.*
Corrected sentence: *I thought he was here<u>;</u> I was wrong.*

SUMMARY: Run-on sentences are two or more sentences that have been joined together without a conjunction or the correct punctuation. You can usually correct them by using punctuation or conjunctions.

WORD ERRORS

Noun Forms

A noun is usually defined as a *person, place,* or *thing.*

Person: *man, woman, waiter, John, book*
Place: *home, office, town, station, Hong Kong*
Thing: *table, car, apple, money, music, love, dog, monkey*

Learning a few basic rules will help you to use nouns effectively:

1. In English, some nouns are countable. That is, they are things that we can count. For example: *house.* We can count *houses.* We can have one, two, three, or more *houses.* Here are more examples of countable nouns:

dog, cat, animal, man, person, bottle, box, pound, coin, dollar, bowl, plate, fork, table, chair, suitcase, bag

Countable nouns can be singular or plural.

Singular: *I have <u>a friend.</u>*
Plural: *I have <u>two friends.</u>*

2. Usually, to make nouns plural, add *-s,* as in the examples given above (*friend–friends*).

However, there are special cases where you do not add *-s.*

➤ When a word ends in *-ch, -s, -sh, -ss* or *–x,* the plural is formed by adding *-es. (ben<u>ch</u>es, ga<u>s</u>es, di<u>sh</u>es, dre<u>ss</u>es, ta<u>x</u>es)*

➤ When a word ends in *-y preceded by a consonant (b, d, m, n, p),* the plural form is *-ies. (par<u>t</u>ies, bo<u>d</u>ies, poli<u>c</u>ies)*

➤ When a word ends in *-y preceded by a vowel,* the plural is formed by adding *-s. (tra<u>y</u>s, jo<u>y</u>s, ke<u>y</u>s)*

➤ When a word ends in *–o,* the more common plural ending is *-oes. (tomatoes, potatoes, zeroes, heroes)*

➤ When the final -o is preceded by a vowel, the plural ending is -os.(videos, studios)

➤ When a word ends in -f, the plural is formed

◆ either by adding -s (beliefs, puffs)
◆ or by changing the -f to -v and adding -es (wife, wives; leaf, leaves; loaf, loaves).

➤ When a word ends in -ex or -ix, the plural ending is usually -es. (appendixes, indexes)

➤ In certain cases the plural form of a word is the same as the singular. (deer, sheep, fish, series)

3. Some nouns are uncountable.—The represent things that cannot be counted. For example, we cannot count *coffee*. We can count "cups of *coffee*" or "pounds of *coffee*," but we cannot count *coffee* itself. Here are more examples of uncountable nouns:

music, art, love, happiness, advice, information, news, furniture, luggage, rice, sugar, butter, water, electricity, gas, money

We usually treat uncountable nouns as singular.

Incorrect: *These <u>furnitures</u> are beautiful.*
Correct: *This <u>furniture</u> is beautiful.*

4. Some uncountable nouns refer to abstract ideas or emotions. Abstract ideas may refer to qualities that we cannot physically touch. For example:
madness, health, justice

We cannot count abstract nouns, so they are always singular.

Incorrect: *<u>Healths</u> are more important than <u>wealths</u>.*
Correct: *<u>Health</u> is more important than <u>wealth</u>.*

Incorrect: *Have <u>funs</u> at the reunion.*
Correct: *Have <u>fun</u> at the reunion.*

5. Some nouns can be countable *and* uncountable. For example, *paper, room, hair, noise, time*. With these nouns, the singular and plural forms often have different meanings.

Countable: *The Christmas <u>lights</u> make the mall very pretty.*
Uncountable: *This room does not get enough <u>light.</u>*

Countable: *Othello is one of Shakespeare's most famous <u>works</u>.*
Uncountable: *I have a lot of <u>work</u> to do tonight.*

6. Singular nouns that are countable usually come after an article or other determiner (*a, an, the, this, my, such*).

Incorrect: *His mother is doctor.*
Incorrect: *Boy standing over there is brother.*
Incorrect: *We saw child in playground.*
Correct: *His mother is <u>a</u> doctor.*
Correct: *<u>The</u> boy standing over there is <u>my</u> brother.*
Correct: *We saw <u>a</u> child in <u>the</u> playground.*

SUMMARY: Nouns are important words in a sentence because they form the subjects or objects. Some nouns can be counted and some can't. Learning a few rules will help you to use nouns effectively.

Verb Forms

Verbs are parts of speech that express action (*jump, show*) or a state of being (*are, was*). Here are a few tips that may help you to use verbs effectively:

1. Helping verbs (also called *auxiliary verbs*) precede the main verb. All of the following verbs may be helping verbs:

   be, am, is, are, was, were, being, been, has, have, had, do, does, did, can, will, shall, should, could, would, may, might, and *must*

   Here are examples of sentences with helping verbs:

   Many people don't know what they <u>are</u> going to do after college.
   I <u>am</u> going to give you step-by-step instructions.

2. Words such as *might, must, can, would,* and *should* are also called modals. They express a wide range of meanings (ability, permission, possibility, necessity, etc.)

   The following examples show one use of modals:

   Tom <u>might</u> have gone to the party if he had been invited.
   If I had a million dollars, I <u>would</u> buy a house for my parents.

   This use of modals is called the conditional use. One event relies on another or it cannot take place. In the first example, Tom cannot go to the party without being invited. In the second example, I can buy a house for my parents only if I had a million dollars.

3. The infinitive form of the verb is formed by using the word *to* plus the simple form of the verb.

   He is too tired <u>to go</u> to the barbecue.
   The manager wants <u>to hire</u> a new secretary.

   The infinitive can also be used as the subject or object of a sentence.

   <u>To invest</u> now seems risky.
   The teacher told him <u>to leave.</u>

   In the first example, *To invest* is the subject of the sentence, while, in the second example, *to leave* is the object.
   We can use the infinitives to show an action that is occurring at the same time as, or later than, the action of the main verb.

   We like <u>to play</u> video games.
   My best friend wants <u>to shop</u> at that mall.

   In the first example, the *liking* is happening at the same time as the *playing*. In the second example, the *shopping* is going to happen at a later time than the *wanting*.

4. Do not use *of* after a helping verb. In some verb phrases, there are two or more verbs being used (*should have happened, might be eaten, could have decided*). Here are examples in which the word "*of*" is used incorrectly:

Incorrect: *They would of stayed one more month if possible.*
Incorrect: *In that time, he could of finished the project.*

Correct: *They would have stayed one more month if possible.*
Correct: *In that time, he could have finished the project.*

     Of is a preposition, not a verb, and in each of these sentences *of* should be replaced with the helping verb *have*.

SUMMARY: Verbs are very important parts of a sentence. There are a few rules that you can learn to make your use of verbs more effective.

Subject–Verb Agreement

In English, the subject and verb must always agree in number. Below are a few rules that will help you:

1. A singular subject takes a singular verb:

   The teacher was happy with my answer.
   My cell phone is not working.

   In the first example, the singular subject *teacher* agrees with the singular verb *was*. In the second example, the singular subject *cell phone* agrees with the singular verb *is*.

2. A plural subject takes a plural verb:

       My parents were happy with my grades.
       Many television stations have reported that story.

   In the first example, the plural subject *parents* matches the plural verb *were*, and in the second example, the plural subject *television stations* matches the plural verb *have*.

   You should never have a plural subject with a singular verb.

   Incorrect: *Many students thinks tomorrow is a holiday.*

   This sentence can be edited to make the subject and verb agree:

   Correct: *Many students think tomorrow is a holiday.*

   Similarly, you should never have a singular subject with a plural verb.

   Incorrect: *The student think tomorrow is a holiday.*

   This sentence can be edited to make the subject and verb agree:

   Correct: *The student thinks tomorrow is a holiday.*

3. Sometimes subjects and verbs are separated by a word or a phrase. When that happens, students sometimes forget to make them agree in number.

   Incorrect: *Your suggestions about the show was excellent.*
   Incorrect: *The use of cell phones during concerts are not allowed.*

Correct: *Your <u>suggestions</u> about the show <u>were</u> excellent.*
Correct: *The <u>use</u> of cell phones during concerts <u>is</u> not allowed.*

In the first example, since the subject of the sentence is *suggestions,* which is plural, the plural verb *were* is used. In the second example, the singular subject *use* needs the singular verb *is.*

4. A compound subject needs a plural verb.

When you proofread your work, correctly identify the subject in your sentences. For example, the following sentences have more than one subject:

The camcorder and the tripod were returned yesterday.
Both Chantel and Rochelle are nice names.

In the first example, the complete subject is compound (*camcorder* and *tripod*), and so the verb must be plural (*were*). In the second example, the compound subject is *Chantel and Rochelle* and therefore needs the plural verb *are.*

5. A collective noun must agree with the verb. Collective nouns are nouns that name a group (*committee, herd, board of directors*). In American English, collective nouns are usually singular:

Correct: *The <u>committee is</u> made up of twelve people.*
Correct: *The <u>jury has</u> not arrived at a verdict.*

When you use a collective noun to refer to a group acting as an individual unit, you should make the verb singular. In the first example, the subject (*committee*) is singular, so it takes the singular verb *is.* In the second example, the singular subject (*jury*) takes the singular verb *has.*

However, sometimes you might want to emphasize that the group acted as individuals, each for himself or herself. Then you could write the following:

Awkward: *The <u>committee were</u> divided in their opinions.*
Awkward: *The <u>jury have</u> been listening to the tapes for two days.*

In these examples, the individuals in the groups are emphasized, so the plural verbs are used. However, while correct, these sentences sound awkward. You might want to change the words *committee* to *committee members* in the first example, and from *jury* to *jury members* in the second example.

SUMMARY: A verb should always agree with its subject. A singular subject takes a singular verb, and a plural subject takes a plural verb. Sometimes a phrase separates the subject and the verb, making it hard to find the real subject.

Pronouns

A pronoun is a word that takes the place of one or more nouns. Pronouns are words like *he, his, she, her, hers, it, they, their, them, these, that, this, those, who, whom, which, what, whose.*

If we didn't have pronouns, we would have to repeat a lot of nouns. We would have to say things like:

Do you like <u>the new manager</u>? I don't like <u>the new manager</u>. The <u>new manager</u> is too unfriendly.

With pronouns, we can say

Do you like <u>the new manager</u>? I don't like <u>him</u>. <u>He</u> is too unfriendly.

Learning a few rules will help us use pronouns correctly and effectively:

1. Pronouns must agree with the nouns they refer to. If your pronoun refers to a girl or woman, you use a feminine pronoun (*she, her, hers*). If your pronoun refers to a boy or man, you use a masculine pronoun (*he, his, him*).

   Any pronoun you use must also agree in number with the noun it refers to. If you are using a pronoun to refer to a singular noun, you must use a singular pronoun; if you are using a pronoun to replace a plural noun, you use a plural pronoun.

   Julia reminded us that that <u>she</u> would not stay late.
   Bob bought two computers and had <u>them</u> delivered to his office.

   In the first example, the singular pronoun *she* is used to stand for Julia, a female person. In the second example, the plural pronoun *them* is used to refer to the plural noun *computers*.

2. Some indefinite pronouns are always singular. Indefinite pronouns like *each, one, every, everyone, everybody, anyone, anybody, anything, someone, somebody, either, neither, nothing, nobody, none,* and *no one* are always singular, so other pronouns that refer to them must also be singular, as in these examples:

   <u>Neither</u> of the boys sent in <u>his</u> report.
   <u>Everyone</u> must buy <u>her</u> own ticket.

   Note the construction of the second sentence, in which the writer decided to use the pronoun *her*. Some people would prefer the pronoun to be *his or her* to indicate explicitly that each person, regardless of his or her gender, is purchasing a ticket. Some instructors consider his or her constructions awkward and allow *everyone* to be treated as plural (*<u>Everyone</u> must buy their own <u>ticket</u>*). Other instructors consider the plural construction not acceptable in good writing.

3. Some indefinite pronouns are always plural. These include *both* and *many*. Other pronouns that refer to *them* must also be plural.

   <u>Both</u> of <u>them</u> are here tonight.
   <u>Many</u> of the managers have moved into <u>their</u> new offices.

   In the first example, *both* is plural, and so the plural pronoun *them* is used. In the second example, the plural pronoun *their* is used because *many* is plural.

4. Some indefinite pronouns can be singular or plural. Indefinite pronouns like *all, any, more, most, none,* and *some* can be singular or plural, depending on their meaning in a context.

Most of my time *is* spent reviewing for the test.
Most of the students *have* turned in *their* reports.

In the first example, *most* refers to *time*, a singular noun. It thus takes the singular verb *is*. In the second example, *most* refers to the plural noun *students*. This is why it takes the plural verb *have* and is referred to by the plural pronoun *their*.

5. Overusing pronouns can cause confusion:

Confusing: *The President informed the Vice President that all of his supporters should be meeting with him.*

Whose supporters, the President's or the Vice President's? Whom are they meeting with? This sentence needs to be revised to fix the confusion caused by the use of *him* and *his*. This can be accomplished by replacing the pronouns with the appropriate nouns.

Clear: *The President informed the Vice President that all of the President's supporters should be meeting with the President.*

Excessive use of *it* weakens writing, especially when *it* is used to introduce a sentence, as in this example:

Confusing: *We were visiting the museum. I saw it. It was interesting and unusual. I was amazed by it.*

You can improve *it* by explaining what the first *it* refers to.

Clear: *We were visiting the museum. I saw the space exhibit. It was interesting and unusual. I was amazed by it.*

In this example, can you figure out what *it* stands for?

Although the car hit the tree, it was not damaged.

Does *it* refer to the car or the tree? You can make the sentence clear by rewriting it.

The car was not damaged, although it hit the tree.

6. When you have nouns joined by a conjunction (*and, or,* or *nor*), don't forget to make a pronoun that refers to them agree in number, as in these examples:

If Bob and Rick want to go, they will need to take the bus because I don't have room in my car.
Whether I buy a dishwasher or dryer, it will have to go in the kitchen.

In the first example, there is a compound noun, as *Bob* and *Rick* are joined by the conjunction *and*. So the plural pronoun *they* must be used. In the second example, the noun is singular (*dishwasher* or *dryer*). Thus the singular pronoun *it* is used.

7. You should know when to use *who, whom, which,* or *that*.

Who and *whom* refer to people. *Which* refers to things, and *that* can refer to either people or things.

The committee interviewed all the candidates who applied.
Do you still have the magazine that I lent you last week?
Which courses should I take in the fall?

In the first example, *who* refers to a group of people (*candidates*). In the second example, *that* refers to a thing (*magazine*). In the third example, *which* refers to a thing (*courses*).

SUMMARY: A pronoun is a word used to take the place of one or more nouns. Singular pronouns must be used to refer to singular nouns, and plural pronouns must be used to refer to plural nouns. Some indefinite pronouns can be singular or plural, according to their meaning in the sentence.

Possessive Pronouns

Possessive pronouns are used to show possession or ownership. Here are a few rules that will help you to use possessive pronouns effectively:

1. When you are using possessive pronouns like *his, hers, mine, theirs, yours,* or *ours,* make sure that the possessive pronoun agrees in number with the noun to which it refers.

   Incorrect: *I have my car, and my husband has theirs.*
   Incorrect: *This is the children's room. All those toys are <u>hers</u>.*

   Correct: *I have my car, and my husband has <u>his</u>.*
   Correct: *This is the children's room. All those toys are <u>theirs</u>.*

   In the first sentence, the singular pronoun *his* should be used to show that the car belongs to the singular *husband*. In the second sentence, *theirs* should be used to show that the toys belong to the plural noun *children*.

2. Possessive pronouns don't take an apostrophe. *His, hers, its, ours, yours, theirs,* and *whose* are pronouns that already convey possession, so don't add an apostrophe to them.

   Incorrect: *Each art room has <u>it's</u> own sink.*
   Incorrect: *<u>His'</u> office is on the third floor.*

   Correct: *Each art room has <u>its</u> own sink.*
   Correct: *<u>His</u> office is on the third floor.*

   In the first sentence, a possessive pronoun is needed (*its*) not *it's,* which means *it is*. In the second sentence, the possessive pronoun *his* is needed; *his'* is never used.

Other Ways to Show Possession

Besides possessive pronouns, there are other ways to show possession, such as using an apostrophe and an s (-'s).

My neighbor<u>'s</u> house is bigger than mine.
Henry<u>'s</u> cat likes to play with our baby.

Below are some rules for indicating possession.

1. When a noun ends in -*s* and the addition of *'s* makes the word sound odd, some writers add only an apostrophe, as in these examples:

   I like James' company.
   This is Harris' wife, Anna.

2. Make sure you put the apostrophe in the right place. Put the apostrophe *before* the *-s* if the word is singular:

The teacher's desk is right in front. (one teacher)
My sister's haircut cost $70 dollars. (one sister)

You will put the apostrophe *after* the *-s* only if it is a plural word:

We borrowed our parents' car. (more than one parent)
I went to a party at my friends' house. (more than one friend)

3. When two or more people share ownership, you use an apostrophe and s on the last noun. When each person has separate ownership, you need to indicate that, as in these examples:

John and Jack's room is very messy. (John and Jack share one room.)
Ian's and George's dreams are very different, even though the two boys come from the same family. (Ian and George have different dreams.)

4. Don't use an apostrophe when you want to make a noun plural. An apostrophe shows possession, not the plural of a noun. These sentences are wrong: They should not have apostrophes.

The new student's look confused.
There are too many car's on our street's.

SUMMARY: Possessive pronouns are used to show possession, or ownership. There are a few rules that can help you to use them correctly.

Prepositions

A preposition is a word that is used before a noun (or noun phrase) to give more information in a sentence. Prepositions are usually used to show where something is located or when something happened. Examples of prepositions include *in, among, between, across, at, with, beside, behind, in, into, from, during, before,* and *after.* entre

Prepositions are used to show al lado de, junto a

➤ place:

The main office is in New York.
I'm meeting my colleagues at the coffee shop.

Besides → además

➤ time:

Let's try to get there by 3:30.
Please do not talk during the show.

➤ action or movement:

He jumped into the river.
We flew from Los Angeles to Toronto.

Some verbs and adjectives are usually followed by certain prepositions.

They always argue about money.
I borrowed a book from the library.

Here are more examples of words and prepositions that usually go together:

familiar with, afraid of, far from, close to, believe in, borrow from, lend to, absent from, nice to, argue with, made of, take off, turn on, happy with, sad about, famous for

The following sentences contain *incorrect* use of prepositions:

Incorrect: *I am <u>afraid at</u> losing my textbooks.*
Incorrect: *The student <u>argued at</u> the teacher.*

Correct: *I am <u>afraid of</u> losing my textbooks.*
Correct: *The student <u>argued with</u> the teacher.*

The first sentence can be corrected by changing *at* to *of*. In the second sentence, the preposition that should go with *argued* is *with*.

SUMMARY: Prepositions are used to show relationships between a noun and other parts of a sentence. There are a few rules that can help you to use prepositions correctly.

OTHER ERRORS

Wrong or Missing Word

Especially when writing or typing quickly, people often use the wrong word or misspell words. When you begin to revise, edit, and proofread, read carefully for wrong words or words that you have left out.

One of the most frequent problems is the use of *the* instead of *they*.

Incorrect: *<u>The</u> went to the store each Monday.*

The writer most likely intended the following:

Correct: *<u>They</u> went to the store each Monday.*

Another common error is a missing noun after the word *the*.

Incorrect: *<u>The</u> go to the store each Monday.*
Correct: *<u>The brothers</u> go to the store each Monday.*

SUMMARY: Wrong or missing words commonly occur but are easy to correct. Proofread your sentences carefully. The spell checker on the computer should be able to catch these errors, too.

Keyboard Errors or Typos

Sometimes while writing the first drafts of an essay, you might leave out words or make keyboarding errors. They might be grammar, usage, or mechanics errors, or they could be omitted words or typos. Proofread carefully to correct these errors when you edit and revise your writing.

USAGE

This section provides information on the following usage errors:

➤ Article Errors
➤ Confused Words
➤ Wrong Form of Word
➤ Faulty Comparison

ARTICLE ERRORS/DETERMINER ERRORS

The following are rules and explanations for using articles and examples of how articles are used correctly when you are writing in English.

What Are Articles?

A, an, and *the* are called *articles.* These are words that come before a noun or its modifier. (A *modifier* is a word that makes a noun clearer or more specific. Modifiers tell how many or which one.)

a thinker	*an* apple	*the* house
a car	*an* old house	*the* newspapers

There are two types of articles in English. *A* and *an* are called indefinite articles. *The* is called a definite article.

When to Use *a* or *an*

A or *an* is used before a **singular** noun when the noun refers to *any* member of a group.

James must write *an essay* for his writing class today.
A newspaper is a good source of information on current events.

If the noun or the modifier that follows the article begins with a consonant sound, you should use the article *a:*

a basketball   *a* new automobile

On the other hand, if the noun or its modifier begins with a vowel sound—a, e, i, o, u—you should use the article *an*:

an elephant   *an* old truck

A/an is used before a noun if the noun can be counted. For example:

I received *a letter* from my sister.
Sending *an e-mail* is a fast way to communicate with classmates.

Sometimes a noun or a modifier can begin with a vowel *letter* but not a vowel *sound*. For example, here the vowel *o* in the word *one* sounds like the consonant *w* in *won*:

This will be *a* one-time charge to your account.

When to Use *the*

The is used before singular and plural nouns when the noun is a particular or specific noun. Use the article *the* if you can answer the question "Which?" or "What one?"

The art class that I want to take is taught by a famous painter.
The students in Mrs. Jones' class do not want to participate in *the debate*.

In addition, *the* is used in the following ways:

➤ To refer to things known to everyone (*the* sun, *the* stars, etc.)
➤ To refer to things that are unique (*the* White House)
➤ To refer to time (*the* past, *the* present, *the* future)

When Not to Use an Article:

A/an is not used before a noun if the noun cannot be counted:

I like to drink milk. (*Milk* is not counted.)

If a quantity of milk is specified, then the article would be used:

I like to drink *a glass of milk* before I go to bed.

Sometimes nouns used to represent abstract general concepts (such as anger, beauty, love, poverty, employment) do not take *a* or *an* before them:

Love is a difficult emotion to describe in words.
Money alone cannot buy happiness.

The is not used when a plural noun is used in a general sense:

Computers are helpful tools for student writers. (*Computers* refers to the general concept of computers, not to specific computers.)
The computers in that classroom are used for writing class. (*The computers* refers to a specific set of computers.)

OTHER DETERMINER ERRORS

The adjectives *this, that, these,* and *those* modify nouns that follow them by telling "which one." These adjectives must agree in number with the nouns they modify. *This* and *that* are used to describe a singular noun. *These* and *those* are used to describe plural nouns.

Incorrect: *I would buy <u>these house</u> for <u>those reason</u>.*
Incorrect: *<u>This kinds</u> of technologies will affect people's behavior.*
Correct: *I would buy <u>this house for that reason</u>.*
Correct: *<u>These kinds</u> of technologies will affect people's behavior.*

HOMONYMS

Certain words are known as *homonyms.* These are words that sound the same but may differ in meaning, spelling, or usage. Homonyms can be of two types—words that are spelled alike and words that sound alike. Words that are spelled alike but differ in meaning are called *homographs.* An example of a homograph is the word *bear,* which can mean a type of animal, or the verb *bear,* which means "to carry." Words that sound alike but differ in meaning and spelling are called *homophones.* The words *whole* and *hole* are homophones. *Whole* is an adjective meaning "complete," and *hole* is a noun meaning "an empty place." What follows are examples of some common homonyms. Always check your writing to make sure you are using the appropriate words.

here *adverb* meaning "in this place"
*We have been waiting **here** for an hour.*

hear *verb meaning "to listen"*
*Do you **hear** the birds singing?*

hole *noun* meaning "an empty place"
*The children dug a big **hole** in their sandbox.*

whole *adjective* meaning "with no part removed or left out, complete"
*Our **whole** project will involve cooperation from everyone.*

its *pronoun* possessive form of *it*
*The kitten hurt **its** paw.*

it's contraction of *it is*
***It's** not fair to leave her behind.*

know *verb* meaning "to feel certain, or to recognize"
*Do you **know** how to get to the subway?*

no *adverb* used as "a denial or refusal"
*The employee said **no** to the job offer.*

knew *verb* past tense of the verb *to know*
*The boy **knew** how to count to ten.*

new *adjective* meaning "not old"
*At the start of the school year, the students bought **new** books.*

desert *noun* meaning "a dry and sandy place"
*It rarely rains in the **desert.***

desert *verb* meaning "to abandon"
*The officer commanded the troops to not **desert** their posts.*

dessert *noun* meaning "the final course of a meal"
*After a big meal, I enjoy a simple **dessert** of vanilla ice cream.*

to *preposition* meaning "toward"
*The man pointed **to** the sun.*

two *adjective* or *pronoun* meaning "the number 2"
*Five is **two** more than three.*

too *adverb* meaning "also"
*Tom and Eleanor wanted to go with them **too.***

they're *contraction* meaning "they are"
***They're** both coming to the party.*

their *possessive pronoun* meaning "belonging to them"
*That is **their** blue house on the corner.*

there *adverb* meaning "at that place"
*Did you see anyone you knew **there**?*

> **through** *adverb* meaning "completed or finished"
> When she was **through** eating, she put her plate in the sink.
>
> **threw** *past tense of the verb throw* meaning "tossed"
> The boy **threw** the ball to his sister.

Other Confused Words

Besides homonyms, other words are confused in English because they are similar in spelling, sound, or meaning. Examples of some commonly confused words include *accept/except, advice/advise, affect/effect,* and *loose/lose.*

Computer spellcheckers will not catch these words if you have misused them. When you review your work, proofread to see whether you have used the correct word. Even native speakers of English often make mistakes with confused words when they are writing, especially when they are in a hurry.

Review the meanings of some commonly confused words.

accept *verb* meaning "to receive, "to agree or to take what is offered"
I **accept** your kind invitation.

except *preposition* meaning "other than or leaving out," "excluding"
Everyone **except** Phil can attend the conference.

advice *noun* meaning "an opinion given about what to do or how to behave"
He has always given me valuable **advice** regarding my future plans.

advise *verb* meaning "to recommend or counsel"
I **advise** you to stay in school and study hard.

affect *verb* meaning "to influence" or "to produce an effect on"
The weather can **affect** a person's mood.

effect *noun* meaning "result"
When students study for tests, they see a positive **effect** on their test results.

effect *verb* meaning "to bring about"
The governor can **effect** change in state education policies.

loose *adjective* meaning "detached, not rigidly fixed," "not tight"
She lost her bracelet because it was too **loose** on her wrist.

lose *verb* meaning "to be deprived or to no longer have," "to not win"
If you don't pay attention to the signs, you might **lose** your way.

quiet *adjective* meaning "not loud or noisy"
Please be **quiet** when other people are speaking.

quit *verb* meaning "to give up or abandon," "to stop"
The boys will **quit** their jobs the week before school starts.

quite *adverb* meaning "to some extent"
Moving to a new city will be **quite** a change for my family.

sense *noun* meaning "conscious, awareness, or rationality" or "the faculty of perceiving by means of sense organs"

*My brother had the good **sense** to keep out of trouble.*
*The doctor explained that my **sense** of smell is not functioning well.*

since *adverb* meaning "from a definite past time until now;" *conjunction* meaning "later than"

*Ginny has lived in the same house ever **since** she moved to town.*
*Karl has worked as an accountant **since** graduating from college.*

than *conjunction* used when comparing two elements
*Her puppy is smaller **than** mine.*

then *adverb* meaning "at that time, or next"
*First I will stop at the store, and **then** I will go home.*

These are just a few examples of words that are often confused in English. When you are unsure of the proper usage of a word, consult an English dictionary.

Wrong Form of Word

When you write quickly, sometimes you use a word form that is different from the one that you intended to use. One reason why this error occurs is that a word can be used in different ways in a sentence depending on its purpose.

When you revise, read your writing very carefully to find these errors. Or get someone else to read your work and to help you see where you are not clear. Here are examples of wrong word forms that can occur:

Incorrect: *But certain types of businesses will continue to grow to <u>an extend</u>, he thinks.*
Extend is a verb, and this writer meant to use the noun *extent*.

Correct: *But certain types of businesses will continue to grow to <u>an extent</u>, he thinks.*

Here is another example of a wrong word form in a sentence:

Incorrect: *I want to work with <u>disable</u> children.*
This writer should revise *disable* to *disabled*.

Correct: *I want to work with <u>disabled</u> children.*

Learning the parts of speech can teach you how each functions in a sentence. Proofreading your own work can help you correct these errors as well.

FAULTY COMPARISON

A faulty comparison error occurs when the word *more* is used with in a comparison with a word that ends in *-er,* or when the word *most* is used within a comparison with a word that ends in *-est.*

Incorrect: *The boy with the red hair is <u>more taller</u> than the girl with the black hair.*
Incorrect: *James thinks that Mary is the <u>most prettiest</u> girl in school.*

To avoid making these kinds of errors in your writing, you should review the following rules.

When comparing one thing to another, add the ending *-er* to short words (usually of one syllable).

Correct: *The boy with the red hair is <u>taller</u> than the girl with the black hair.*
Correct: *Today it is hot, but yesterday it was even <u>hotter</u>.*

When comparing three or more things, add the ending *-est* to short words (usually of one syllable).

Correct: *The girl in the back of the room is the <u>tallest</u> girl in her entire class.*

Correct: *Yesterday was the <u>hottest</u> day ever recorded by the National Weather Service.*

In many cases, with words of two or more syllables, you do not add *-er* or *-est* to the word; instead, use the word *more* before the word when comparing two things, and use the word *most* when comparing three or more things.

Correct: *The judges must decide which of the two remaining singers is <u>more talented</u>.*

Correct: *Of the three new students, John is the <u>most intelligent</u>.*

Comparisons that are negative use *less* for comparisons of two things and *least* for comparisons of three or more things.

Correct: *The third floor apartment is <u>less costly</u> than the first floor apartment.*
Correct: *Of the three colleges that I've visited, this one is the <u>least expensive.</u>*

NONSTANDARD VERB OR WORD FORM

The words you use in everyday conversation are often different from the words you use in standard written English. While a reader might understand these informal words—*gotta, gonna, wanna, kinda*—you should not write them in an essay. Here are two examples of nonwords used in sentences:

Nonstandard: *I told her I <u>gotta</u> go to school now.*
Correct: *I told her I <u>have got to</u> go to school now.*
Nonstandard: *Do you <u>wanna</u> go to college?*
Correct: *Do you <u>want to</u> go to college?*

Even though you can understand what the writer means, the words *gotta* and *wanna* do not exist in standard written English.

Mechanics

This section provides information on the following types of mechanics errors:

➤ Capitalization
➤ Spelling
➤ Punctuation
➤ Other Errors

CAPITALIZATION

To *capitalize* means to use capital letters. Below are some guidelines for capitalization:

1. Capitalize the first word of every sentence:

   <u>H</u>e is the most famous director in Hollywood right now. <u>N</u>o doubt about it.
   <u>G</u>ive it to me. <u>I</u>t looks like mine.

2. Capitalize all proper nouns, for example names of individuals, objects, titles, and places:

Francis Lloyd Mantel lives on Moore Street.
The class is reading The Adventures of Huckleberry Finn.

In the first example, "Francis Lloyd Mantel" is the name of an individual, so it is capitalized. "Moore Street" is the name of a place, so it is also a proper noun. The second example contains the title of a book, so it is capitalized.

All names are proper nouns and must be capitalized. Other examples:

➤ Names of institutions, places, and geographical areas:

She is a new faculty member at Stanford University.
Their main office is in New Delhi, India.

➤ Names of historical events, days, months, and holidays:

Martin Luther King Day is a school holiday.
Classes don't meet until October.

➤ Names of languages and proper adjectives:

He speaks Spanish and Italian fluently.
They teach Korean dances at the academy.

3. The first person pronoun *I* is always capitalized, even when it is in the middle of a sentence.

It is I who sent you that letter.
They told me that I should call for an appointment.

4. Capitalize words like *father, mother, aunt,* and *uncle* when used with proper names or when addressing a particular person.

Aunt Bessie and Uncle Jesse just bought a country house.
Yes, Mom, I'm going after dinner.

However, when these words are used with possessive pronouns, they are not proper names and therefore are not capitalized.

My father is not at home.
Their mother is my aunt.

In the above examples, *father, mother,* and *aunt* are not capitalized because they are used with the possessives *my* and *their.*

SUMMARY: In English, the first letter of the first word in a sentence is always capitalized. You must also capitalize all proper nouns. Proper nouns include all names and titles. The first person pronoun I is always capitalized too.

SPELLING

English spelling rules are complex. Here are a few rules that may help you:

1. Write *i* before *e* (*fiery*, *friend*, *dried*), EXCEPT

   ➤ after *c* (*rec**ei**ve*)
   ➤ when sounding like *a* as in *neighbor* (*w**ei**gh*, *h**ei**r*, *for**ei**gn*)

   Note these examples:

   *All applicants will rec**ei**ve a response within three weeks.*
   *The breakfast special is fr**ie**d eggs and sausage.*

Adding Endings to Words

2. If a word ends with a silent *e*, drop the *e* when adding a suffix that begins with a vowel (for example, the *-ing* suffix). However, do <u>not</u> drop the *e* when the suffix begins with a consonant (for example, the *-ful* suffix).

   *I like to skat**e**. I enjoy skat**ing**.*
   *I could use a dictionary. A dictionary is very us**eful**.*

   In the first example (*skate–skating*), the *e* is dropped because the *-ing* suffix begins with the vowel *i*. In the second example, the *e* is not dropped because the *-ful* suffix begins with the consonant *f*.

3. When *y* is the last letter in a word and the letter before *y* is a consonant, drop *y* and add *i* before adding a suffix.

   *The beaches in Thailand are extremely beaut**iful**.*
   *They hurr**ied** to the gate because they were so late.*

   In both examples, the *y* is replaced with *i* (*beauty–beautiful*; *hurry–hurried*).

4. When forming the plural of a word that ends with a *y* preceded by a vowel, just add *s*. But if the letter before *y* is a consonant, drop *y* and add *i* before adding the suffix.

   FAO Schwartz is a famous <u>toy</u> store. It sells all kinds of toy<u>s</u>.
   *Lad**ies** and gentlemen, please be seated.*

   In the first example, *o* (a vowel) comes before *y*. So you only need to add *s* to form the plural noun. But in the second example, in the word *lady*, *d* (a consonant) comes before *y*. You have to drop *y* and add *i* to make the word plural.

5. When a word ends in a consonant preceded by one vowel, double the final consonant before adding a suffix that begins with a vowel.

   *The children sw**im** at the community pool. They love sw**imming**.*
   *You should beg**in** at the beg**inning**. Start by writing the title.*

   In the first example, the word *swim* ends with *m*. In the second example, the word *begin* ends with *n*. Both *m* and *n* are consonants. When adding *-ing*, a suffix starting with a vowel, you just need to double the final consonant.

   Remember: When the ending begins with a vowel and the word ends in an *e*, do not double the consonant. Instead, drop the *e* and add the ending.

Incorrect: *The children go <u>skatting</u> in the winter.*
Correct: *The children go <u>skating</u> in the winter.*

The following examples contain *incorrect* spelling:

Incorrect: *We visited the monkey house at the zoo. There were <u>monkies</u> from all over the world.*
Incorrect: *My <u>neice</u> is a student in your class.*

In the first sentence, the plural form of *monkey* is *monkeys*. This is because when forming the plural of a word that ends with a *y* preceded by a vowel, you should just add *s*. In the second sentence, *niece* is the correct spelling. Remember, "*i* before *e* except after a *c*" is a very useful rule!

Correct: *We visited the monkey house at the zoo. There were <u>monkeys</u> from all over the world.*
Correct: *My <u>niece</u> is a student in your class.*

These are all useful rules for learning English spelling. However, there are also some exceptions that are not covered by these rules, so it is a good idea to learn a few strategies for spelling as well.

For example, there are times when we make mistakes because we type too fast. It is easy to make the following errors on the computer:

Incorrect: *A letter <u>frrom</u> her former neighbor came in the mail today.*
Incorrect: *<u>Becuase</u> I lost my homework, I had to do it again.*

Both sentences contain typos, or mistakes we make when we type. One strategy for dealing with typos is to use the spell check function on the computer.

However, there are mistakes that will not be caught by the spell checker. For example,

Incorrect: *W   ͞er he is at work today?*
Incorrect: *A͞   ͞n restaurants in this area?*

In these examp   ͞rlined word is spelled correctly, the use of the word in the ser   ͞he spell checker will not be able to find such errors, so after s   ͞ould check for these errors as you read each sentence for meani

Another str   ͞ of words that you often misspell. Memorize as many as you ca   ͞ specifically for these words.

You could al   ͞hile you write to check the spelling of words that you are unsure

SUMMARY: Englis   ͞ and may sometimes seem strange. There are rules that can b   ͞rned, and there are strategies that can help you to spell better.   ͞ictionary and the spell check function on your computer.

PUNCTUATION

Punctuation refers to the use of punctuation marks. Some punctuation marks, like the *apostrophe*, are used with individual words. Some, like *commas*, are used either to separate parts of sentences or to separate digits in numbers. Others, such as *periods, question marks,* and *exclamation points* are used to separate sentences. They help us to make the meaning of our sentences clear.

Apostrophe

Use an apostrophe when you write a contraction. A contraction is the joining of two words by eliminating some letters and adding an apostrophe. It's a kind of short form. For example, *can't* is the contraction of *cannot, shouldn't* is the contraction of should *not,* and *let's* is the contraction of *let us.* Other contractions are *won't, it's, wouldn't,* and *couldn't.*

> They <u>won't</u> be able to enter without their tickets.
> We could hear them, but we <u>couldn't</u> see them.

In the first example, *won't* is the contraction of *will not,* and in the second sentence, *couldn't* is the contraction of *could not.*

Some people write contractions without the apostrophe. They are incorrect. The following sentence shows an incorrect use of a contraction.

> Incorrect: <u>Lets</u> go to the park tomorrow.
> Correct: <u>Let's</u> go to the park tomorrow.

Let's is the contraction of *let us.* Without the apostrophe, the word means "allow," as in this sentence:

> Correct: *She <u>lets us</u> use the computer when she's not using it.*

In order to be used correctly, the apostrophe must be in the proper position. Below are examples of misplaced apostrophes:

> Incorrect: *We <u>could'nt</u> understand the lecture.*
> Incorrect: *Students <u>were'nt</u> in school in the summer.*
> Correct: *We <u>couldn't</u> understand the lecture.*
> Correct: *Students <u>weren't</u> in school in the summer.*

Note that the apostrophe should replace the vowel that is being deleted.

SUMMARY: The apostrophe is used to show contraction and possession. For other uses of the apostrophe, see the section on "Possessive Pronouns."

Comma

The comma is the most common form of punctuation within a sentence. It's a signal for the reader to pause. In fact, if you read the examples below carefully, you'll notice a natural pause where the commas are situated.

Learning a few basic rules will help you to use the comma effectively:

1. Use a comma and conjunction (such as *and* or *but*) to join two clauses in a compound sentence:

> *The causes of the civil war were many, <u>and</u> the effects of the war were numerous.*
> *The experiment was incomplete, <u>but</u> the lessons learned were important.*

In the above examples, because the two clauses are independent clauses (or complete sentences) joined together by a conjunction, they need a comma between them.

2. Use a comma to connect words to the front or back of your sentence. We often add information to our sentences by attaching one or more words to the front or back. When you do that, you can use a comma to help your reader find your main message.

   Last night, my friend and I celebrated his 58th birthday.
   Many years ago, I studied French and German.

   Each of these sentences begins with a phrase that indicates time. This information is separated from the main sentence by a comma.

3. Use a comma between each item of a list when you are listing three or more items in a sentence:

   The flag was red, white, and blue.
   I bought milk, bread, cheese, and butter.

   The commas in the above examples clearly mark where one item on the list ends and the next one begins.

4. Use a comma between adjectives. If you have two adjectives together before the noun they describe, they must be separated by a comma:

   The cold, wintry wind chilled me to my bones.
   The complex, diverse cultures in the city add to its excitement.

   In the above examples, the adjectives describing *wind* and *cultures* are placed before the noun, separated by commas.

5. Use commas to set off additional information in the middle of a sentence: Some information, often telling details about the subject of the sentence, needs to be distinguished from the main part of the sentence (the verb and object). We place commas in front and in back of these groups of words.

   Ms. Johnson, the company president, will announce the winner.
   My brother, who loves to read, uses the library every day.

   In the above examples, if you take away the parts that are set off by commas, you still have a complete sentence.

6. Use commas to separate quoted matter from the rest of the sentence:

   "Take a break," said the instructor.
   Nancy announces, "I'm getting married tomorrow."

   In each example, the quotation is set apart from the rest of the sentence by a comma.

7. Use commas to set off the name of a state or country when it follows a city, county, or equivalent:

   The newspaper is based in Chicago, Illinois.
   Her flight to Beijing, China, took twelve hours.

   In the above examples, the comma is used to set off the name of a state or country from a city within it.

8. In written American English, use commas to set off numbers in groups of four or more digits and between the words for the day, month, and year of a date.

He won $1,000,000 in the lottery.
The date is March 15, 2003.

In the first example, commas are used because of the numbers (of four or more digits). In the second example, it is used in a date.

The following sentences are missing commas:

Incorrect: *Conrad Redding the father of the bride cried at the wedding.*
Incorrect: *In conclusion I believe that technology will be the main factor affecting life in the 21st century.*

In the first sentence, "the father of the bride" should be set off by a pair of commas. In the second sentence, there should be a comma after "In conclusion."

Correct: *Conrad Redding, the father of the bride, cried at the wedding.*
Correct: *In conclusion, I believe that technology will be the main factor affecting life in the 21st century.*

SUMMARY: Commas are used to separate parts of sentences and make meaning clearer. There are rules that can help us to use commas more effectively.

Hyphen

The hyphen is the punctuation mark used to join two words together to form a compound word. The most common uses of hyphens are as part of an adjective phrase, in numbers, and as prefixes.

1. Hyphens with compound adjectives. Use a hyphen to join two or more words serving as a single adjective *before* a noun. For example,

   His uncle is a <u>well-known</u> author.

   However, when compound adjectives come *after* a noun, they are not hyphenated. For example,

   The author is <u>well known</u> for his mystery stories.

2. Hyphens with compound numbers. A hyphen should be used in fractions and in the numbers twenty-one and above.

   The cup is <u>three-quarters</u> full.
   Our teacher is <u>sixty-three</u> years old.

   In the above examples, the compound numbers are joined with hyphens.

3. Hyphens with prefixes. A *prefix* is a syllable or word added to the beginning of another word to change its meaning. The prefixes *self-*, *ex-*, and *great-* always require a hyphen when they are added to words.

   The instructions are <u>self-explanatory</u>.
   The children are with their <u>great-grandparents</u>.

   However, for prefixes such as *dis-*, *pre-*, *re-*, and *un-*, a hyphen is normally not used.

   My aunt <u>dislikes</u> loud music.
   The answer to that question is <u>unknown</u>.

SUMMARY: We use hyphens to link some compound words, but not all compound words are hyphenated. In fact, American English is tending to use fewer and fewer hyphens. Always check a recent dictionary to be sure you are hyphenating correctly.

FINAL PUNCTUATION

There are a few punctuation marks that help us to end our sentences. These are the question mark, the period, and the exclamation point.

Question Mark

Use a question mark at the end of a direct question.

> *When did World War II begin?*
> *What were the key stages in the Romantic Art movement?*

Period

Periods are used to mark the end of a sentence that is a not a question. A period is also used at the end of an indirect question.

> *I just completed the project.*
> *Cindy asked me who would be taking notes at the meeting.*

Exclamation Point

Use an exclamation point after a sentence that expresses strong feeling or requires emphasis. An exclamation point also serves to make a sentence stand out.

> Correct: *That was utter nonsense!*
> Correct: *What absolutely gorgeous flowers! Thank you!*

The following examples contain *incorrect* use of final punctuation:

> Incorrect: *Have you called Mrs. Han yet.*
> Incorrect: *Oh, that's an amazing story?*

The first example is a question and needs a question mark. The second example should have either an exclamation point or a period, not a question mark.

> Correct: *Have you called Mrs. Han yet?*
> Correct: *Oh, that's an amazing story!*

SUMMARY: Question marks, periods, and exclamation points are used to end sentences. Use question marks to end direct questions, periods to end other sentences, and exclamation points when you want to express strong emotions or emphasis. Don't use too many exclamation points in your writing, or you may sound like you are shouting!

OTHER ERRORS

Compound Words

A *compound word* is a word that has two or more parts. For example, the word *everywhere* is made up of two distinct words: *every* and *where*. But as a compound word, everywhere has a new meaning that is different from the meanings of *every* and *where*. Although there are times when experts can't agree if a word should be a compound, in most cases there are clear rules. In the following sentences, you can see where student writers make mistakes when using compound words:

> Incorrect: *I work to support <u>my self</u> and my family.*
> Incorrect: *You can learn from <u>every thing</u> happening today.*

In each of these sentences, compound words have been written incorrectly as two separate words. The two underlined words in each sentence should be written as one compound word.

> Correct: *I work to support <u>myself</u> and my family.*
> Correct: *You can learn from <u>everything</u> happening today.*

SUMMARY: In English, words, especially adjectives and nouns, are sometimes combined into compound words in a variety of ways. Compound words have a meaning that is different from the meanings of the two words that form them. Not all words can be joined this way. When you are not sure whether a word is a compound, check your dictionary.

Fused Words

Sometimes writers fuse two words together to form an incorrect compound word. The sentences below show examples of fused words:

> Incorrect: *Some people say that <u>highschool</u> is the best time of your life.*
> Incorrect: *I like to play soccer <u>alot</u>.*

Each of the underlined fused words should be two separate words.

> Correct: *Some people say that <u>high school</u> is the best time of your life.*
> Correct: *I like to play soccer <u>a lot</u>.*

SUMMARY: When you join words together incorrectly, you get fused words. When you are not sure whether two words should be compounded, check your dictionary.

Duplicate Words

When writing a first draft, you might make errors simply because you are thinking faster than you can write or type. As a result, you might write the same word twice.

Sometimes you might write two words in a row that, though different, function in the same way. It is very common for writers to type two verbs, pronouns, or articles in a row in early drafts.

> Incorrect: *Sally's older sister <u>can may</u> help her pay for college.*
> Incorrect: *He was as silly as <u>a the</u> clown.*

In each sentence, one of the underlined words should be deleted.

> Correct: *Sally's older sister <u>can</u> help her pay for college.* (meaning that the sister is able to help Sally)
> Correct: *Sally's older sister <u>may</u> help her pay for college.* (meaning that the sister might decide to help Sally)

> Correct: *He was as silly as <u>a</u> clown.* (meaning that he generally acts clownish)
> Correct: *He was as silly as <u>the</u> clown.* (meaning that he acts like a specific clown)

SUMMARY: You "duplicate" when you write the same word twice or when you use two different words that serve the same function. A real duplicate is easy to correct, as the spell checker will usually identify it. But if you have typed two words that serve the same function and are not sure which to keep, check a dictionary to help you choose the word with the most appropriate meaning.

Style

This section provides information on how you can address the following kinds of problems in writing:

➤ Word Repetition
➤ Inappropriate Words or Phrases
➤ Too Many Passive Sentences
➤ Too Many Long Sentences
➤ Too Many Short Sentences
➤ Sentences Beginning with Coordinating Conjunctions

WORD REPETITION

Repeating some words to emphasize your key points is a good writing technique. However, repeating the same words or sets of words too often gives your writing an immature style. It can also make your essay seem boring.

To write more effectively, try using a variety of vocabulary words. Here are a few ideas that can help you:

1. Use synonyms (words that have similar meanings) to replace repeated words. For example, instead of repeating a common verb like *make*, where appropriate, use synonyms like these:

   create, produce, perform, do, execute, bring about, cause, form, manufacture, construct, build, put up, set up, put together, compose

   You can find synonyms in a thesaurus.

   In the following paragraph, the noun *student* is repeated too many times:

   Think about this situation. A <u>student</u> interviewed another <u>student</u> and many <u>students</u> about what it is like to be an only child. If the teachers in charge of the school paper did not edit names of <u>students</u> from the paper or facts that would give that particular <u>student</u> away to other <u>students</u>, then serious problems could be caused for the <u>students</u> who gave their information.

   We can improve this paragraph by using a variety of other words to refer to *student*. For example,

   Think about this situation. A <u>reporter</u> interviewed many <u>students</u> about what it is like to be an only child. If the teachers in charge of the school paper did not edit the <u>individuals'</u> names from the paper or facts that would give <u>each person</u> away to the <u>readers</u>, then serious problems could be caused for the <u>students</u> who gave their information.

2. Use phrases like *the former*, *the latter*, *the first one*, and *the other* to avoid repeating the same nouns. In the following paragraph, the same names are repeated several times:

Of the two sisters, <u>Grace</u> is confident and at ease with everyone. <u>Lily</u> is shy and cautious. <u>Grace</u> always gets what she wants. <u>Lily</u> waits patiently for whatever comes her way. <u>Grace</u> never misses a chance to show off her many talents. <u>Lily</u> never says "boo" unless someone asks her a question.

This paragraph can be improved by using a variety of phrases:

Of the two sisters, <u>Grace</u> is confident and at ease with everyone. <u>Lily</u> is shy and cautious. <u>The former</u> always gets what she wants. <u>The latter</u> waits patiently for whatever comes her way. <u>Grace</u> never misses a chance to show off her many talents. <u>Her sister</u> never says "boo" unless someone asks her a question.

SUMMARY: When you look over your writing, think about how you can replace overused words and phrases. You can use a thesaurus to help you add variety to your writing.

INAPPROPRIATE WORDS OR PHRASES

Language that is too informal, such as slang expressions, is not appropriate for academic writing. It's not always easy to tell when an expression is too informal. Some expressions are used so often in spoken English that we may think it is all right to use them in academic writing, too.

Too informal: *No way would I ever vote.*
Much better: *There is no way I would vote.*
Too informal: *People just need to get it all together and participate in democracy.*
Much better: *People need to consider their beliefs and opinions and participate in democracy.*

SUMMARY: Written language is usually more formal than spoken language. Try to avoid expressions that are too informal when writing academic essays. Use a dictionary when you are not sure if an expression is appropriate.

TOO MANY PASSIVE SENTENCES

A sentence is active when the subject is the *doer* of the action. It is passive when the subject is the *receiver* of the action.

Active sentence: <u>*Two hundred million people*</u> *saw the movie.*
Passive sentence: <u>*The movie*</u> *was seen by 200 million people.*

In the above examples, the action is *seeing*. In the active sentence, the subject (*two hundred million people*) is the doer of the action. In the passive sentence, the subject (*the movie*) is the receiver of the action.

Because passive sentences are usually longer and harder to read, using too many passive sentences can make your writing slow and uninteresting. Many experts think that passive sentences should make up only about 5 percent of your writing.

Active sentences, on the other hand, are generally clearer, more direct, and seem stronger. However, this does not mean that you should stop using passive sentences. Appropriate use of passive sentences can make your writing more powerful.

Here are a few suggestions about when to use passive sentences:

1. When the *action* is more important than the doer:

   The <u>theater was opened</u> last month.
   <u>New students are invited</u> to meet the dean in Room 226.

   In these sentences, the theater being opened and the new students being invited are more important than the "doers" (the people who opened the theater or invited the new students). In fact, the "doers" are not important enough to mention.

2. When the *receiver* of the action is more important than the doer:

   <u>Everyone</u> was given a key to the gym.
   <u>The letters</u> were faxed this morning.

   In the first sentence, we care more about the people who were given a key than the people who were doing the giving. In the second sentence, the letters that were faxed are more important than the person who did the faxing.

3. When the *result* of the action is more important than the doer:

   <u>Our advice was followed</u> by our clients.
   <u>The new computers were installed</u> by the systems staff.

   In the first sentence, our advice being followed is more important than the people giving the advice. In the second sentence, the installation of the computers is more important than the people who installed them.

4. When you don't know who did an action, don't care, or don't want your reader to know:

   Passive: *A mistake was made, and all the scholarship application files were lost.*
   Passive: *This report was written at the last minute.*

   The active forms of these examples would be as follows:

   Active: *I made a mistake and lost all the scholarship application files.*
   Active: *I wrote this report at the last minute.*

   If you were the person who made the mistake in the first sentence, or the person who wrote the report in the second, would you choose the active or passive voice?

5. When you want to sound objective:

   Using passive sentences is a common practice in scientific and technical writing. When you are reporting the results of an experiment or describing a study, it helps to sound objective and fair. Thus, reports are filled with sentences like

   The pigeons were observed over a period of three weeks.
   The subjects were divided into three groups.

   The use of the passive voice in lab reports also keeps the reader focused on the experiment itself, rather than on the researchers.

SUMMARY: When you look over your writing, think about whether you have used too many passive sentences. Passive sentences are longer and more difficult to read and understand, so use them only when they help you to emphasize something important.

TOO MANY LONG SENTENCES

Experts believe that the average sentence length should be between 15 and 20 words. This length allows your reader to absorb your ideas more easily. For example, the following sentence may be confusing to read because of its length:

My favorite place to visit is my grandparents' house near the lake where we love to fish and swim, and we often take the boat out on the lake.

Breaking the sentence into two (or more) can make your writing clearer and more interesting:

My favorite place to visit is my grandparents' house near the lake. We love to fish and swim there, and we often take the boat out on the lake.

Good writers usually mix longer sentences with shorter ones to make their writing more effective. You may even want to try a short sentence (or a single-word sentence) after a few long ones to help you to emphasize what you are saying.

Benjamin Franklin, who was one of America's "founding fathers," helped write the Declaration of Independence. He also invented many things such as bifocals and the Franklin stove, and he discovered electricity. Think about that discovery.. Where would we be without electricity?

In the example above, the paragraph starts with long sentences and ends with short ones. This combination makes the paragraph more lively and effective. Compare it with the paragraph below, which is made up of only long sentences:

Benjamin Franklin, who was one of America's "founding fathers," helped write the Declaration of Independence. He also invented many things such as bifocals and the Franklin stove, and he discovered electricity, which became very important to modern life.

Which paragraph do you prefer?

SUMMARY: It is a good idea to mix long sentences with short ones. A good combination of long and short sentences makes writing lively.

TOO MANY SHORT SENTENCES

You may have too many short sentences in your writing. Good writing usually contains a variety of sentence lengths to make the writing more interesting. Too many short sentences often makes the writing sound choppy. You should combine some of your short sentences to make the writing smoother. Here is an example of a paragraph with too many short sentences:

I knew my friends would throw me a party. It was for my birthday. There was something in the air. I felt it for a whole week before that. I was nervous. I was also very excited. I got home that night. My friends didn't disappoint me. I walked in my house. All my friends yelled, "Surprise!"

The paragraph can be improved by joining some of the short sentences using sentence connectors:

<u>Because</u> it was my birthday, I knew my friends would throw me a party. There was something in the air <u>for</u> a whole week before that. I was nervous <u>but</u> excited <u>when</u>

I got home that night. I wasn't disappointed. <u>When</u> I walked in my house, all my friends yelled, "Surprise!"

SUMMARY: Good writing usually contains a variety of long and short sentences. A good mix of sentence lengths makes the writing more interesting. Too many short sentences often make the writing sound choppy.

SENTENCES BEGINNING WITH COORDINATING CONJUNCTIONS

Coordinating conjunctions are words such as *and, but, as, or, yet, for,* and *nor.* They link or join thoughts together in the middle of a sentence. For example:

I love pizza, <u>so</u> I eat it for breakfast.
Mother drove to town to buy groceries, <u>but</u> she came home with a present for me.

Coordinating conjunctions can also be used to begin sentences, as in these examples:

<u>And</u> I didn't like parties.
<u>So</u> I did not do well on that test.

When you have too many sentences beginning with coordinating conjunctions, your writing becomes choppy. To make your writing smoother, use coordinating conjunctions only when joining ideas within sentences.

In the paragraph below, the writer uses a lot of coordinating conjunctions to begin sentences:

Baseball is the great American sport. <u>And,</u> it is thought of as a summer pastime. <u>So</u> as soon as the weather turns warm, all the neighborhood kids find a field to toss a ball around. <u>And</u> soon they form teams and play each other. <u>But</u> all summer, they always find time to listen to pro games on the radio. <u>And</u> they watch them on TV.

The paragraph can be improved by getting rid of beginning coordinating conjunctions:

Baseball, the great American sport, is thought of as a summer pastime. As soon as the weather turns warm, the neighborhood kids find a field to toss a ball around. Soon, they form teams to play each other, but all summer, they always find time to listen to pro games on the radio and to watch them on TV.

SUMMARY: Coordinating conjunctions are very useful for joining thoughts together in the middle of a sentence. However, try to avoid using them to begin sentences in academic writing.

Organization and Development

The purpose of this section is to explain how a strong essay is typically organized and how to develop your ideas in an essay. It will provide answers to the following questions:

Introduction

➤ What is an introduction?
➤ How do I write an introduction?

Thesis

➤ What is a thesis?
➤ How do I know that my reader understands my thesis?

Main Ideas

➤ Does each of my main ideas begin with a topic sentence?
➤ Have I discussed each main idea completely?
➤ Have I arranged my ideas in an orderly method?

Supporting Ideas

➤ Have I done my best to support and develop my ideas?
➤ Do I include enough details in each paragraph so that the main idea and topic sentence are explained fully?

Transitional Words and Phrases

➤ Do I use words and phrases that help the reader think about relationships among different ideas in the essay?

Conclusion

➤ Do I restate the importance of my ideas based on what I have written in my essay?

INTRODUCTION

What Is an Introduction?

An introduction is the first paragraph or two of an essay. It tells the reader what the essay is about and provides background for the thesis (main idea).

A good introductory paragraph does several things:

➤ It makes the reader want to read the essay.
➤ It tells the reader the overall topic of the essay.
➤ It tells the reader the main idea (thesis) of the essay.

How Do I Write an Introduction?

Introductions can be written in many different ways. Here are some ideas you can use to write a good introduction:

➤ Background about the topic
➤ Narrative
➤ Quotation
➤ Dramatic statistics/facts
➤ Shocking statement
➤ Questions that lead to the thesis

The following are examples of these ideas. The essay's thesis sentence is high-lighted in bold.

Background about the Topic
Since the beginning of time, there have been teachers. The "classroom" teacher has many important tasks to do. A teacher has to teach information while keeping things interesting. She also sometimes has to be a referee, a coach, and a secretary. At times, a teacher has to be a nurse or just a good listener. **This career demands a lot, but it's a career I most want to have.**

Narrative
My fourth grade teacher, Miss Vela, was not a big woman. She was about five feet tall and was no longer young. Even though she did not look very strong, she never had trouble controlling all her students. She could quiet us down with just a stare. We always wanted to make her happy because we knew how much Miss Vela cared about us. She expected us to do the best we could, and we all tried our hardest. **Miss Vela was the kind of teacher who made me know that I wanted to be a teacher.**

Quotation
"Teaching is better than tossing a pebble into a pond of water and watching those ripples move out from the middle. With teaching, you never know where those ripples will end." I remember those words of my fourth grade teacher. Miss Vela once told me that years after they left her class, her students would come back to tell how much she helped them. Miss Vela's students said that it was because of her that they learned to work hard and to feel proud of what they did. **I would like to teach because I would like to make that kind of difference.**

Dramatic Statistics/Facts
Three out of four people said that they thought it didn't matter how many students were taught in one class. However, our class researched this and found that the opposite is true. Studies completed at a university show that having small class sizes, especially in the primary grades, makes a big difference in how much students learn. **Before we decide how many students to assign to a primary school teacher, we need to think more carefully about how important smaller class size is.**

Shocking Statement
Some teenagers today say that they think that wives should earn money and that husbands should help with child care and other household tasks. Recent studies indicate that 13 percent of teenage boys would prefer a wife to stay at home, while 96 percent of the teenage girls surveyed wanted to work outside of the home. **However, couples who marry today may have grown up in very traditional households and therefore may find it difficult to accept wives of equal, not to mention greater, job status.**

Questions That Lead to the Thesis
What exactly is "voice"? Is it a speaking voice or a singing voice? When someone says that they have a voice in their head but no way to get it out, what does that mean? **"Voice" has less to do with throats and mouths than it has to do with being human, being alive.**

THESIS

What Is a Thesis?

The thesis statement tells the main idea—or most important idea—of the essay. It emphasizes the writer's idea of the topic and often answers the question, "What important or interesting things do I have to say?" Thinking about the thesis statement can help you should decide what other information needs to be presented or omitted in the rest of the essay.

A good thesis statement

➤ gives the reader some hint about what you will say about the topic
➤ presents your opinion about the topic and is not just a fact or an observation
➤ is written as a complete statement
➤ does not formally "announce" what your opinion about the topic is

A good thesis statement gives the reader some hint about what you will say about the topic.

Weak Thesis: *Mahatma Gandhi was an interesting man.*
Good Thesis: *Mahatma Gandhi was a person of contradictions.*

Weak Thesis: *Television is a total waste of time.*
Good Thesis: *Parents should carefully choose appropriate, educational television shows for their children to watch.*

A good thesis statement presents your opinion about the topic and is not just a fact or an observation.

Weak Thesis: *London is the capital of England.*
Good Thesis: *For tourists interested in British history, London is an ideal travel destination.*

Weak Thesis: *Many movies today are violent.*
Good Thesis: *The violence in movies today makes children less sensitive to other people's suffering.*

A good thesis statement is written as a complete statement.

Weak Thesis: *Should something be done about bad drivers?*
Good Thesis: *Bad drivers should have to take a driving course before being allowed to drive again.*

Weak Thesis: *There is a problem with the information on the Internet.*
Good Thesis: *To make sure information found on the Internet is valid, computer users must make sure the sources of the information are credible.*

A good thesis statement does not formally "announce" what your opinion about the topic is.

Weak Thesis: *In my paper, I will write about whether schools should require uniforms.*
Good Thesis: *Public schools should not require uniforms.*

Weak Thesis: *The subject of this essay is drug testing.*
Good Thesis: *Drug testing is needed for all professional athletes.*

How Do I Make Sure That My Reader Understands My Thesis?

Sometimes you might use a word in your introduction or thesis that you should define or explain. For example, if you are writing about "Who is a hero?" you should first explain what you think the word hero means. Is a hero a person who risks his life to save others? Is a hero a person whom you admire for any reason? People might have their own way of thinking about a certain word. When you define the word, you help your reader better understand what you mean.

Do You Have Enough Main Ideas to Support Your Thesis?

A main idea is a point that you feel strongly about. It is important to you, and you want the reader to understand this idea. Some writers like to give the reader three main ideas. However, the number of main ideas will vary among good essays. The important thing to remember is that your main ideas need to support your thesis adequately.

If you don't have enough main ideas, you may want to do some rethinking. Here are five suggestions for how to think of more ideas about your subject.

Ask yourself these questions to get you started again:

➤**Who?**

Who in my life has influenced me to consider becoming a teacher?

➤**What?**

What do teachers do?

➤**When?**

When did I start thinking about becoming a teacher?

➤**Where?**

Where are teachers needed the most?

➤**Why?**

Why would a person want to become a teacher? Why do I want to become a teacher?

➤**How? How much?**

How does a teacher learn how to teach?
How has my idea of becoming a teacher changed over the years?
How much does a teacher influence her students?
How much time does a teacher have to work outside of school?

➤**What if? Why not?**

What if teachers do not have all of the materials they need?
Why teach in the classroom and not just over the Internet?

Talk to others about your topic

Lots of people are happy to share what they know. Take good notes because you may want to quote them in your essay.

➤ Other students in your school probably have opinions.
➤ A teacher who knows about the issue or subject could give you some opinions.
➤ Other people who are experts may have valuable information or opinions.
➤ Research your subject on the Internet or in a library.
➤ Send an e-mail to someone who may be an expert.

Think about the kind of writing that you are doing.

Consider the questions below to help you figure out which ideas you need to add or how you should arrange those ideas.

> ➤ Are you explaining how things are alike (comparison) and different (contrast)? You can use this purpose when you are describing something *(such as how to teach primary school students compared to how to teach high school students)* or when you are analyzing different viewpoints *(such as whether or not children should go to school year-round)*.

> ➤ Are you putting your ideas in categories? You might be able to describe something in general and then describe its particular qualities. *For example, you might want to talk about what it takes to be a good teacher and then talk about the unique qualities of a particular teacher you've had.*

> ➤ Are you giving reasons to show how a problem developed and what the effects of the problem are? *For example, if you were discussing how students' attitudes are affected by their environment, you might want first to describe what has caused a particular attitude to develop. Then you might want to discuss the effects of that attitude.*

> ➤ Are you trying to convince someone to think like you or to do something that will improve a situation in the way that you want it to be improved? *For example, if you are trying to persuade a friend to think about an issue the way you think about it, you might want to start by saying what the issue is and why your ideas are the best.*

Start all over and see where you go this time in your writing!

> ➤ Don't be afraid to start over. Lots of writers get new and better ideas when they write about something more than once.

Reread your draft.

Look at your previous draft and start where the writing is the most interesting or at the point that you think is your best statement.

> ➤ Try to write three more sentences to explain your best sentence.
> ➤ Look at the three new sentences, pick the best one, and write three more sentences that explain the most important idea in that best sentence.

MAIN IDEAS

Does Each of Your Main Ideas Begin with a Topic Sentence?

Each main idea needs to be discussed fully. The main idea is part of a sentence that explains the idea. This sentence is called the topic sentence, and its goal is to help the reader think of questions about the topic.

Pretend that you're the reader of this topic sentence:

Not passing a test in fourth grade in Miss Vela's class made me think about what a teacher is.

What questions do you have?

Do you want to know more about what happened to this writer in fourth grade? Do you think that you will learn what the writer thought or meant by the words "what a teacher is"?

Use your topic sentence to prepare the reader for understanding what is written in the essay.

You can look at your sentences to see which words are the influential words. They are the words that seem more important in your sentence.

In this topic sentence, which words or phrases are important?

Teachers don't get paid for every hour that they work.

Would you say that "every hour that they work" are the important words?

Here are the other sentences in this paragraph:

Teachers sometimes do work even when they are not in the classroom. Sometimes my mother grades papers and projects all day on Sunday. Even though she does not get paid, she says that that is the only time she can grade all of her students' work. My neighbor spends three weeks of his summer vacation on a ship that does scientific experiments. He doesn't get paid for any of that work, but he says the things that he learns help him be a better teacher.

Use topic sentences to connect two paragraphs or two main ideas.

Here's a sample paragraph that begins with a topic sentence:

Teachers get many benefits in their careers. My neighbor has children and likes having the summer off when his children are home. Some teachers say their work is very enjoyable. At least that's what my mom says when she mixes up her magic bubble formula for science class. My mom also says that one of the benefits of teaching is that she is using her college education every day. She also gets paid to take refresher courses. But she works hard.

Can you see how the next topic sentence connects to another thought?

In fact, teachers don't get paid for every hour that they work, but the teachers that I know say that they love their work.

What do you expect the writer to tell you about in this paragraph?

Have You Discussed Each Main Idea Completely?

In good writing, you (the writer) and the reader feel as if all of your questions/concerns have been discussed. Remember that your reader needs to understand what you are writing, so discuss each idea completely. Here are a few suggestions for making your main ideas worth reading about.

Give each main idea its own paragraph.

However, if a main idea is very broad, it will need more than one paragraph because it is too complicated to be discussed in one paragraph.

Have You Arranged Your Ideas in an Orderly Manner?

You can arrange your ideas in many different ways. You can organize your ideas in chronological order, which means the order in time in which they occurred. You can begin with the oldest point first and then use paragraphs to discuss what happened next or later.

Here are two main ideas that will be developed into paragraphs:

Idea 1
I have wanted to be a teacher ever since I failed a test in Miss Vela's class in fourth grade.

Idea 2
Then in eighth grade I had an assignment to teach a science lesson to a class in my former primary school, and that experience showed me how good I felt when the students didn't want the class to be over.

You can organize your ideas by importance, either most important to least important or the other way around.

TIP: If your writing assignment has to be completed in a short time, as in an essay test, you probably want to begin with the most important parts or reasons first.

Here are what two different writers think is their most important idea:

Writer 1
The most important reason to be a science teacher is to help the next generation learn about the Earth.

Writer 2
Getting to do fun activities is the reason why I want to be a science teacher.

SUPPORTING IDEAS

What Are Some Ways to Develop Supporting Ideas?

Supporting ideas help to convince your reader that your main idea is a good one. Here are some things that professional writers do:

➤ Tell a story that clarifies the main idea.
➤ Give examples of the main idea to explain what the paragraph is about.
➤ Give reasons that support the thesis. These can be facts, logical arguments, or the opinion of experts.
➤ Use details that are very specific so the reader can understand how this idea is different from others.
➤ Tell what can be seen, heard, smelled, touched, felt, or experienced.
➤ Try to see the idea from many different angles.
➤ Tell how other events, people, or things might have an influence on the main idea.
➤ Use metaphors or analogies to help the reader understand an idea by comparing it to something else.

Have You Done Your Best to Support and Develop Your Ideas?

Think of your reader as a curious person. Assume that your reader wants to know everything that you can say about this subject.

Here are some specific questions that are appropriate for certain types of writing:

➤ **If you are describing a problem or issue, you might was to complete the following:**

What type of problem or issue is it?
What are the signs that a problem or issue exists?
Who or what is affected by the problem or issue?
What is the history of the problem or issue—what or who caused it or contributed to it and what is the state of the problem now?

Why is the issue or problem significant? What makes this issue or problem important or less important?

➤ **If you are arguing or trying to persuade your reader to agree with your opinion, consider the following:**

What facts or statistics could you mention as support?
What ideas could you discuss to prove your points?
What comparison could you make that would help your readers understand the issue?
What expert opinion would make your opinion more valid?
Could you support your point with some examples?
Could you describe the views of someone holding a different opinion?

TIP: Strong arguments are often made by discussing what is good in the opponent's view. You can use expressions like *although that is a point well taken, granted, while it is true that,* or *I agree that* to discuss an opposite view.

➤ **If you are analyzing literature or writing a review of a story or movie, consider these questions:**

Can you summarize the story so that your reader knows what happens?
Can you give the details about the place or time so that your reader has a context for understanding the story?
What can you say about the main characters so that the reader can understand what makes them special or interesting?
Can you describe the point where the main character(s) is in a crisis and has to make an interesting choice?
Can you quote what characters say about each other or about what they are experiencing?
Does the story have a deeper theme that you could discuss?
Can you describe the style in which the story is told or the camera angles of the movie?
Are there interesting images or symbols?

➤ **If you are describing something or providing a definition, consider the following:**

Can you tell what the thing looks like or what its parts are?
Can you say what it does or means?
If what it does or means has changed over time, can you describe what it used to mean or used to do and what it now means or does?
If what you are describing has a different name or meaning, can you tell the reader the different name or meaning?

➤ **If you are telling how to do or make something, consider these points:**

Have you started at the right place—the first step—and proceeded logically?
Have you defined any terms that might be unfamiliar to your reader?
Have you given an example that might help your reader understand what you mean?
Have you tried to explain your instructions clearly? Have you numbered these instructions so that the reader knows the order in which it is best to do them?

TIP: You may want to think of a way to arrange your material so that your reader can understand it better. For example, in a recipe the ingredients are listed at the top and the instructions are in short paragraphs or are numbered as steps.

CONCLUSION

What Is a Conclusion?

The concluding paragraph is separate from the other paragraphs and brings closure to the essay.

➤ It discusses the importance of your ideas.
➤ It restates the thesis with fresh wording.
➤ It sums up the main ideas of the paper.
➤ It can also include an anecdote, quotation, statistics, or suggestion.

Concluding Approaches

You might consider some of the following approaches to writing concluding paragraphs:

➤ Summarize main points.
➤ Provide a summarizing story.
➤ Include a provocative or memorable quotation.
➤ Make a prediction or suggestion.
➤ Leave the reader with something to think about.

Here are two different concluding paragraphs:

Good teaching requires flexibility, compassion, organization, knowledge, energy, and enthusiasm. A good teacher must decide when a student needs to be prodded and when that student needs mercy. Good teaching requires knowing when to listen and reflect and when to advise or correct. It requires a delicate balance of many skills, and often a different mix of approaches for different students and different situations. Is this profession demanding? Yes! Boring? Never! Exciting? Absolutely!

When I become a teacher, I want fourth graders like Miss Vela's. We adored her and wanted to please her. But more importantly, I want to be a Miss Vela for my students. I want to challenge my students to become good citizens. When the river in our town flooded its banks and some classmates had to be evacuated, Miss Vela asked us to think about what we could do. We came up with three decisions. We packed lunches for our classmates, we shared our books and pencils in class, and we gave them clothing. Later when we studied civics, we realized that we were taking care of our classmates the way the local or federal government does in a disaster. Miss Vela was helping her fourth graders become more civic minded. I'm hoping to help my students think like that when I'm a teacher.

TRANSITIONAL WORDS AND PHRASES

Do You Use Transitional Words and Phrases to Take the Reader from One Idea to the Next?

Transitional words and phrases connect what a reader has already read to what the reader is going to read. They give the reader an idea of the relationships between the various ideas and supporting points. They also help to show the relationship between sentences.

You can guide the reader as he or she reads an essay by using transitional words or phrases in paragraphs and sentences.

These words can help you talk about time and the relationship between events:
today, tomorrow, next week, yesterday, meanwhile, about, before, during, at, after, soon, immediately, afterward, later, finally, then, when, next, simultaneously, as a result

These words can help you show the order of ideas:
first, second, third, finally, lastly, most importantly, of least importance

These words can help you show location:
above, over, below, beneath, behind, in front of, in back of, on top of, inside, outside, near, between, beside, among, around, against, throughout, off, onto, into, beyond

These words can help you compare or demonstrate similarity:
also, as, similarly, in the same way, likewise, like

These words can help you contrast or demonstrate difference:
in contrast, however, although, still, even though, on the other hand, but

These words can help you add information:
in addition, for instance, for example, moreover, next, likewise, besides, another, additionally, again, also, in fact

These words can help you clarify a point:
in other words, for instance, that is, just to reiterate, in summary

These words can help you add emphasis to a point that you are making:
truly, in fact, for this reason, again, just to reiterate

These words can help you conclude or to summarize:
all in all, lastly, as a result, in summary, therefore, finally

Does Each of Your Paragraphs Support and Develop/Explain the Main Idea/Topic Sentence?

Paragraphs are a group of sentences about a thought or discussion. Each paragraph is about a main topic.

Some paragraphs are long and some are short. Some paragraphs are just one sentence, which can be a very interesting way to present information.

Some contain an interesting story that can take several sentences to tell.

Some paragraphs answer all of the topic issues. Others are more like transitions between two main ideas.

Here are some questions to help you evaluate your paragraphs:

➤ **Have you said enough so that each paragraph is complete?**

TIP: Try giving each paragraph a title and see if, read by itself, it could be something meaningful. If the reader asked you a specific question, would this paragraph be the answer? If some of the sentences don't fit as an answer, then you should probably delete them.

➤ **Have you used words that need to be explained or defined?**

If you're trying to sound important and don't explain what you mean, your reader might feel frustrated. Try using more than one sentence to define or explain something. Three sentences might really explain your idea!

➤ **Have you provided evidence (proof)? Would an example show what you mean?**

Use a good example to show that what you say is true. This is important.

➤ **Is there a personal experience or quotation from another source that would validate what you are trying to say?**

TIP: Personal experiences are appropriate in some essays but not in others. Make sure you understand the type of information that is expected in each essay you write.

TIP: If you are quoting from another source, make certain that you are quoting (reproducing the words) accurately. Also be sure that you are using quotation marks correctly.

➤ **Have you used clear transitions that establish connections between sentences and ideas?**

You might think of your paragraph as a train and the sentences as cars (and the topic sentence as an engine). Do all the parts of the paragraph link or fit together?

Advice to Writers

This section provides information about the different kinds of essays you may be asked to write.

➤ Persuasion
➤ Informative Writing
➤ Comparison–Contrast
➤ Description
➤ Narration
➤ Cause and Effect
➤ Description of a Process
➤ Writing for Assessment
➤ Response to Literature
➤ Problem and Solution
➤ Writing in the Workplace

PERSUASION

When you write a persuasive essay, you are trying to make the reader agree with you. You thus have to offer good reasons to support your opinion, deal with opposing views, and perhaps offer a solution.

Here's how to start:

➤ List specific arguments for and against your opinion (i.e., the pros and cons).
➤ Decide whether you need to find more information (e.g., *statistics* that support your argument, *direct quotes* from experts, *examples* that make your ideas concrete, *personal experience, facts*).

➤ Think of good arguments from someone who holds the opposite view. How could you respond to that person?

TIP: In this kind of writing, you might want to keep your best argument for last.

SUMMARY: When you write a persuasive essay, you have to be clear and convincing. Any kind of writing improves with practice. Try to practice writing and revising, and expose yourself to as many good models of persuasive essays as you can.

INFORMATIVE WRITING

This kind of writing presents information that helps your reader understand a subject (e.g., global warming, jazz music, pollution). Informative writing can be based on formal research (reading, interviews, Internet browsing). Sometimes you may also be asked to write about a personal experience or observation.

Here's how to start:

➤ Find a specific focus (e.g., not *recycling in general* but *the recycling of paper*).
➤ Choose several important points to discuss (*how paper is recycled, what recycled paper is used for, etc.*).
➤ Think about the supporting details for each point. These details can be facts, observations, descriptions, and/or examples (*items that use recycled paper are paper towels, greeting cards, etc.*).

COMPARISON–CONTRAST

Writing a comparison-contrast paper involves comparing and contrasting two subjects. A comparison shows how two things are alike. A contrast shows how two things are different.

You can use comparison and contrast to describe, define, analyze, or make an argument—for in fact, almost any kind of writing.

Here's how to start:

➤ Select two subjects that have some basic similarities or differences.
➤ Look for how these subjects are similar and different.
➤ Decide how you want to present your information. Choose one way and stick with it throughout your essay.

◆ Do you want to discuss a point for one subject and then the same point for the second subject?
◆ Do you want to show all the important points of one subject and then all the important points of the second subject?
◆ Do you want to discuss how your two subjects are the same and then how they are different from each other?

➤ Remember to make clear to your reader when you are switching from one point of comparison or contrast to another. Use clear transitions. Some transition words that you may find useful are as follows:

For similarities: *similarly, likewise, furthermore, besides*
For differences: *in contrast, in comparison, on the other hand, although, however, nevertheless, on the other hand, whereas, yet*

DESCRIPTION

In descriptive writing, you write about people, places, things, moments, and theories with enough detail to help the reader create a mental picture of what is being described. You can do this by using a wide range of vocabulary, imaginative language, interesting comparisons, and images that appeal to the senses.

Here's how to start:

➤ Let the reader see, smell, hear, taste, and feel what you are writing about. Use your five senses in the description (e.g., *The ancient driver nervously steered the old car down the red mud road, with me bouncing along on the back seat.*).

➤ Be specific (not *this dessert is good* but *the fudge brownie is moist, chewy, and very tasty*).

➤ Show the reader where things are located from your perspective (e.g., *As I passed through the wooden gates I heard a cough. A tiny woman came out from behind the trees.*).

➤ Decide whether you want to give a personal view (subjective) or a neutral viewpoint (objective).

> TIP: What seems unusual or contradictory can make your subject more interesting (e.g., *Martin Luther King probably contributed more than anyone else to changes in civil rights, but he hardly earned any money for his speeches and work*).

NARRATION

This kind of essay offers you a chance to think and write a story about yourself, an incident, memories, and experiences. Narratives or stories usually include a plot, a setting (where something happened), characters, a climax, and an ending.

Narratives are generally written in the first person, using *I*. However, as the storyteller, you can choose to "speak" like different people to make the story more interesting.

Here's how to start:

➤ If you are writing about a quarrel with a friend:

- ◆ Think of what caused the quarrel.
- ◆ Think of who is involved and how.
- ◆ Think of how the quarrel developed, was settled, or whether you and your friend are talking now.

➤ Remember the details that make the event real to you (e.g., what your friend said to you and the tone of voice your friend used).

➤ Try to answer the question, "What did this event mean to me?"

➤ Choose a way to begin; you can

- ◆ build your story in scenes (the way you see in movies)
- ◆ summarize what happened and tell only the most important scene
- ◆ begin at the ending and tell why this was such an important event

CAUSE AND EFFECT

Cause and effect essays are concerned with why things happen (causes) and what happens as a result (effects). In the cause and effect essay, it is very important that your tone be reasonable and that your presentation looks factual and believable.

Here's how to start:

➤ Think about the event or issue you want to write about.
➤ Brainstorm ideas.
➤ Introduce your main idea.
➤ Find relevant and appropriate supporting details to back up your main idea. You can organize these details in the following ways:

◆ *chronological,* the order in which things/events happen
◆ *order of importance,* from least to most important or vice versa
◆ *categorical,* by dividing the topic into parts or categories

➤ Use appropriate transition words and phrases such as the following:

because, thus, therefore, due to, one cause is, another is, since, for, first, second, consequently, as a result, resulted in, one result is, another is,

PROBLEM AND SOLUTION

A problem–solution essay starts by identifying a problem (or problems) and then proposes one or more solutions. It is usually based on topics that both the writer and the reader care about (like the quality of cafeteria food).

Here's how to start:

➤ Think of all the reasons that the problem exists:

◆ Why did it happen?
◆ How did it begin?
◆ Why does it exist now?

➤ List possible solutions to the problem.
➤ Evaluate your solutions—which ones will most likely work?
➤ Write the pros and cons of one or more good solutions, but give the most space in your essay to the best solution.
➤ Explain why the best solution is the one to choose.

DESCRIPTION OF A PROCESS ("HOW-TO")

This kind of essay explains how to do something (e.g., *how to bake your favorite cake*) or how something occurs (e.g., *how movies are made*).

For how to do something, here's how to start:

➤ Think about all the equipment, skills, or materials needed.
➤ How many steps are there in the process? Put the steps in the right order. Why is each step important?
➤ What difficulties are involved in each step?
➤ How long does the process take?

TIP: Give any signs or any advice that can help the reader accomplish the step with success!

For how something occurs, here's how to start:

➤ Give any background that can help your reader understand the process.
➤ Tell what happens in the order that it happens.

TIP: Don't forget to explain any terms that your reader might not understand!

Process essays are usually organized according to time: that is, they begin with the first step in the process and continue until the last step. To indicate that one step has been completed and a new one will begin, we use transitions. Some common transition words and phrases used in process essays are as follows:

first of all, first, second, third, etc., next, soon after, after a few hours, afterwards, initially, at the same time, in the meantime, before, before this, immediately before, in the meanwhile, currently, during, meanwhile, later, then, previously, at last, eventually, finally, last, last but not least, lastly

WRITING AS PART OF AN ASSESSMENT

This kind of writing may be more difficult because you are trying to write your best in a certain place and a limited amount of time. There are a few tricks, however.

Here's how to start:

➤ Take a few moments to understand the question and to note down some ideas that come to mind.
➤ Before beginning to write, take a few moments to plan. How are you going to organize your main ideas and supporting details? Some students find making an outline to be a helpful strategy.
➤ During your writing, if other ideas come to mind and they feel right, use them.
➤ Keep track of your time, but don't panic.
➤ Revise. Look at the paper from the reader's point of view; reorganize and add explanations if necessary.
➤ Proofread if you have time.

TIP: Like any other kind of writing, writing on a test improves with practice. You can practice this skill by writing and revising essays while working within a set time limit.

RESPONSE TO LITERATURE

When you write about literature, you are telling why that literature (story, movie, poem, or play) is interesting and what makes it effective (e.g., why it makes you laugh, why you care about the character).

You can write about why the literary work seems true, you can analyze the character or actions, or you can analyze how the literary work accomplishes its effect.

There are many ways to respond to literature, but here are a few ways to start:

➤ Write for a while about your own personal feelings about the literature. Are you most interested in the setting, the situation, the characters, or the atmosphere that the work creates? These are clues to what you can write about.

- ➤ What is the situation or the mood?
- ➤ What clues does the author give you about the true meaning of this story, poem, or movie? (For example, the many "Cinderella" stories in the world have the same meaning: kindness is rewarded no matter how poor you are.)
- ➤ Organize your thoughts and support them with examples from the literary work. Don't assume that your reader knows the story or movie that you are writing about!

WRITING IN THE WORKPLACE

Letters, memos, and reports are the kinds of writing that are most often done when we do business with each other. In this kind of writing, you want to make your points as quickly and clearly as possible. So try to be brief and direct.

Here's how to start:

- ➤ Organize your thoughts. Most business letters should take one page.
- ➤ Think about whether there is a special format you should follow.
- ➤ Decide if you want the reader to take action (persuasive), to understand a problem (informative), or to fix something (problem–solution). (*Refer to the relevant sections in "Advice to Writers."*)
- ➤ Write clearly and courteously.
- ➤ Include relevant quotations.
- ➤ Leave the reader with something to think about (e.g., make a prediction or suggestion).

Revising, Editing, and Proofreading

THE WRITING PROCESS

The writing process has several stages: planning, drafting, writing, revising, editing, and proofreading. Many writers and instructors think that improving your essay has three distinct stages: revising, editing, and proofreading. Look at each column of this chart to understand each stage completely.

As you write, you may wish to revise and edit your essay several times, as you clarify and develop your ideas. The Writer's Handbook sections on Style, Organization and Development, and Advice to Writers can be very helpful as you revise and edit your essays. When you have a final version of your essays, be sure to proofread it carefully.

	REVISING	EDITING	PROOFREADING
Purpose	➤ See the complete concept ➤ Decide if your essay says what you want it to say. ➤ Add ideas.	➤ Correct grammar and usage ➤ Make changes in word choice, style, and the way you explain your ideas.	➤ Correct typos, spelling, punctuation, and formatting errors.
When	➤ After you have written your first draft, don't do anything with it, then begin revising.	➤ Begin when you have a complete draft of your essay.	➤ Make this the final stage before you submit your essay.
What	➤ Read your entire essay from beginning to end.	➤ As you read each sentence, revise that sentence before you do the next sentence.	➤ Read word-by-word and line-by-line to make corrections.
Strategies	➤ Identify each part of the essay: introduction, thesis, main ideas, supporting ideas, and conclusion. ➤ Review carefully how the ideas are connected and the order of paragraphs. ➤ Don't be afraid to cut and paste, delete, or add new ideas. ➤ Ask a peer reviewer to say what is good and what could be better in your essay.	➤ Ask your teacher, a peer editor or a friend to give you ideas and advice. ➤ List the kinds of grammar and usage errors you make and look at those errors first. ➤ If a sentence seems right, do not revise it. Just think about the parts that seem to have problems. ➤ Use a handbook to help you correct errors and rewrite sentences.	➤ Print a copy of your essay and make the changes on the paper copy. ➤ Read your essay aloud to your teacher or to someone who is more English-proficient than you and circle identified errors. ➤ Have a peer reviewer who is more proficient in English read your essay backwards. Start with the last sentence, then the second to the last, and so on. ➤ Use a dictionary, handbook, and spell check to help you correct errors.

Step 1: Organization and Development
Think about your topic and change the way your essay is organized and developed.

Step 2: Style
Look at each sentence to see if your ideas are easy to understand.

Step 3: Grammar, Usage, Mechanics
Check each word and sentence for errors.

Step 4: Proofreading
Check spelling and typing as you read your final draft.

USING A COMPUTER TO WRITE

Computers make the writing process much easier than handwriting. Computers let you

- ➤ write faster than you can with a pen
- ➤ save or delete ideas and drafts
- ➤ move words, paragraphs, and sentences
- ➤ try out new ways of expressing yourself
- ➤ locate and correct mistakes

Always remember that the computer is a tool that lets you think about how to write. You will still have to make decisions about how to draft and revise your essays and other writing.

GLOSSARY

active voice—English sentences can be written in either the active or passive voice. In the active voice, the subject is the doer of an action. For example, in *Sam kicked the ball,* the action is *kicked,* and the doer is *Sam*: An active sentence emphasizes the doer of an action.

adjective—Adjectives give more information about nouns. In English, they usually come before the nouns. For example, *a red umbrella, a rainy day, a beautiful woman.*

adverb—Adverbs are words like *quickly, happily,* or *carefully.* They can tell more about an adjective (e.g., *very big*), another adverb (e.g., *very quietly*), or a verb (e.g., *walk slowly*).

antecedent—A noun to which a pronoun refers. In the following sentence, *John* is the antecedent of the pronoun *he*: *John was late for school because he missed the bus.*

apostrophe—This punctuation mark (') shows the omission of letters in contractions (*cannot–can't*), or possession (the *girl's* dress, the *animals'* cages).

article—Articles are *a, an,* and *the,* the little words in English that come before nouns. English has two types of articles. The definite article (*the*) is used to refer to one or more specific things, animals, or people (e.g., *the house on the hill*). The indefinite articles (*a, an*) are used to refer to a thing, animal, or person in a nonspecific or general way (e.g., *a house, an elephant*).

clause—A clause is a group of related words that contains a subject and a verb. There are two kinds of clauses: independent and dependent. An independent clause expresses a complete thought and can be seen as a sentence (e.g., *She saw Jim.*). A dependent clause is a part of a sentence and cannot stand on its own. (*When she saw Jim* is a dependent clause.) To make a complete sentence, you need to add an independent clause: *When she saw Jim, she smiled.*

collective noun—A collective noun refers to a *group* of people or animals: *population, family, troop, committee.*

comma—This punctuation mark (,) is used to separate words (*She bought apples, oranges, and grapes*) or parts of a sentence (*He was here, but he left*).

compound subject—This is a plural subject; a subject that consists of more than one part: *Lions, tigers, and bears are kept in the zoo.*

compound verb—This type of verb consists of more than one part: *The baby started crying*.

compound words—These are words that are made up of two words: *everywhere, boyfriend, himself, weekend.*

conclusion—This is the last paragraph of an essay; the paragraph that closes the essay. In a conclusion, you can restate the thesis or sum up the main ideas of the essay.

conjunction—A conjunction is a word that connects words, phrases, or sentences. It also shows relationships between words or clauses. There are two kinds of conjunctions: coordinating and subordinating. Coordinating conjunctions like *and, but, or, nor,* and *for* connect parts that are equal: In *She bought a desk and a chair,* both *desk* and *chair* are nouns. Subordinating conjunctions like *although, because, if, since,* and *when* connect parts that are not equal: In *Because he missed the train, he was late for work. Because he missed the train* is a dependent clause, and *he was late for work* is an independent clause.

contraction—Contractions are short forms. You make a contraction when you combine two words, shorten one of them, and add an apostrophe: *cannot–can't; does not–doesn't; should not– shouldn't; it is– it's.*

dependent clause—A dependent clause is a part of a sentence and cannot stand on its own. (*When she saw Jim* is dependent clause. To make a complete sentence, you need to add an independent clause: *When she saw Jim, she smiled.*

exclamation point—This mark of punctuation (!) at the end of a sentence is used to show surprise or strong emotion.

fragment—A fragment is a group of words that is not a complete sentence, even though it sometimes starts with a capital letter or ends with a punctuation mark, and often contains a subject and verb.

helping verb—This type of verb is also called an auxiliary verb. Helping verbs are used with main verbs in a verb phrase: *is going; were singing; can talk; may leave; must tell; will see*).

hyphen—This mark (-) is used to separate the different parts of a compound word: *mother-in-law, self-motivated student.*

independent clause—An independent clause has a subject and a verb, expresses a complete thought, and can be seen as a sentence. (e.g., *She saw him.)* It can also be combined with another independent clause to make a compound sentence (*She saw him, so she called him over.*) It can also take a dependent clause to make a complex sentence (*She saw him, even though it was dark.*)

infinitive verb—An infinitive consists of the word *to + verb* (e.g., *to go, to swim, to wish*). It can function as a noun, adjective, or adverb. For example: *To swim the English Channel is my friend's strongest dream.* Here, the infinitive *to swim* acts as a noun. It is the subject of the sentence.

intransitive verb—This type of verb does not need an object to complete its meaning. For example: *John ran*. *Bob left*. *Jane slept*.

introduction—An introduction is the first paragraph of an essay. Effective introductions do two basic things: grab the reader's interest and let the reader know what the whole essay is about. This is why most introductions include a thesis statement that clearly states the writer's topic and main argument.

main idea—Main ideas are the important points of an essay. They state what will be discussed in each paragraph (or set of paragraphs for longer essays). Main ideas develop the thesis statement of an essay and are in turn developed by supporting details.

modal verb—A modal verb is a kind of helping verb. Modal verbs help to express meanings such as permission (*may*), obligation (*must*), prediction (*will, shall*), ability (*can*), and so on.

noun phrase—This type of phrase consists of several words that together function as the noun of a sentence, (e.g., *Talking to my mother made me feel better*. "Talking to my mother" is a noun phrase that is acting as the subject of this sentence.)

paragraph—An essay is made up of smaller sections called paragraphs. Each paragraph should focus on one main idea; you tell your reader what this idea is by using a topic sentence. A good paragraph is one in which every sentence supports the topic sentence.

passive voice—English sentences can be written in either the active or passive voice. In a passive sentence, the verb *to be* is combined with the past participle form of a verb, e.g., *John was kicked*. A passive sentence emphasizes the receiver or the results of an action.

period—In English grammar, this punctuation mark (.) is used to signal the end of a declarative sentence. (A declarative sentence is one that is not a question or an exclamation.) It is also used to indicate abbreviations (e.g., *Mr., St., Ave.*)

phrase—A phrase is a group of related words with a single grammatical function (e.g., a noun phrase, a verb phrase). The noun phrase acts as a noun or subject in this sentence: *The girl in the corner is Mary*.

plural—*Plural* means "more than one." In English grammar, nouns, pronouns, and verbs can take plural forms. For example, *cars* is a plural noun, *we* or *they* is a plural pronoun, and *climb* is a plural verb.

possessive pronoun—These are pronouns that show possession or ownership (e.g., *my, our, his, her, their, whose*). Some possessive pronouns can function as nouns: *Is this yours? That book is mine*.

prefix—A prefix is a word part, such as *co-* in *co-star*, attached to the front of a word to make a new word. For another example, the prefix *re-* can be added to the word *sell* to make the word *resell*, which means to *sell again*.

preposition—Prepositions are words such as *in, of, by*, and *from*. They describe the relationship between words in a sentence. In the sentence *The professor sat on the desk*, the preposition *on* shows the location of the professor in relation to the desk.

pronoun—A pronoun can replace a noun or another pronoun. You can use pronouns such as *she, it, which,* and *they* to make your writing less repetitive.

question mark—This is the punctuation mark (?) used at the end of a direct question. For example, *Is David coming to the party?*

sentence combining—Sometimes writers combine two or more short sentences to make a longer one. The reason for doing this is that too many short sentences often make the writing sound choppy. Using sentence-combining techniques in the revising process can improve the style of your essay.

singular—*Singular* means "single," or "one." In English grammar, nouns, pronouns, and verbs can take singular forms. For example, *car* is a singular noun, *he* or *she* is a singular pronoun, and *climbs* is a singular verb in the present tense.

subject—The subject of a sentence tells who or what a sentence is about. For example, *Stephen ran into the parking lot. Stephen* is the subject of the sentence.

supporting ideas—Supporting ideas are the details that develop the main idea of a paragraph. They can be definitions, explanations, illustrations, opinions, evidence, and examples. They usually come after the topic sentence and make up the body of a paragraph.

tense—Tenses indicate time. Sometimes tenses are formed by changes in the verb, as in *He <u>sings</u>* (present tense) and *He sang* (past tense). At other times, tenses are formed by adding modals, or helping verbs. For example, *He <u>will give</u> me fifty dollars* (future tense); *He <u>has given</u> me fifty dollars* (perfect tense).

thesis—The thesis or thesis statement of an essay states what will be discussed in the whole essay. It offers your reader a quick and easy summary of the essay. A thesis statement usually consists of two parts: your topic and what you are going to say about the topic. Thesis statements are supported by main ideas.

topic sentence—The topic sentence states the main idea of a paragraph. It tells your reader what the paragraph is about. An easy way to make sure your reader understands the topic of a paragraph is to put your topic sentence near the beginning of the paragraph. (This is a good general rule for less experienced writers, although it is not the only way to do it.)

transition words and phrases—Transition words and phrases are used to connect ideas and signal relationships between them. For example, *First* can be used to signal the first of several points; *Thus* can be used to show a result.

transitive verb—Transitive verbs require an object. For example, in *He <u>mailed</u> the letter, mailed* is a transitive verb, and *<u>letter</u>* is its object.

verb—A verb is an "action" word (e.g., *climb, jump, run, eat*). English verbs also express time. (e.g., past tense verbs like *climbed, jumped, ran,* and *ate* show that the action happened in the past). Verbs also show states of being—to be words—mentioned earlier in chapter.

verb phrase—A **verb phrase** is a phrase (or a group of words) that consists of a main verb (e.g., *climb, jump, run, eat*) plus one or more helping verbs (e.g., *may, can, has, is, are*). Examples of verb phrases are *She <u>may go,</u>* or *The students <u>will receive</u> certificates.*

TOEFL® iBT Score Information

The TOEFL iBT Field Test

ETS conducted a field test of the new Internet-based (iBT) TOEFL test to achieve three major goals: to evaluate item (question) properties, to inform decisions about score scales, and to provide a score link between the new TOEFL iBT and the computer-based TOEFL test (CBT). The field test also yielded percentile data about test performance, as well as test taker responses to English language competency descriptors, both of which were thought to be potentially useful to score recipients.

TIME AND SAMPLE. From November 2003 to February 2004, 3,284 test takers participated in the field test. Participants were recruited from 30 countries in North America, Latin America, Africa, Asia, and Europe. Approximately 80 percent of the current TOEFL examinees are from these 30 countries.

TEST ADMINISTRATIONS. Each participant was required to take the TOEFL iBT (Form A) and a computer-based TOEFL test. Approximately 500 of the participants were also required to take a second form of the new test (Form B). Each participant completed an online questionnaire of demographic, self-assessment, and post-testing questions. A total of 2,720 usable responses were obtained from the 3,284 examinees who took Form A of the new test and the computer-based test.

The table titled "TOEFL iBT Field Test Sample" indicates the number of participants from each country, their percentage in the total study, and the percentage of individuals who took the current versions of the TOEFL test in that country between July 2002 and June 2003.

Score Comparisons

ETS has created score comparison tables to help score users establish recommended or required TOEFL iBT scores for their institutions. The field test provided data to compare performance on the new iBT test with performance on the CBT test. It did not compare performance between the new iBT test and the paper-based TOEFL. Paper-based and CBT score comparisons shown in the tables here were developed based upon data from 6,556 examinees who took both the paper-based and computer-based tests between November 1997 and March 1998.

Score comparison tables are provided in score-to-score and range formats for

➤ total score
➤ reading
➤ listening
➤ writing
➤ total score—reading listening, and writing only

Although score comparisons can be useful in understanding the relationship between scores on the three versions of the TOEFL test, it is important to note that differences among the tests make it difficult to establish exact comparisons.

The difference in the three versions of the test can be seen most clearly in the writing component. The new iBT Writing section is composed of two writing tasks: one independent essay and one integrated writing task. The computer-based Structure and Writing section includes multiple-choice questions and an essay. The paper-based Structure and Written Expression section consists of multiple-choice questions only, and the required essay score is reported separately from the total score. Therefore, the scores for these three sections are derived differently.

In addition, when comparing total scores, it should be kept in mind that while the new TOEFL test measures the four skills of reading, writing, listening, and speaking, neither the computer-based nor the paper-based version of the test measures speaking.

Speaking Score Comparisons and ITA Score Standards

There is no speaking score comparison because the TOEFL CBT test does not measure speaking. However, ETS conducted a standard setting study with international teaching assistant administrators in September 2004 to establish cut scores for International Teaching Assistants (ITAs) on the speaking portion of the new TOEFL test.

The panel of 18 experts established two separate cut scores: first, a cut score for minimally acceptable speaking skills in order to have the lowest level of ITA contact with undergraduate students; and second, to establish a Speaking score that corresponds to the TSE (Test of Spoken English) score of 50.

The lowest level of ITA contact with undergraduate students was set as 23 out of 30 scaled score points.

The TSE score equivalent of 50 was established as 26 out of 30 scaled score points.

Percentile Data

Percentile rank information is based on results from 2,720 test takers who participated in the field test and who took both the new TOEFL test and TOEFL CBT. The participants' English ability levels ranged from low to high to replicate the current TOEFL testing population; **however, the field study group performed below the typical testing population on TOEFL CBT. Therefore, this field study percentile data should be used with great caution.**

Using Percentile Data—Considerations for Score Users

Although great care was taken in the design and administration of the next generation TOEFL field test, there are a number of important reasons why score users should view these percentile data as preliminary.

➤ Sample size: Results are based on a field sample of 2,720 participants.
➤ Motivation and performance: Participants typically are less motivated to perform well on field tests than on operational, high-stakes tests.
➤ Unfamiliarity with the test: The field test was administered to test takers who had no familiarity with the new TOEFL iBT, which is based on current theories of communicative competence and uses integrated tasks that require examinees to combine language skills. In July 2004, ETS published a complete version of the new test on its Web site to familiarize teachers and test takers with the new test and its requirements. It is anticipated that increased familiarity will affect performance.
➤ The addition of a speaking measure: The current TOEFL test does not measure speaking ability, and in many parts of the world teachers have not emphasized the development of this skill in their classes. Although the addition of speaking on the new test will initially be challenging for some test takers, learning this skill will improve their ability to communicate effectively in an academic environment.
➤ When taking the TOEFL CBT test, the field study group performed below the typical TOEFL CBT population. Thus, the percentile data should be used with great caution, as they are not reflective of anticipated performance if the field study participants had performed similar to the overall TOEFL CBT population.

Updated percentile data based on the high-stakes operational test will be published after the first testing year.

Score means and standard deviations are also provided and will be updated after the first year of testing.

TOEFL Total Score Comparisons

New Internet-Based TOEFL Total	Computer-Based Total	Paper-Based Total	New Internet-Based TOEFL Total	Computer-Based Total	Paper-Based Total
120	300	677	62–63	177	503
120	297	673	61	173	500
119	293	670	59–60	170	497
118	290	667	58	167	493
117	287	660–663	57	163	487–490
116	283	657	56	160	483
114–115	280	650–653	54–55	157	480
113	277	647	53	153	477
111–112	273	640–643	52	150	470–473
110	270	637	51	147	467
109	267	630–633	49–50	143	463
106–108	263	623–627	48	140	460
105	260	617–620	47	137	457
103–104	257	613	45–46	133	450–453
101–102	253	607–610	44	130	447
100	250	600–603	43	127	443
98–99	247	597	41–42	123	437–440
96–97	243	590–593	40	120	433
94–95	240	587	39	117	430
92–93	237	580–583	38	113	423–427
90–91	233	577	36–37	110	420
88–89	230	570–573	35	107	417
86–87	227	567	34	103	410–413
84–85	223	563	33	100	407
83	220	557–560	32	97	400–403
81–82	217	553	30–31	93	397
79–80	213	550	29	90	390–393
77–78	210	547	28	87	387
76	207	540–543	26–27	83	380–383
74–75	203	537	25	80	377
72–73	200	533	24	77	370–373
71	197	527–530	23	73	363–367
69–70	193	523	22	70	357–360
68	190	520	21	67	353
66–67	187	517	19–20	63	347–350
65	183	513	18	60	340–343
64	180	507–510	17	57	333–337

Continued

TOEFL Total Score Comparisons (Cont.)

Score Comparison, cont.			Range Comparison		
New Internet-Based TOEFL Total	Computer-Based Total	Paper-Based Total	New Internet-Based TOEFL Total	Computer-Based Total	Paper-Based Total
16	53	330	111–120	273–300	640–677
15	50	323–327	96–110	243–270	590–637
14	47	317–320	79–95	213–240	550–587
13	43	313	65–78	183–210	513–547
12	40	310	53–64	153–180	477–510
11	37	310	41–52	123–150	437–473
9	33	310	30–40	93–120	397–433
8	30	310	19–29	68–90	347–393
7	27	310	9–18	33–60	310–343
6	23	310	0–8	0–30	310
5	20	310			
4	17	310			
3	13	310			
2	10	310			
1	7	310			
0	3	310			
0	0	310			

Note: The paper-based total score does not include writing. The paper-based and computer-based total scores do not include speaking.

TOEFL Score Comparisons for Reading

Score Comparison				Range Comparison		
New Internet-Based TOEFL Reading	Computer-Based Reading	Paper-Based Reading		New Internet-Based TOEFL Reading	Computer-Based Reading	Paper-Based Reading
30	30	67		28–30	28–30	64–67
29	29	66		26–28	25–27	59–63
28	28	64–65		21–24	22–24	56–58
28	27	63		17–20	19–21	52–55
27	26	61–62		14–16	16–18	48–51
26	25	59–60		11–13	13–15	44–47
24	24	58		8–10	10–12	40–43
23	23	57		5–7	7–9	34–39
21	22	56		1–4	4–6	31–33
20	21	54–55		0	0–3	31
19	20	53				
17	19	52				
16	18	51				
15	17	50				
14	16	48–49				
13	15	47				
12	14	46				
11	13	44–45				
10	12	43				
9	11	41–42				
8	10	40				
7	9	38–39				
6	8	36–37				
5	7	34–35				
4	6	32–33				
3	5	31				
1	4	31				
0	3	31				
0	2	31				
0	1	31				
0	0	31				

TOEFL iBT Field Test Sample

Country	Number of Study Participants	Percentage of Study Participants	Percentage of TOFEL 2002–03 Volume
Egypt	49	1.80	0.35
Ethiopia	59	2.17	0.07
Israel	69	2.54	0.28
Kuwait	12	0.44	0.36
United Arab Emirates	44	1.62	0.87
France	54	1.99	1.81
Germany	26	0.96	2.5
Greece	22	0.81	0.75
Italy	3	0.11	1.02
Norway	69	2.54	0.65
Romania	37	1.36	0.41
Russia	35	1.29	0.22
Spain	36	1.32	0.62
Turkey	23	0.85	1.55
Australia	121	4.45	0.34
Hong Kong	35	1.29	0.79
India	233	8.57	3.35
Japan	119	4.38	5.61
Korea	193	7.10	2.05
Malaysia	41	1.51	0.57
New Zealand	179	6.58	0.32
Philippines	45	1.65	1.7
Taiwan	81	2.98	1.15
Thailand	47	1.73	0.56
Argentina	55	2.02	0.46
Brazil	64	2.35	0.85
Colombia	84	3.09	0.82
Mexico	65	2.39	0.75
Canada	117	4.30	6.05
United States	703	25.85	23.32
Total	2,720	100.00	60.15

TOEFL Score Comparisons for Listening

Score Comparison			Range Comparison		
New Internet-Based TOEFL Listening	Computer-Based Listening	Paper-Based Listening	New Internet-Based TOEFL Listening	Computer-Based Listening	Paper-Based Listening
30	30	67–68	29–30	28–30	65–68
30	29	66	26–28	25–27	60–64
29	28	65	22–25	22–24	56–59
28	27	63–64	18–21	19–21	53–55
27	26	62	15–17	16–18	50–52
26	25	60–61	12–14	13–15	47–49
25	24	59	9–11	10–12	44–46
23	23	58	5–7	7–9	40–43
22	22	56–57	1–4	4–6	34–39
21	21	55	0–1	0–3	31–33
19	20	54			
18	19	53			
17	18	52			
16	17	51			
15	16	50			
14	15	49			
13	14	48			
12	13	47			
11	12	46			
10	11	45			
9	10	44			
7	9	42–43			
6	8	41			
5	7	40			
4	6	38–39			
2	5	36–37			
1	4	34–35			
1	3	32–33			
0	2	31			
0	1	31			
0	0	31			

TOEFL Score Comparison for Writing

Score Comparison			Range Comparison		
New Internet-Based TOEFL Writing	Computer-Based Structure Writing	Paper-Based Structure and Writing/ Written Expression	New Internet-Based TOEFL Writing	Computer-Based Structure Writing	Paper-Based Structure and Writing/ Written Expression
30	30	68	28–30	28–30	65–68
29	29	67	22–26	25–27	59–64
28	28	65–66	17–20	22–24	55–58
26	27	63–64	13–16	19–21	51–54
24	26	61–62	11–13	16–18	47–50
22	25	59–60	10–11	13–15	43–46
20	24	58	8–9	10–12	39–42
19	23	56–57	7–8	7–9	33–38
17	22	55	3–6	4–6	31–32
16	21	54	0–1	0–3	31
14	20	52–53			
13	19	51			
13	18	50			
12	17	48–49			
11	16	47			
11	15	46			
10	14	44–45			
10	13	43			
9	12	42			
9	11	40–41			
8	10	39			
8	9	37–38			
7	8	35–36			
7	7	33–34			
6	6	31–32			
5	5	31			
3	4	31			
1	3	31			
0	2	31			
0	1	31			
0	0	31			

Note: The new Internet-based TOEFL Writing section is composed of two writing tasks: one independent essay and one integrated writing task. The computer-based Structure and Writing section includes multiple-choice questions and an essay. The paper-based Structure and Written Expression section consists of multiple-choice questions only, and the required essay score is reported separately from the total score. Therefore, the scores for these three sections are derived differently.

TOEFL Total Score Comparisons for Reading, Listening, and Writing Only

This table presents another way of comparing scores between the new Internet-based TOEFL test and the computer-based and paper-based versions of the test. While the new TOEFL test will measure speaking ability, the computer-based and paper-based versions of the test do not. Therefore, this table compares total scores for the Reading, Listening, and Writing sections of the new test with total scores for the computer-based and paper-based versions of the test. The Internet-based scores are presented on a 0–90 scale because the Speaking section, which is worth up to 30 points, is not included in the comparison. Please note that the paper-based total score does not include Writing.

Score Comparison			Score Comparison, cont.		
New Internet-Based TOEFL Reading, Listening, and Writing Only Total	Computer-Based Total	Paper-Based Total	New Internet-Based TOEFL Reading, Listening, and Writing Only Total	Computer-Based Total	Paper-Based Total
90	300	677	53	197	527–530
90	297	673	51–52	193	523
90	293	670	50	190	520
89	290	667	49	187	517
88	287	660–663	48	183	513
87	283	657	47	180	507–510
86	280	650–653	46	177	503
85	277	647	45	173	500
84	273	640–643	44	170	497
83	270	637	43	167	493
82	267	630–633	42	163	487–490
80–81	263	623–627	41	160	483
79	260	617–620	40	157	480
78	257	613	39	153	477
76–77	253	607–610	38	150	470–473
75	250	600–603	37	147	467
74	247	597	36	143	463
72–73	243	599–593	35	140	460
71	240	587	34	137	457
70	237	580–583	33	133	450–453
68–69	233	577	33	130	447
67	230	570–573	32	127	443
65–66	227	567	31	123	437–440
64	223	563	30	120	433
62–63	220	557–560	29	117	430
61	217	553	28	113	423–427
59–60	213	550	27	110	420
58	210	547	26	107	417
57	207	540–543	25	103	410–413
55–56	203	537	24	100	407
54	200	533	23	97	400–403

Continued

TOEFL Total Score Comparisons for Reading, Listening, and Writing Only (Cont.)

Score Comparison, cont.			Range Comparison		
New Internet-Based TOEFL Reading, Listening, and Writing Only Total	Computer-Based Total	Paper-Based Total	New Internet-Based TOEFL Reading, Listening, and Writing Only Total	Computer-Based Total	Paper-Based Total
22	93	397	84–90	273–300	640–677
21	90	390–393	72–83	243–270	590–537
21	87	387	59–71	213–240	550–587
19–20	83	380–383	48–58	183–210	513–547
19	80	377	39–47	153–180	477–510
18	77	370–373	31–38	123–150	437–473
17	73	363–367	22–30	93–120	397–433
16	70	357–360	14–21	63–90	347–393
15	67	353	6–13	33–60	310–343
14	63	347–350	0–5	0–30	310
13	60	340–343			
12	57	333–337			
11	53	330			
11	50	323–327			
10	47	317–320			
9	43	313			
8	40	310			
7	37	310			
6	33	310			
5	30	310			
5	27	310			
4	23	310			
3	20	310			
2	17	310			
1	13	310			
1	10	310			
0	7	310			
0	3	310			
0	0	310			

Scale: 0–90

Percentile Ranks, Means, and Standard Deviations for TOEFL® iBT

Total Scale Score Reading, Listening, Writing, Speaking	Percentile Rank	Total Scale Score Reading, Listening, Writing, Speaking	Percentile Rank
120	100	89	77.9
119	99.98	88	76.9
118	99.9	87	76.1
117	99.9	86	74.5
116	99.8	85	73.1
115	99.5	84	71.9
114	99.3	83	70.6
113	98.7	82	69.1
112	98.2	81	67.8
111	97.6	80	66.2
110	96.8	79	64.8
109	96.1	78	63.5
108	95.5	77	62.0
107	95.1	76	60.5
106	94.2	75	59.0
105	93.6	74	57.4
104	92.9	73	56.3
103	92.3	72	54.6
102	91.1	71	53.7
101	90.1	70	52.3
100	89.0	69	51.0
99	88.3	68	49.6
98	87.3	67	48.3
97	86.6	66	46.7
96	85.9	65	45.5
95	85.0	64	44.3
94	83.8	63	42.7
93	82.8	62	41.6
92	82.0	61	40.4
91	81.0	60	38.9
90	79.7	59	37.4

Continued

Percentile Ranks, Means, and Standard Deviations
for TOEFL® iBT

Total Scale Score Reading, Listening, Writing, Speaking	Percentile Rank	Total Scale Score Reading, Listening, Writing, Speaking	Percentile Rank
58	35.6	25	4.2
57	34.6	24	3.7
56	33.5	23	3.2
55	32.7	22	2.9
54	31.2	21	2.5
53	29.9	20	2.1
52	28.6	19	1.7
51	27.4	18	1.2
50	26.5	17	0.8
49	25.6	16	0.7
48	24.5	15	0.6
47	23.2	14	0.4
46	22.1	13	0.4
45	20.9	12	0.3
44	19.5	11	0.2
43	18.8	10	0.2
42	17.8	9	0.1
41	16.7	8	0.04
40	15.8	7	0.04
39	14.8	6	
38	14.2	5	
37	13.1	4	
36	12.2	3	
35	11.1	2	
34	10.1	1	
33	9.2	0	
32	8.5		
31	7.8		
30	7.4		
29	6.5		
28	5.7		
27	5.2		
26	4.7		

Total—Reading, Writing, Listening, Speaking

N = 2,720
Mean = 67.04
SD = 24.58
Minimum Score = 6
Maximum Score = 119

Percentile Ranks, Means, and Standard Deviations
for TOEFL® iBT

Reading Scale Score	Percentile Rank	Listening Scale Score	Percentile Rank
30	99.5	30	99.7
29	97.6	29	98.6
28	95.3	28	96.1
27	90.1	27	92.9
26	87.2	26	88.7
25	83.8	25	84.1
24	76.7	24	79.3
23	73.6	23	74.0
22	70.6	22	69.4
21	66.6	21	64.6
20	59.8	20	59.6
19	55.6	19	54.9
18	51.2	18	49.7
17	44.1	17	45.6
16	39.9	16	40.2
15	36.9	15	36.5
14	33.0	14	29.3
13	27.0	13	26.3
12	23.7	12	22.8
11	21.3	11	19.9
10	15.6	10	16.8
9	13.3	9	14.0
8	11.1	8	11.5
7	9.0	7	9.4
6	5.9	6	6.4
5	3.8	5	4.6
4	3.0	4	3.2
3	1.1	3	2.1
2	0.7	2	1.4
1	0.2	1	0.6
0		0	

Reading
N = 2,720
Mean = 17.04
SD = 6.99
Minimum Score 0
Maximum Score 30

Listening
N = 2,720
Mean = 16.98
SD = 6.95
Minimum Score 0
Maximum Score 30

Percentile Ranks, Means, and Standard Deviations
for TOEFL® iBT

Writing Scale Score	Percentile Rank	Speaking Scale Score	Percentile Rank
30	97.9	30	98.6
29	95.9	29	96.2
28	93.4	28	93.4
27	90.5	27	90.2
26	90.5	26	86.2
25	87.2	25	86.2
24	82.9	24	81.3
23	82.9	23	75.7
22	77.4	22	70.5
21	72.4	21	70.5
20	66.9	20	63.9
19	66.9	19	56.3
18	60.2	18	49.3
17	53.6	17	42.1
16	53.6	16	42.1
15	46.3	15	35.9
14	37.3	14	30.3
13	37.3	13	24.5
12	30.0	12	24.5
11	21.4	11	20.1
10	14.9	10	15.4
9	14.9	9	12.1
8	5.4	8	9.2
7	5.0	7	9.2
6	5.0	6	6.8
5	1.1	5	4.8
4	1.1	4	3.2
3	1.1	3	1.9
2	1.1	2	1.9
1	1.1	1	0.9
0		0	

Writing
N = 2,720
Mean = 16.05
SD = 6.67
Minimum Score = 0
Maximum Score = 30

Speaking
N = 2,720
Mean = 16.97
SD = 6.98
Minimum Score = 0
Maximum Score = 30

English Language Competency Descriptors

English Language Competency Descriptors
TOEFL iBT

These English Language Competency Descriptors are based on the self-evaluation of approximately 2,300 test takers who took the TOEFL iBT. Examinees were asked to respond to questions related to their English language abilities in Reading, Writing, Listening, and Speaking. Descriptive statements were derived from several sources and instruments, including analyses of the academic language demands placed on students in North American educational institutions. Score recipients and English language programs can use these descriptors to help interpret the language ability of test takers at each major score level for each of the skill sections as well as the total score. The shaded areas indicate the likelihood that a test taker with that score would be able to perform the language task described.

Overall Language Competency Descriptors

Descriptor	<30	30–39	40–49	50–59	60–69	70–79	80–89	90–99	>=100
My instructor understands me when I ask a question in English.									
When I speak in English, other people can understand me.									
When my instructors speak English, I can understand their directions about assignments and due dates.									
I can understand major ideas when I read English.									
I can understand a speaker's attitude or opinion about what he or she is saying.									
I can write a summary of information that I have read in English.									
I can write an essay in class on an assigned topic.									
I can recognize why an English speaker is saying something (for example, to explain something, to complain about something, or to agree with someone).									
I can talk in English for a few minutes about a topic I am familiar with.									
When I read English, I understand charts and graphs in academic texts.									
When I write in English, I can support ideas with examples or data.									
I can understand how the ideas in an English text relate to each other.									
I can understand important facts and details of lectures and conversations.									
I can speak for about one minute in response to a question.									
When I write in English, I can organize my writing so that the reader understands my main and supporting ideas.									
I can relate information I hear in English to what I already know.									
I can give prepared presentations in English.									
I can understand the main ideas of lectures and conversations.									
I can understand English vocabulary and grammar when I read.									

Continued

Total Score Scale: 0–120

	<30	30–39	40–49	50–59	60–69	70–79	80–89	90–99	>=100
I can understand the relationships among ideas in a lecture.									
After I hear a lecture in English, I can recognize which points are important and which are less important.									
I can state and support my opinion when I speak English.									
When I read academic texts written in English, I understand the most important points.									
I can understand the relative importance of ideas when I read an English academic text.									
I can organize or outline the important ideas and concepts in English academic texts.									
I can participate in conversations or discussions in English.									
I can talk about facts or theories I know well and explain them in English.									
When I read an academic teat written in English, I can remember major ideas.									
I can write a summary of information that I have listened to in English.									
When I listen to a lecture In English, I can remember the most important points.									
I can orally summarize information I have read in English.									
When I write in English, I can write more or less formally depending on the purpose and the reader.									
When I read academic texts in English, I can understand them well enough to answer questions about them later.									
I do not have any problem understanding what people say in English.									
When I read a text in English, I am able to figure out the meaning of words I do not know by using the context and my background knowledge.									
I can quickly find information that I am looking for in academic texts written in English.									
I can express ideas and arguments effectively when I write in English.									
When I read academic texts in English, I can understand them well enough to answer questions about them later.									

Continued

Overall Language Competency Descriptors (Cont.)

Total Score Scale: 0–120

	<30	30–39	40–49	50–59	60–69	70–79	80–89	90–99	>=100
I can use correct grammar, vocabulary, spelling, and punctuation when I write in English.									
I can orally summarize information from a talk I have listened to in English.									
I can read English academic texts with ease.									
I can read and understand texts in English as easily as I can in my native language.									

Likelihood of Being Able to Perform Each Language Task:

<50% Very unlikely

50–65% Unlikely

66–80% Borderline

81–95% Likely

>95% Very likely

Overall Language Competency Descriptors (Part 2)*

Total Score Scale: 0–120

Score ranges: <60 · 60–69 · 70–79 · 80–89 · 90–99 · >=100

Statements (language tasks):

- When I read English, I often have to reread something to understand it.
- On occasion, I've misunderstood the main idea of a lecture I've heard in English.
- I can understand people only when they speak English very slowly.
- Writing even a short text in English takes a long time for me.
- I need to use my dictionary a lot when I read English.
- It is very difficult to express what I mean when I speak English.
- I cannot figure out what an author's opinion is in texts written in English.
- I cannot express at all what I want to say when I write in English.
- Speaking English even for a short time is exhausting for me.
- It is hard for me to ask questions in class or make presentations in English.
- When people speak to me in English, I can understand almost nothing.
- I have no idea how to structure what I write in English.
- My spoken English is so bad that nobody understands me.

Likelihood of Difficulty with Each Language Task:

<10% Unlikely | 10–29% Slightly likely | 30–49% Somewhat likely | >50% Very likely

*These statements indicate language tasks that examinees said they had difficulty with.

Reading Competency Descriptors

Total Score Scale: 0–30

Score ranges across the top of the chart: 1–5 | 6–10 | 11–15 | 16–19 | 20–23 | 24–27 | 28–30

Reading competency descriptors (rows):

- I can understand major ideas when I read English.
- I can understand how the ideas in an English text relate to each other.
- When I read English, I understand charts and graphs in academic texts.
- I can understand English vocabulary and grammar when I read.
- When I read academic texts written in English, I understand the most important points.
- I can understand the relative importance of ideas when I read an English academic text.
- I can organize or outline the important ideas and concepts in English academic texts.
- When I read an academic text written in English, I can remember major ideas.
- When I read a text in English, I am able to figure out meanings of words I do not know by using the context and my background knowledge.
- I can quickly find information that I am looking for in academic texts written in English.
- When I read academic texts in English, I can understand them well enough to answer questions about them later.
- I can read English academic texts with ease.
- I can read and understand texts in English as easily as I can in my native language.

Likelihood of Difficulty with Each Language Task:

(white)	<50% Very unlikely
(light gray)	50–65% Unlikely
(medium gray)	60–80% Borderline
(dark gray)	81–95% Likely
(black)	>95% Very likely

Listening Competency Descriptors

Total Score Scale: 0–30

Columns (score ranges): 1–5 | 6–10 | 11–15 | 16–19 | 20–23 | 24–27 | 28–30

Descriptors:

- When my instructors speak English, I can understand their directions about assignments and due dates.
- I can understand the main ideas of lectures and conversations.
- I can recognize why an English speaker is saying something (for example, to explain something, to complain about something, or to agree with someone).
- I can relate information I hear in English to what I already know.
- I can understand a speaker's attitude or opinion about what he or she is saying.
- I can understand important facts and details of lectures and conversations.
- After I hear a lecture in English, I can recognize which points are important and which are less important.
- I can understand the relationships among ideas in a lecture.
- When I listen to a lecture in English, I can remember the most important points.
- I do not have any problem understanding what people say in English.

Likelihood of Difficulty with Each Language Task:

- <50% Very unlikely
- 50–65% Unlikely
- 60–80% Borderline
- 81–95% Likely
- >95% Very likely

Speaking Competency Descriptors

Total Score Scale: 0–30

Speaking Competency Descriptors	1–5	6–10	11–15	16–19	20–23	24–27	28–30
My instructor understands me when I ask a question in English.							
When I speak in English, other people can understand me.							
I can give prepared presentations in English.							
I can talk in English for a few minutes about a topic I am familiar with.							
I can participate in conversations or discussions in English.							
I can state and support my opinion when I speak English.							
I can talk about facts or theories I know well and explain them in English.							
I can speak for about one minute in response to a question.							
I can orally summarize information I have read in English.							
I can orally summarize information from a talk I have listened to in English.							

Likelihood of Difficulty with Each Language Task:

<50% Very unlikely	50–65% Unlikely	66–80% Borderline	81–95% Likely	>95% Very likely

Writing Competency Descriptors

Total Score Scale: 0–30

Writing Competency Descriptors	1–5	6–10	11–15	16–19	20–23	24–27	28–30
I can write a summary of information that I have read in English.							
When I write in English, I can organize my writing so that the reader understands my main and supporting ideas.							
When I write in English, I can support ideas with examples or data.							
When I write in English, I can write more or less formally depending on the purpose and the reader.							
I can write an essay in class on an assigned topic.							
I can write a summary of information that I have listened to in English.							
I can express ideas and arguments effectively when I write in English.							
I can use correct grammar, vocabulary, spelling, and punctuation when I write in English.							

Likelihood of Difficulty with Each Language Task:

- <50% Very unlikely
- 50–65% Unlikely
- 66–80% Borderline
- 81–95% Likely
- >95% Very likely

CD-ROM WARRANTY

This software is protected by both United States copyright law and international copyright treaty provision. You must treat this software just like a book. By saying "just like a book," McGraw-Hill means, for example, that this software may be used by any number of people and may be freely moved from one computer location to another, so long as there is no possibility of its being used at one location or on one computer while it also is being used at another. Just as a book cannot be read by two different people in two different places at the same time, neither can the software be used by two different people in two different places at the same time (unless, of course, McGraw-Hill's copyright is being violated).

LIMITED WARRANTY

Customers who have problems installing or running a McGraw-Hill CD should consult our online technical support site at http://books.mcgraw-hill.com/techsupport. McGraw-Hill takes great care to provide you with top-quality software, thoroughly checked to prevent virus infections. McGraw-Hill warrants the physical CD-ROM contained herein to be free of defects in materials and workmanship for a period of sixty days from the purchase date. If McGraw-Hill receives written notification within the warranty period of defects in materials or workmanship, and such notification is determined by McGraw-Hill to be correct, McGraw-Hill will replace the defective CD-ROM. Send requests to:

McGraw-Hill
Customer Services
P.O. Box 545
Blacklick, OH 43004-0545

The entire and exclusive liability and remedy for breach of this Limited Warranty shall be limited to replacement of a defective CD-ROM and shall not include or extend to any claim for or right to cover any other damages, including, but not limited to, loss of profit, data, or use of the software, or special, incidental, or consequential damages or other similar claims, even if McGraw-Hill has been specifically advised of the possibility of such damages. In no event will McGraw-Hill's liability for any damages to you or any other person ever exceed the lower of suggested list price or actual price paid for the license to use the software, regardless of any form of the claim.

McGRAW-HILL SPECIFICALLY DISCLAIMS ALL OTHER WARRANTIES, EXPRESS OR IMPLIED, INCLUDING, BUT NOT LIMITED TO, ANY IMPLIED WARRANTY OF MERCHANTABILITY OR FITNESS FOR A PARTICULAR PURPOSE.

Specifically, McGraw-Hill makes no representation or warranty that the software is fit for any particular purpose and any implied warranty of merchantability is limited to the sixty-day duration of the Limited Warranty covering the physical CD-ROM only (and not the software) and is otherwise expressly and specifically disclaimed.

This limited warranty gives you specific legal rights; you may have others which may vary from state to state. Some states do not allow the exclusion of incidental or consequential damages, or the limitation on how long an implied warranty lasts, so some of the above may not apply to you.